GW00645529

The Adentures
of the
Communist Manifesto

Originally published in 1994 by Center for Socialist History

This edition published in 2020 by
Haymarket Books
P.O. Box 180165
Chicago, IL 6618
773-583-7884
www.haymarketbooks.org
info@haymarketbooks.org

ISBN: 978-1-64259-038-8

Distributed to the trade in the US through Consortium Book Sales and Distribution (www.cbsd.com) and internationally through Ingram Publisher Services International (www.ingramcontent.com).

This book was published with the generous support of Lannan Foundation and Wallace Action Fund.

Library of Congress Cataloging-in-Publication data is available.

Cover photograph of barricades of the Paris Commune, April 1871,
Corner of the Place de l'Hôtel-de-Ville and the Rue de Rivoli,
by Pierre-Ambroise Richebourg.

The Adentures
of the
Communist Manifesto

Hal Draper

Haymarket Books
Chicago, Illinois

Editor's Note

This book is a much expanded edition of an earlier publication of the Center for Socialist History. That book—*The Annotated Communist Manifesto*—comprised Part II and Part III of the current work and a much shortened version of Part I. The textual analysis of the Manifesto by Hal Draper in *The Annotated Communist Manifesto* and Part III of the current work refers often to the publishing history of the Manifesto and cannot really be understood without it. Hence the condensed version of Part I in the earlier work. In preparing a new edition of *The Annotated Manifesto* the editorial board of the Center decided that, rather than publish *The Adventures of the Communist Manifesto* separately, we would integrate the two works.

The text of Hal Draper's New English Translation has not, of course, been altered. Neither has the text of the annotations that make up Part III nor that of *The Adventures* itself. The two prefaces that Hal Draper wrote have had to be revised since the originals reflected the division of the work into two separate (although cross-referenced) books. The condensed version of the publishing history of the Manifesto found in *The Annotated Communist Manifesto*, now redundant, has been eliminated.

The Annotated Manifesto included the German original of the Manifesto as an appendix. We have included it here as a parallel text for easy comparison with the new translation by Hal Draper and the Authorised English Version by Frederick Engels and Samuel Moore. Another new feature of the present publication as compared to *The Annotated Manifesto* is the inclusion of the first English translation by Helen Macfarlane as one of the parallel texts for reasons which should be clear from the discussion of that translation in Chapter 11 of Part I.

For similar reasons, it might have been a good idea to include the French translations by Laura Lafargue. They also were done in close collaboration with Engels and throw some light on the problems he faced in translating the Manifesto into English. Unfortunately, there were three versions by Laura Lafargue and their inclusion would have made comparison of the texts difficult if not impossible and thus defeated the whole purpose of parallel translations. Nevertheless, as the discussion in Part I makes clear, these three translations are important for understanding the difficulties with the Authorised English Version of Engels and Moore.

The editors wish to acknowledge the assistance of Martin Lipow who transcribed the texts of the original German edition of 1848 and the Macfarlane translation into machine-readable form. This painstaking task required him to preserve the misprints and grammatical slips in the originals without adding any of his own. These conflicting requirements made it impossible to use any grammatic or spelling checkers since they would have eliminated the original mistakes as well as any introduced by the typist. We cannot thank Mr. Lipow enough.

We also want to acknowledge the work of Michael Friedman and Eugene Darling who proofread the manuscript.

Contents

PART I:
THE ADVENTURES OF THE COMMUNIST MANIFESTO

Preface

At this date, it is unnecessary to explain the continuing concern with a short pamphlet published nearly a century and a half ago. Page for page, no other publication in our time has rivaled the historical impact of the *Manifesto of the Communist Party* by Karl Marx and Friedrich Engels.

The oft-repeated statement that the Manifesto gained no attention whatever when it first came off the press is, as we shall see, inaccurate.

But it is certainly true that, decade by decade, the significance of the Manifesto increased both in quantity and extension, until now it blankets most of the globe. The number of books and essays which, in whole or part, devote long discussions and evaluations to the views of the Manifesto—for or against—is enough to fill this book from cover to cover in a mere listing. But this book is not one of them. It is, logically, anterior to all of them for the following reason.

Before you can discuss the views in the Manifesto, you have to know what it says; and this is not quite as simple a requirement as it may seem. Firstly, there is the language problem, if you do not read German; and if you do, there are still some questions about textual changes in the German editions from 1848 on. Secondly, there are problems with any writing from the first half of the 19th century, for some German words were still altering in meaning (as in the case of *Idiotismus*). Thirdly, the language of politics was changing even more rapidly and extensively—for example, the word "democracy"—and the language of socialism was in process of being born; and this was the case in all national tongues. Fourthly, the authors of the Manifesto were writing for their contemporaneous public, who could be expected to know, say, who Guizot was; but this allusion, like many others, has dimmed out today even for more or less educated readers.

Above all, there are the problems that cluster about the "Authorized English Translation," which is the English version you have undoubtedly read.

The new English version presented in the second part of this book follows the text of the first edition of 1848. The Authorized English Translation of 1888 (the A.E.T.) was made from what was then the latest German edition, published in 1883, or perhaps from the 1872 edition (which amounts to the same thing for translation purposes). Our Annotations—presented in the third part—will not only be concerned with the differences between the A.E.T. and the first edition, but also with the differences among the various German editions. It will also be necessary from time to time to refer to the other translations—in English and French—for which Marx and Engels bore some responsibility.

A necessary introduction to our subject is the history of the Communist Manifesto as a publication—the publication which has had the liveliest impact of any that ever came out of a bindery.

Books or essays dealing with the Manifesto are usually, in reality, essays on Marx and Marxism in general; but this is not our purpose. You will not find here a summary of Marx's, or Marx's and Engels', theoretical and political development or relations to the early socialist movement, or of the ideological themes in the Manifesto. Such material, of course, is a necessary introduction, and for the purpose I would recommend a substantial biography of Marx, say, David McLellan's. The present work *assumes* that the reader already has some acquaintance with the basic facts.

This caveat applies to essays on the Manifesto such as E. H. Carr's in his *Studies in Revolution*, A. Labriola's in his *Essays in the Materialistic Conception of History*, Sweezy and Huberman's "The Communist Manifesto After 100 Years" in an edition of the Manifesto itself, or H. J. Laski's much-reprinted article. (You should be warned, however, against a consumer fraud titled *The History of the Communist Manifesto* by V. Adoratsky, New York, 1938.) Naturally, I do not mean to derogate the enterprise of discussing Marx's ideas via an inquiry into the Manifesto. But the present project is something else.*

Nor will we duplicate another type of book: the documentary collection on the Manifesto's background. There are two that deserve notice. The older one is a volume titled *The Communist Manifesto of Karl Marx and Friedrich Engels*, edited with an introduction and notes by D. Ryazanov (London, 1930). This is still of some interest for its section of "Explanatory Notes" and its Appendixes (documents). We will return to it in the last chapter. Newer is a collection titled *Birth of the Communist Manifesto*, with an introduction, notes and translations by Dirk J. Struik (New York, 1971). This is very useful.

But there is only a single work that explores the history of the Manifesto as a publication, and I must emphasize it because it provides much of the factual framework of this book. It provides a great deal of raw material for what we are calling a "close-up history" of the Manifesto. If you are a camera, you need a broad focus to see the sweep of the sociohistorical forces in whose context the Manifesto was produced; you need a somewhat narrower one to focus in on the development of the two authors themselves in the context of the early socialist movement. And we must narrow the focus considerably more in order to follow the vicissitudes of the Manifesto as a published document, on the background of all the preceding.

The factual detail for this enterprise is supplied by Bert Andréas' outstanding work of scholarship, *Le Manifeste Communiste de Marx et Engels. Histoire et Bibliographie 1848–1918* (Milan: Feltrinelli, 1963).

This notable work seems to have largely escaped the attention of researchers in socialist history or Marx studies: one seldom encounters substantial use of its material, even in the scholarly literature. Part of the reason must be its form. It consists of bibliographical entries and tables, drily informative, and approximately as readable as a telephone directory; it does not offer a narrative account. The story of the Manifesto's adventures in the world has to be mined and quarried from its pages.

---

* My own inquiry into the development of the political ideas that went into the Manifesto is contained in the first part of my *Karl Marx's Theory of Revolution*, Volume I, titled "The Political Development of the Young Marx."

While Andréas' work provides much of the framework, I have also utilized a number of other sources, including the annotation of the Marx-Engels Werke (MEW), the Marx-Engels *Gesamtausgabe*, and other basic editions of the Marx-Engels works; added political background information and interpretation, wherever necessary; and reorganized and rearranged the whole into a connected account. The result is a history of the Manifesto for which Andréas cannot be held responsible; all interpretations and opinions are naturally my own.

Because Andréas is such a reliable guide in general, I have not dared to depart from his conclusions without warning the reader; and so in a few cases where I have differed with his interpretations, I have noted and explained the issues. For that matter, I have done this also with other sources which are so important that, when they do make an error, it is necessary to note it: the *MEW* annotation, for example. Instead of page references to Andréas' entries, I usually give his entry numbers; for example: A#100 means his item No. 100.

THE MANIFESTO IN 1848

1. THE LONDON-BRUSSELS CONNECTION

The Manifesto was published in 1848 under the title *Manifesto of the Communist Party*. It is seldom remarked that this title should seem odd to us. For no organization called the Communist Party existed in 1848. More: the organization that *did* sponsor the publication of the Manifesto was nowhere mentioned in its pages. The explanation lies in the immediate genesis of the Manifesto.

The idea of writing a communist credo (*confessio fidei, Glaubensbekenntnis*) arose in 1847 out of the interaction of two currents of German émigré revolutionaries. In Brussels, Marx and Engels had established a political center which they called the Communist Correspondence Committee. It was not conceived as a sect battling for the field against all other sects, nor was it conceived as a German group, though Germans formed its cadre; it sought to include not only Belgians (in the Brussels C.C.C.) but also to encourage the formation of similar Correspondence Committees in other countries, above all Paris and London.

In London, the revolutionary German émigré workers (who were mainly artisans) were grouped largely around the League of the Just (*Bund der Gerechten*). Its Central Committee was in London; there were scattered branches and members on the Continent (Paris, again, in the first place), and it invited non-Germans to join. Its very name savored of its past, the direction from which it was coming: sentimental artisan-revolutionism. But ideologically it was on the move; its leaders were exploring the marketplace of revolutionary ideas for something better. By 1847 they were definitely through with the man whose ideas had been most important at the beginning: Wilhelm Weitling and his messianic utopianism, based on "artisan-communism" (Marx's term). Outgrown by his own movement, Weitling had left London, to no one's regret. The "Just" were becoming increasingly hostile to any notion of building socialistic "colonies" or communities in the American wild in order to get out from under capitalistic civilization; later in 1847 they were going to make a definitive break with utopian-community notions after a round of arguments with Etienne Cabet.

Since 1843 Engels had been on friendly personal terms with the League of the Just leaders, Karl Schapper, Heinrich Bauer, Joseph Moll, et al. Then he had published a highly regarded book, *The Condition of the Working Class in England*, which made him one of the most prominent figures in this burgeoning movement. Marx's brief career of 1842–1843 as the crusading editor of the most important organ of leftist bourgeois democracy in Germany in the decade of the forties, the *Rheinische Zeitung* of Cologne, was well known to the Just, as was his subsequent publication of the ambitious *Deutsch-Französische Jahrbücher* in Paris, though its ambitions crumbled after one issue. In this single issue Marx and Engels, together, had had four seminal articles, plus interesting letters about radical reorientation. Since then they had published a work on philosophy, *The Holy Family*, and had written articles for the Paris *Vorwärts!* and the Brussels *Deutsche Brüsseler Zeitung*, articles that discussed questions which people like Schapper were eager to take up.

In short, the London communists, looking around for new and better revolutionary ideas, could not fail to be attracted to these two men, who furthermore had formed themselves into a sort of partnership since 1845. The Just moved to make contact.

Marx told about it as follows, thirteen years later: as a result of the work done in Brussels,

> ...[T]he London Central Committee [of the League of the Just] entered into correspondence with us, and at the end of 1846 sent one of its members, the watchmaker Joseph Moll (who later fell on the battlefield in Baden as a soldier of the revolution) to Brussels to invite us to join the League. The misgivings that assailed us regarding this proposal were quashed by Moll's announcement that the Central Committee planned to call a congress of the League in London, where the critical views we had urged would be established as the League's doctrine in a public manifesto; that however our personal participation was indispensable as against the outdated opposition elements, but this was dependent on our joining the League. We therefore joined. The Congress took place, with representatives of League members in Switzerland, France, Belgium, Germany, and England; and after lively debate over several weeks, the Manifesto of the Communist Party written by Engels and myself was adopted...[1]

Notice that, as Marx remembered the events, he was induced to join the League—despite "misgivings" about this step—by the opportunity to issue a "public manifesto," one which would set forth what Marx had called his "critical communism." Mere membership in this communist group was not itself the inducement; on the contrary, this is what aroused the misgivings. In fact, the group itself was going to have to be remodeled in accordance with this outlook. These were not *arrière-pensées* held by Marx but an open agreement with the League leaders.

Engels' account (published in 1885) tells us more about the conditions under which he and Marx joined:

> ...[I]n the spring of 1847 Moll showed up in Brussels to see Marx, and right afterwards in Paris to see me, in order to repeatedly urge us on behalf of his comrades to join the League. They were, he said, convinced of the general correctness of our way of thinking as well as of the need to rid the League of the old conspiratorial traditions and forms. If we were willing to join, we would be given the opportunity at a League congress to set forth our critical communism in a manifesto, which would then be published as the manifesto of the League...

We interrupt to underline two things. First: Engels, like Marx, recalls the *primary* role played in the decision to join by the project of issuing the Manifesto. Second: though writing a few decades later (or perhaps because of this) he says it was to be "published as the manifesto of the League." *But in fact it was not so published,* and this is precisely what we are inquiring into.

Engels' account continued, with the second of the conditions:

> ...[A]nd we could likewise make our contribution toward replacing the League's obsolete organization with a new one befitting our times and aims.[2]

He emphasized two things about the projected recasting of the organizational side of the League. (1) The whole idea of a conspiratorial organization was to be dropped. It had to be admitted that the League was forced to be a secret organization in, say, Germany, for the simple reason that the government outlawed it and sent its members to jail; but this was a practical necessity, not a political orientation. In other words, while the League had no option but to be a secret organization *in Germany*, it would reject the perspective of a conspiratorial movement. (2) The organization was thoroughly democratized and converted into a "propaganda group," rather than a group organized to make putsches.

Everything left over of the old mystical terms belonging to the conspiratorial days was now abolished [at the June 1847 congress]... The organization itself was [now] democratic throughout, with an elected leadership always subject to removal; and this by itself debarred all hankerings for conspiracy, which require dictatorship; and the League was converted into a pure propaganda society—at least for ordinary times of peace.[3]

For Marx and Engels, then, the Communist League offered itself primarily as a medium through which to issue a statement about a new view of communism, a "manifesto."

2. THE COMMUNIST LEAGUE

n June 1847 the League of the Just held a congress in London and reorganized itself as the Communist League, in accordance with the agreement with Marx and Engels. (Its name, *Bund der Kommunisten*, literally means League, or Federation, of the Communists; the shorter form has become customary in English.) Meeting from June 2 to 9, it adopted new by-laws ("statutes") for submission to the branches for discussion—"so democratic was the procedure now," Engels comments—preliminary to their endorsement by the second congress to come. Engels attended this founding congress as delegate of the Paris branch; Wilhelm Wolff represented the Brussels people. Marx was unable to go to London for lack of money, he said. (No doubt he was short of money, but he was never an eager congress-goer anyway.)

Engels took an active role in the congress, and during its early days drafted a "Communist Credo." It must have been done hastily, and there is no reason to believe that this draft was intended to be a final version. At its last session on June 9, the congress approved the draft as a basis for discussion, that is, as a document to be sent out to the branches.*

We know little more in detail about the discussions at this congress, but we know the outcome: the League speeded up its new orientation and prepared expeditiously for a second congress the very same year.

For the next five months, Marx and Engels were quite busy with both literary and organizational work. In early July Marx published an important book in Paris, his polemic against Proudhon, *The Poverty of Philosophy*—important, for one thing, in establishing Marx's reputation even more firmly in revolutionary circles. Marx became a prominent contributor to the *Deutsche Brüsseler Zeitung*, which the Londoners read too; Engels began to collaborate with the leading leftist paper in Paris, *La Réforme*. In Brussels they set up a branch of the Communist League on August 5; also, toward the end of that month, a Brussels equivalent of the Workers' Educational Association for German émigrés, which had been so useful for the London CL. Then on September 27 a Democratic Association was founded in Brussels, with Marx and Engels and their circle very active in its ranks.

On October 18 the London Central Committee notified Brussels of the coming Second Congress. Besides asking for Belgian delegates, the C.C. urged Marx himself to come this time. Around this date, in mid-October, Engels went back to Paris, and was again involved in busy journalistic and propagandist activity.

In Paris, Moses Hess—whom Marx and Engels regarded as a muddleheaded sentimental-socialist—had drafted a Communist credo of his own. Engels thought it very bad. At a meeting on October 22 of the Communist League district committee (a body established by the Paris branches), Engels began to dissect Hess's draft "question by

---

* This "Communist Credo" was discovered only in 1968, by Bert Andréas. There is an English translation in MECW 6:96.

question" (as he reported to Marx) "and had not gone through the half of it when the people declared themselves *satisfaits*."

> I had myself commissioned to draft a new one, which now will be discussed next Friday in the district committee, and *behind the branches' back* will be sent to London.[1]

As far as one can make out, this stratagem had to do with the pressure of time. The new draft, after approval by the district committee, would not go back to the branches (in line with the ordinary procedure) but would be shipped directly to London because little more than a month remained before the congress was to convene, and the district committee did not want it bottled up in Paris branch discussions.

Engels' letter indicates that it was only at the end of October that he set down his new draft, which is identified with the document we know as his "Principles of Communism." Andréas, to be sure, gives reasons to believe that this draft had been written during the summer*. Perhaps there was an interim version; we cannot be certain.

The Second Congress of the CL was scheduled to open in London on November 29. About two weeks before, on November 14, the Paris district committee elected Engels as its delegate. Less than a week before, Engels wrote Marx from Paris to arrange to meet on the way to London, at Ostend: the two would stay overnight at the Hôtel de la Couronne and consult on congress problems. This letter by Engels, dated November 23–24, reflects the fact that the partnership had been unable to function closely while its members were in different cities, Engels in Paris and Marx in Brussels. Engels put pressure on Marx to do more in the way of immediate preparation: "This congress must be decisive," he wrote, adding (in English), "as this time we shall have it all our own way." After signing the letter, he bethought himself that evening to add another passage:

> Give a thought to the Credo. I believe we would do best to drop the catechism form and entitle the thing: Communist *Manifesto*. Since a certain amount of history has to be related in it, the present form is quite unsuitable.

He then informed Marx how far he had got:

> I am bringing with me what I wrote here [meaning, presumably, his "Principles of Communism"][1]; it is simply narrative, but wretchedly drafted, in frightful haste. I begin: What is communism? and then right on to the proletariat—history of its genesis,

---

* Andréas points to evidence that its text was known to friends of the CL in Sweden by the summertime (page 20). Or perhaps this concerned an earlier version. In September the CL's one-issue organ, *Kommunistische Zeitschrift*, stated that a credo had been sent "to friends on the Continent" for discussion. Was it Engels' draft that was sent, or was it someone else's? If Engels', was it the text we now call "Principles of Communism"? These are the uncertainties.

difference from earlier workers, development of the opposition of proletariat and bourgeoisie, crises, consequences. In between, all kinds of incidental matters, and finally the party policy of the communists insofar as it belongs in the public's eye. What I have here has not yet been quite submitted for approval, but, except for some quite small details, I mean to get it through so that there will at least be nothing in it contrary to our views.[2]

Marx must have agreed with the idea of substituting a "manifesto" for a catechism, for that is what he did do.

On November 27 Marx set out for London, accompanied by the Belgian radical Victor Tedesco (whom we will meet again). As arranged, Marx and Engels stopped off in Ostend, stayed overnight, and thus had some hours to discuss the congress. Marx went on to London the next day, Engels on the day after that, taking the Channel ship *Onyx* to Dover.

Engels arrived on the day the congress began, November 29; it went on through December 8. Again we know little in detail about the discussions at the congress. Engels wrote in 1885 that Marx championed the new theory in the longish debate—the congress lasted at least ten days. All opposition and doubts were finally disposed of; the new principles were adopted unanimously; and Marx and I were commissioned to work out the Manifesto.[3]

The unanimity of the decision was also attested by the memoirs of Friedrich Lessner. Lessner, a tailor who had come to England from Hamburg only that April, was not a delegate to the congress and therefore (he tells us) could not attend. (Unnoted by everyone concerned, this was plainly a remnant of the old conspiratorial attitude of the League, designed to make it difficult for police spies; in practice it was usually more effective in keeping not the secret police but League members in ignorance.) "We soon heard," Lessner related, "that the congress had unanimously declared for the principles expounded by Marx and Engels, and had charged them with writing a Manifesto."[4]

Unfortunately, no one has offered information on what form this unanimous decision took. What did the congress actually vote on? A motion summarizing a point of view? (Unlikely.) A general motion of confidence? (Possibly.) A proposal simply to entrust the Manifesto to the newcomers? To *both* of them? The accounts by Engels and Lessner agree that the congress assigned the writing of the Manifesto to Marx and Engels as a team; but we will look back on this question in the next chapter.

When Marx and Engels drafted their first preface to the Manifesto almost a quarter century later (1872), they stated in the first sentence that the November 1847 congress of the CL "commissioned the undersigned [the two of them]...to draw up for publication a detailed theoretical and practical party program."

3. WHO WROTE THE MANIFESTO?

rom start to finish, Marx and Engels both consistently always referred to the Manifesto as their joint product.* The only question I raise is—what this statement means. There are various ways in which two authors can collaborate on a work, and indeed Marx and Engels had already demonstrated two different cases. *The Holy Family* was published under joint authorship, "by Friedrich Engels and Karl Marx"; but its parts were written separately, each part by one or the other author. In *The German Ideology,* on the other hand, we cannot distinguish separate authorship with certainty; the degree of responsibility by Marx or Engels for one or another section is speculative. What was the case with the Manifesto?

The question is sharpened by this fact: during much of the time when the Manifesto was being written, and especially when it was finished, Engels could not have collaborated directly because he was not even in the same city with Marx.

Between the First and Second Congresses—that is, *before* the Manifesto was commissioned—there certainly were times when the two men could jointly consult, plan, sketch, perhaps even draft. Engels left London in mid-June to return to Paris; then toward the end of July he moved back to Brussels, where he worked with Marx on many activities till mid-October. As we have seen, he then saw Marx briefly at Ostend on the way to the Second Congress. No doubt they chatted about the contents of a Credo at one or another of these times, but it is unlikely that Marx started writing a draft until the Second Congress had acted.

When the Second Congress was over, Marx began working on (which perhaps meant: thinking about) the Manifesto while still in London, from December 9 to about the 13th, when he left England for Brussels. Engels was available during these days, for he stayed in London until December 17, when he too left for Brussels. But while Marx remained in Brussels, Engels went to Paris again around the end of the month. At any rate, on New Year's Eve he was already in Paris, giving a talk at festivities held by the German émigré community.

How much of the Manifesto had Marx drafted by the end of the year? We don't know, but he certainly did not get the job finished before the end of January. Nor did he assure the London Central Committee that he was making some progress. He had to be prodded, first gently by Engels, then brusquely by the Londoners.**

---

* For a qualification, but not really an exception, see Chapter 10, in connection with Marx's communication to the *NDZ.*

** Marx's inventive biographers sometimes turn pure speculation into "probable" fact: "The writing of the Manifesto did not progress rapidly, probably because Marx kept on consulting Engels, who had gone back to Paris from London," says Padover's *Karl Marx* (page 246). This is a purely imaginative conjecture, based on no factual indication whatever. Marx's delay in finishing the Manifesto needs no such guesswork.

On January 14, reporting on Paris affairs to Marx, Engels wrote that the condition of the CL branches was "wretched": the people were sleepyheads, the petty squabbling was fierce. He added:

I will now make one last try; if it does not succeed, I'll withdraw from this kind of propaganda work. Hopefully the London documents [*Papiere*] will come soon and liven things up a bit; then I will make use of the occasion. Since up to now the chaps have seen no result of the congress at all, they are naturally becoming altogether slack.[1]

What were the London *Papiere* which were eagerly awaited in Paris? MEW editorially interprets this to refer to copies of the Manifesto. Perhaps it was a broader reference to other CL documents as well. But certainly there could be no misunderstanding Engels' jab of the needle when he complained about "no result of the congress." He was reminding Marx that the branches were looking forward to getting the Manifesto.

On January 24, having heard nothing from Marx, the London Central Committee of the League adopted a motion in an effort to put a fire under him. They sent this motion out the next day, not to Marx directly but to the district committee of the League in Brussels, no doubt in order to make it an official démarche. The communication was received in Brussels by Philippe Gigot, one of the local League leaders. Since Marx was out of town at the time, Gigot copied the London communication into a note of his own (which had the Marxlike distinction of including three languages in the course of a few lines) and sent it to Marx on January 28. Since the mails were efficient in those days, it may well have reached Marx's house the same day. It is Gigot's copy of the London note that is extant:

London, Jan. 25, 1848

Central Committee to the Brussels district committee
Motion of Jan. 24, 1848

The Central Committee hereby instructs the Brussels district committee to notify K. Marx that, if the "Manifesto of the C. Party," the writing of which he undertook at the *last* congress, has not arrived in London by Tuesday, February 1 of this year, further measures will be taken against him. In the event that K. Marx does not write the manifesto, the Central Committee demands the immediate return of the documents handed over to him by the congress.

In the name and on behalf of etc.

Signed: Schapper. Bauer. Moll[2]

We will return to this note later to consider a couple of its features,* but for the nonce let us continue with the course of events. Since there is no record that "further measures" were taken, it may be assumed that the Londoners received the finished manuscript by February 1, hence that Marx finished it at the very end of January. This is a risky assumption, since we cannot exclude the reasonable possibility that the Londoners were not eager to act in hairtrigger fashion, that they would allow a week's leeway or so before they would begin to think of what measures to take. The completion of the Manifesto, then, may be assigned to the last days of January or the first days (or first week) of February. Then it would take another two or three days before the London people had it in their hands.

Meanwhile, we should note, Engels was expelled from France on January 29, by a government that was getting increasingly jittery as the political temperature mounted toward revolution. He returned to Brussels on January 31. Did he have an opportunity to look over the manuscript before it was hastily shipped off to London? Assuming, of course, that it had not been already been sent off by the time he arrived. There is no information on this point. Neither he nor Marx, certainly, ever mentioned such a last-minute collaboration. At the most, Engels might have had a day or two or three to go over the manuscript with Marx. I suspect not.

Engels' undoubted contribution to the writing of the Manifesto, therefore, may be summarized as follows:

(1) *General influence.* He played a definite part—along with Marx as well as independently, e.g., through his *Condition of the Working Class in England*—in developing the basic ideas that permeate the Manifesto. While he always ascribed the major role to Marx, his own contribution was considerable. (But this is an issue we cannot pursue here.)

(2) *Discussion.* He certainly discussed with Marx the contents of the projected document: orally, possibly also in nonextant letters**. But we know nothing about these discussions, except that they must have taken place.

(3) *Drafts.* Engels' most tangible contributions were his drafts, the two catechisms, "Communist Credo" and "Principles of Communism." Perhaps they summarize everything else he did for the project.

(4) *Negative conclusions.* On the negative side there is no evidence or indication that Engels drafted any part of the Manifesto as we know it. The only manuscript page of the Manifesto is mostly in Marx's hand, with some lines in his wife's hand; and an extant outline of Section III is also by Marx.[3] There is also no evidence that Engels ever took part in revising Marx's draft at any point. He may have, to be sure, but a firm conclusion either way is not possible.

Overall conclusion: the probability is great that the actual text of the Manifesto was solely from Marx's pen, however much weight we give to Engels' contributions preliminary to the final draft.

---

* For the reference to the "immediate return of the documents," see Chapter 6 below.

** During the 1848 revolution Engels, faced with possible arrest, destroyed a number of papers, including letters from Marx. The reference to "nonextant letters" is therefore not speculative.

Certainly in the eyes of the Londoners it was Marx who was personally responsible for producing the Manifesto; for their threatening motion of January 24, as well as the accompanying note of January 25, never mentioned Engels. There is a problem in reconciling this fact with the reiterated statements that the CL congress had commissioned both to prepare the programmatic statement. The answer may be: the London C.C. wrote in this vein because it had already been informed that Marx assumed responsibility for finishing the document, Engels being in Paris.

4. A DARK-GREEN PAMPHLET

Friedrich Lessner's memoirs of 1898 give us the following vignette: "When at the beginning of 1848 the manuscript of the *Communist Manifesto* arrived from Brussels I was to play a modest part in the publication of this epoch-making document: I delivered the manuscript to the printer and took the proof sheets from him to Karl Schapper for checking."[1]

An interesting feature of this account is what does not appear there. When Marx's manuscript of the long-awaited manifesto arrived in London, wasn't there any provision for the London C.C., or any other body of the Communist League, to review it for approval as a statement of the League? The answer seems to be no—certainly not as far as is known. We will have to come back to this point.

The printer to whom Lessner took the manuscript put his own name on the cover. This dark-green cover bore the following information:

Manifest
der
Kommunistischen Partei.
Veröffentlicht im Februar 1848.
Proletarier aller Länder vereinigt Euch!
London.
Gedruckt in der Office der Bildungs-Gesellschaft
für Arbeiter
von J. E. Burghard.
46, Liverpool Street, Bishopsgate.[2]

[Manifesto of the Communist Party. Published in February 1848.—Proletarians of all countries, unite!—London. Printed in the office of the "Educational Society for Workers" by J. E. Burghard. 46, Liverpool Street, Bishopsgate.]

The pamphlet comprised twenty-four pages, the last one unnumbered; octavo, 215 x 134 mm. It is often called the "twenty-three page edition."

A notable feature of this cover (which is also the title page) is that the name of the real publisher, the Communist League, does not appear; nor does it appear elsewhere in the brochure. The imprint, instead, gives the name of the printer, and it states that the printing has been done on the premises of the named society. This statement was not really true. The address given was that of Burghard's printshop; the society's "office" or headquarters was at 191 Drury Lane, High Holborn.

This organization, here called the "Educational Society for Workers," had more different names—simultaneously and successively, in German and English—than any other I have heard of; and the name used in the Manifesto's first edition was not its commonest variation. The organization later was usually known by the name it settled on about 1871: the Communistischer Arbeiter-Bildungs-Verein (with or without the hyphens)—the Communist Workers' Educational Association. But in the 1840s it did not usually use "Communist" as part of its title.

The *Verein* (association) or *Gesellschaft* (society) this was one of the elements of variation—had been founded on February 7, 1840, on the initiative of Karl Schapper, then recently expelled from France for revolutionary activity in connection with a Blanquist putsch. In London he found two organizations meeting at the Red Lion pub (20, Great Windmill Street, Haymarket), both operating since 1835: a society of German liberal émigrés, called the Deutsche Gesellschaft, and one comprising more radical French refugees, republicans and Babouvist-type revolutionaries ("Blanquists" in the generic sense), called the Société Démocratique Française. Dissatisfied with the tepidness of the German group, Schapper, together with friends like Joseph Moll and aided by the French, founded a new *Arbeiterverein* (workers' association) with communistic principles. Apparently it was originally named the Deutsche Demokratische Gesellschaft (German Democratic Society—similar to the name of the French society). But it was soon renamed the Deutsche Bildungsgesellschaft für Arbeiter (German Educational Society for Workers). Then it started its career of taking on new names, for reasons which no one has bothered to explain as far as I know. For a long time it remained in Great Windmill Street, "a short street running from Coventry Street, Piccadilly Circus end, northwards to Brewer Street."[3]

In 1848, when the Manifesto was heading for Burghard's press, the organization was celebrating its eighth anniversary, and a leading German paper in London, the *Deutsche Londoner Zeitung*, had an article which called it the Londoner Bildungsverein für Arbeiter.

A version of the name that occurs in historical accounts is Deutscher Arbeiter-Bil-dungsVerein (with or without the hyphens), that is, German Workers' Educational Association. For present purposes, let us use the last-named version (GWEA) without taking account of the variation.

At this time the GWEA was a "front organization" for the Communist League; under Schapper's leadership, it had played a similar part from the beginning. During the summer of 1847 it had collected 25 and bought a supply of German type necessary to set up its own printshop; but it could not yet afford to buy a press. The *Communist Manifesto* was typeset with the GWEA's own type, no doubt by compositors who were members, but the pamphlet had to be printed off-premises. Burghard too was a member of the GWEA, having joined in mid-1846, but he was a commercial printer first. Perhaps he gave the association a low price for his services.

Some time between February 22 and 29, Burghard presented the association with his bill: he had probably run off a thousand copies, and had probably asked for about £5; we can probably figure that the printing had taken place between, say, February 14 and the week of 22–29; probably the date of February 24 would be close to the real printing date. Among other probabilities is the surmise that the GWEA was reimbursed by the real publisher, the Communist League.

5. WHOSE MANIFESTO WAS IT?

aving just gotten the Manifesto off the press, let us now go back over some ground.

What exactly was Marx trying to do when he sat down to draft the Communist League's manifesto at his desk in Brussels? Well, his desk was not precisely in Brussels (he was living just outside the city proper, in the Faubourg d'Ixelles) and the manifesto he was drafting was not precisely the CL's.

As we have seen, not only was it not published as the manifesto of the League, but the organization's name did not appear at all. Was this done perhaps because the League was a secret and illegal organization? It was perfectly legal in England. Perhaps omission of its name would legalize, or facilitate, distribution in Germany? Not likely. The "illegal" word on the cover was in the largest and blackest type of all: Communist. No policeman would stay his truncheon, nor censor his shears, because of the difference between the "League of the Communists" and the "Communist party," nor would the government know or care what the difference was.

The pamphlet said it was a manifesto of the "Communist party"—but the title did not assert that an organization of this name existed. At this time, well before the development of modern party systems in politics, the word 'party' (in any European language) meant primarily a tendency or current of opinion, not an organized group.* The title said: This is the communist point of view. Certainly, the Communist League assumed a certain responsibility by making this point of view available to the public, but that was all it was doing. We can believe that this was at least one reason why the manuscript went to the

---

* Writing in 1884 on "Marx and the *Neue Rheinische Zeitung*," Engels put it in language that must have been quite unclear to the Social-Democratic party members to whom it was then addressed: "At the outbreak of the February Revolution the German 'Communist party,' as we called it, consisted only of a small cadre, the Communist League, organized as a secret propaganda society."[1] This was ambiguous at best, in fact quite misleading. Even in 1872, when Marx and Engels drafted their first preface, one wonders how many readers understood the nuance when they read that "The Communist League ... commissioned the undersigned ... to draw up a ... program of the party."[2] (Emphasis added.)

printer without going through some approval procedure, or indeed without going to the next congress for a vote.

The title, we know, must have been decided well in advance, for when the London C.C. prodded Marx with its motion of January 24, it already referred to the document as the "manifesto of the Communist party."

This ties up with the fact that, from the beginning, Marx and Engels went into the CL with the announced intention of moving it away from the traditional sect format, a step which Schapper and his friends were ready to take. A sect defines a hard line between its inner mysteries and the outside world precisely by adopting a sect program, acceptance of which brings sanctification. The decision to issue a manifesto not of the League itself but of a communist point of view in general reflected an attitude looking away from sectism. A few months later, when Marx's *Neue Rheinische Zeitung* in Cologne became the de-facto communist political center, Marx had the CL shelved in practice for the duration of the revolution. (Here I leave aside the question whether this step was justified; I am pointing out that all these measures were part of a single approach.) The title of the Manifesto was an advance notice of the de-emphasis of the sect.

This approach ties up with still another aspect of the history we have sketched here. In the light of later socialist history, one has reason to wonder about the way the organizational question was posed in 1847. Marx and Engels were asked to join the CL, as individuals. Why didn't they raise the question of unifying two groups, the League of the Just centered in London and the Brussels C.C.C. led by Marx? Certainly there is no record that "fusion" or "merger" was ever brought up.

The explanation is this: Marx did not think in terms of "unification," "merger" or "fusion" because he had not in the first place thought of the C.C.C. as one sect in competition with other sects. For him, the C.C.C. was exactly what its name implied--a "correspondence committee" only, a means of contact between various communists, not a programmatic sect.* He never drafted a platform or program or manifesto for the C.C.C.

When Marx was convinced to join the CL for the motive we have seen, he gave up the C.C.C. format in order to recast the CL type of organization into something different, into the kind of political center for communists that he looked to. So when a manifesto was to be written, it was not a manifesto *of* the CL, but a manifesto presented on behalf of a broader current of politics than was contained within the organizational walls of any league. Of course, this new orientation was never followed through, since the coming of the revolution washed away all existing boundary signs.

Thus, at his desk a little outside Brussels, Marx was not under the kind of constraint that would be imposed by the need to get a draft through an overseeing committee, or to get a majority vote in some congress. Still, he was not free of all constraint. Engels had put some of it into words when he wrote to Marx that "I mean to get it through [the League] so that

---

* By a programmatic sect we mean, as before, a group whose membership boundary lines are set by a programmatic statement distinctive to it and held by no one else; the sect establishes its program as its defining wall.

there will at least be nothing contrary to our views."[3] After all, even if Schapper and the London leadership reposed great confidence in Marx, their membership was more heterogeneous and less advanced. Marx later (1860) wrote that "after vehement debates [in the CL] over several weeks, the *Manifesto of the Communist Party* written by Engels and me was accepted..."[4] He must have meant that what was accepted was the body of ideas that went into the writing of the Manifesto. He could not have gotten away with putting anything and everything he believed into the document, as if he were writing an article over his own signature; he was setting down a statement of common ground, though from his own standpoint. Everything in the Manifesto certainly represented Marx's view; but not every view held by Marx can be found in the document.

As the Manifesto was changed by the passage of time from a politically *actuel* document into (what Marx more than once called) a "historical document," this original characteristic tended to be dropped down the Memory Hole. It even took some years before the names of Marx and Engels became indelibly associated with the pamphlet. What started as the manifesto of the "communist party" eventually became the communist manifesto of Marx and Engels.

6. SOME HISTORICAL CONTROVERSIES

Among the questions that subsequently got tangled up with the Manifesto was this: Was it written as a "propaganda work" or a "scientific study"?*

For example, in 1893 the Rumanian Social-Democrats published a new edition of the Manifesto, apparently translated by I. Nadejde, with the title *Socialist Manifesto*. In an afterword headed "The Revolution and the Revolutionary Tactic," Nadejde stated that the Manifesto was a study piece, not a propaganda piece. He advised that for practical propaganda one should use the German party's Erfurt program of 1891.

Andréas, recounting this episode, comments: "Marx himself was of a contrary opinion."[1] This is certainly true. In Herr Vogt (1860) Marx explicitly remarked that the Manifesto "was intended directly for workers," as distinct from "scientific works" like his *Poverty of Philosophy*.[2] Of course, we would know this even if Marx had not written it down in *Herr Vogt*, for after all the CL issued the Manifesto as a propaganda tract. (Which does not gainsay the Manifesto's scientific content.)

Nadejde was, then, wrong in implying that the Manifesto was *issued* as a "study piece" as counterposed to a propaganda work. It might have been juster to maintain that *in 1893* it was

---

* The word 'scientific' here is a little misleading in English, which has no word clearly equivalent in broadness to the German *wissenschaftlich*. Misunderstanding of this German word is frequent in connection with Marx's view of 'scientific' socialism as well as in references to "scientific" articles. A "scientific article" by Marx is, in English radical jargon, a "theoretical" article—an article intended as theoretical analysis, not with a propaganda or agitational aim.

no longer a propaganda work, though in fact it was still frequently published as part of the propaganda arsenal of the movement. In point of fact, the dichotomy "study piece" or "propaganda piece" had become superannuated; and this is exactly what Marx and Engels meant by their reiterated statements that the Manifesto had become a "historical document."

Marx and Engels put the "historical" tag on the Manifesto in order to explain their steadfast refusal, against repeated pressures, to bring the Manifesto "up to date" in some sense, to revise it so that it was once again a politically *actuel* statement. Passage of time made the Manifesto a "historical document" by changing the meaning of the language used, by dimming the meaning of historical references, by changing readers' expectation in the way political ideas were expressed, as well as in changing the political context in every country. This effect of time is most insidious when a reader fails to realize that a change has occurred, as when he reads the word 'Democracy.'

Actually, disputes of this sort often masked other issues. The language of the Communist Manifesto breathed a revolutionary spirit which made many Social-Democrats uneasy by the end of the century: how explain it away? A few years after Nadejde's edition, Eduard Bernstein solved the problem by telling the movement that the Manifesto was one of Marx's early "Blanquist" aberrations.

This issue entered into the general battle over "Revisionism," and it is not our present subject. However, it illustrates the way in which the Manifesto became covered with a crust of controversy to which the Manifesto *per se* was incidental. Another illustration is the way in which the question of the genesis of the Manifesto became a device to downplay the role of Marx in the history of socialism.

Thus, in an essay "Karl Marx" which has been much reprinted as an introduction to the Manifesto, Harold J. Laski painted a picture of Marx's contributions that makes one wonder why anyone pays much attention to a dreary old bearded German. The *Communist Manifesto*, he explained, was not an "original" document, for it owed "much" to Victor Considérant's *Manifeste de la Démocratie* of 1843. His explanatory footnote informs us only that Considérant's "picture of the economic situation" was "like that of Marx."[3] It would be rash to believe that Laski thought this said very much. At any rate, Laski found in Considérant references to poverty, crises, oppression by capital, industrial evils—in fact, everything which by this time was the common coin of virtually all socialist propaganda. If this is all one requires of a "picture of the economic situation," then one can find the contents of the Communist Manifesto by poking a finger blindfold at the name index of any history of early socialism.

But in Considérant's "picture" of society, the basic counterposition was between the "Industrial Feudalism" of the financial oligarchy and Big Capital (meaning great wealth), on the one hand, and on the other the good bourgeoisie leading the proletariat. The economic situation is an inferno, to be sure, but there is hope:

> Fortunately the ranks of the Bourgeoisie are numerous, and its intelligences are rousing: feeling is appearing about the material and moral miseries of the working classes and the necessity for remedying this; social charity permeates them and stirs them; and the bourgeois classes are beginning, moreover, to see that they are not less

interested than the proletarians in introducing guarantees into the industrial order and in resisting the encroachments of the financial Aristocracy .

Will enlightenment come to the French bourgeoisie in time? he asks. The war of labor and capital can lead only to the victory of "feudal capital" against "small and medium capital" plus labor, or (horrors) to workers' insurrection; the solution is "to stop the struggle." The hope lies in this:

> The French bourgeoisie will not let itself be shorn and stripped with impunity of its property and of its political influence, and cast down into the proletariat...

His "picture of the economic situation" is that "there is no basic antinomy in the nature of things; there is no contradiction, no necessary war between the principles and elements of production."

> Let's talk [cries Considérant] about making the machines work FOR the capitalists and FOR the people and not FOR *the capitalists* AGAINST *the people*![4]

There is hardly any document of the early movement that so unequivocally painted a "picture of the economic situation" in which the social struggle arrayed the bourgeoisie itself ("small and medium capital") as the champion of progress, justice and the enserfed workers themselves. Here Considérant was not dealing with common ideas but with a distinctive feature of his Fourierist group which made it the most prominent representative of "petty-bourgeois socialism."

It need hardly be added that the originality of the *Communist Manifesto* comprised more than a "picture of the economic situation." There is plenty of room for serious inquiries by competent social historians into the common stock of socialistic ideas which already by 1847–1848 lay behind Marx's manifesto as behind many another socialistic production, including Considérant's.

It has been the fate of the Manifesto to suffer the brunt of this sort of historical work because of its prominent position among Marx's works. It started before Marx was in his grave. In 1881 a German scholar, Hugo Eisenhart, came out with the disclosure that the *Communist Manifesto* was "a wretched...imitation of Babeuf's manifesto of 1796"—by which he meant Marchal's "Manifesto of the Equals." The edifying tale of Eisenhart's methods is mentioned in Chapter 20. In 1901 Charles Andler, in a once much-read "Introduction and Commentary" to his own French translation of the Manifesto, argued that it was inspired by Sismondi, Buret and especially Pecqueur[5]—all good representatives of French culture, be it noted (even if Sismondi was Swiss). In 1936 Arnold Winkler came out with the thesis that the Manifesto was borrowed from Lorenz Stein.[6] This is by no means a complete list of such vagaries. By its very terms it is a game that can go on indefinitely. All that is needed is ignorance of the background of the Communist Manifesto as a "historical document."

Another aspect of this question can be introduced by coming back to a remark made in the London C.C.'s motion of January 24, 1848 (quoted in Chapter 3 above). If Marx won't do the job, the Londoners threatened, then he must immediately return "the documents handed over to him by the congress."

Evidently Marx was given documents to help him draft the Manifesto. These documents must have included a file of proposed drafts—perhaps Moses Hess's (which is not extant) as well as Engels', and perhaps others we know nothing about. The file no doubt included previous programmatic statements by the CL and its predecessor League of the Just. The CL had sent out "addresses" *(Ansprachen)* to its membership, in November 1846 and February 1847, expressing its viewpoint; the C.C. of the CL had sent out a circular on June 9, 1847, and an "address" of September 14; the first and only issue of the CL's *Kommunistische Zeitschrift* (Communist Journal) had appeared in early September with important programmatic articles.* The first congress of the CL may have produced documents on the program discussion that took place, documents not now extant.

Marx had to keep an eye on these documents because he had to satisfy the people who had recently written and discussed them, as we have explained. More important were his own recent writings and Engels' as well, for the Manifesto condensed much of their contents. It is easy to find a list of this material: it is the table of contents of the volumes of the Marx-Engels *Collected Works* for 1845–1847.

7. THE MISDATING PROBLEM

The Communist Manifesto often has the date of publication 1847 attached to it, not only in printed references but even in formal bibliographical and in scholarly publications. This error is so common that we must ask if there is any good reason for it. The answer is no; but there is a reason why the error keeps cropping up.

The date of publication is not in doubt; and even the date when the writing was completed is not doubtful as far as the year is concerned: for the London C.C.'s prodding letter of January proves that this date was late January 1848 at the earliest. Indeed, the *Communist Manifesto* is the only work one can easily think of which actually bore its date of publication as part of its title!** In the first edition, "Published in February 1848" appeared in the position of a subtitle, and this was repeated up until the 1866 edition (for

---

* All these documents, and more, are now easily available in a valuable volume of almost 1200 pages: *Der Bund der Kommunisten. Dokumente und Materialien. Band 1: 1836–1849* (Berlin: Dietz, 1970).

** Why the date of publication was given such special prominence in the first edition is a question I have never seen raised. Later on, it served to say, in effect: "This manifesto was published on the very eve of the revolution"; but if it served this purpose in the first edition, then this edition must have been published very late in February.

which see Chapter 14 below) and was adopted in a number of translations. Why then the common error in dating?

The trouble probably stems from a mistake in *Capital*.

In the first volume of *Capital*, published 1867, the Manifesto was quoted in two passages. The first constituted a footnote in Chapter 13, Section 9, note 306 (MEW 23:511); in English editions this is Chapter 15, Section 9. In this footnote the Manifesto was duly dated 1848.

The second passage was a footnote in the best-known chapter of the work, "Historical Tendency of Capitalist Accumulation"—Chapter 24, Section 7, note 252 *(MEW* 23:791); in English editions, Chapter 32, last note. And in this *footnote the Manifesto was erroneously dated 1847.*

This mistake appeared not only in the first edition of *Capital*, but in all the subsequent German editions revised by Marx or Engels; also in the French translation by Joseph Roy which Marx intensively revised; also in the first Italian edition, the first Roumanian edition, perhaps in other translations, and likewise in the English translation published in 1887 under Engels' editorship. The Kerr edition of Volume 1 (English translation) retained the 1847 mistake; but in later English editions (IML editions, the Pauls' translation, and Fowkes') as well as in modern German editions, the error has been silently corrected to 1848.

The chapter on the "Historical Tendency [etc.]" was not only a prominent locus but also the single chapter most often excerpted in anthologies and selected-writings editions. We can assume that a great many, doubtless most or all, of these reprints reproduced the error.

Now the error itself requires no special exegesis—a slip is a slip, and this is not the only one of the kind that Marx made. The fact that the other passage in *Capital* quoting the Manifesto bore the date 1848 saves us, at least, from theories that Marx *intended* to claim 1847 as the date of the Manifesto. But casual readers, acquainted only or mainly with the second passage, may be pardoned for believing that the dating statement made by Marx himself was reliable. But editors may not be pardoned.

Thus the error got wide circulation, and took on a persistent life, which is by no means over. It appeared, perhaps for the first time after *Capital*, in the anti-Bakunin pamphlet drafted mainly by Engels and Lafargue that was published by the International in 1873.[1] It appeared in an 1873 book by Wilhelm Bracke, a close associate of Marx and Engels in the German party[2] and in the first Italian book that gave a presentation of the Manifesto's contents, a work by V. Cusumano published in 1875.[3] H. M. Hyndman's memoirs (1911) referred to "the famous Communist Manifesto of 1847."[4]

Editions of the Manifesto itself began bearing the erroneous date: for example, the first Polish translation of 1883, which bore "1847" right after the title.[5] The book by Mermeix which contained Laura Marx Lafargue's second French version (see Chapter 25 below) had a chapter titled "Le Manifeste de 1847."

Engels himself helped to spread the mistake, not only in the above-mentioned editions of Capital and of the Manifesto which he edited, but in at least two other loci. In 1885 he was in correspondence with Pasquale Martignetti, who did translations of works by Marx and Engels. On June 13 Engels sent Martignetti a copy of the Manifesto, "un esemplare [he wrote] del *Manifesto del partito comunista di 1847* (da Marx e Engels)."[6] Martignetti may be pardoned for taking his word for it.

Two years later, much worse: Engels gave the erroneous date a mighty publicity boost when he published a new preface to the American edition of his *Condition of the Working Class in England.* The preface, dated January 26, 1887, ended with a longish quote from "the *Communist Manifesto* of 1847." This preface received very wide distribution, being reprinted several times in English and translated into a number of languages. The "1847" mistake in this work has never been corrected to the present day. Even *MEW* (which generally follows the unwise editorial policy of silently correcting errors of this sort by Marx and Engels) perpetuates the mistake in two separate volumes, without a note[7]; and even current English translations of this 1887 preface continue publicizing the "1847" date of the Manifesto.[8] This may be the immediate source of many contemporary mistakes.

The chapters that follow will show many examples of the erroneous 1847 dating, cropping up as an incidental part of the story. It is no part of our aim to collect such cases, but we should stress that the mistake has been made even by the most knowledgeable writers. It is perhaps piquant to mention that Karl Kautsky, at the height of his eminence as an authority on Marxism, in his 1909 book *The Road to Power,* stated that "the Communist Manifesto announced in November 1847 the coming revolution of 1848."[9] The date he gave was that of the Communist League congress which commissioned the manifesto; he may have been under the impression that the congress actually adopted a finished text. To keep the political scales even, we can add that Kautsky's "Revisionist" opponent, Eduard Bernstein, also misdated the Manifesto, not in some obscure article but in his chief work launching the controversy.[10]

8. THE MANIFESTO IN THE REVOLUTION OF 1848

If we figure that the Manifesto came off the press during the last week of February 1848, then its appearance almost exactly coincided with the outbreak of the first edition of the international revolution, that is, the first international revolution in world history.

The rumblings of revolution were already heard in 1847—well summarized in an article Engels published in Brussels on January 23.[1] A few days later, he published an article titled "The Beginning of the End in Austria," which was more anticipatory than reportorial.[2] On January 12 a revolt in Palermo against the Bourbon monarchy of the "Two Sicilies" brought repercussions in the other "Sicily," i.e., Naples: on February 10, King Ferdinand II ("King Bomba") proclaimed a constitution after turbulent demonstrations. On February 20, an article by Engels was able to chortle that "In less than a fortnight three absolute monarchies have been transformed into constitutional states: Denmark, Naples and Sardinia."[3]

Then the dam burst. On February 22, Paris saw demonstrations and barricades; fighting began in the streets. On February 23, Louis Philippe dismissed Guizot—a wolf sacrificed to the lambs. The workers continued fighting, and by morning controlled the streets. On February 24, the king abdicated, and the Second Republic was proclaimed.

And quite possibly at this very moment the Manifesto was coming off Burghard's press in London.

The stormy events of February accounted for much of Europe's subsequent history; *parvis componere magna*—the same storm also conditioned the publishing history of the Manifesto. In ordinary times the (estimated) thousand copies of the first printing might have sufficed for a while. As it was, four printings of the first edition were run off, and a second edition called for, by April or May.

The four printings (which Andréas calls editions IA to ID) probably followed each other at short intervals, so that there was no time in-between to make corrections of even bad typographical errors. There was a large number of typos and defective letters in this first edition, remaining uncorrected through the printings.*

We know where some bundle orders went: at the beginning of March, a hundred copies went to the Amsterdam GWEA; about March 20, a thousand copies went to Paris; at about the beginning of April, the Paris communists supplied Manifestos to three or four thousand German émigré workers returning to their homeland-in-revolution. The spread of uprising to Berlin on March 18 meant a demand for more copies, not only because of the radicalization of the situation but also because distribution could now be legal. If we assume an interval of about a week between printings, the fourth printing (edition ID) came about the end of March or early April, and was probably exhausted during April.

Not long after the first edition came out, the Manifesto had its first serial newspaper publication. The émigré weekly *Deutsche Londoner Zeitung* started publishing the entire text in installments, thirteen in all. It began in the March 3 issue, and ended July 28. The *DLZ* had published documents of the League of the Just before, also those of the GWEA—not because it was itself communist in sympathy, but because of the interest of the German community. The picture that is sometimes painted of a Manifesto that came out to total indifference and disappeared to oblivion is far from true.

This newspaper publication reached another circle of readers, and made the Manifesto known to people who would otherwise not have seen it. They were reading it in the newspaper's columns all during the months when the revolution spread over Germany and most of Europe.

The first Continental reaction to the Manifesto came in March—in Amsterdam. As mentioned, a hundred copies had been sent to the workers' association in that city, called the Vereenigung tot Zedelijke Beschaving van de Arbeidende Klasse, founded in 1847. On March 24 the association held a big meeting on the central plaza to discuss workers' conditions; it drew a few thousands. The police broke it up on a pretext, arrested the leaders, and actually put three of them on trial, even demanding the death penalty. The jury's

---

* Andréas has a table comparing the distinctive features (misprints, defective type, etc.) of the four printings of the first edition. If you run across one, you should have no trouble identifying it.

response was to acquit them. One of the three, Christian Gödeke, sent out an invitation to a number of people to come to a gathering to take up "the brochure discussed March 24." The government prosecutors published a report on the affair in which they devoted considerable space to summarizing and denouncing the *Communist Manifesto*. Evidently the bundle of a hundred Manifestos had played a role in focusing the political orientation of the Amsterdam demonstration and the subsequent thinking of its leaders.

A second edition of the pamphlet was needed because of the extensive use of the Manifesto by members of the CL who did propaganda work in several German cities during April and concentrated in Cologne by May.[4] This second edition probably came out in April or May. The cover—still dark green—bore the same words as the first edition, but the text type was reset, this time in thirty pages, a bit smaller in size (208 x 134 mm). There were fewer errors. (Andréas has a table for this edition too.) It was this second edition—the "thirty-pager"—which, as things developed, became the basis of most subsequent German editions.

In April, as the CL émigrés were preparing to leave Paris for their return to Germany, Marx and Engels published what was in effect a timely supplement to the Manifesto. The Manifesto already had a ten-point program (see end of Section III) but this, written in advance of the revolution, was directed at large. What was needed now was a program for a specific country, Germany, and for this specific time, *now*. What they produced was a flysheet bearing seventeen demands. It was headed "Demands of the Communist Party of Germany," using "party" in the same way as the Manifesto itself. It was distributed along with the Manifesto in the course of the CL's activity.

Distribution of copies of the Manifesto was an important part of the work of the Marx group—that is, the activists around the *Neue Rheinische Zeitung*—in Cologne during the revolution. One episode provides a vignette: at an important juncture in 1848, when Wilhelm Weitling was making a bid for influence in the Cologne movement, "many copies of the Manifesto of the Communist Party were distributed" as an educational-propaganda bar to illusions about Weitlingism.*

A contrary impression is given by many works on Marx, which assert, on the basis of misinterpreted evidence, that Marx and Engels suppressed or shelved the Manifesto or its views during the revolutionary period in Cologne. I have dealt with this myth in my Karl Marx's Theory of Revolution (2:214–219); and it need only be added that, if the claims were true, it would be hard to explain why so many editions and printings of the Manifesto were called for in 1848.

Before the revolution was over, Germany saw the first publication of a substantial part of the Manifesto within the country itself. It came in a leftist paper, *Die Homisse* (Kassel), edited by Gottlieb Kellner. In March 1849, with the revolution plainly on the defensive, it published, under editor Kellner's signature, a free adaptation of the first three sections of the

---

* The quote is from *Karl Marx, Chronik seines Lebens*, page 55, which cites two Cologne newspapers. Andréas (page 13, note 6) also refers to Hermann Becker's memoirs.

Manifesto in a three-article series. In another three issues during April and May, it published the complete text of Section I, with slight changes.[5]

9. THE PHANTOM TRANSLATIONS OF FORTY-EIGHT

The Manifesto itself stated, at the end of the preamble, that translations "will be published" in five languages: English, French, Italian, Flemish, and Danish. This was not a prediction but undoubtedly reflected specific plans to get these translations made. Indeed, efforts followed in 1848 to get versions done in Spanish and Polish too, and possibly in Hungarian. But not one of these was published in 1848–1849. And the first translation that did appear was none of the foregoing.

Obviously, from the CL's standpoint, the most important translations would be in English and French. The French translation seems to have been assigned initially to Victor Tedesco, a Belgian CL member of Luxemburgian origin, whom we saw accompanying Marx to the CL congress in November 1847. He was a 27-year-old lawyer in Liège, who later in 1848 was going to be framed up by the Belgian police for involvement in the Risquons-Tout riot, and imprisoned until 1854. At his trial he testified that he had been asked to do such a translation; in prison, without documents, he composed a "Catéchisme du Prolétaire" based in part on passages from the Manifesto and from Engels' "Principles of Communism," reprocessed through his own mind and memory. (It was published in Liège in 1849.) But he never did a translation of the Manifesto itself, presumably because of his imprisonment.

In November Hermann Ewerbeck, a member of the CL in Paris, was assigned the task of getting a French translation done. According to Andréas, it *was* done—by Charles Paya, a French left-republican journalist, formerly editor of the Toulouse *Emancipation;* he was possibly aided by the German communist Friedrich Wolff and others. It was finished about the end of February 1849, and was to be published as a brochure with a biographical note on Marx and a translator's preface—but it did not appear, and in fact was never heard from. Later in 1849, one Morel, a French socialist, worked on a translation, but did not finish it. We will not hear again about a French translation until after the Paris Commune.

In April 1848, the English translation was undertaken by Engels himself. After getting to Cologne with Marx, he left town on a fund-raising trip to his home town, Barmen (to sell shares for the forthcoming *Neue Rheinische Zeitung*). It was a depressing expedition, for he found that his father and bourgeois acquaintances were in a bitterly antirevolutionary mood; nor was the trip productive financially, naturally. Perhaps to cheer himself up, or to do something useful, he devoted time to working on the Manifesto.

I am working on the English translation [he wrote to Marx on April 25], which presents more difficulties than I thought. Still, over a half is finished, and the whole thing will be finished soon.[1]

That is the last we hear of it. There is no indication that this manuscript (whether completed or not) was preserved even to 1850, when Engels might have made it available to Helen Macfarlane—if he had it. (See Chapter 11 below.) There is no evidence at all on what he did with it; it may well have been destroyed in Barmen in anticipation of searches by the police.

In the same letter to Marx, Engels wrote that "Ewerbeck is having the Manifesto translated into Italian and Spanish in Paris..." But he expressed a dim view about expectations from this quarter. The dim view was justified; nothing came of either an Italian or a Spanish version.

Nor was there any sign of a Flemish translation. There is more hope about a Danish version: the London CL had some Swedish and Danish members; and Engels later (in 1880–1890s) wrote as if a Danish translation had appeared. But none has been found. It is possible to point to several later statements by Marx and Engels about 1848–1849 translations of the Manifesto that do not in fact exist—or anyway have never been found. As likely an explanation as any is that Marx or Engels was simply relying on the statement in the Manifesto's preamble.

A Polish translation (not mentioned in the Manifesto preamble) may possibly have been done. Marx and Engels were in close touch with the Polish Democratic emigration in Brussels, Paris and London, and had participated in more than one meeting celebrating the Polish uprising of 1830–1831. Also, Poland was one of the countries about which the Manifesto's Section IV discussed a specific policy. In this case too, Ewerbeck was acting as a go-between: on December 12 he wrote Marx that a Polish translation was being prepared. Andréas even concludes that "It seems probable this Polish translation did in fact appear a little later," perhaps because Marx and Engels mentioned such a publication in three prefaces to the Manifesto. But in fact no copy of a Polish edition of this time has been found. And so, in the end, a Polish translation of 1848 is as spectral as the rest of the list; as spectral as the Hungarian translation of 1848 which an anonymous columnist in a Czech socialist paper once referred to—in 1890.*

So, as far as anyone knows, there was only one translation issued in this period. It came out, probably at the end of December 1848—in Swedish.

The title was rewritten as follows: *The Voice of Communism. Declaration of the Communist Party, Published in February 1848.—The voice of the people is the voice of God.*** The motto added here was the Swedish touch, replacing the watchword "Proletarians of all countries, unite," which was deleted from the ending of the Manifesto. A paragraph was also deleted from Section II.

The translator was widely believed to be Per Götrek, a Stockholm teacher and bookseller; he had a bookseller's advertisement on the verso of the cover. In 1847 he had written a book

* An editorial note in MECW 6:698 alleges that a Danish edition and a Polish (Paris) edition were published, but it gives no reference.

** In Swedish: Kommunismens Röst. Förklaring af det Kommunistiska Partiet, offentliggyord i Februari 1848. —Folkets Röst är Guds Röst. The imprint: Stockholm, f.d. Schultzes Boktryckeri, 1848, in 8o, 44 pages.

on communism which had made use of Engels' "Principles of Communism." He had started as a Saint-Simonian, turned Cabetist in the 1840s, and later helped found a communist society, the

Kommunistiska Sälskapet. (It should be recalled that the Cabetists, a.k.a. "Icarians," called themselves communists.)

But Götrek denied that he was the translator. On January 28, 1849, the editor of the *Folkbladet*, K. J. Ekeblad, published a virulent blast against the newly published Manifesto; Götrek, denying responsibility, replied in an article on February 4. The Manifesto was drawing first blood in, of all places, Stockholm.

There was more controversy about the Manifesto in April 1851, when the organ of the Stockholm workers' association, *Demokraten,* wrote about the translation. (Per Götrek was one of the leading contributors to this paper; one can see a possible connection). A conservative organ attacked the Manifesto. In this connection, *Demokraten* itself commented that "there was no communist movement in our country"; Swedish socialism, it assured, had no intention of shaking the established order.[2] This was no doubt true; Sweden's priority was something of a fluke. There was a hiatus of over a third of a century before a translation of the Communist Manifesto came out in Swedish under its own name.[3]

The fact that the translations promised in the Manifesto's preamble did not appear has little to do with the question of the work's reception. A revolutionary storm is not good weather for literary work. In the revolutionary period the impact of the Manifesto was limited to the German left

.FROM 1848 TO THE PARIS COMMUNE

10. THE MANIFESTO AFTER THE REVOLUTION

arx was settled in England by August 1849, followed by Engels in November. Their immediate project was the publication of a periodical named after their Cologne daily newspaper but planned as a monthly magazine: *Neue Rheinische Zeitung, politisch-ökonomische Revue*—for short, *NRZ Revue*. Its first issue, dated January 1850, came out in March; its fifth and last issue was a double number labeled "No. 5/6, May to October," which appeared on November 29.

The revolution was over. By late summer Marx decided that it was not just in a lull (as many in the CL still believed) but finished for the period. Still, CL members were active here and there in Germany; and wherever there was CL activity, there was also a demand for copies of the Manifesto. The police kept finding "a small brochure with green covers" as they executed home searches to stamp out the "Communist Conspiracy"—so reported the Wermuth-Stieber textbook for Prussian police communist-hunters.*

Refugees from the German revolution were still living in countries of exile around Prussia. The Manifesto was in demand for workers' educational associations and reading-and-study circles in cities like Geneva, Hamburg, Stockholm, and other cities where there was émigré activity. There are some scattered indications of the sporadic demand. In Berlin, an active CL member, Carl J. A. Htzel, distributed about a dozen copies at the beginning of 1849; Wilhelm Liebknecht gave lectures during 1849–1850 at the workers' association in Geneva—on the Manifesto; in March 1851, a CL member in Brunswick acknowledged receipt of fifty copies; in Frankfurt a *Leseverein* (reading circle) received a package of brochures, including Manifestos, to be read in the course of a study class. In October—six months after the police had started their mass arrests of CL members and sympathizers in Prussia—the Berlin police prefect wrote: "The *Communist Manifesto* forms the basis of the League and ... is everywhere distributed."[1]

The demand for a new edition traveled back to Marx's dwelling in London. In September 1850 the cigar worker Peter Röser, a leading CL member in Cologne, wrote Marx asking for a new edition on behalf of the Cologne Communists. He repeated the request in early November.

By the end of 1850, Marx was involved in a wider publishing project: he was arranging with Hermann Becker of Cologne for the publication of his *Collected Essays*, writings going back to 1842. This multivolume enterprise was going to include the Manifesto too. But it collapsed, after publishing an initial volume only, when the arrests of the Cologne Communists started in 1851.

During this period, it is entirely possible that Marx began thinking of a third edition of the Manifesto. Andréas argues that Marx, or Marx and Engels, drew up a revised text, embodying changes in preparation for such a new edition. His argument hinges on certain corrections and verbal alterations which *did* later show up—in Macfarlane's English version, in the "Hirschfeld edition" of the 1860s (see Chapter 13), and in Marx's quotes from the Manifesto in his *Herr Vogt*. As a matter of fact, Andréas goes much further, proposing that a third edition may actually have been published. But there is no evidence whatever for this latter hypothesis, nor even the existence of a revised manuscript. This shadowy "third edition" may have existed only in the form of a few proposed changes penciled in on a copy by Marx; at any rate, this is a more reasonable conjecture. But it is only a conjecture.

In the course of 1850, the fact of the authorship of the Manifesto was allowed into print for the first time, on three occasions. The first, a partial case, came in June. Otto Lüning, a "petty-bourgeois socialist" (in Marx's view) who edited the *Neue Deutsche Zeitung* in Frankfurt, reviewed Marx's articles in the *NRZ Revue* on the revolutionary period in France, the articles later entitled *The Class Struggles in France 1848–1850*. Lüning's main objection was to Marx's emphasis on the working class, especially on the goal of working-class power in society; he

---

* The Wermuth-Stieber book is discussed in Chapter 12.

thought that the abolition of all classes should be stressed instead. Marx sent in a letter to the editor, tersely making the point that he always coupled the one with the other: his letter was a series of citations from his writings to show he had emphasized the abolition of class as the aim of working-class victory. It was in this context that he quoted from the Manifesto.[2]

Marx, then, was plainly citing the Manifesto along with his other writings, and a reader could have assumed that he was *the* author. The terse form of the letter left this question ambiguous.

The authorship was made explicit when, in the last issue of the *NRZ Revue*, off the press November 29, Marx republished all of Section III of the Manifesto. An editorial note stated: "We give here an excerpt from the *Manifesto of the Communist Party* written by Karl Marx and Friedrich Engels, published before the February Revolution."

The title of this reprint was the title of the corresponding section of the Manifesto: "Socialist and Communist Literature." The text was that of the first edition, with some corrections of typographical errors. Even these corrections, however, were not perpetuated in subsequent editions, because Marx and Engels later based themselves on the Meyer edition of 1866, which in turn was based on the second edition. In fact, this reprint of Section III was ignored in later editorial work to such an extent that it can be explained only by the unavailability of *NRZ Revue* copies. (Even Engels did not own a complete set in later years.)

Marx's choice of Section III for this reprint deserves some notice. We can understand that he did not want to take the space to republish the entire Manifesto; but why *this* section? This is the section that was later often dismissed as the "obsolete" part of the Manifesto because it discussed rival schools of socialism which no longer existed. Indeed, the specific targets of Section III were hardly in existence by 1850. Clearly Marx must have felt that the critical ideas expressed in Section III were important at a conjuncture when the triumph of reaction was reviving conservative attitudes, viewpoints which the revolutionary upheaval had temporarily swamped. To be sure, "feudal socialism" as such was obsolete in 1850, but the critique of this school was not. "Bourgeois socialism" and "petty-bourgeois socialism" lived on in other forms.*

The third place where the Manifesto's authorship was publicized was in connection with the English translation by Macfarlane, which is the subject of the next chapter. In fact, this English announcement came out about three weeks before the *NRZ Revue*, and therefore was the first linkage of the names of Marx and Engels with the Manifesto.

I think there was a particular reason why at this time Marx and Engels wanted to publicize their authorship of the Manifesto. The Communist League had gone through a split in September 1850, after growing dissension by a faction following Karl Schapper and August Willich, who wound up establishing a rival Communist League. In the discussions

---

* Many years later, Engels was led to make a similar point about the relevancy of Section III, in a letter criticizing Liebknecht's weakness for catering to bourgeois intellectuals who wanted to blunt the party's revolutionary character: "The petty-bourgeois element in the party," wrote Engels in 1885, "is more and more getting the upper hand... Well now, will the section [of the Manifesto] on German or True Socialism again become applicable after 40 years?"[3]

Marx had taken the position that the Willich-Schapper group was departing from the orientation laid down by the Communist Manifesto and other League programmatic documents. In effect, Marx and Engels came forward as the continuators of the policies of the Manifesto; and in this connection they put the spotlight on the fact that they, after all, had written it.

This situation may also have been the reason in whole or part why Marx chose Section III for reprinting. At this time he was arguing that the Willich-Schapper group was repudiating proletarian socialism, like the schools criticized in that section.

11. HELEN MACFARLANE AND THE FIRST ENGLISH TRANSLATION

The month of November 1850 saw not only the *NRZ Revue* reprint in German but also the publication of the first English version of the Manifesto. This translation appeared in the weekly *Red Republican*, in four issues, November 9 to 30.

This was a left Chartist organ published by George Julian Harney, then the leading voice of the revolutionary wing of the English movement. Harney had been a good friend of Engels since 1843, and had long been associated with the CL (and of the preceding League of the Just) as a British ally of Continental revolutionaries. He was a leading non-German member of the London GWEA; his international enterprise, called the Fraternal Democrats, had included Schapper and his friends even before the latter made common cause with Marx; and in mid-1850 he joined with Marx and the French Blanquist group in London in a projected Société Universel des Communistes Révolutionnaires which in actuality never got off paper.

Harney was in steady personal contact with Marx, and unquestionably he must have run the Manifesto in his weekly with the agreement of, and by arrangement with, its authors. His short editorial introduction to the translation stated that it had been "drawn up in the German language, in January 1848, by Citizens *Charles Marx* and *Frederic Engels*." As mentioned, the original title clearly said "Published in February," but this note by Harney referred to the date when it had been "drawn up." We must presume that Marx or Engels had told Harney that the writing had taken place in January.

The translation was done by Helen Macfarlane. She is something of a mystery woman—only because we know so little about her and would like to know more. In early 1850 she appeared on the socialist scene as a contributor to Harney's journalistic enterprises, and then vanished from it by the end of the year, not to be heard from again. Harney's biographer Schoyen writes that she was "an ardent feminist, thoroughly emancipated and advanced in her expression; wellread in philosophy and an admirer of Hegel; and evidently a traveled woman as well, having witnessed the Vienna revolution in 1848." (These are all deductions from her articles.)

She lived in Burnley, a town twenty-two miles north of Manchester, and therefore may have met Engels first; but she also knew Marx, who had a high opinion of her abilities.* A letter by Harney referred to her as "Miss" Macfarlane; she must have lived with someone of the same name, perhaps her mother.

Macfarlane wrote a number of articles for Harney during this year, using also the pen name Howard Morton. (Schoyen is surely correct in identifying this name with her.) Some of these articles had paraphrased the Manifesto. Her articles, in Harney's weekly *Red Republican* and monthly *Democratic Review,* showed acquaintance also with the "Demands of the Communist Party in Germany" of 1848. It would be hard to see how this Burnley resident knew of this document unless we assume that Marx or Engels showed it to her.

Her translation of the Manifesto followed the first edition, like the *NRZ Revue* reprint. The question we have to ask is this: to what extent does her version reflect help from Engels or Marx?

There is no information at all about any relationship between Macfarlane and the authors *on this translation,* but we know they were in touch in general. Thus, when the last issue of the *NRZ Revue* came out, containing the Section III reprint, Mrs. Marx wrote to Engels: "On behalf of Karl I am sending you herewith six copies of the *Neue Rheinische Zeitung [Revue].* Harney ... wishes you to send one to Helen Macfarlane..."[2] This copy was evidently not being sent to her for use in translating, for her translation had already begun appearing in the November 9 issue. But we have a right to ask this key question: given these relations, would Macfarlane have been loath to ask Engels' or Marx's advice on how to translate one of the many difficult passages? And wouldn't the authors have been very, very eager to help?**

There is, then, an open question about whether this or that feature of the Macfarlane translation may have been due to consultation with one of the Manifesto's authors. Little attention has been paid to this possibility, in part because of the inaccessibility of the text; the Macfarlane version has never been reprinted. On the other hand, it would be quite

---

* When Harney's narrowminded wife forced him into a personal break with Macfarlane, Marx deplored Harney's "very discreditable way of breaking with the only contributor...who really had ideas. A *rara avis* in his sheet."[1] This episode, in fact, ended Macfarlane's writing. There is no reason to believe that Mrs. Harney had any ground for her animosity other than the belief that any woman who associated with radicals was a loose hussy. Harney's shameful behavior toward Macfarlane prefigured his subsequent way of breaking with Marx and Engels; the reference is not to the political but to the moral pattern.

** Andréas, as mentioned, seems to think that Engels must still have had a copy of the translation which he had worked on In Barmen in 1848, and, if so, must have made it available to Macfarlane. In a footnote he says that "we have it from Dr. F. de Jong of the I.I.S.H. that Harney's letters to Engels confirm Harney's intention to publish the 1848 translation by Engels; this correspondence itself has not been accessible." But the Harney letters have now been published,[3] and I do not find such a statement. Nevertheless: even if the Barmen manuscript was not extant, Engels could still have aided Macfarlane just as well as the manuscript. Andréas' strongest case is made on the basis of textual considerations: emendations which she could hardly have made without getting special advice from the authors. But this case does not require the hypothesis that Engels' manuscript was still extant.

erroneous to leap to the opposite sort of conclusion, namely, that Marx or Engels was responsible for everything and anything in Macfarlane's text. It is very likely, in my opinion, that their contribution was most important for preventing bad (or worse) mistakes in the translations.

We do know that Marx's and Engels' first view of the Macfarlane translation must have been that it was generally acceptable, with whatever reservations; for they proposed to make use of it more than once. In January 1851 Engels reported that he was discussing with "friends of Harney" in Manchester: "I will see," he remarked, "about organizing a small club or regular get-togethers with these chaps and discussing the Manifesto with them."[4] This would have entailed using the *Red Republican* translation.

Later that year, Marx tried to promote publication of the translation as a brochure. From the United States, he received a request for copies of the Manifesto from a former German Catholic priest, Eduard Ignaz Koch. Of about the same age as Engels, Koch had taken part in the 1848 revolution and in the Baden-Palatinate uprising of 1849, then emigrated to America in 1850; there he occasionally wrote for the *New Yorker Staatszeitung*. Marx sent him twenty copies of the Manifesto in German and a copy of the Macfarlane translation, then heard nothing more from him. (Koch had other interests: he distributed Blanqui's writings too, and after 1851 was involved with the "Free Community" in New York.) In October, Marx wrote to his friend Weydemeyer about a "task for you":

> Ask him [Koch] for an explanation (1) of this very suspicious silence after he had written me so urgently, and (2) get the English translation from him and see if you can't launch it as a brochure, i.e., print, distribute, and sell it. It goes without saying that whatever revenue there is goes to you, but we want 20–50 copies for ourselves.[5]

Weydemeyer tried to get such a brochure published with the help of Charles A. Dana, editor of the *New York Daily Tribune*, who knew Marx; but nothing came of it.

In England, the Macfarlane translation had an unexpected echo: an editorial in *The Times* of September 2, 1851 devoted itself to deploring the "literature of the poor"; and to exemplify the horrors of this socialistic literature, the paper cited some passages from the Macfarlane version as well as from Proudhon. The *Quarterly Review* reprinted the editorial the same month. Later, an antisocialist flyer published in London by a group of industrialists carried a caricature showing a monster, communism, besetting the bourgeoisie. This cartoon-communism was shown with the device, "Proletarians of all countries, unite!" The language of the Manifesto made its way through odd channels.

But we will see below that later, when Marx and Engels encountered the Macfarlane translation in other guises, without realizing its provenance, their reaction was unfavorable: they thought it quite defective—and this, by the way, is true.

P ublication of the English translation was virtually the last positive development of the decade in the career of the Manifesto.

To be sure, in New York the complete text *almost* got republished in (of all places) the paper run by Marx's old enemy, Wilhelm Weitling, *Die Republik der Arbeiter*. Weitling was as hostile to Marx as ever; but while he was away on a propaganda tour of the country, his temporary editor (unidentified) started publishing the Manifesto in installments, beginning with the issue of October 11, 1851. The paper ran four installments, the last coming on November 8, presenting Section I and most of Section II; then no more. One presumes that Weitling returned and put a stop to it.

In general, the fifties formed a low point in Marx's life as well as in the fortunes of the Manifesto (and of the movement as a whole). As mentioned, the Prussian government launched an anticommunist witchhunt in 1851; the preceding November, King Friedrich Wilhelm IV himself had intervened to promote it with a letter to his minister Manteuffel. Arrests of CL members and friends took place during 1851; after months of imprisonment they were haled before the court in a framed-up show-trial, in October 1852. The scenario called for a Communist Conspiracy to Overthrow the Government by Force and Violence; and the conspiracy was invented to order by the police impresario, Wilhelm Stieber.

Stieber was a lawyer who had entered police administration in 1844; in 1851 he became head of the security Polizei in Berlin, under police chief K. L. F. von Hinckeldey; from 1852 to 1860 he functioned as head of the Prussian political police, an institution whose development he pioneered. Eclipsed for a while in the 1860s as a result of the bad odor that settled over his police operations, Stieber served the czarist government for a few years, then was recalled by Bismarck, who used his practiced hand to prepare the outlawing of the Social-Democratic Party in 1878. He went to his reward in 1882.

The *Communist Manifesto* naturally played a role in the conspiracy. Stieber arranged for forged documentation as needed; but he also introduced whatever else suited his purpose, in particular CL documents and letters from Marx and Engels seized in house searches. The prosecution cited the real documents, including the Manifesto, in partly falsified or distorted quotes. In the court session of November 4, 1852, one of the defendants, Heinrich Bürgers, devoted himself to exposing the falsifications and expounding the history and real contents of the Manifesto.*

The government conspiracy was a great success. Three defendants were given six years; another three, five years; one got three years; three were acquitted, and one was tried again; but all of them had been in prison for a year and a half before the trial had even taken place. Most important, workers' groups were intimidated; study groups and circles had already been broken up by police raids and intimidation. Hardened communists might shake their

---

* About the Cologne Communist trial, much information can be gained from the collection, Marx and Engels, *The Cologne Communist Trial;* edited by Rodney Livingstone with a historical introduction (1971). It contains the pamphlet written by Marx to expose the trial, and much more material.

fists, but miasmic fear settled over dissentient elements of the Lower Orders, who were finding out what a police state meant. On Marx's proposal, the Communist League itself decided to dissolve, its organization in Germany smashed.

During 1853–1854 Stieber collaborated with another ornament of the German gendarmerie to produce a two-volume work on the conspiracy from which they had saved the nation; his partner was K. G. L. Wermuth, the police chief of Hanover.* This book was not intended to become a public best-seller; it was published with a small press run as an official textbook for the use of German police authorities confronted by the Communist Menace.

Part of the educational material offered here comprised passages from the *Communist Manifesto*, many of them distorted or falsified. Engels later wrote about "this crude compilation, which bristles with deliberate falsifications, fabricated by two of the most contemptible police scoundrels of our century..." [1] (This comes up again in Chapter 21 below.)

One of the troubles that crowns success in communist witchhunting is that the operation removes the need for the operators. After the working-class movement had reached a nadir of inactivity and silence, and after the law of November 1854 had decreed the dissolution of workers' organizations, one might suppose that Wermuth and Stieber would direct their energies to constructive channels. But these defenders of civilization knew a good thing when they saw it: they continued their creative literary efforts; and a new subversive circular was discovered in Hanover (Wermuth's bailiwick). The Hanover daily published it; the August Augsburg *Allgemeine Zeitung* republished it; and in this latter paper Marx could read it and see that it consisted of some shards from the Manifesto and other CL documents, including an eight-point program inventively paraphrasing the Manifesto's ten-point program. Marx commented in a letter that it was "a falsification, a wretched compilation from our writings, written by Herr Stieber, who in Prussia in recent times has not been properly appreciated, and now in Hanover wants to set himself up as a big man..." [2] When the circular's authenticity was questioned by a Bremen paper, Stieber himself rushed to defend it in the press. [3]

As the last flickers of the revolutionary period guttered out, the *Communist Manifesto* too faded from view. Engels later wrote in retrospect along these lines:

The Manifesto has had a history of its own. ...[I]t was soon forced into the background by the reaction that began with the defeat of the Paris workers in June 1848, and was finally excommunicated "according to law" by the conviction of the Cologne Communists in November 1852. With the disappearance from the public scene of the

---

* The title of this opus, sometimes called the "Black Book," was *Die Communisten -Verschwörungen des neunzehnten Jahrhunderts* (The Communist Conspiracies of the Nineteenth Century). Volume 1 dealt with "The historical presentation of the investigations in question." Volume 2 was an index of 760 persons suspected of subversive activity; Engels was No. 155, Marx No. 404.

workers' movement that had begun with the February Revolution, the Manifesto too passed into the background.[4]

13. THE SIXTIES: LASSALLE AND HIRSCHFELD

The Manifesto revived in the sixties along with the movement. It still remained far from well known. Liebknecht thought in 1865 that he possessed "probably the sole copy in Germany." (So he wrote in 1900, but the claim need not be taken literally.) In 1866 a member of the International in Hamburg, F. Meinecke, tried to find a copy, without success, and wrote to J. P. Becker in Geneva to get one.

The sixties began with Marx's publication of his defensive polemic *Herr Vogt* (1860), which made two contributions to the history of the Manifesto. For one thing, Marx included a passage briefly relating the genesis of the Manifesto.[1] For another, he quoted from the pamphlet in such fashion as to suggest that he was quoting a revised text.[2] But the emendations he gave (if that is what they were, rather than simply mistakes) never appeared in any edition of the Manifesto he supervised. As I hypothesized previously, maybe it was merely a question of alterations tentatively penciled in, but not carried further.

In the early 1860s Lassalle was beginning his new career as a workers' political leader; and much of Lassalle's ideological-theoretical equipment depended on his knowledge of the *Communist Manifesto*. As Engels had occasion to remark: Lassalle "knew the Manifesto by heart." But Lassalle never accepted, or understood, Marx's economic theory, political approach, or consistent materialist method of historical analysis; he used pieces, or bits and pieces, of Marx's theory as suited his own purposes—like many another "Marxist" since then.

On April 12, 1862, Lassalle gave a lecture to a Berlin workers' group, published at the beginning of the following year as the *Arbeiterprogramm* (Workers' Program); it became one of the most popular of Lassalle's agitational pamphlets. Its ideological content was largely based on Section I–II of the *Communist Manifesto*—which however was not mentioned (typically). Marx expressed the opinion that the lecture was a "bad popularization of the Manifesto and other things so often preached by us that they have already become sort of commonplaces."[3]

If the beginning of Lassalle's agitation marked the starting point of the German Social-Democracy as an organized movement, then the second epoch-making event of the sixties was the founding in September 1864 of the International Working Men's Association (IWMA), later called the First International.

No wonder, then, that the sixties also saw the publication of two significant editions of the *Communist Manifesto*. Unfortunately, we do not know exactly when the first of these editions came out; and in fact this date may have been well before both Lassalle's agitation and the founding of the International, hence not a response to either.

We are talking about the so-called "Hirschfeld edition," which may have been published as early as 1859 or as late as 1865.

The following confusing words appeared on the blue cover of this twenty-four-page pamphlet:

Manifest der Kommunistischen Partei.—Veröffentlicht in Februar 1848. London, Druck von R. Hirschfeld, English and Foreign Printer, 48, Clifton Street, Finsbury Square, 1848.

It is the date at the very end that is confusing; for we see that this cover reproduced not only the title of the first edition but also its year date: 1848. But Hirschfeld could not have done the printing in that year.

The printer, Rudolf Hirschfeld, had been in London only since 1854, and his shop had been located at the address in Finsbury Square only since 1856. In 1858–1859 he was the printer of the London paper *Neue Zeit*, organ of the London GWEA. In July 1859 Marx proposed that Hirschfeld print *Das Volk*, the GWEA's new paper. In 1860 Marx turned the printing of his *Herr Vogt* over to Hirschfeld's shop. There is no record of subsequent relations between Marx and this printer.

Was then the Hirschfeld edition of the Manifesto authorized or sponsored by Marx? There is no information bearing directly on this point. Andréas argues that Hirschfeld, operating in London and with good relations with Marx, would not be likely to reprint the Manifesto without the authors' knowledge or toleration. He suggests a possibility: that Hirschfeld was merely acting as printer for the GWEA, which was the actual publisher. According to this hypothesis, we can imagine that the GWEA people asked Marx: "Do you mind if we republish the Manifesto?" and Marx agreed—enthusiastically, reluctantly, or by shrugging his shoulders (pick one). While we are writing this scenario, we can imagine furthermore that Marx added a proviso: that the Manifesto should be reprinted only "as a historical document, printed just a it originally appeared." (This is actually a quote from a letter of 1866 in which Mrs. Marx conveyed Marx's views to a prospective reprinter.[4]) Perhaps this injunction, carried out more literally than was intended, explains why Hirschfeld put the 1848 date on the pamphlet.

Although the Hirschfeld edition might have been published some time in 1859–1860 (when, we know, relations between Hirschfeld and Marx were good), there are reasons to favor the later end of the spectrum of possibilities.[5] In fact, Andréas' index lists this edition as 1864 without qualification,[6] despite the fact that this date is not vindicated elsewhere. We can assume that Andréas regards 1864 as the best guess.

14. THE MEYER EDITION OF 1866

ne of the arguments in favor of a later date for the Hirschfeld edition is a letter written by Marx to J. P. Becker, who, based in Geneva, was trying to organize German-language sections of the IWMA (First International). The letter, undated, was probably written about January 13, 1866.[1] It concerns Marx's arrangements to send Becker a package of literature comprising chiefly copies of the Manifesto. What edition of the Manifesto could have been involved here? The simplest answer is that it just have been the Hirschfeld edition, and so this edition must have come out fairly recently, say, within a year or two.

Leaving aside the problem of dating the Hirschfeld edition, Marx's letter certainly shows him concerned to make the Manifesto available in the 1865–1866 period. Marx proposed that Becker publish parts of it in his monthly *Vorbote*. In the summer of 1866 Becker was indeed planning to publish the whole of the *Communist Manifesto* in installments, together with an introduction; but he never carried out this intention.

A new edition of the Manifesto was certainly needed, from Marx's standpoint. But it need not be thought that it was needed mainly because of the activity of the IWMA, or activity in the IWMA. There could not have been much demand from English and French workers for a German pamphlet. There was, however, a new demand for the Manifesto growing out of the development of the Lassallean workers' organization, the General German Workers Association (GGWA).

A dissident group had gotten under way in the GGWA, especially in Berlin, in reaction against the dictatorial conduct of the leadership which J. B. von Schweitzer had taken over from Lassalle, also in reaction against the Lassalleans' sectist attitude to the working-class movement, particularly its claim to political control over the new, growing tradeunion movement. The Berlin dissidents—Liebknecht, August Vogt, Sigfrid Meyer, Theodor Metzner, A. Reimann, and others—looked to Marx for support.[2] When Liebknecht was expelled from Berlin by the Prussian police in July 1865, he moved to Leipzig, where his team-up with August Bebel marked a historic new beginning in the evolution of the Social-Democracy. It was the Bebel leadership (or, as some would put it, the Bebel-Liebknecht leadership) which eventually superseded Lassalleanism.

But what basic literature did the anti-Lassallean dissidents have to represent their viewpoint, or at any rate a viewpoint other than Lassalleanism? Little. They used the "Inaugural Address" of the International; written by Marx, it breathed an atmosphere altogether alien from the Lassalleans' sectism, but it did not speak of socialism or communism. They had the recently published *Herr Vogt*, which however was hardly suitable for their purposes. They badly needed something like the *Communist Manifesto*.

The need was met by one of the dissidents, Sigfrid Meyer.* Some time in the early spring of 1866 (about March or April), the first complete edition of the Manifesto ever published inside Germany for socialist propaganda purposes came off the press. The title said:

Manifest der Kommunistischen Partei. Veröffentlicht im Februar 1848. — Proletarier aller Länder, vereinigt Euch!—London, Neu herausgegeben durch Sigfrid Meyer, Im Selbstverlage, 1866.

---

* Meyer's first name is often spelled Siegfried (the usual form) especially after he emigrated to America.

This imprint claimed: "London, newly published by Sigfrid Meyer, self-published, 1866." "London" was a bit of deliberate mystification, a misdirection, a modest attempt to mislead the German authorities, who were becoming more repressive as war with Austria loomed. It was only a modest effort, for the last page indicated that the pamphlet had been printed in Berlin at the printshop of Gustav Muthschall.

There were no separate covers; it began with the title page. Like the second edition whose text it followed, it comprised thirty pages.

Meyer informed Marx in advance—probably in January 1866—of his intention to put out a new edition of the Manifesto. Since Marx was ill, Mrs. Marx replied: "As far as the M[anifesto] is concerned, he would like it, as a historical document, to be printed just as it appeared in the beginning; the misprints are so obvious that anyone can correct them."[3] Marx and Engels subsequently repeated more than once that they refused to recast or revise the Manifesto because it was a "historical document."*

The press run of the edition was probably small: "after all," Andréas says, "Meyer paid for the printing with the monthly advance which he got from his father as a student at the Berlin Polytechnic School." We know that there were movement activists in Germany who never saw it. Meyer no doubt put it out with the idea of supplying a cadre, not for mass distribution. It was distributed in Germany and Austria by relatively few IWMA and Social-Democratic propagandists.

The following year Meyer emigrated to America, probably importing some copies with him. The American GGWA had been founded in October 1865; the German-American socialist movement was shot through with Lassalleanism; but around this time—doubtless with Meyer's aid—"it was no longer true that the propaganda of Lassallean principles was the only one going," related Schlüter as historian. "Along with the writings of Lassalle the Communist Manifesto was also read and studied."[5]

The most lasting result of this edition came from its subsequent use by Marx and Engels: through them, it served as the main basis for German editions to come.

15. THE LATE SIXTIES: LIEBKNECHT'S MODEST PROPOSAL

he publication of the first volume of Capital in September 1867 gave new importance to Marx's name in left-wing circles; and it is a regular feature of the history of the Manifesto that interest in it was almost automatically boosted whenever interest in Marx got a lift. (The biggest example of this pattern will come along shortly—after the Paris Commune.) Besides, there were two passages in *Capital* itself with extensive quotes from the Manifesto.[1]

---

* For example, at the end of their preface to the German edition of 1872 (their first preface), Marx and Engels referred to some dated aspects of the Manifesto that would "be very differently worded today."

But, then, the Manifesto has become a historical document which we no longer have any right to alter.[1]

Two incidents of this period point to a trend: the forthright revolutionary language and ideas of the Manifesto were beginning to be embarrassing to some people. The first instance was not surprising.

This case involved a circle of Austrian IWMA people, whose Vienna organ, the *Arbeiter-Blatt*, was also the organ of the city's Arbeiter-Bildungs-Verein (workers' educational association). This paper appeared as a semiweekly supplement to the daily *Telegraf*. In mid-1868, the Arbeiter-Blatt reprinted the entire text of the Manifesto. in ten installments, from June 7 to July 10. If this was a plus from Marx's view, there were two other features less gratifying. (1) The text used for the reprint came straight from the Wermuth-Stieber compilation, with its distortions (see Chapter 12); and (2) the Vienna editors added notes disclaiming agreement with the idea of workers' power and repudiating the use of revolutionary force. They proclaimed that they wanted no class domination of any sort, only equality for all and the elimination of class differences. The counterposition of "equality" to workers' power was a hallmark of reformism.

Around the same time, Liebknecht was writing to Marx with a proposal of his own to republish the Manifesto in the paper he edited, the *Demokratisches Wochenblatt*. This too had an aspect that was far from gratifying.

The background fact is that at this point Liebknecht was still following a political line that Marx strongly condemned—one of the chief reasons, especially initially, why Marx had such a low opinion of Liebknecht's political capacity. This line was the policy of politically subordinating the working-class movement to a bourgeois (petty-bourgeois and small-bourgeois) liberal party. In Saxony the workers' movement had made great progress especially under the practical leadership of Bebel, who was still a socialist neophyte looking to Liebknecht as his political teacher. The result was the Federation of German Workers' Associations (Verband Deutscher Arbeitervereine).

But instead of striking out on the path of independent workers' political action as Marx advocated, the FGWA acted as the working-class wing of the Saxon People's Party (Sächsische Volkspartei)—a typical petty-bourgeois-cum-smallbusiness liberal party (called a "democratic party" in the language of the time). It was (also typically) run by intellectuals and educated master artisans or petty businessmen, with a left-democratic rhetoric, the whole leavened by its anti-Prussian orientation which set it in opposition to Berlin. The working-class wing could not hope to move this party to the left, that is, in the direction of socialism, since victory in this effort meant an automatic split. Here, then, in Leipzig, the most important center of working-class organization, the developing forces of proletarian socialism (as Marx saw it) were still stuck in the mire of bourgeois liberal politics.

On the socialist side, Liebknecht was the political mentor of this mixed-class popular front, and he edited the paper representing the coalition, the *Demokratisches Wochenblatt*. Originally the organ of the People's Party (from January 1868 on), in December it became *also* the organ of the FGWA. To be sure, this class unity was wearing thin, and in fact in August 1869, at Eisenach, the working-class wing was going to organize itself independently for the first time as the Social-Democratic Workers Party ("Eisenachers").

We have had to give this part of the background because of the legend, assiduously nurtured in the ensuing decades by the party and by Liebknecht himself, that Liebknecht ("Soldier of the Revolution") represented not only Marx's politics in Germany in this period but also was a stern champion of revolutionary politics, whose bold watchword was "No Compromise!"* When Liebknecht urged a new edition of the Manifesto in a letter of June 29, 1869, what he wanted was a *revised* Manifesto that would not run counter to his current compromising politics of coalition with the People's Party.

Marx and Engels, on the contrary, for whom the central axis of the Manifesto was precisely its view of working-class independence, thought that the People's Party coalition had to be condemned. Engels wrote a friend explaining Marx's position in face of the two bisymmetrically erroneous courses in Germany: the sectarianism of the Lassalleans and the opportunism of Liebknecht's policy, both of which were on the brink of breaking down. "The dissolution of the Lassallean sect and, on the other hand, the separation of the Saxon and South German workers from the leading strings of the 'People's Party'—these are the two basic conditions for the emergence of a real German workers' party." Lassalleanism, fortunately, was destroying itself,

> but the narrow South German-republican-babbitt ideas systematically pumped into the workers by Liebknecht are much harder to shuck off. Just look at the stupidity of heading his paper Organ of the People's Party, i.e., of the South German babbitts! ... And here comes Liebknecht and demands that we should take sides directly for him and the People's Party against Schweitzer!

No, Engels wound up, we have less in common with the bourgeois of the People's Party than with the sectarians of the Lassalleans' working-class sect.[2]

As it happened, just *before* receiving Liebknecht's modest proposal that the revolutionary content of the Manifesto should be revised out, Engels had already commented, in the course of a letter to Marx, on the unacceptable demand that the two of them should take sides for Wilhelm [Liebknecht] and the People's Party.

> It would be well for Wilhelm to read the Manifesto on the position of the workers' party. if reading or anything else would help him at all![3]

Well, obviously Wilhelm did read the Manifesto with an eye to this question—only, he decided that it was the Manifesto that should be changed, not his own policy. His letter to Marx of June 29 first assured him that the anti-Lassalleans had *already* won an overwhelming majority of the Lassallean GGWA and would take over the organization in August. (Marx's terse comment on this, to Engels, was that Liebknecht was a "liar"—an indubitable truth.[4])

---

* No Compromise...! was the silly title of a pamphlet published by Liebknecht in 1899, about parliamentary work. Despite its militant clang, the slogan was an empty bit of rhetoric, to which Liebknecht gave lip service only at moments of elocutionary excitement.

Breathing hard over this fictitious victory, Liebknecht then laid down, in a series of injunctions, what Marx "must" do right now, including this:

> You MUST *revise the Communist Manifesto for agitational use*. For *enemies* I have never had any regard; but friends, and those who would like to be friends, deserve to be taken into consideration.[5]

This meant: the "friends" represented by the People's Party liberals had to be kept placated, and must not be scared off by revolutionary talk in the Manifesto; the historic Manifesto "must" be rewritten in order not to get in the way of Liebknecht's political maneuvering in his corner of Germany...

Marx reacted with predictable anger to Liebknecht's tone and content, both. Wilhelm now is telling me what I "must" do, Marx wrote indignantly to Engels: "I *must* come to their August congress," etc.—and "I *must* fuck up the Communist Manifesto!" Further down, he repeated that Liebknecht's aim was "giving a beating to the Manifesto."[6]

Liebknecht's plans for some sort of republication of the Manifesto did not end there, and we will encounter his operations again. In fact, he did not leave off hoping that the Manifesto might be redrafted to embody the opposite of its contents, viz., the politics of class collaboration instead of class struggle, in order to cover his lib-lab coalition.

16. ENGLISH SIDESHOW

The least known English version of the Manifesto is an abridgment that was published by Cowell Stepney in 1869.

William Frederick Cowell Stepney (1820–1872), a nephew of Lord Carnarvon, had become a dedicated social reformer despite his upper-class background. He had been a member of the Reform League and the League for Peace and Freedom before he became active in the International. He sat on the General Council of the IWMA for several years (1867–1872), and was its treasurer for part of that time (1868–1870); he was a delegate to its congress in 1868 and 1869 and to the London Conference in 1871, and a member of the British Federal Council of the International in 1872. Clearly he was a devoted participant in the organization of the International and must have worked closely with Marx, who indeed had originally proposed him for the treasurer's post.

In 1868 Stepney established a monthly, *The Social Economist*, as a spokesman of the cooperative movement, under the editorship of George Holyoake, an ex-Owenite. Marx thought Stepney was squandering his money by supporting this "extraordinarily stupid publication of old Holyoake."[1] In general Marx had a high opinion of Stepney's heart and dedication to the popular movement and a low opinion of his head.[2] During 1868-1869 the *Social Economist* devoted pages to excerpts from Bakunin and Proudhon; this was not calculated to improve Marx's opinion of it.

In 1869 the August and September issues—which turned out to be the last issues—came out with an abridged translation of large portions of the *Communist Manifesto;* more accurately, translations and paraphrases. The first installment in the August issue was headed: "The Middle Class. (From the French.)" (We will comment later on the reference to French.) This installment covered part of the preamble and went up to a mid-point in Section I. The September issue continued with "The Proletariat," offering most of the rest of Section I and a good part of Section II. It is reasonable to suppose that Stepney was planning to finish up with at least one more installment, if the magazine had continued.

An editor's note at the end of the first installment admitted that "We have abridged the foregoing historical discussion," and censured the Manifesto for its lack of brevity. ("We English are not very brilliant, but we are briefer than our foreign friends.") It then criticized the Manifesto's alleged misuse of the word 'bourgeoise' (sic: it meant 'bourgeoisie') with a comment which it would be unkind to quote. This note, with its simpleminded arrogant ignorance, has the hallmarks of editor Holyoake.

The second installment was hedged fore and aft by notes signed "Ed. S.E.," that is, Holyoake. The introductory note said, as if Holyoake did not know the Manifesto's authors:

> The gentleman to whom we owe the translation of these extracts [doubtless Stepney] has not marked upon them the name of the writer, whom we understand to be an eminent expositor of social ideas. We omit so much that we mar the proper expression of his ideas; but if we quoted in full he would scare our readers, whom we are told we have already terrified...

The text of this installment ended with the following signature note, written in all likelihood by Stepney himself: "—*Translated by W.F.C.S. from the Genevan Manifesto of the Communistic Party.*" To this, the "Ed. *S.E.*" appended a parting shot: "We only mention the 'Communistic Party' in a note thus, that it may not attract the attention of the reader." Wry humor, suitable for an editor who thought that Marx and Engels were confused about the meaning of 'bourgeoise.'

The invention of a "Genevan Manifesto of the Communistic Party" may well have been Stepney's idea. The initials W.F.C.S. were plainly Stepney's and could not have been intended to conceal his identity; other parts of the magazine referred to its valued contributor W.F.C.S. The mystification concealed the identity of the Manifesto's authors and even their nationality; hence the misleading reference to "French" in the heading of the first installment.

Stepney, without any doubt, knew all about the *Communist Manifesto* and its authorship. In fact, his translation-abridgment was probably made from a copy of the Hirschfeld edition made available to him by Marx. Stepney knew German as well as French.* Why then the horseplay?

Andréas (A#52) thinks that Stepney concealed the authorship of the manifesto "in order not to compromise the International, of which Marx was the best-known leader, in the eyes of the English public." This may have been a factor, but it would not be as strong a motivation in 1869 as it was going to be after the Paris Commune (when the world press proclaimed Marx to be the monster who instigated all the Paris outrages). There is another possible explanation. The pattern reminds us of the motivation of H. M. Hyndman in plagiarizing Capital without mentioning Marx's name, when he published *England for All* in 1881: namely, "The English don't like to be taught by foreigners."[4] And there is a third possibility: Holyoake, who as "Ed. *S.E.*" had claimed that Stepney failed to write down the author's name, was virulently hostile to Marx and his ideas. The omission of Marx's name may have been his doing, directly or indirectly.

Holyoake's anti-Marx bias makes it doubly probable that it was Stepney who decided to devote his magazine's space to the Manifesto. Stepney must have thought the Manifesto a significant document: did he also admire or agree with its political contents?

It is hard to say anything about Stepney's motivation because he was so shadowy a figure in the activity of the International—not for any "mysterious" reasons but simply because he stayed out of political discussions. Consider: although his attendance at General Council meetings was better than average, the GC Minutes record not one instance, in the course of well over a hundred meetings, in which he took part in the discussion of any substantive question whatsoever. Perhaps he was conscious of his outsider status in class terms. When he resigned as treasurer, someone else explained "that he [Stepney] considered [it] impolitic that a man of his social position should occupy so prominent a place in a working men's association..."[5]

His sole political statement in the IWMA records came at the Brussels Congress of 1868, where the minutes summarize his talk as follows: "In England, as elsewhere, there are two classes, the exploiters and the exploited, who are engaged in a relentless war; I long ago took the side of the disinherited." The chairman, Hermann Jung, thereupon introduced him to the other delegates: "the speaker [said Jung] is a member of the highest aristocracy... closely related to a minister, who had to give up his cabinet post as being too reactionary. He [Stepney] began by being a bourgeois philanthropist, and became, despite his great fortune, one of the most zealous adherents of the advanced socialist party."[6]

The Stepney version of the Manifesto has never been reprinted.

---

* In a letter to a friend early this same year, Marx wrote that "The treasurer of our General Council here, Cowell Stepney—a very rich and prominent man, but wholly devoted to the workers' cause, though in somewhat foolish fashion—inquired from a friend in Bonn about the literature (German) on the labor question and on socialism."[3]

or a couple of decades, virtually no attention was paid to the Manifesto in the Russian language. About all that requires mention is a piece by Lavrov in the St. Petersburg magazine *Zagranichnii Vestnik* (1864, No. 6), in which Marx's friend paraphrased the beginning of Section I—without mentioning the source.[1]

Then in 1869 a more or less complete Russian translation was published in the West. This edition was really only a historical curiosity, but it is also a historical puzzle. This is the translation which was long attributed to Bakunin, erroneously.

This *Manifest Kommunisticheskoi Partii* had no cover, no title page, and no mention at all of publisher, place of publication, date, author, or translator. It was a twenty-four page brochure, with the last page blank. The type and the very thin paper used were the same as were employed in February 1869 by Herzen's organ *Kolokol*, published at Geneva and printed by L. Czerniecki's shop. But this Russian edition of the Manifesto was not published by *Kolokol*.

Let us summarize the real history of this edition, as ascertained by Andréas, before taking up the widespread mistakes about its provenance, especially those that were embodied in prefaces by Marx and Engels.

This uncommunicative brochure probably appeared around the end of September. Andréas implies (but does not directly say) that it was drafted by Nechayev, who was then working closely with Ogarev. In early September Ogarev sent the manuscript to the printer, Czerniecki, asking him to print a thousand copies - "although," added Ogarev on September 27, "the writing is not at all in accord with the propaganda we are printing at this time." The order to the printer, according to the evidence, came from the Russian group in Geneva in which Nechayev was active along with Bakunin and Ogarev.

To be sure, the brochure came out after Nechayev had returned to Russia (in August), but we must assume that he had already made all arrangements by that time, arrangements which Ogarev carried through. Andréas believes that the initiative toward the publication was also Nechayev's, not Bakunin's. In fact, Andréas sees no role at all in the enterprise on Bakunin's part. (It is not recorded that Bakunin ever made any statement about the paternity of the Manifesto translation.)*

The translation was based on the Hirschfeld edition; there was a copy in Geneva, we know, owned by J. P. Becker, who at this time was collaborating with the Bakuninist group. But, says Andréas, "The translation in general is incorrect and alters the text in several cases;

---

* Bakunin is given as the translator even in the editorial notes to *MECW* (6:698), but this note is not reliable in other respects as well. Struik (in *Birth of the Communist Manifesto*, 212) has the misfortune of writing the following:

> Some inadequacies in the translation were removed by G. V. Plekhanov in a new translation of 1882—almost as if Plekhanov's translation (for which see Chapter 22) was based on the 1869 version

for example, the word 'Klasse' is regularly translated *sosloviem*, that is, social estate (Stand) as in 'third estate'; and Klassengegensatz [class antagonism] is rendered as *soslovniye razlichiya*, that is, 'differences in rank (or estate)'; several passages are omitted." [2]

As for misinformation about this translation: the story begins with the fact that its producers never told Marx or Engels about the project, either before or after publication. Marx learned about its existence in April 1870 from an advertisement in *De Werker* of Antwerp, founded in 1868 by Philipp Coenen as the Flemish organ of the IWMA.[3] Marx, who proceeded to order six copies, evidently thought it had just been published, and connected the edition with the fact that Herzen had died recently (January) and left the Kolokol publishing enterprise to Bakunin—so Marx was erroneously informed by J. P. Becker from Geneva.[4] The ad and the circumstances led him to believe that the brochure had been published by *Kolokol*, hence under Bakunin's control. This whole train of deduction was off the rails: Kolokol was not the publisher; Bakunin was not the new owner of the Kolokol firm (this was Ogarev); and, as we have seen, Bakunin had nothing to do with this translation.

When in 1872 Marx and Engels wrote a preface for the new German edition, and listed some translations, they merely stated that a Russian translation was published in Geneva "in the sixties."[5] A few months later, Marx and Engels were told of Nechayev's role when they (especially Engels) were gathering material for the IWMA's exposé of the Bakuninist machinations in the movement, later published as *L'Alliance de la Démocratie Socialiste et l'Association Internationale des Travailleurs* (1873). On November 1, 1872, Nicholas Utin, who headed the Geneva opposition to the Bakuninist cabal, wrote Marx about the activity of Nechayev and Bakunin in the period from 1869 to early 1870, and said *inter alia* that "in fact they translated the Manifesto and published it together with other Russian brochures." (This referred to a series of seven propaganda pamphlets drafted and published by Nechayev and Bakunin in Geneva in August 1869.)* Engels and Lafargue, who were working on the exposé pamphlet, may have gotten such advice from other sources as well.

Chapter 8 of this pamphlet, headed "L'Alliance en Russie," exposed the nature of Nechayev's "barracks-communism" and his dictatorial aspirations, and then stated:

> To give the semblance of a theoretical basis to this absurd plan of organization, a little note is attached to the title itself of this article: "Those who want to know the complete theoretical development of our principal theses will find it in the work which we published: *Manifesto of the communist party*." —In point of fact, the Russian translation of the (German) manifesto of the communist party of 1847 [sic] is being advertised,

---

* Utin may well have based this information on a statement made in the periodical *Narodnaya Razprava*, No. 2, published by Nechayev, to which Bakunin contributed. This periodical referred to the "Manifesto of the communist party, published by us [and containing] the complete theoretical development of our principal theses." This issue appeared at the end of December 1869 or the beginning of 1870. Compare the statement quoted by Engels-Lafargue in the next excerpt cited. Utin's information, then, had a certain basis from his own standpoint.

priced at one franc, in every number of the 1870 *Kolokol*, side by side with Bakunin's appeal "To the Officers of the Russian Army" and the two numbers of the *People's Judgment*. The same Bakunin who misused this manifesto to gain credit for his Tartar fantasies on Russia also had it denounced by the Alliance in the west as an ultra-heretical work, preaching the baneful doctrines of authoritarian German communism (see the resolution of the Rimini Conference [of the Bakuninist Alliance], Guillaume's speech at the Hague, *Bulletin Jurassien*, No. 10–11, the Barcelona *Federación*, etc.).[5]

The emphasis, above, on "our" and "we" was, of course, added by Engels-Lafargue to point out how the Russian publishers, who had suppressed the authorship of the Manifesto, were now claiming the document as their own. The "we" was in effect interpreted to mean Nechayev and Bakunin as a team. This jibed with the information supplied by Utin, though Engels/Lafargue were interested in putting the spotlight on Bakunin.

But a decade later—when Marx and Engels wrote a preface for the first authorized Russian translation in January 1882—Nechayev's name was dropped out of the picture. Nor was this the only inaccuracy: "The first Russian edition of the *Manifesto of the Communist Party*, translated by Bakunin, appeared at the beginning of the sixties [actually 1869] in the *Kolokol* printshop."[7] This statement, erroneous both about the authorship of the translation and the place of publication, was the continuing source of numerous later misstatements of the same sort. If the brochure had been published "at the beginning of the sixties ... in the *Kolokol* printshop," then it would have been published in London, for the enterprise was moved to Geneva only in April 1865.

In his preface to the English edition of 1883, Engels introduced new inaccuracies: "The first Russian translation, made by Bakounine, was published at Herzen's 'Kolokol' office in Geneva, about 1863..."[8]

We said that this particular edition was mainly a "historical curiosity." This statement should not be confused with the point that was later made by Marx and Engels: "The West could, at that time [in the sixties], see in this (the Russian edition of the Manifesto) only a literary curiosity. Such a conception would be impossible today." They went on to discuss the growing importance of the Russian movement as "the vanguard of revolutionary action in Europe" in the 1880s and beyond.[9] What they were criticizing here was the notion of Russia as a social wasteland so backward as to be irrelevant to revolutionary prospects.

But the Geneva Russian edition of 1869 *was* pretty much irrelevant to the growing movement. Nechayev's efforts to get it into Russia were largely as futile as the rest of that adventurer's busywork. There were border seizures, police confiscations, losses in transportation. Andréas opines that the edition had a low distribution. Only three copies have been preserved in Russia itself; a handful elsewhere. However, handwritten copies of the Manifesto were passed around in the 1870s in Russia, and these may have been copied from the 1869 pamphlet. Nothing is ever completely lost.

FROM THE COMMUNE TO THE DEATH OF MARX

18. IN THE WAKE OF THE PARIS COMMUNE: 1871–1873

As mentioned, whenever the light of publicity fell on Marx, a certain reflection also hit the *Communist Manifesto*. This pattern was especially clear in the period after the bloody suppression of the Paris Commune, when Marx—the Red Doctor who headed the Sinister International Conspiracy --was being denounced throughout the European and world press as the diabolical director of communist terrorism. The more enterprising journalists and pundits asked where these fiendish doctrines had been written down, and so were led to read the Manifesto. (Of course, they also found the Inaugural Address, but this was less fiendish.)

There was a reverse effect: some socialists were moved to make the Manifesto more easily available so that its actual contents could be compared with what was being said about the specter of communism, which more than ever was haunting Europe. Unfortunately the translations listed in the preamble of the Manifesto did *not* exist, and at this time the document could be read mainly in German.

A couple of new translations were stimulated. The first was a Serbo-Croatian version, "Manifest Komunisticke Partije," which came out in ten installments in *Pancevac* (published in the town of Pancevo) from April 8 to May 23, 1871. It will be noted that this started appearing before the Commune's fate had been decided; an unsigned postscript explained that an exposition of communism was made necessary by the press campaign against the Commune. The authors' names were not given; the translator is unknown. The translation then appeared in pamphlet form as an offprint, announced in the periodical on June 6.

In Chicago, in July of the same year, a German-American socialist group issued a new edition reprinting the Meyer edition of 1866—"Published by the Social-Politische Arbeiter-Verein in Chicago," printed at M. Hofmann's shop, in a twenty-page format, with a 3000-copy press run. A publisher's note "To Party Comrades in the United States!" stressed that this was first in a series of brochures which aimed to combat the worldwide campaign against the International.

Sigfrid Meyer himself may well have been responsible for this publication. He had emigrated to the United States in the first half of 1867, and (at any rate in October 1871) was living near Chicago, in Joliet, Illinois. He was active in the International, acted as its correspondent for the U.S. to the General Council in London by the end of 1868, and so remained in contact with Marx by mail. As we saw, he had taken copies of his 1866 edition with him across the ocean, to seed the New World.

It was probably a copy of this Chicago edition of the Manifesto which was given to Samuel Gompers by an IWMA member in New York, Karl Laurell, who furthermore translated and interpreted it for Gompers. The latter was much impressed—his auto-biography emphasized how much: "This insight into the hidden world of thought aroused me to master the German language."[1]

Writing to Marx on October 22, Meyer proposed that the 1850 Macfarlane translation be published as an English brochure (as Marx himself had once suggested). Meyer may well have put out the idea to other quarters; and others may well have gotten it independently. For one thing, Meyer's letter to Marx mentioned that the *New York World* had just (September 21) published an article about the International and about Marx which quoted a number of passages from the Manifesto in Macfarlane's old version. This was the sort of article which stimulated interest in the Manifesto.*

The *World* article was undoubtedly also read with interest by the energetic woman in New York who was making plans to take over (more or less simultaneously) the International in America, the Stock Exchange, the women's suffrage movement, and the spiritualist world. This was Victoria Woodhull, who had gotten Cornelius Vanderbilt to bankroll her organ, *Woodhull & Claflin's Weekly*. As leader of Section 12 of the IWMA, Woodhull aspired to take over the American sections, and probably figured that judicious exploitation of Marx's name would help her case. And so, although she and her section were explicitly opposed to the communist class struggle and to the working-class emphasis of the International, she seized the opportunity to reprint the Manifesto in her *Weekly*. She was not hampered by principles; in a broadminded way, her group was oriented toward converting the International into a catch-all repository (like Section 12 itself) of funny-money schemers, spiritualists, bourgeois Free Love prophets, professional atheists, occultists, necromancers, Universal Language panacea-mongers, magi of Universology and Pantarchy, and other marginal dissentients and cranks, along with good liberal-progressives who advocated important reforms like women's rights, cooperatives, etc.**

Woodhull & Claflin's Weekly reprinted virtually the whole of the Macfarlane translation in one issue, December 30, 1871 (pages 3 to 6), under the title, "German Communism—Manifesto of the German Communist Party."*** Thus Woodhull's momentary ambitions made the Manifesto available to some in the American English-speaking movement for the first time.

---

* Datelined September 15 from Washington, D.C., the article cited information on "Dr. Karl Marx—Some Reminiscences" gained from unnamed friends of his (meaning Adolf Cluss, thought Sigfrid Meyer; Hermann Meyer, thinks Andréas). It called the Manifesto "a remarkable paper," and said that "one can readily, in perusing it, discover the philosophy animating the 'International'..." Other eminent newspapers were quoting the Manifesto that year: for one, the London Times for October 27, 1871; for another, the Augsburg *Allgemeine Zeitung* for March 15, 1872.

** For Woodhull's career, see Emanie Sachs, *The Terrible Siren* (New York, 1928); for her operation in the International, see Samuel Bernstein, *The First International in America*.

*** An editorial note in *MEW* 33:780, note 447, says that the Manifesto was published "shortened," and that the authors were not named. This is incorrect, according to Andréas' account: the *Weekly* omitted only part of a single sentence (the one about the lumpenproletariat) and the title of Section II was abridged to "Communism." Moreover, the Weekly editorially named Marx as the author.

Woodhull gave no credit to Macfarlane for the translation, and did not mention its actual source. Interestingly enough, Marx and Engels did not now recognize the translation as the one published in 1850. In a letter Engels was derogatory about "Woodhull's English."[2] In his preface to the English edition of 1888, he wrote: "In 1872 [sic], it was translated into English in New York, where the translation was published in *Woodhull and Claflin's Weekly*," that is, he viewed it as a new translation.[3] Despite its defects, Engels asked Sorge to send him fifty copies of the *Weekly*. Though the translation left much to be desired, he wrote, "we have to make use of [it] for propaganda for the time being..."[4]

The English translation in Woodhull's weekly was soon used to produce a French version for the New York organ of the French-speaking IWMA sections, *Le Socialiste*. This version comprised only Sections I and II, published in nine installments from January 20 to March 30, 1872, under the heading "Manifeste de Karl Marx." (Engels' collaboration was mentioned in an editorial note preceding the text.) The translator is not known. The changes introduced by Woodhull's weekly were continued here; indeed, the abridgment of Section II's title to "Communism" was accompanied by a special footnote explaining "that the French, who above all are bent on being clear [the classic Gallic delusion], have preferred the name of socialists rather than communists."

Engels asked Sorge to send copies of this translation too—"50–100 copies" if he could obtain that many. Referring to both the Woodhull/English version and this one, he wrote what we have partly quoted above: "No matter how much both translations still leave to be desired, we have to make use of them for propaganda for the time being..." He added: "and in particular the French translation is quite indispensable to me for the Latin countries of Europe, in order to counteract the nonsense spread by Bakunin, as well as the Proudhonist variety, which is propagated there."[5]

Both of these New York publications had been made without the authors' authorization or help; but their appearance was one of the signs encouraging Engels to think that the political situation was picking up. When he told Liebknecht about the New York publications, he added: "You see, we are beginning to get going. But all this makes for a lot of work."[6]

At this time, Marx and Engels were involved in Liebknecht's plans for the new German edition which in fact appeared in the middle of 1872; this will be described in the next chapter. But—a little out of order—let us continue with other publications of 1872–1873, in particular the Spanish edition of 1872, since it partly evolved from the New York *Le Socialiste* translation just discussed.

This Spanish translation was undertaken by Jos Mesa, a printing worker who had been a founder of the IWMA sections in Spain and a leader in the struggle against Bakuninism in that country, where he became one of the first propagandists of Marxism. Since 1871 he had been a member of the Spanish Federal Council, and the founding editor of the pioneer socialist organ *La Emancipación*. As an émigré in Paris in the 1866–1868 period, he was well acquainted with the international movement. With this background, he naturally undertook to collaborate with the authors of the Manifesto whose translation he undertook—unlike the publishers of the two New York editions. Engels, in turn, wanted to help him as much as possible.

As one might expect, Mesa's German was evidently much inferior to his French; Engels wanted to provide him with a French "trot." There was the *Le Socialiste* version now, to be sure; but Engels was told by Sorge that a "Frenchman living in America" (not further identified) had done a revision which, while still based on the Woodhull/English version, was superior. Sorge brought this manuscript with him to the Hague Congress in September 1872, and Engels agreed with his estimate: it is "mostly quite good, insofar as 'Woodhull' [the Woodhull/ English version] was good"—so Engels wrote in a letter.[7] In addition, Engels set about himself revising the French translation, especially for Mesa's use:

> The fact that Mesa has begun to translate the Manifesto has forced me to send him a revision of the Le Socialiste French translation, in connection with which the one you brought in manuscript turned out very useful, since it is much better, though still based on "Woodhull's" English. I am taking the opportunity to generally fix up the French translation.[8]

Like the version in *Le Socialiste*, the revised French translation covered only Sections I–II. (It is probably this revision that was referred to in the 1872 preface to the German edition, which, after mentioning the New York Le Socialiste version, said: "A new translation is in the course of preparation."[9]) Mesa did the rest from the 1872 German edition.

The result was published in *La Emancipación* in six installments from November 2 to December 7, 1872, as the "Manifiesto Comunista de 1848, precedido de un prólogo de sus autores." The *prólogo* was Mesa's translation of the new Marx-Engels preface to the aforementioned German edition of 1872. The installments were printed as a feuilleton in each issue, and were arranged so that they could be cut out to form the pages of a pamphlet. Note that Mesa used the title which had just been introduced by the 1872 German edition: *Communist Manifesto* instead of *Manifesto of the Communist Party*—to be discussed in the next chapter.

Andréas points out changes made by Mesa in the text of the Manifesto; they make one wonder if he had cleared them with Engels. (There is no information on this point.) His version omitted the entire subsection on "German or True Socialism" on the ground, explained in a note, that its transitory importance had been that "of a purely local kind of literature" only. This was one of the earliest statements of the claim that parts of the Manifesto were obsolete. Also, Mesa rendered some passages so freely that they were, in effect, slightly revised in language, not in order to affect the sense but to lessen readers' puzzlement over now-obscure allusions. A note was added to Section IV explaining that the Manifesto had been written "in 1847 [sic] when the proletariat, in all countries (except England), was in tow by the bourgeoisie," whereas now the developed situation "allows us to adopt a very different position." Mesa, we see, certainly did not follow (if he ever heard) Marx's injunction that the Manifesto should be published unchanged as a "historical document."

In its turn, Mesa's Spanish version served as basis for a Portuguese translation. Now, the Mesa/Spanish version had been mostly based on Engels' revision of someone else's revision of a French translation which had been made from Macfarlane's English. The Portuguese version, made from the Spanish, was thus about four or five removes from the original, perhaps a record of some kind. Headed "Manifesto do Partido Communista," it was published in six installments in the organ *0 Pensamento Social* of Lisbon, from March 2 to April 5, 1873, as a feuilleton. The paper suspended publication while the series was in the midst of Section II; the translation remained incomplete.

To finish the story of 1873 before turning back: we record that a Hungarian translation of Section I (only) was published during August in the country's twin socialist organs of the Workers Party. The German-language paper *Arbeiter-Wochen-Chronik* ran it August 3–17; the Hungarian-language paper with a corresponding title, *Munkás-Heti-Krónika,* ran it August 10–24; in both cases in three installments, translated from the 1872 German edition. This publication was headed "On the History of the Workers' Movement. I. Bourgeois and Proletarians." Neither the Manifesto nor its authors were actually mentioned.

The text had probably been supplied by Leo Frankel, who was still an émigré in London in close association with Marx and Engels. No doubt it was the Budapest editors who published it in such uncommunicative fashion and so incompletely. Perhaps they broke it off because they did not like what it was saying. Once more, I think, the Manifesto was beginning to embarrass certain elements of the developing Social-Democracy.

19. LIEBKNECHT'S FAKE EDITION OF 1872

We have seen, in Chapter 15, that in 1869 Wilhelm Liebknecht tried to promote a politically bowdlerized edition of the Manifesto. Following this attempt, he continued to press Marx and Engels to prepare a republication of the pamphlet.

He now argued that the original text would be banned in Germany mainly because of the ten-point program of demands in Section II and the peroration about "forcible overthrow." So during 1870–1872 he kept proposing to Marx and Engels "the printing of a revision ... in a changed form corresponding to present-day conditions," a revision which he could legally publish in his *Volksstaat*.[1] To be sure, Marx and Engels recognized that the 1848 pamphlet would be banned by the German authorities,[2] but they refused to revise the text on that account. They did agree, however, that they should write an "explanatory preface" to an unmodified version.[3]

At the beginning of April 1871, Liebknecht again proposed to Marx: "Could you write a short preface to the Communist Manifesto, which I can print with the Manifesto?"[4] Marx agreed: "The C. Manifesto can naturally not be written [error for published?] without a new preface. Engels and I will see what we can fix up along these lines."[5]

The date of this letter, April 13, explains why the promise was not kept. The Paris Commune was in full swing; Marx was working on what was going to be the International's statement on *The Civil War in France*, and was feverishly involved with the fate of the Paris revolt; internal conflicts in the International were heating up; he was busy producing new "historical documents" and had no mind to write prefaces to old ones.

As we have seen in the preceding chapter, the following period saw new publications of the Manifesto, especially in America. At the same time that Engels asked Sorge to send bundles of *Woodhull & Claflin's Weekly* and *Le Socialiste*, he also informed him: "As soon as we have time, M[arx] and I will prepare a new [German] edition of the Manifesto with a preface etc., but we have our hands full at the moment."[6]

The following month, the question was given new actuality by the trial of Bebel, Liebknecht and Hepner, as leaders of the socialist movement, for high treason, opening in Leipzig on March 11, 1872, and ending on the 26th. The prosecution insisted on reading the *Communist Manifesto* into the court record; this took place in the third session, on March 13, using the Meyer edition of 1866. With this action, the government made the text of the Manifesto (as read in court) an integral part of the court proceedings, and thus provided an unlooked-for opportunity to publish this part of the court record—legally, for the first time.

Liebknecht drew up a detailed account of the trial, with documents, and this started appearing in serial fascicules beginning about April 17. The party organization distributed each fascicule as it came out, in thousands of copies, as propaganda publications. The third fascicule, containing the text of the Manifesto as entered by the prosecution, came out in mid-June. This yellow-covered publication bore a long title beginning: *Leipziger Hochverraths-prozess. Ausführlicher Bericht* (Leipzig High Treason Trial. Detailed Report); and it continued: "edited by the defendants; appearing in six to seven fascicules. —3rd fascicule," published by the Volksstaat press, comprising pages 97–144. The Manifesto took up pages 97–119 of this publication.*

With a view to an offprint edition of the Manifesto, Liebknecht had started pressing Marx and Engels for the promised preface soon after the end of the trial. In a letter of April 20, he told Engels about plans to issue an offprint from the trial proceedings.[7] Engels wrote back on April 23:

> To send you an introduction for the Manifesto off the cuff in that way won't do. For this we would need studies on the socialist literature of the last twenty-four years, in order to supplement Section III and bring it up to date. This, then, must remain reserved for a later edition, but we are willing to send you a short "preface" for the offprint, and this will do for the present.[8]

Around the beginning of June, the proofs of the third fascicule arrived in London for Engels' checking. On June 6 Engels wrote Liebknecht: "The proofs of the Manifesto together with a short preface will go out as fast as possible, hopefully tomorrow." He must have sent

---

* There were, in all, twelve fascicules, the last one published at the beginning of 1874. The twelve were then put together in a single volume and distributed as a 600-page book, with the imprint Leipzig, 1874.

the proofs back on the 7th or 8th for, as mentioned, the publication took place around the 15th. But he did not send the promised preface with the proofs. In any case, the preface could not have been printed in the third fascicule as such; it was not part of the court record. Did Liebknecht make this clear to Engels? Probably not. Actually, the preface was intended for the offprint edition.

Marx's and Engels' preface was finished, and dated, June 24. It was undoubtedly sent off to Liebknecht immediately, for the offprint pamphlet containing the preface came off the press before the end of June. It is this offprint edition which is usually called the "German edition of 1872."

There are three aspects of this edition that require attention.

(1) *The preface.* This was the first of the seven prefaces for the Manifesto by Marx and Engels, only two of which were signed by Marx in addition to his collaborator. In this first preface, they attempted to set down an answer to the problem which Liebknecht had been flogging in an attempt to persuade them to revise the text, a problem they knew others were raising in different ways. Was the document obsolete as it stood? Did everything still apply? Hadn't conditions changed?

Their answer, in few words, was: The principles remain; what changes is application in practice.

No matter how much conditions have changed in the last twenty-five years, the general principles set forth in this Manifesto still on the whole retain their complete correctness today. Details might be improved here and there. The practical application of these principles—so the Manifesto itself states—will depend everywhere and every time on the historically existing state of affairs, and therefore no special weight at all is given to the revolutionary measures proposed at the end of Section II. This passage would today read differently in many respects. In view of the immense progress of large-scale industry in the last twenty-five years and of the concomitant advance of the party organization of the working class, in view of the practical experiences gone through—in the first place the February Revolution [of 1848] and then, far more, the Paris Commune, where for the first time, for two months long, the proletariat held political power—this program is out of date today in some places. In particular the Commune has provided the proof that "the working class cannot simply lay hold of the ready-made State machinery and wield it for its own purposes." (See *The Civil War in France* [Chapter 3] ... where this is developed further.) Furthermore, it is self-evident that, for today, the critique of socialist literature is incomplete because it extends only to 1847; likewise that the remarks on the attitude of the communists to the various opposition parties (Section IV), although in their principles still correct today, yet in their execution are already out of date today because of the fact that the political situation has been totally transformed and historical development has removed from the face of the earth most of the parties there enumerated.[9]

They thus restated their ground for refusing to revise the text: "Still and all, the Manifesto is a historical document which we no longer claim the right to change." And they repeated the promise—or aspiration—that Engels had already stated to Liebknecht in his April letter: "A later edition may perhaps appear with an introduction which will bridge the interval between 1847 and now..."

(2) *The new title.* The offprint edition was the first one that was published with the title *The Communist Manifesto*

> Das Kommunistische Manifest. Neue Ausgabe mit einem Vorwort der Verfasser. Leipzig, Verlag der Expedition des "Volksstaat," 1872.
> (The Communist Manifesto. New edition, with a preface by the authors. Leipzig, Volksstaat Press, 1872.)

This pamphlet had 27 pages, plus a blank unnumbered page; it had no separate cover, beginning with the title page. It was printed with the same type that had been used for the third fascicule.

The old title, *Manifesto of the Communist Party*, was retained as a subheading preceding the preamble. This pattern was followed by subsequent German editions, and also by many editions in other countries.

To be sure, the title change was not very startling in itself; informally the document had been called the "Communist manifesto" before this, in a natural shortening. In fact, the very first suggestion by Engels, in his letter to Marx of November 1847 (see Chapter 2 above), had given the title in this short form. Letters passed between Marx and Engels had used the short title at least twice.* No doubt, others did the same.

But was there a special reason for the short title at this point? Yes, there was a legal consideration which Liebknecht had already shown himself anxious about. From the standpoint of legality inside Germany, the title *Communist Manifesto* now had the advantage of not flaunting the existence of a Communist *party* which the police would find more objectionable than mere ideas. More than in 1848 or the fifties, the word 'party' now tended to invite an organizational interpretation, not only by socialist readers but especially by the guardians of public morality; for socialist, i.e., "subversive," party organization now existed. The old title complicated the legal problem; demoted to an inside heading, it was de-emphasized. The new title was less immediately linked to the old illegal pamphlet which the police under Stieber and Wermuth had once hunted down; it removed the reference to an obviously illegal *organization,* guaranteed to catch the eye of the stupidest gendarme.

This consideration was not peculiar to Germany; and in fact we have already seen that Mesa's Spanish edition, which came along very soon, adopted the new short title.

---

* In 1851 Engels made a parenthetical reference to "certain people [who] think they are up to the mark, yet do not even understand the 'Communist Manifesto'..."[10] In 1869 Marx told Engels about Lafargue's sending "his French translation of the 'Communist Manifesto,' which we are to look over."[11]

Henceforward, the new short title was going to become rather more common than the original title, which however was never entirely displaced.

There is no record that Liebknecht discussed the title change with Marx or Engels, or informed them in advance. But in any case neither Marx nor Engels commented on it—not in any extant letter or other record—and we may assume they found it unobjectionable; otherwise we would probably be aware of some echo of their dissatisfaction. No doubt they appreciated the legal considerations behind the change.

(3) *The Potemkin's Village.* Andréas' work for the first time put the spotlight on the strange nature of this offprint edition called the "German edition of 1872." The strangeness can be put briefly: *there was no such edition in actuality.*

Liebknecht, in point of fact, produced only a few copies of the offprint pamphlet containing the Marx-Engels preface—as distinct from the third-fascicule version of the Manifesto which had been legally printed and distributed in thousands of copies. This explains, for example, why Franz Mehring (for one) was aware only of the fascicule format, not of the offprint, which he had never heard of as late as 1877. Nearly a year later, Bebel's letter to Marx explained that it was *not* after all legally practicable to distribute the offprint in mass; that it existed only in "several" copies; that these few copies were probably distributed only to functionaries and leading propagandists of the party. Any public distribution would "immediately bring down a treason trial on [our] necks."[12]

Besides, the market had probably been filled by the several thousands of copies in the form of the third fascicule, available since mid-June. What sense was there in pushing another printing of exactly the same pages in July–August?

All this was evidently unknown to Marx and Engels in 1872. The very fact that they took the time, under pressure, to do a preface means that they were not told by Liebknecht that an edition with that preface would be legally out of the question. This concealment confronted Liebknecht with a problem immediately, for Engels ordered a bundle of "author's copies," especially to give a batch to the London GWEA in recognition of its past aid in publishing the Manifesto. There is reason to believe that Liebknecht did not have a bundle to send, and that he had to get it printed up to order. The evidence for this is deductive: Liebknecht sent Engels a bundle of one hundred copies and also a bill *demanding payment for them.* Engels was so indignant at this that he wrote two strong denunciatory letters about it (very unusual for him). He told the manager of the party press, A. Hepner: Here Marx and I supply pieces for the press without asking for any pay, and then into the bargain you make us buy our own copies at the bookstore! (This had recently happened with a new edition of *The Peasant War in Germany* and other material.[13]) He wrote to Liebknecht: this "boorish behavior" must come to a halt.[14] Liebknecht was apparently unable to explain that the hundred copies constituted most of the "edition."

If this view of the episode is essentially correct, it may be asked why Liebknecht had pressed Marx and Engels so hard for a preface in the first place. The answer must be that he had begun by believing his own huffing-and-puffing. (His problem was not hypocrisy but muddleheadedness, if we trust Marx's and Engels' estimate.) Then when it dawned on him that the legal offprint was impracticable, he tried to cover up the fact that he had bothered

54

them uselessly. Besides, he had started pressing for a preface before the court proceedings had made publication of the Manifesto legal in the form of the third fascicule *without* a preface.

Andréas' account has the virtue of explaining why not a word about the offprint edition (the alleged "German edition of 1872") got into the *Volksstaat* itself, and why the new Marx-Engels preface was not given separate periodical publication. The latter would have made the offprint known to the party membership and the public (not to speak of the authorities), and there would have been embarrassing requests for copies. This was virtually a secret edition, what there was of it, if it can be called an edition at all. Andréas says flatly that it "cannot be considered as constituting an edition."[15] It was a fake by Liebknecht.

And yet—here the irony of history doubles back on itself—this fake edition became the father of many real ones. For Marx and Engels used the bundle of copies to answer requests from many countries; and the Manifestos they sent out to correspondents became the models for a number of translations and other publications. Their own preface, which had not gotten to the general German public in its original form, was read by millions, in a score of tongues, before long.

It was as if Potemkin's Village was subsequently furnished out by real inhabitants and turned into a real hamlet.

20. IN THE WAKE OF THE PARIS COMMUNE: II

T he last two chapters reported on editions of the Manifesto appearing in 1871-1873. Another activity that picked up after the Paris Commune was the pattern of discussing, or merely mentioning, the Manifesto in books and articles on current politics or political history. This inaugurates the time when the Manifesto started gaining its status as a necessary part of any cultured person's stock of knowledge on sociopolitical matters, meager as that might be. To identify this status, one might say that it is the process which reached its apogee when the Manifesto was hallowed by membership on the Hundred Great Books list in university courses.

At our present point, this process was only in its first stages. Two developments were needed before the culmination in England and America: a usable English translation had to be available (a condition that was fulfilled in 1888) and the socialist movement had to become strong enough to justify chronic fear of the Red Menace. The latter condition started taking life during the 1890s, and the corresponding state of mind became permanent with the First World Revolution period of 1917–1923. (One of the side effects of the Ten Days That Shook the World was the establishment of the Manifesto as one of the books that shook the world—in retrospect.)

In the 1870s this process was still mainly at the level of mentions, rather than full-length discussions. Andréas' criterion for inclusion is actual citation from the Manifesto; he does not list mentions as such. Even so, his is a long list, even before we come to the twentieth century.

Here we give only a general overview.

We have already noted that as a result of the Commune Marx became notorious as the Red Doctor who was the head of the International Conspiracy to Subvert Civilization. The International was the conspiracy itself. There were also less extreme tirades against the threat of socialism. Among the books purporting to reveal the "truth" behind the dread International, and quoting from the Manifesto to do so, were the following:

■ Oscar Testut, *L'Internationale* (Paris, 1871).

■ Edmond Villetard, *Histoire de l'Internationale* (Paris, 1872).

■ M. B. [probably Moritz Busch], *Geschichte der Internationale* (Leipzig, 1872).

■ Eugen Jäger, *Der moderne Socialismus. Karl Marx, die Internationale Arbeiter-Association, Lassalle und die deutschen Socialisten* (Berlin, 1873). Copious citations from the Manifesto.

Books that discussed the new socialist movement were likely to refer to the Manifesto for illumination. For example, Rudolph Meyer's *Der Emancipationskampf des vierten Standes* (Volume 1, 1874) was a much-praised work that we will meet again. There were: Georg Brandes' biography *Ferdinand Lassalle*, which first ran in a Danish periodical in 1875 before its book publication in Germany (but not in Denmark) in 1877; Emile de Laveleye's *Le Socialisme Contemporain*, first published in the *Revue des Deux Mondes* in 1876, later as a book in 1881, followed by numerous editions; and, not least, the violent anti-Marx and anti-Social-Democratic diatribes of the still unconverted Franz Mehring, steaming in a series of articles in 1876, collected into a book *Die deutsche Socialdemokratie* (Bremen, 1877), and reprinted in many editions.

In English, the Reverend Moritz Kaufmann published a survey of *Utopias, or Schemes of Social Improvement. From Sir Thomas More to Karl Marx* (London, 1879), which had first appeared as a series in *The Leisure Hour* of 1878. In French, Benoît Malon's *Histoire du Socialisme* (Lugano, 1879) carried a translation of most of Section I and II of the Manifesto, done by Malon himself with the aid of Katerina Katkov.

A Dutchman, A. Kerdijk, wrote one of the first substantial biographical sketches of Marx, published as the first part of a collective work edited by N. C. Balsem, *Mannen van Beteekenis in Onze Dagen*, Volume X (Haarlem, 1879). We come back to the International with a German work, L. Friedlieb's *Die rothe und die schwarze Internationale* (Munich, 1874). An unsigned brochure of 1878, *Prinzipien der Social-Demokratie und Lassalle'sche Lehren*, an antisocialist polemic, did much quoting from the Manifesto. Also in 1878, when the influential Augsburg *Allgemeine Zeitung* ran a series on "The Philosophy of the Social-Democracy," the first article (March 29) gave long excerpts and summaries from the Manifesto's first section. Unsigned, the series was by Johannes Huber, who also published a summary article with the same title in a Berlin magazine in May. (See A#111.)

Socialists too were referring to the Manifesto more and more often, even in articles for the general press. It was probably J. G. Eccarius, Marx's long-time collaborator, who wrote the article published in the London *Times* (October 27, 1871) on the International, with excerpts from the Manifesto.[1] At this time Eccarius was earning some money as the *Times* correspondent on the affairs of the International. The article was good propaganda for the International; certainly Engels thought so when he recommended its reading to a comrade in Italy.[2] For this reason, it was reprinted in the March 16, 1872 issue of the *International Herald* (London), a paper which acted as an International organ.

As Marx's name became more common in the press, socialist periodicals sometimes sought to explain that he was not really Beelzebub in person. For example, the Austrian party's *Workers' Calendar for 1874*, which offered articles by party leaders, carried an essay by Leo Frankel on "Karl Marx as Thinker and Agitator"; it quoted from the Manifesto. This article, probably prepared with the help of Engels, came out while Frankel was still living in London. The Vienna Socialdemocratic *Volkswille* reprinted Section III of the Manifesto (after the *NRZ Revue* text) in its issue of January–February 1874. This year was a vintage year for Manifesto quotes: in March they also appeared in the Chicago *Vorbote* and in the *Braunschweiger Volksfreund* (Brunswick) and in June in the Leipzig Volksstaat.

In the well-circulated *Hamburger-Altonaer Volksblatt* for May 5, 1878, Marx's comrade Carl Hirsch reported on the Paris world's fair, and in the course used excerpts from the Manifesto to explain the historical achievements of the bourgeoisie. The Manifesto was well on its way to becoming the inevitable source of suitable pithy quotes for various socialist occasions.

21. IN THE WAKE OF THE PARIS COMMUNE: III

The burgeoning notoriety of the Manifesto continued into the early 1880s, though with less of the virulent hatred that was in evidence right after the Paris Commune. Here let us keep an eye only on the period before Marx's death. The Manifesto received important notice, including citation, in a number of books:

■ Theodore Woolsey's antisocialist work, *Communism and Socialism in Their History and Theory* (London, 1880) had first been published in a New York weekly, the *Independent*, the year before.

■ John Rae's article on "The Socialism of Karl Marx and the Young Hegelians" in the *Contemporary Review* (London) for October 1881 was later incorporated into his widely read book *Contemporary Socialism* (published in 1884).

■ Adolf Held, *Zwei Bücher zur socialen Geschichte Englands* (Leipzig, 1881) told its readers that "there is, still today, no better source than the *Communist Manifesto*" for getting to know socialist ideas.

■ Hugo Eisenhart's *Geschichte der Nationalökonomie* (Jena, 1881) was the first history of economics to take note of the Manifesto.

■ And there were new editions of some works already cited.

As for periodical literature, in addition to John Rae's article, there were: an essay by Laveleye on the International, in the *Revue des Deux Mondes* (March 15, 1880), which went into his 1881 book along with the 1876 material already noted[1]; an article in the Polish leftist organ *Rownosc* (Geneva), January–February 1881, unsigned; and the memoirs by the kaiser's policeman Stieber in the *Berliner Tageblatt*, where the October 7, 1882 article dealt with the Manifesto.

There is a certain peculiarity about two of the above-listed items which reminds us of another tendency that blossomed especially after the Paris Commune, and about which a word may be said at this point. Namely: there was a notable increase in the frequency with which the Manifesto was cited or reported in a falsified way, or at any rate falsely.

"Falsified" usually implies lying intent, but it is often hard to distinguish falsification from merely incompetent and careless quoting. There are two points to be kept in mind:

(1) When a book carries false or distorted quotations in its first edition, the distinction may well be difficult. But when the falsity has been pointed out to the author, who then issues revised editions of the book without correcting these errors, judgment becomes considerably easier.

(2) In the case of Marx in general and of the Manifesto as a case in point, there is a frequent phenomenon that lies in-between outright falsification and simple error; and, personally, I am convinced that this is the most common case of all. This is a mind-set which encourages careless statement without conscious falsification, a mind-set which may be labeled: "Against Marx, anything goes," or "Who'll object, anyway?"

However, there was no question about the intent of the first prominent falsifiers. Chapter 12 has already introduced the "Black Book" by the Prussian police chiefs Wermuth and Stieber, produced as a police training manual after the Cologne Communist trial of 1852, which railroaded to prison the German cadre of the Communist League and broke its movement. This "crude compilation" bristling with "deliberate falsifications" (as Engels said) included the text of the Manifesto with a number of distortions; it also confused the end of Section I with the beginning of the pamphlet. For example, where the Manifesto said that the proletariat in power will "increase the mass of productive forces as rapidly as possible," the Wermuth-Stieber version replaced "mass" with "lack," that is, reversed the meaning. (See A#33.)

This treatment was part of the aftermath of the 1848–1849 revolution. After the Paris Commune, the Manifesto came to be trotted out to explain the wild, bloodthirsty destruction of civilization by the Communards: the "Anything goes" syndrome went into operation. Some errors were relatively harmless—for example, when the Augsburg *Allgemeine Zeitung* ran a feature article, March 15, 1872, which thought that the famous watchword at the end of the Manifesto was its first sentence. This sort of thing merely showed that the writer had not bothered to study, or perhaps read, the document he was attacking. He could therefore be uninhibited by any knowledge of its actual contents.

A stickier case was that of the eminent publicist Rudolph Meyer, whose book *Der Emancipationskampf des vierten Standes* (Berlin, 1874) became a very popular work, highly touted as an authority even in right-wing social-democratic ranks. (Engels thought that Mayer was a feudal socialist,[2] i.e., antibourgeois from a reactionary *pre*capitalist standpoint.) Meyer quoted part of the beginning of Section II, and summarized the ten-point program; but his quoting was erroneous and the text was altered in several places (see A#86). These regrettable errors remained uncorrected in a couple of new editions, including a second enlarged edition in 1882.

In the same year, a twist was added to the case: an Italian, Valentino Steccanella, published a book *Del Comunismo* (Rome, 1882) which quoted the Manifesto *in German* in the same way as Meyer but with still more alterations! Obviously these improvements were due to an original mind that was not satisfied merely to copy Meyer's distortions. Steccanella's work was published by the press Della S. C. di Propaganda Fide.

It has already been mentioned that the history of economics by Hugo Eisenhart (1881) was the first such work to discuss the Manifesto. Alas, it was also the first to falsify, or bungle, its citation from the Manifesto, aside from two short excerpts that were given accurately. A second enlarged edition ten years later left this accomplishment unchanged. (See A#129.)

The 1882 memoirs by Stieber, listed above, gave Manifesto citations partly falsified as in the Wermuth-Stieber book of 1853, thirty years being insufficient for correction. The book publication of these memoirs in 1884 (A#171) carried on the tradition.

In 1886 the German Reichstag was discussing the prorogation of the Anti-Socialist Law, which had outlawed the Social-Democracy in 1878. In the session of April 2, a conservative deputy, Friedrich Kalle, quoted the Manifesto on marriage. Unfortunately he actually quoted not from Marx's and Engels' Manifesto but from a commentary on the Manifesto written by a pastor, Richard Schuster, in his book *Die Social-Demokratie* (1875, second edition 1876). And Schuster had falsified the content of the Manifesto. The next day in the Reichstag, Liebknecht demonstrated the case, citing the real text. (See A#198.)

In 1890 professor William Graham made a contribution to the gaiety of nations with a book called *Socialism New and Old*, which went through several editions both in England and America. While its summary of the history of the International is outstanding in making at least two factual errors per sentence, it earns a place in our present account by its quotations from the Manifesto.

[The Manifesto states] "that the transformation of society would not take place according to the preconceived ideas of any reformer, but on the initiation of the entire labouring classes"--whatever the last vague clause may mean, which is both mysterious and partly contradictory to the preceding [etc.]...[3]

The "mysterious" contradiction is cleared up when we find out that the alleged quotation from the Manifesto (complete with quote marks) is in fact part of the statement about the Manifesto in Laveleye's *Socialism of To-Day*; for it seems that Graham had no time to read the

Manifesto itself and got his notes from his authority Laveleye mixed up. But Graham's book attained such eminence as an authority on socialism that it was translated into Japanese—only the second book on socialism published in Japan when it came out in 1894. Thus, the Japanese reader could find out that Marx had no system of his own but only echoed the "communism of Louis Blanc." Inscrutable Westerners!

Falsifications—or distortions, or misquotations --of the Manifesto were not the monopoly of Marx's bourgeois opponents. A case in point was H. M. Hyndman, whose leadership of the first British "Marxist" group was one of the major disasters that beset the early rise of Marxism. In the May 1, 1886 issue of his organ *Justice*, Hyndman's article "Social Democrats in Politics" attributed to the Manifesto the Lassalle thesis that "opposed to us all other parties form a reactionary mass" (A#201a). This Lassalleanism had appeared in the text of the Gotha Program of the German party in 1875, and had been denounced in Marx's critique of that program. While Marx's critique was not yet known in 1886, the important point is that the thesis was nowhere in the Manifesto.

Another Lassallean idea often assigned to the Manifesto was the so-called iron law of wages. For example, Kirkup's *History of Socialism* (1892), a book much praised by Eduard Bernstein, revealed that in the Manifesto "The Iron Law of Wages is stated in its hardest and most exaggerated form." This baseless claim remained in all editions of Kirkup's history, including the fifth edition which was revised in 1920 by the Fabian leader E. A. Pease.

We have already put a question mark over the term 'falsification.' The same point can be made from another angle. In its issue of December 18, 1895, the Swiss Social-Democratic organ *Berner Tagwacht* carried an article titled "Die Bourgeoisie," signed by Marx and Engels, neither of whom was then in position to protest that they had never written this piece (A#342). In fact, this article "by Marx and Engels" had been invented by the editors, who took some passages out of the Manifesto and carpentered them together freehand, under a new title.

Now let us assume that the overall effect was not distorting, for this operation was carried out by friendlies. But if the same method were used by hostiles, who were often not loth to use it to prove whatever needed proving, the outcome might be quite a different matter. And in all likelihood, this could be done with the same subjective feeling of honesty as no doubt filled the breasts of the good Swiss social-democratic editors. The important point, therefore, is not so much the incidence of falsifiers but, rather, the frequency of uncorrected distortions which pepper all literature about Marx more than any other body of literature extant.

While we are on the subject, let us take the opportunity to mention a notable falsification of the Manifesto much nearer our own times—one sponsored by the eminent sociologist Robert Michels. After 1923 the Mussolini regime in Italy had all copies of the Manifesto removed from public and university libraries; in their place appeared an edition edited by Michels, with a commentary. Michels claimed to be presenting the Bettini translation; but in fact the text had been changed in several places.[4] Even so, Michels' sanitized version of the Manifesto was reserved exclusively for students who could get advance authorization to consult it.[5] There is perhaps an Iron Law of Falsification under fascism.

I n 1882, two friends of Marx in America proposed editions of the Manifesto. The first project began in the 1870s.

(1) *Friedrich A. Sorge.*

Sorge's efforts had begun some years before 1882 on the basis of an English translation made by Hermann Meyer, a member of the International in America who was an old friend of Weydemeyer and a correspondent of Marx and Engels. Meyer had made the translation in 1870–1871. When Sorge went to Europe for the Hague Congress in 1872, he gave Marx and Engels the manuscript of this translation, for revision. Evidently they originally considered that the Meyer draft offered a basis for publication, and promised to work on it.*

The International, its General Council having been moved to New York, declined in its American exile; and in 1874–1875 Sorge, its general secretary, feared the growth of antirevolutionary trends especially among the "natives," the English-speaking elements. These had little to read in English about the ideas and ideals that had inspired the movement in Europe, and even less about the ideas of Marx. An IWMA Congress was scheduled for Philadelphia for 1876. (This congress was going to dissolve the organization, in fact.)

Concerned about educating native members, Sorge made plans with Meyer for the publication of the Manifesto in English that winter or the following spring, apparently without waiting for a revision from London. But Meyer's death in December scotched that plan. On March 17, 1876, Sorge wrote to Marx and Engels appealing for help. "The movement is getting stronger daily," he wrote optimistically, but we need literature to inspirit the English-speakers. Meyer's death killed our plan, "and now you have to help. You have Meyer's translation ... look it over, do *the promised Supplement*, send it to me soon, and I will take care of its speedy publication and distribution here. Do what you can, and fast!"[1]

On April 4, Marx replied positively: "We will set about" doing the revision, "but as for the Appendix, we can't say yet."[2] This Appendix—what Sorge had called a Supplement—was to be an afterword designed to bring the Manifesto up to date. The idea of the authors' updating the original kept cropping up for decades. But while "updating" the work sounded like a simple job, it actually entailed a review of world history and politics since 1848. It is easy to see why Marx and Engels were reluctant to undertake such a project in the illusory form of a Manifesto appendix.

Sorge received no revised translation from London. He wrote again on April 17, and repeated his request in several letters during 1876–1880.[3]

And so it was that in mid-1882 Sorge again proposed the publication of Hermann Meyer's English version. This time (if not before) Engels replied negatively. Marx was

---

* An obituary article on Meyer, probably by Sorge, said that Marx approved the translation, presumably as a basis for revision. (*Vorbote*, Chicago, December 4, 1875, quoted by Andréas.)

sojourning in Algeria in a vain attempt to regain his health; he was in fact slowly dying. Engels wrote on June 20: "The English translation of the Manifesto sent to us is utterly unpublishable without total revision. But you understand that under the present circumstances this is out of the question."[4]

The phrase "sent to us," used here by Engels, raises a question: was he really referring to the Meyer translation, which had been handed over in London?

Whatever the answer, this was indubitably not the time for either Marx or Engels to work on an English translation. We will come back to Sorge's renewed efforts in June 1883.

(2) *Adolf Hepner.*

Hepner, an old comrade of Marx now in America, had a different proposal to make in 1882: publication of the first *German* edition of the Manifesto on this side of the ocean.

Writing to Engels on May 3, he asked for authorization to publish it as No. 1 in a collection (publisher's series) to be called "Hepner's Deutsch-Amerikanisches Arbeiter-Library." Engels was able to consult with Marx only with difficulty, since Marx was on the Continent; but on June 25 he replied with a cautious yes. Hepner (wrote Engels) should simply go ahead and reprint *without* any formal consent by the authors; we would not think of protesting against it so long as no changes or omissions, which are inadmissible in a historical document anyway, or improper notes, compel us to do so. But he refused to write a new preface or do anything else to formally link himself to an undertaking about which they had no say.[5]

In fact, Hepner did not carry his project out. A New York edition of the Manifesto in German appeared only in April 1902 (see A#396).

o   o   o   o   o

And thus it came about that the publication of an authorized English translation was easily beaten out by the first authorized Russian edition.

We have seen (in Chapter 17 above) that a very defective Russian translation had appeared in 1869. By 1875 the Narodnik, N. I. Kibalchich,* was preparing to put out a new translation, probably done by himself from a German text. This manuscript was seized by the police in a raid on his house in St. Petersburg; it was incomplete, ending in the course of Section I of the Manifesto. When Kibalchich was arrested again in 1881, the police again found a manuscript translation of the Manifesto in his possession; but the extent of this second manuscript is not known.

During its first third of a century, the Manifesto had garnered little notice in the Russian press, judging by Andréas' survey. An 1864 piece by Lavrov has been mentioned (Chapter 17). Besides the 1872 Russian edition of Marx's *Capital*, which quotes from the Manifesto,

---

* Nikolai Ivanovich Kibalchich (1854-1881), an inventor as well as a revolutionary, was a member of the populist Narodnaya Volya (People's Will) organization. Imprisoned in 1881, he was executed for participation in the assassination of Alexander II.

62

there was only the January 1879 number of the St. Petersburg magazine Vestnik *Evropi*, which carried a long article by L. A. Polonsky on Mehring's anti-Social-Democrat and anti-Marx book.[6] This included material on the Manifesto, with citations. Mehring's attack was vicious enough to gladden the czarist censors, but Polonsky's knowledge of the subject was not profound. He disclosed, for example, that the end-motto was a translation from the French.

The first adequate edition of the Manifesto in Russian was produced by the beginnings of the first Russian Marxist group. The leading founder of this group, G. V. Plekhanov, was also the Manifesto's translator.

Back in December 1880, Marx had given the Russian Narodnik, N. Morozov, visiting him in London, a number of his writings, including a copy of the 1872 German edition of the Manifesto. In Geneva, Morozov gave these materials to Plekhanov, who was working with Lavrov on the publication of a "Russian Social-Revolutionary Library" (publisher's series), to be edited by Lavrov.

Plekhanov—not yet a Marxist but on the road—read the Manifesto and was fired by enthusiasm for it. Lavrov himself was indifferent to the idea of publishing it, for he wanted Plekhanov to write an original work. The enterprise therefore fell to Plekhanov, who got the idea of asking Marx and Engels, via Lavrov, to do a new preface for the Russian edition. Marx and Engels agreed immediately.

The new preface, dated January 1882, was written in German, and in fact Marx told Lavrov that "since it is to be *translated* into Russian, it is not written in the style that would be necessary for its publication in the German vernacular."[7] I presume he meant that the language was somewhat more simply formulated, to lessen the chance of mistranslation.* Plekhanov translated this preface too.

The preface is very important for the study of Marx's views on Russian development, but it makes no contribution to our knowledge of the history of the Manifesto itself, which is our present subject.

The blue-gray-covered pamphlet probably came out in June. Here is the bibliographical data:

Manifest Kommunisticheskoi Partii. Karla Marksa i Fr. Engelsa. Perevod s nemeckago izdaniya 1872. S predisloviem avtorov. Zheneva, Volnaya Russkaya Tipografiya, 1882, in 8o, x-50 p. (Russkaya Socialno-Revolutsionnaya Biblioteka. Kniga tretya.) [This series note is at the head of the title page.]

---

* I must enter a demurrer against Andréas' interpretation of Marx's statement, an interpretation embodied in his translation of it: "le style...n'est pas aussi soigné que cela aurait été nécessaire [etc.]" (page 91). This inserts the implication, which is not present in Marx's words, that stylistically it was not as *carefully* done as if intended for German publication. In fact, Marx was careful to simplify the style to aid the translator.

Besides the text of the Manifesto itself, the pamphlet included the following materials:

■ A Foreword by Plekhanov, titled "A Few Words by the Translator," emphasizing the importance of the Manifesto for the revolutionary movement and for the activity of illegal workers' groups in Russia, as well as of their unification.

■ Prefaces by Marx and Engels: the new preface, followed by their preface to the 1872 German edition.

■ An appendix offering excerpts from Marx's Civil War in France (included because the 1872 preface referred to the lessons of the Paris Commune) and from the "Rules of the IWMA," which organization (says Plekhanov inaccurately) was the first successful attempt to establish an international organization on the principles proclaimed in the Manifesto. (But in fact the International did *not* proclaim the principles of communism.)

Engels thought that Plekhanov's translation was by far the best of the translations done.[8] Plekhanov was on the road to organizing the group called "Emancipation of Labor" *(Ozvobozhdeniya Truda)*, and the Manifesto edition was mainly distributed by this first Russian Marxist group, once it got under way. In the ensuing years, it was illegally distributed inside Russia by reprinting, lithographing, mimeographing, etc. For example, not long after the original publication in Geneva, a clandestine edition was printed in Moscow in a lithographic printshop run by one Yankovskaya (A#138). References in the illegal press, police records and reports, and memoirs show that the Manifesto was distributed in all regions of Russia and was widely read.

It was not until 1906 that another Russian translation was published: done by V. V. Vorovsky, writing as P. Orlovsky, perhaps in collaboration with Maxim Gorky, in the period of relative freedom following the 1905 upheaval. (See A#461.) Before the revolution of 1905, local socialist and revolutionary circles had few alternatives to turning out copies by their own limited means—not only mimeographing and hectographing on primitive apparatus but also by manuscript copying.

AFTER THE DEATH OF MARX

23. MARX'S DEATH. EDITIONS OF 1883. AUTHORIZED GERMAN EDITION

arx died March 14, 1883. The news snapped the world to attention: editorials, feature articles, and obituaries proliferated.[1]

There was one important new translation of the Manifesto which happened to come along just as Marx's death notices were appearing. This was the first Polish translation.[2] Like the Russian edition of 1882, it came out of the Geneva emigration. The translation, based on the 1872 text, was made by Witold Piekarski—in 1881 one of the founders of the émigré Polish socialist organ *Przedswit* (Dawn) and its editor in chief. The printing work was done in the periodical's printshop.

The following bibliographical data describes the red-covered pamphlet:

K. Marx i Fr. Engels. Manifest Komunistyczny 1847 r. Przelozyl Witold Piekarski. Genewa, 1883, 4°, 32p.

The cover carried a subtitle, "The Principles of Modern Socialism," and a sponsor's listing, "Warsaw: Publications of the Workers' Committee of the Social-Revolutionary Party Proletariat." Note that the date 1847 mistakenly appears. The contents included the authors' prefaces to the German edition of 1872 and the Russian edition of 1882, preceded by a foreword signed by Piekarski, plus bio-bibliographies of Marx and of Engels.

Though the foreword was dated April 1883, there was no reference to Marx's death, suggesting that the edition was completely set up by mid-March.

o   o   o   o   o

Few of the press notices evoked by Marx's death could have failed to mention the Manifesto, along with *Capital*. The list of mere mentions, indeed, becomes unmanageable and need not concern us. With reference to German and English only, let us give a few examples of the first books, published in the years immediately following Marx's death, which treated the Manifesto as an important part of social history, in the manner that subsequently became general.

■ In 1883 Richard T. Ely published his *French and German Socialism in Modern Times* (New York); it cited the Manifesto, and had a new edition in 1886. Ely was a sort of American Katheder-socialist, a University of Wisconsin professor whom Engels characterized as "a well-intentioned philistine" who "at least takes more trouble than his German comrades in affliction and stupidity, which is always to be appreciated."[3]

■ John Rae's book[4] was published this year after previous periodical publication; and Laveleye's work[5] appeared in English as *The Socialism of To-Day*, to be dissected by E. B. Bax in *Commonweal*, May 1885.

■ In 1885 Gustav Gross published *Karl Marx. Eine Studie* (Leipzig), one of the first full-length studies devoted to Marx. It was based on his piece on Marx in the multivolume encyclopedia *Allgemeine Deutsche Biographie*; the Manifesto was summarized and excerpted.

■ The same year, Georg Adler's *Die Geschichte der ersten sozialpolitischen Arbeiterbewegung in Deutschland* (Breslau, 1885) gave Manifesto citations and summaries relying on the

Wermuth-Stieber compilation. Kautsky, with Engels' help, wrote a critical review for the *Neue Zeit*.

■ Johannes Huber put his articles of 1878[6] into book form (Munich, 1885), with a second edition in 1887.

■ In 1886 Peter Resch, a high Catholic dignitary, dealt with the Manifesto in a book *Die Internationale* (Graz, Leipzig).

■ In 1887 Georg Adler returned to the charge with *Die Grundlagen der Karl Marx'schen Kritik der bestehenden Volkswirtschaft* (Tübingen), which disposed of the economic theory of this "impotent and wretched fellow," and dismissed the Manifesto as a "ridiculous and grotesque pamphlet."

■ In 1888 William H. Dawson's *German Socialism and Ferdinand Lassalle* cited from the Manifesto in the author's own translation; second edition 1891.

■ In 1889 Georg Brandes' *Ferdinand Lassalle* (Leipzig) came out in a second edition, twelve years after the first.

The following publications by persons closer to Marx should also be mentioned for this decade:

■ In the London monthly *Progress,* Eleanor Marx's articles included a biographical sketch of her father in the May 1883 issue; it gave a summary of and quotes from the Manifesto. The July issue carried her article giving a résumé of *Capital*.

■ For the first anniversary of Marx's death Engels published an essay on "Marx and the *Neue Rheinische Zeitung,*" which began by citing passages in the Manifesto looking to revolutionary strategy and tactics in the coming revolution. He concluded with a bid for the judgment of history:

> Never has a tactical program justified itself as well as this one. Put forward on the eve of the revolution, it stood the test of this revolution; whenever, since this period, a workers' party has deviated from it, the deviation has met its punishment; and today [1884], after almost forty years, it serves as the guiding line of all resolute and class-conscious workers' parties in Europe, from Madrid to St. Petersburg.[7]

Published in the German party's organ on March 13, 1884, this essay was widely reprinted and translated.

■ A few months later, Engels published an essay "On the History of the Communist League," first in October 1885 as an introduction to a reprint of a work by Marx, and then in installments in November in the German party organ. Its reference to the Manifesto was very brief and not very informative:

> [At the Second Congress of the Communist League] Marx and I were commissioned to draw up the Manifesto. This was done immediately afterwards. A few weeks before the February Revolution it was sent to London to be printed. Since then it has traveled round the world, has been translated into almost all languages, and today still serves in numerous countries as a guide for the proletarian movement.[8]

o   o   o   o   o

Soon after Marx's death, the German Social-Democratic Party began its series of "authorized" editions of the Manifesto. This was not an act of memorialization, and probably would have been undertaken in any case. Pirated editions had been cropping up to an unwelcome extent, as in the case of the Most group's edition of 1880.[9] An editorial statement in this edition had claimed that it was necessary because the Manifesto was not easily available.

The German party's publishing arm was, like the administration of the party, located in the Zurich area, since Bismarck's Anti-Socialist Law of 1878 had outlawed the organization in Germany. Its press manager was Hermann Schlüter, aided by Julius Motteler; it used the imprint Schweizerische Volksbuchhandlung of Hottingen-Zurich (Hottingen being a suburb on the east side of the city). The Manifesto may have been its first big publication project.

The new edition of 1883 was labeled "Third Authorized German Edition," counting the 1872 edition (erroneously) as the second one. It was based on the 1872 text, with small changes, including some spelling modernizations. Engels probably did not work on the text for this edition; for one thing, at this point he was overwhelmed by the task of sorting out Marx's papers and manuscripts.

But Engels did contribute a new preface, the first one signed by him alone and the shortest of all, dated June 28. Since Marx's death, he emphasized, "there can be even less thought of revising or supplementing the Manifesto." And, summarizing "the basic thought running through the Manifesto," that is, the viewpoint of historical materialism, he asserted that "this basic thought belongs solely and exclusively to Marx."[10]

This edition retained the 1872 title *Das Kommunistische Manifest*, rather than the title including the name Communist Party. It had been announced for May but, probably delayed by the preface, appeared in July, with a press run of 10,000 copies. This run was exhausted in a rather short time, probably by early 1884, showing that there had indeed been a need to be filled. An additional printing of at least 5000 was made in July-August 1884.

In 1887 the unsold copies were bound together with two other pamphlets when the socialists of Western Switzerland made it mandatory for new members to read all three. (The other two were Lassalle's *Workers' Program* and an unsigned agit-prop pamphlet on socialism written by Bernstein.) This combination was out of print in 1890.

To complete the story of the "authorized editions": In early August 1890 the party press issued the "Fourth Authorized German Edition" as No.33 of the Sozialdemokratische Bibliothek, a pamphlet series launched in 1885. This was the last German edition seen through the press by Engels. He augmented it with five notes, which with one exception had already appeared in the English edition of 1888 (which comes up in Chapter 26).

Engels again contributed a new preface, dated May 1. It quoted the Marx-Engels preface to the Russian edition of 1882, and included a somewhat revised version of Engels' own preface to the English edition of 1888. The new edition also included the prefaces of 1872 and 1883, plus an excerpt from the 1888 preface.

The pages were stereotyped by the printshop, and the plates were used to produce the subsequent editions printed in Berlin up to 1909. The "Fifth Authorized German Edition" came in the first half of 1891. It was the first "authorized" edition published in Germany itself, for the Anti-Socialist Law had fallen the previous year. The party publisher was now called the Vorwärts Press of Berlin. The sixth edition was published about June 1894. Then the party publishers stopped numbering editions for a while; and all editions made from the stereotype plates were labeled the sixth—until in 1908 a "Seventh Authorized Edition" was printed from the old 1890 plates.

It is of some interest to note that in 1895 the Hamburg party organization, through its publishing arm Auer & Company, went into business competition with the national office by putting out its own edition of the Manifesto, printed in its own shop.

After Engels' death in 1895, and after the subsequent outbreak of Bernstein's so-called Revisionism, the Manifesto figured prominently in the storm of controversy. Bernstein's major Revisionist work, for example, denounced the Manifesto as "Blanquist." But this belongs to the history of the Social-Democracy at large.

In the chapters to follow, we will take up only major editions of the Manifesto, especially those that Engels was involved with in some way. This points above all to the editions in English and French. This will be followed by a summary of editions in various languages belonging to the period from the death of Marx to the death of Engels.

24. JOHANN MOST HIJACKS THE MANIFESTO

Johann Most is mainly known today for the notoriety he gained as a rhetorician of anarchism in America; but at the time Marx died he was just entering on this vocation. In his youth a bookbinder, he was a Social-Democratic journalist and agitator from 1871 on. In his first period he was known as Professor Eugen Dühring's chief Social-Democratic disciple, and indeed led the cabal that tried to get the party to scuttle its serial publication of Engels' *Anti-Dühring*.

The government expelled him from Berlin in 1878; he moved to London, and published *Freiheit* as an émigré organ, specializing in virulent public attacks on the German party and its leaders. As a result of other antiparty activity, a party congress expelled him in August 1880. When he published an article in praise of the assassination attempt on Alexander II in 1881, the English government sentenced him to prison; and Marx joined those who supported his civil liberties. In 1882 Most fled to America, re-established *Freiheit* in New York, and came out with increasing openness as the kind of anarchist reveling in wild rhetoric and sanguinary "r-r-revolutionary" elocution. But in 1883 his political character was not yet publicly crystallized.

A couple of years before, Most and his London circle had made an initial démarche on the Manifesto. In or about November 1880, they published an edition which, for uncommunicative anonymity, was rivaled only by his fellow anarchist Nechayev's production of 1869.[1]; This was an edition without covers or title page, without date or place of publication or publisher. But it did advertise *Freiheit*, which the old Communist Workers Educational Association* in London had by now adopted as its organ. This edition also had some anonymous notes, by the anonymous editors, imposing Most's anarchizing line on the Manifesto. It was printed at the *Freiheit* shop and probably paid for by the CWEA. The following January-February, CWEA and the *Freiheit* printshop used the same type metal for a new printing, this time with the CWEA named as publisher.

When Marx died, it was in America that memorial meetings and obituary publications were most plentiful. (Germany was in the midst of the Anti-Socialist Law repression; in France the movement had split; in England labor was still in the doldrums.) Johann Most saw an opportunity to use Marx's ghostly coattails to push himself forward as the chief disciple of the dead leader, who could no longer protest.

In New York a broad committee of trade-unionists and socialists was formed to hold a memorial meeting. It was sponsored by the Central Labor Union, in the large hall of Cooper Union, on March 19. This memorial meeting filled the hall, and another 5000 were turned away. Prominent trade-unionists and socialists presided and spoke; there was even a letter from Henry George. Johann Most and his *Freiheit* sectlet set out to capture this broad movement and turn the affair into a tail to the anarchist kite. We will now see the steps in this operation, which intimately involved the *Communist Manifesto*.

In the first place, Most appeared as the concluding speaker at the memorial meeting. His speech was one of fulsome flattery of Marx, tricked out with quotations from the Manifesto. It seems that before Marx died, he had handed on the torch to his best disciple Most: "When I saw Marx for the last time ... he said to me: 'I will not see the triumph of our cause, but you are young enough [etc., etc.]...'"[2] The historian Foner describes his speech as follows:

---

* This is the organization described in Chapter 4 under the name German Workers Educational Association (GWEA). By this time it was mainly known by the Communist name (or some variation thereof), and we will call it the CWEA.

Johann Most spoke of having been the popularizer of Marx's works in Germany, and related that when he had met Marx in London before coming to the United States, he had literally received his blessings. His assertion left the impression with the audience that Marx's writings were part of the foundations of anarchism, and soon Most's friends were boasting of him as "the most competent and hard-working distributor of the ideas which Marx had given to the German proletariat."[3]

The effect of this operation may be seen in what happened to Philip Van Patten, one of the few "native" socialist leaders in what was still mainly a German émigré movement. Van Patten had been national secretary of the Socialist Labor Party since 1879, and was a leading participant in the Cooper Union meeting. On learning that Most was Marx's corporeal representative on this earth, he was extremely upset. On April 2 he wrote to Engels, asking whether Marx had really sympathized with "the anarchistic and disorganizing methods of Most."

> Most's ill-advised, stupid chatter [he wrote] has already done us too much harm here, and it is very unpleasant for us to hear that such a great authority as Marx approved of such tactics.[4]

Engels replied quickly and strongly, and his letter of April 18 to Van Patten, repudiating Most and anarchism, is now well known.[5] Engels furthermore had it immediately published in the German press.

What is less well known is what happened to Van Patten. On April 22—well *before* Engels' reply could possibly have reached him—Van Patten suddenly walked out of the movement and disappeared, citing his disgust with the behavior of the German-American socialistic elements. He felt, he said, that these German-Americans did not care about making American workers understand their ideas[6]—a condemnation which Marx and Engels had been making for years. Like many another eviscerated militant, Van Patten's subsequent life is a sad story, but it is not our present concern.

Johann Most's operation did not end with his annexation of Marx's mantle. The fund raised by the trade-unionist and socialist committee to organize the memorial affair wound up with a surplus, which was supposed to go for the publication of an English edition of the Manifesto, to be circulated in the labor and socialist movement. The sponsoring organizations were to receive 300 free copies. The fund was fattened by the sale of a special Marx portrait.

This enterprise was taken over by Most and his anarchist circle, and turned into an anarchist benefit. An English edition of the Manifesto was published; it was taken from the Macfarlane translation of 1850, in the form of the 1871 reprint in *Woodhull & Claflin's Weekly*, but with some Mostite changes. Hepner, Engels' old friend and comrade, wrote him on May 7-12 that the Most clique had made the arrangements for publication "naturally without asking you or putting the translation before you..."[7]

The "Mostites" made some deliberate omissions in the Macfarlane text. One change deleted the ten-point program in Section II: these demands, said the pamphlet's editors, were "not applicable at the present time, as more radical measures are necessary." This statement was made as a "Translator's note"—one of the falsifications designed to convey the notion that this was a new translation. To the same end, an editorial note also said: "we have resolved to translate and publish it," the "we" being the present publishers, Most's sect. The introduction of a number of Americanisms into the text also gave the impression of a brand-new translation.*

Even the title was revised:

Manifesto of the Communists. Published by the International Workingmen's Association. New York, Schaerr & Frantz, in 8o, 28 p.

The name "International Workingmen's Association" had been expropriated from the First International by its anarchist rump in Europe, and Most made his own use of it.

This edition of the Manifesto—which had originally been decided on, sponsored, and financed by the broad movement behind the memorial meeting, was now not only labeled "Published by" the anarchist sect, but the text was followed by this advertisement: "This pamphlet and the organ of the I.W.A. *Freiheit* for sale at Justus H. Schwab [etc.]." Schwab was the *Freiheit* publisher and Most's lieutenant.

The brochure appeared at the beginning of June; its sale was announced on June 9. The former secretary of the broad Marx Memorial Commission, George G. Block, protested against the fact that the anarchist "International" and the anarchist organ *Freiheit* were advertised on the first and last pages. In the ensuing argument, Schwab freely embroidered the original pretense that the translation was a new one. He asserted that the translation had been prepared by his group already three months before Marx's death, in an effort at the "most accurate possible translation of the original German text ... made by wage-workers," members of the I.W.A. group. (This rattled the bones of the old anarchoid "proletarianism," according to which the translation was sanctified if made by certified "workers.")

While both Hepner and Engels had failed to recognize the source of the translation, there can be little doubt that Schwab knew where it came from. A *Freiheit* announcement had said that the Manifesto "will shortly be published separately for the first time in the English language..." This statement was technically true only because of the word "separately," which indicated that the *Freiheit* staff knew of the previous *nonseparate* publication of the translation.

---

* Engels did not recognize the Macfarlane source of this version, especially since (as we will see) he was told it was a new translation, gotten up by Most's people. He thought it was quite bad. The translation, he wrote, again shows that there does not seem to be anyone there who can translate *our* German at least into literary and grammatical English. This takes practice as a writer in both languages, and moreover practice not merely in the daily press. Translating the Manifesto is terribly difficult... [8]

The bowdlerization of the ten-point program of demands was the target of further criticism and protest in the German-American socialist press during June. Of course, the issue was not whether these demands were presently applicable, but rather whether the anarchist editors had any right to excise them from the text on their own say-so. *Freiheit* finally printed the ten points in its June 23 issue, together with an anarchist-style attack on them.

This edition had a press run of some thousands of copies. Instead of the 300 copies promised to contributing unions and organizations, the Most-Schwab operation sent only 100—swindlers even in detail. When there was a temporary holdup of about two weeks in the printing of the pamphlets, the copies that came off the press after the interruption were labeled "Second Edition," with some changes in ads and other details. Also added was the announcement that the pamphlet was available in Chicago through August Spies and the *Arbeiter-Zeitung*, that is, the anarchists in that city.

Thus the English edition of the Manifesto was "captured" as the property and instrument of the Mostite anarchist sect alone, with a distorted text, lies about the translation, and charges and countercharges flying about among the former participants in the Cooper Union memorial meeting, to the delight of the antisocialist press.

Our "r-r--revolutionary" swindlers and wreckers had one other exercise in chicanery that should be mentioned. The anarchists' introduction to the Manifesto stated that "It was written by K. Marx, assisted by Fr. Engels."[9] Johann Most, of course, knew perfectly well that Engels was its coauthor.

Why did Engels have to be demoted to a "mention"? Because he, unlike Marx, was still quite alive and in position to repudiate and denounce the swindlers—as indeed he did in his letter to Van Patten.

25. THE THREE VERSIONS OF LAURA MARX LAFARGUE

ight up to the 1880s, no adequate translation of the Manifesto had been produced in French. This was a serious lack, since it held back the growth of Marxist influence not only in France but in other Latin countries whose socialists tended to know French but not German. The first adequate French translation was finally made by none other than Marx's daughter Laura, who was married to the French socialist leader Paul Lafargue.

Just as her younger sister Eleanor was long undervalued because the label "Marx's daughter" obscured her independent contributions, so too Laura has rarely been given due credit. To be sure, Laura was not independently active in the French movement in the way that Eleanor was in England. But this can be stated: the correspondence between Engels and the Lafargues (published only in 1956) shows that Laura's political intelligence was substantially superior to that of the French party leader who was her husband. Engels often urged her to use her abilities for political writing; but (for whatever reason) what Laura mainly undertook was translation. She wrote not one French version of the *Communist Manifesto* but three.

The story of the three Laura-versions (which we will call Laura-1, Laura-2, and Laura-3) will raise the question of Engels' views on the interpretation of particular passages in the Manifesto; but unfortunately it cannot answer these questions. However, we will find suggestive material. No doubt Engels discussed such problems with Samuel Moore as he worked on the revision of Moore's English translation (for which see the next chapter), but we possess neither any preliminary draft nor any record of such discussion. In Laura's case, something of a spoor remains. We can examine the three versions—and conjecture.

Up to the eighties, the French side of the Manifesto's history had been a record of frustration. During the several decades when France was a hotbed of socialist sentiment as compared with the rest of the Continent, it was still true that the names of persons who even contemplated translating the Manifesto were overwhelmingly the names of foreigners in France, or of not-quite-native Frenchmen (like Paul Lafargue himself). To explain this state of affairs, we would have to, but will not, digress to a subject which often distressed the French, namely, chauvinist attitudes.

For a couple of decades there was hardly a sign of a French translation in the offing. As we saw in Chapter 9, French figured among the "phantom translations" of 1848, involving a Belgian with an Italian name, Victor Tedesco, and a German émigré, Hermann Ewerbeck. In September 1851 the Russian journalist N. I. Sazanov, a former editor of the Paris *Réforme*, did half of a translation, in Geneva. The German communist Ernst Dronke was assigned to do the rest, but his laziness asserted itself.[1] The translation was probably not finished; anyway, no translation appeared; no manuscript is extant.[2]

In 1869 there was a draft that involved Paul Lafargue, Marx's semi-French son-in-law. On April 15 Marx wrote to Engels as follows:

Lafargue has sent me his French translation of the *Communist Manifesto*, which we are supposed to check over. I am sending the manuscript to you by post today. To begin with, the thing is not pressing. In no wise do I want Lafargue to burn his fingers prematurely. But should the thing get printed in France sooner or later, certain parts would be reduced to a few lines, like the part on German or True Socialism, since it is not of interest to them there.[3]

Engels replied on April 19:

The Lafargue manuscript is here; I have not yet been able to look at it; I also believe he should do his examination *avant tout*.[4]

That is, Engels thought that Lafargue should get ahead with his medical schooling, in preparation for the looming examination, rather than work on the Manifesto. Both Marx and Engels appeared to be far from eager to see a French edition of the Manifesto come out at this moment. I conjecture that this attitude was conditioned by the delicate situation in the

International, where the Proudhonist leadership of the French section was unfriendly not only to Germans but to communism. If Lafargue sponsored publication of a German communist manifesto, he might "burn his fingers" with his Proudhonist connections. Marx's willingness even to edit the Manifesto's text in order to avoid rubbing French sensibilities the wrong way can scarcely be duplicated in any other case.

It contrasts with Marx's often-repeated injunction that the Manifesto must be republished only integrally as a "historical document."

There are two puzzling points about this French translation.

(1) Marx refers to it as "his" (Lafargue's) translation. Andréas takes this literally, and concludes that Lafargue actually wrote a translation, probably assisted by Laura. But we know that Lafargue could not even read an article in German; it is hard to imagine him doing a difficult translation, even with assistance. By "his" translation Marx may simply have meant a manuscript that Lafargue sent in, or perhaps one that he had promoted. To be sure, there is no mention of any other translator; of course, the possibility nearest to Lafargue was Laura.

(2) Whoever the translator was, what happened to the translation? It was not heard from again.

In 1872—as we saw in Chapter 18—the New York organ *Le Socialiste* published a French translation of Sections I and II of the Manifesto; and, faute de mieux, Engels welcomed it as helpful for propaganda in Europe. Also, around this time, Engels received, via Sorge, a revised version done by a "Frenchman living in America"; and he made use of this material to help Mesa's Spanish translation-in-progress.* "As occasion offers," Engels wrote to Sorge, "I will put the French translation in general in order."[6] Perhaps it is because of this promise that Andréas thinks that "it is certain that at this time Marx and Engels had decided to do a French edition of the Manifesto themselves." But Engels was planning only to work on revising the *Le Socialiste* translation.

In their preface to the 1872 German edition, the authors announced that "A new translation [in French] is in the course of preparation." But the urgent press of work prevented them from carrying out their intention, and there is no evidence that Engels kept at it after the Hague Congress had precipitated another critical period. Engels wrote to Sorge on November 16, "I am up to my ears in work," and reported that he had given the revised French translation to Mesa,[7] but this is most easily understood as explained above. If, as Andréas believes, Engels had an unfinished draft of a translation of his own by the end of 1872, there is no sign of this manuscript later.

In 1879 the Bakuninist-turned-reformist Benoît Malon published his *Histoire du Socialisme* (Lugano), which devoted a half-score of pages to a defective translation of Sections I and II of the Manifesto with substantial omissions. This version had been done by Malon, with the

---

* See Chapter 18, page 76. On May 23, 1872, Marx wrote to Sorge: "It will do no harm to send me the French translation of the *Communist Manifesto.*"[5] It would appear, as *MEW*'s note says, that Marx was referring to the translation in *Le Socialiste*. Andréas thinks he was referring to a new translation, but I do not see why this hypothesis comes up .

assistance of Katerina Katkov, from the 1866 German edition. Subsequent editions of Malon's history (Paris, 1880 and 1884) did not correct the translation.

o   o   o   o   o

Around the beginning of 1883, Mme. Gendre, a RussoFrench socialist living in France, proposed to do a translation of the Manifesto.* Via the Lafargues, she asked Engels for a preface (like everyone else). Engels replied to Laura on April 11, in English:

> If Mme. Gendre will translate the Manifest [sic] into French and let me revise the translation (it's no child's play, you know) I will write her a preface sufficient to explain the historical circumstances etc. But as I know nothing much of the lady, I am bound to say at present: no revision, no preface. A right to stop any proceedings of her in that direction I have not.[8]

But nothing further is heard of a translation by Mme. Gendre.

Two years later, the French "Guesdist" party (the Parti Ouvrier Français), which published the Paris *Le Socialiste*, thought that a man for the job had been found in a Paris member named Lavigne,** who had translated a couple of Marx writings in manuscript. On November 4, 1885, Lafargue informed Engels of the outcome: "We commissioned him to translate the Manifesto. But after going over the translation for the first number [of *Le Socialiste*] we decided that it had to be thrown into the wastepaper basket. It was then that Laura took on the task."[9]

Laura not only took on the task but for the first time completed it. When Lafargue wrote these words, Laura's new translation (i.e., Laura-1) had been appearing serially in the press since August.

Her unsigned translation was published in *Le Socialiste* in eleven installments, from August 29 to November 7, 1885. Based on the German edition of 1872 or 1883, it appeared under the rubric "Variétés." In preceding issues, under this same rubric the paper had published biographical sketches of Marx and Engels, inaugurating a series called "Galerie Socialiste Internationale." The translation was immediately reprinted, also serially, in a number of Guesdist organs in the provinces.

Laura naturally wanted Engels to write a special preface, evidently for an expected pamphlet edition of the translation. She wrote:

---

* Barbe Gendre (1842–1884), Russian-born daughter of French émigrés, called herself Mme. Gendre, but was married to a Russian named Nikitine. She lived in Paris from 1878 on; was a friend of Lavrov; was acquainted with Marx's writings; authored a work *Etudes Sociales*, and contributed to periodicals.

** His full name is given as Paul Lavigne in the index to *MEW* 36, which contains a letter to him by Engels (December 1, 1885). The index to the Engels/Lafargues Correspondence does not know his first name.

I will translate the one of 1872, if you like, but I think it is hardly suitable for the present publication ... I don't know whether our Parisian readers will appreciate the preface in question. I should say that a few lines would suffice by way of introduction...[10]

She added that when subsequent editions of the pamphlet came out, "all former prefaces can, and shall be, published." She hinted that the French public was too chauvinist-minded at present to be well-suited by the 1872 preface. Engels, however, wanted to know specifically which passages in the 1872 preface might shock the sensitive Gallic ears of the "Parisian readers." He thought his French comrades should not yield to this "sensitivity"—that is, the chauvinist sensitivity of patriotic Frenchmen who believed "that all light necessarily comes from Paris." Every edition of the Manifesto had to explain, he thought, how the document had come into being, otherwise parts of Section II and all of Sections III and IV would be incomprehensible.[11]

But no pamphlet edition of this Laura-1 version was ever published—for reasons not recorded by extant documentation—and certainly Engels wrote no new preface.

o   o   o   o   o

Laura had undoubtedly sent Engels a copy of her translation in manuscript, and—probably by September, certainly in October—he sent her his suggested revisions and criticisms.* The printer was holding the type for the projected pamphlet edition; Paul Lafargue pressed Engels for his revisions *in toto* on October 11, and Engels came through immediately.[12] Unfortunately, his letter (or any other letter with suggestions for change) is not extant. In her reply of October 23, Laura promised to incorporate the proposed changes in the pamphlet edition, but spiritedly objected when (it seems) he used harsh terms to criticize a couple of formulations in the translation.[13] However, in his 1890 German preface, Engels called the Laura-1 translation "the best one published to date."[14]

Engels' criticisms and suggestions can only be conjecturally reconstructed from the revisions made by Laura for her second version (Laura-2). We certainly cannot assume that all of these revisions stemmed from Engels alone.

The Laura-2 translation, probably finished in November or December 1885, was not published as the pamphlet edition of the series in *Le Socialiste;* indeed it was never published in any pamphlet form. It appeared, in the first months of 1886, in the Appendix of a book by a radical journalist who used the pen name Mermeix: *La France Socialiste. Notes d'Histoire*

---

* This means that, as far as is known, Engels did not check over Laura's draft translation before it started running in *Le Socialiste.* The statement—for example, in the editorial notes in MECW 6:699—that Engels reviewed the manuscript of Laura-1 before publication must be simply a matter of speculation.

Contemporaine (Paris).* The translation was titled "Le Manifeste du Parti Communiste," and was preceded by an explanatory note headed "Le Manifeste de 1847 [sic]."

This Laura-2 version included 126 corrections (by Andréas' count). We can add that about 100 of these were later retained in Laura-3. Although there was no separate pamphlet edition, the Laura-2 translation was reprinted in 1890 in the Possibilist (i.e., reformist) organ *Le Prolétariat* (Paris), in installments appearing from July 26 to October 11.

o   o   o   o   o

Laura did another, and final, revision eight years later. Virtually nothing is known of the circumstances which led her to do so, or under which she carried out the project. There is no reference to it in the extant correspondence between herself and Engels; but they must have exchanged letters about it, or discussed it on Laura's visits to London, or both. We do not know whether Engels proposed any new changes, that is, other than those he had made in 1885. Yet, unlike Laura-2, this Laura-3 version was specifically labeled "revue par Frederick Engels." (Yes, the English form Frederick was used in the French context.) Perhaps this was done because in a number of respects Laura-3 followed the Authorized English Translation of 1888, which had indeed been published as revised by Engels.

Laura-3 ran first in three monthly issues of the socialist journal *L'Ere Nouvelle* (Paris),** September to November 1894, still titled as before. A preface signed "La Rédaction" (The Editors), based on the prefaces of 1872 and 1888, stated that "the French translation ... made by Laura Lafargue, has been revised by Frederick Engels." The use in French of the English spelling Frederick suggests to Andréas that the preface was written by Laura. An alternative conjecture is that whoever wrote it must have had an eye fixed on the English pamphlet of 1888.

Laura-3 includes the majority of the 126 corrections embodied in Laura-2, and adds another 300 or so supplementary changes; as a result Laura-3 is farther away from Laura-1 than was its predecessor. There is no way of knowing how many of the additional changes, if any, were made by Laura on her own or in discussion (by letter or during visits) with Engels. There is no record that Engels objected to any of them.

The Laura-3 translation was the one that finally made it to pamphlet publication. It came out as a 36-page yellowcovered brochure with the same title, published by *L'Ere Nouvelle* itself,

---

* His name was Gabriel Terrail (1859–1930). Elected a Boulangist deputy in 1889, he subsequently wrote an exposé, *Les Coulisses de Boulangisme* (1890). *La France Socialiste* was considered, both by the Guesdists and their enemies, as favorable to the former but Mermeix himself was no Guesdist. In 1906 he published another book on socialism, *Le Socialisme* (Paris), which in its appendix reprinted the same version (Laura-2) of the Manifesto, preceded by his own introduction citing some passages from the 1872 and 1890 prefaces. Of course, by this time the Laura-3 version monopolized the field; Laura-2 was obsolete.

** This magazine, published only from July to November in 1894, was founded and edited by the Rumanian Georges Diamandy, and managed by Leo Frankel. It had previously published translations of three pieces by Marx or Engels.

undated but probably in early 1895. Laura did not succeed in getting a new preface from Engels; the same preface appeared, shorn of the signature "La Rédaction."

The next year, the Belgian socialists (Parti Ouvrier Belge) put out their own edition of Laura-3; and in 1897 the Paris publishers V. Giard & E. Brière began their series of editions of the translation. From 1901 the Giard & Brière edition was marked "Traduction de Laura Lafargue, revue par Engels," which information had previously appeared in the editors' preface. The Laura-3 translation continued to appear, either as a separate brochure or as an inclusion in a number of books, well into the twentieth century, though in time revised variants by Amédée Dunois or Jean Fréville also appeared. In 1901 Charles Andler's independent translation made its bid... But we are now beyond our time frame.

26. THE AUTHORIZED ENGLISH TRANSLATION OF 1888

From the standpoint of Marxist studies, we now come to the translation which is undoubtedly the most important one of all, because of Engels' special relation to it. The pressure for this translation built up during the 1880s.

When the decade began, the sole English translation was still essentially the 1850 Macfarlane version, though it had gone through some handling and mishandling by various hands. Writing concerning the years 1880–1881, H. M. Hyndman emphasized in his memoirs that there was little socialist literature available in English:

> ...there was then no literature to refer to, no books in English which could be obtained and read, either by the educated class or by the workers. At most, a few ill-printed copies of the famous Communist Manifesto of 1847 [sic] by Marx and Engels done into English could be found by searching for them in the most advanced revolutionary circles.[1]

Though Hyndman seems to be referring to pamphlets, Andréas thinks he was alluding to old copies of the *Red Republican* now thirty years old. A more probable explanation is that Hyndman, writing from memory, was misdating his recollection by a few years. The situation he described, however, was a strong motivation for any socialist.

In 1885, the *Communist Manifesto* received conspicuous attention in the "Manifesto of the Socialist League" written by William Morris.* The new manifesto not only quoted the old one but paraphrased parts of Sections I and II. It was much reprinted and translated, cited and mentioned, throughout the European movement; new editions came out in 1885 and 1886.

---

* The Socialist League was formed in December 1884 by the anti-Hyndman opposition in the Social Democratic Federation, led by William Morris and including Eleanor Marx and other friends of Engels. For a while Engels thought the SL was the only socialist group in England with which he could "thoroughly sympathize"; but by 1889 its anarchist wing captured the organization and quickly destroyed it.

In 1886, early June, the English anarchists put out their own edition of Johann Most's hijacked American edition of the *Communist Manifesto* with the imprint London, International Publishing Company. According to the anarchist historian Nettlau, it was actually published by *The Anarchist*, edited by Henry Seymour. This British edition kept the title invented in America, *Manifesto of the Communists*. The falsified statement of authorship, which in America had been printed in the first sentence of the preface, was now in the by-line: "By Karl Marx. Assisted by Frederick Engels." The pamphlet advertised the anarchist press, books and magazine. No doubt this event exerted pressure on Engels to put out an adequate edition.

In early 1887 (actually off the press in mid-December) the English edition of *Capital*, Volume 1, came out at last. The significance for our account was not so much that it cited from the Manifesto as that it removed a great deal of the pressure from Engels and his translator Moore. They could say: *Now for the Manifesto...*

Sorge started pressing again from America. Writing to Engels on February 20, 1887, he offered another candidate for the task, Mrs. Florence Kelley Wischnewetzky.*

> How about entrusting the translation of the Communist Manifesto to her? You possess various badly done translations of the Manifesto, and moreover the manuscript of a translation that H. Meyer made here is in your hands (from Marx's papers). You could send this manuscript here, outfitted with some notes by you; Mrs. W. would revise it, send it to you for review, and then it could be published here.[2]

Engels replied on March 10:

> W. is not up to translating the Manifesto. This can be done only by one person, namely Sam Moore, and he is indeed at work on it; I already have the first section in manuscript.[3]

This is the first notice we have that Engels had turned the Manifesto over to Moore.

Of course, Samuel Moore was a choice to be expected, in view of his work on *Capital*. In any case, Engels had a low opinion of Mrs. W.'s ability as a translator. Ability aside, Moore had a special advantage in Engels' eyes: his physical closeness to Engels, who could work with him and guide him every step of the way; in addition, Moore was not only willing but eager to be supervised in this way. As a translator Moore was happy to be Engels' right arm and had no illusions or pretenses about his own capacity. This fact, plus Engels' acknowledged role in reviewing and revising ("editing") the manuscript, points to an

---

* At this time Florence Kelley (1859–1932) was still using her married name. She had done the first English translation of Engels' *Condition of the Working Class in England*; this was in course of publication and was going to come off the press in May 1887. Her translation of Marx's address on free trade came the following year.—Andréas (page 131) is mistaken, I believe, in saying that Mrs. Wischnewetzky had already drafted a translation of the Manifesto. Sorge's letter clearly referred to the old manuscript translation by Hermann Meyer.

important conclusion: the English translation was going to be the sole version of the Manifesto for which Engels was 100 percent responsible, hence a document of independent authority. It is the only translation of which this can be said without qualification.

For Engels' thoughts on the enterprise, let us return to his letter to Sorge of March 10:

> However, in this connection it should be remembered that the Manifesto, like almost all the shorter pieces by Marx and myself, is at the moment still far too hard to understand for America. The workers there are just now coming into the movement; are still altogether raw; in particular they are tremendously backward, in general because of their Anglo-Saxon, and specifically of their American, nature and previous training. There the lever has to be applied directly In practice, and for that purpose a whole new literature is necessary. ... Once the chaps get pretty well set on the right road, the Manifesto will not fail to have its effect; right now it would be effective only among a few.[4]

Engels' expectation that the ideas of the Manifesto could penetrate Anglo-Saxon skulls only with difficulty was going to have an important effect on the formulations in the English translation.

In urging the importance of an English edition, Sorge stressed that the Manifesto "had had an effect on us boys even forty years ago."[5] Engels replied, in a letter announcing Moore's completion of the draft: "The Manifesto has been translated, and only my accursed eyes [eye trouble] prevent me from going over the work."[6] His reply to Sorge's argument again showed how much he feared that the theoretical level of the Manifesto was still too high for American and English workers:

> ...[F]orty years ago you were Germans with a German mind for theory, and that is why the Manifesto had an effect at that time, whereas, though translated into French, English, Flemish, Danish, etc., it remained absolutely without effect among the other peoples. And for the untheoretical matter-of-fact Americans, I think, plainer fare would be all the more wholesome since *we* went through the history presented in the Manifesto but they didn't.[7]

This statement is especially clear evidence that Engels thought all of those "phantom translations" of 1848 had really been published, doubtless relying on the assertion in the Manifesto's preamble. On the basis of this mistake, it is also a source of the belief that the publication of the Manifesto was "absolutely without effect," at least outside of the Germans.

There is another defect in Engels' argument, once we know that the "phantom translations" did not exist. It was *only* the German movement that was given the Manifesto while it was still hot with revolutionary ardor. The 1850 English translation, for example, was put before a defeated movement that was rapidly declining, and it came as the manifesto of another defeated movement. The Swedish translation appeared in a country that was not in revolution. Even if the French, Flemish, Danish, etc. translations of 1848 could be shown to exist, they must have been hole-in-the-corner productions at best, whereas in Germany the Manifesto was used as a propaganda instrument by a very active revolutionary group in the Rhineland with connections in Berlin and elsewhere.

Nevertheless one must grant two of Engels' points: the German workers *were* amenable to revolutionary theory to an extent not found in America and England, for a historical reason that Marx and Engels explained more than once; and in any case "plainer fare" *was* needed, whether or not the Manifesto came out. In any case, it is clear that Engels was full of apprehension about the existence of a radical public capable of appreciating and using the coming English edition.

In May 1887, Florence Kelley Wischnewetzky's translation of Engels' *Condition of the Working Class in England* came out in America, with a new preface by the author, dated January 26; written in English. Toward its close, Engels quoted a longish passage from the Manifesto. It consists of five paragraphs of Section II followed by a sentence from Section IV; no break is indicated; only the word "Thus" is inserted to make the bridge. (Incidentally, I know of no edition of this essay which informs the reader that this "excerpt" from the Manifesto is not, as such, in the Manifesto.)

Now at the time Engels wrote this January 26 preface, it is unlikely that Moore had yet given him a draft of the passages quoted. The translation, then, is probably Engels' own. To be sure, it is very close to the final version, differing only in details. This preface was very widely reprinted and translated all over Europe both in periodicals and as a separate brochure.

On the very eve of the publication of the Moore-Engels translation, whose preparation for over a year had been no secret, H. M. Hyndman once more acted out the nature of Hyndmanism. Up to this point, his Social Democratic Federation and its organ *Justice* had been able to resist all temptation to make any English version of the Manifesto available to the public before which it posed as a Marxist group, despite the need for literature which Hyndman's memoirs recall. Now, at the last minute, *Justice* jumped in to anticipate the new publication. For this purpose it used the worst English text available, viz., the British anarchist edition of 1886 based on Johann Most's American despoilment. This ran for six installments, January 7 to February 11, under the Mostite title. However, *Justice* reinstated the ten-point program which the anarchists had bowdlerized, and, in an introduction, reassigned the authorship back to Marx *and* Engels.

This pre-emptive coup by *Justice* had one positive result. Seeing the publication, in late January the socialistic publisher William Reeves approached Engels about an "authorized translation." As we know, this was already in the works. But now, besides, Reeves would pay good money for it! "So," Engels wrote on February 22 to Mrs. Wischnewetzky, "we revised it, and sold it to R[eeves]— he [Moore] received the corrections last week, and as soon as it comes out you will get a copy. Sam Moore is the best translator I know, but not in a position that permits him to work without receiving something for it."[8] Therefore, evidently, Engels let Moore get whatever money was obtainable from Reeves. This chalks up another first: the first publication of the Manifesto by a commercial publisher, albeit one sympathetic to the movement.*

The pamphlet came out a couple of weeks later, in early March 1888. The title page of the coverless brochure read as follows, after the legend "Price Twopence" in the upper left corner:

Manifesto of the Communist Party, / By Karl Marx, and Frederick Engels. / Authorized English Translation. Edited and annotated by Frederick Engels. / 1888. London: William Reeves, 185, Fleet Street, E.C.

The following features deserve a word.

(1) We note that Engels did not follow the 1872 innovation of the short title *Communist Manifesto.* The motivation was probably nothing more than a desire to preserve the "historical document" nature of the publication.

(2) I have wondered about the insertion of the comma after the name of Karl Marx. Was it Engels or the publisher who put it there? No information. It is possible that Engels inserted it to suggest Marx's primary role, a point he made over again in the new preface.

(3) The name of Samuel Moore as translator does not appear on the title page. His name is given in the last paragraph of Engels' preface; and Engels adds: "We have revised it in common, and I have added a few notes explanatory of historical allusions." On the title page it is the editor's name that is featured after the authors. This treatment indubitably reflects the reality. It underlines that Engels took complete responsibility for this edition. True, Moore's draft saved him some labor, but *this is essentially Engels' translation.*

We have seen that Moore drafted Section I before March 10, 1887, and that he completed his draft by the beginning of May, at which time it appears that Engels put the project aside temporarily because of eye trouble. There is reason to believe that it stayed on the shelf until Reeves came up with his offer in late January, and that it was only at this point that Engels seriously went at the labor of revision—that is, at establishing the translation in its definitive final form.

One indication, not conclusive in itself, is the already quoted statement made by Engels to Mrs. Wischnewetzky (letter of February 22, 1888).[9] When Engels said, "So we revised it..." it seems clear that this was done subsequently to, and as a result of, Reeves' offer. *This means that Engels could have devoted only about a week or so to this work,* for by February 7 he was not only

---

* Andréas regards the Swedish edition of 1848 as an exception to this statement (see Chapter 9 above) since the putative translator was also a bookseller and had an advertisement in the pamphlet. But the publisher named in this case was hardly a regular commercial publisher in the sense that Reeves was.

82

all finished but awaiting proofs. On that date he wrote to Paul Lafargue: "The business of the English *Manifesto* is finally concluded and I await the proofs in a few days."[10]

Another indication is that his new preface was dated January 30. In accordance with his usual pattern, this would mean that he finished work on the translation on or before this date.

No wonder Engels felt that it had been done in a rush! He told Paul Lafargue:

> I look to Laura for *improvements* to the translation—my revision had to be done in some haste and it [Laura's criticism] would be of the greatest help to me for a reprint.[11]

Clearly, at this point Engels expected that he would put out a revised edition when the first printing was exhausted. We will see why this did not happen. At any rate, it is certain that *he did not look on the 1888 text as definitive*—not even for the day, let alone for eternity.

Engels' new preface, the longest of all the prefaces, spent few words on the genesis of the Manifesto but lightly sketched the political history of the ensuing years, listing some of the translations that had come out. He was summarizing the circumstances that had made a world document out of this 1848 statement. He concluded:

> Thus the history of the Manifesto reflects to a great extent the history of the modern working-class movement; at present it is undoubtedly the most widespread, the most international production of all Socialist literature, the common platform acknowledged by millions of workingmen from Siberia to California.[12]

The translation was based on the German text of 1872 or 1883 (which are close enough so as to make no difference). If you want to trace the difference between the two hands that worked on it, compare the text with the German original line by line and the following characteristic emerges unmistakably. *The translation is either extremely literal or else boldly revisionary.* Indeed, each sentence or phrase is either one or the other, rarely in-between. I deduce that Moore's draft was a very close type of translation, the kind that follows the original as literally as possible within the bounds of English grammar and style; and that the bold departures from this pattern, sometimes amounting to rewriting the original, were made by Engels, and only by Engels. I think it is out of the question that Sam Moore would, on his own, move so far away from the original.

It has often been noted that the translation contains a number of modifications and changes. There is a list, for one, in the old *Marx-Engels Gesamtausgabe* (MEGA)[13]; Andréas devotes a special table to this listing[14]; but neither list is complete, no doubt because both tried to include only the most significant cases. A complete explanation of all the introduced changes is given in the third part of this work.

Reeves made stereotype plates of the pages, and this would have negated Engels' plans for a revision even if he had done the work. These plates served for all editions of the Authorized English Translation that were put out by this publisher well into the twentieth century. An undated "second edition" was published in 1893. Andréas states that the "sixth impression," still on sale in 1963, was printed in 1927

The Authorized English Translation (A.E.T.)—often called the "standard translation"—was widely reprinted all over the English-speaking world during the ensuing decades and up to the present day. In the following summary, as elsewhere, we limit ourselves to the few years up to Engels' death.

In the United States, the new translation was distributed mainly by the Socialist Labor Party and its publishing agency, called the New York Labor News Company. First it was published in the party's weekly organ, *Workmen's Advocate* (New York), edited by Lucien Sanial: in seven installments, June 7 to July 19, 1890. The paper did not ask for permission to reprint, but perhaps Sorge had reported that Engels would not take measures against republication in the United States. The N.Y.L.N. Co. then published the A.E.T. as a separate brochure, in early November, with the peculiarity that Marx's first name became "Carl." A second edition came out in 1898; and so on into the next century.

Later on, beyond our time frame, editions of the A.E.T. were published by the Socialistic Co-operative Publishing Association, the Debs Publishing Company, and Charles H. Kerr & Company of Chicago.

Australia went in for originality. In Brisbane, the organ of the Australian Labour Federation, *The Worker*, having installed William Guy Higgs as its editor in place of William Lane, ran six installments of something called the "Manifesto of the Socialist Party" by Karl Marx and *Henry* Engels. Published September 9 to October 14, 1893, the text was that of the A.E.T., but all of Section III and almost all of Section IV were omitted (lack of space, said the paper). All forms and cognates of 'communism' were changed to 'socialism.' Engels' notes were shorn of his initials, perhaps because the editors did not know what they were; but by the third installment they got his first name right. The first installment appeared under the heading "Karl Marx's Famous Manifesto," but its fame was evidently by word of mouth, for the editors explained they had managed to obtain "one of the very few copies in Australia." A separate pamphlet edition in November, titled *Karl Marx's Famous Manifesto (Abridged)* never revealed what the infamous title really was. No complete edition of the Manifesto appeared in Australia until 1920.

Up to 1918 (Andréas' boundary line), no new English edition of the Manifesto was published in any other country that was wholly or partly English-speaking.

27. INTERNATIONAL ROUNDUP 1883–1895

The period we are concerned with is that from the death of Marx to the death of Engels. We must report that this last phase of our account is rather anticlimactic. There were no more editions as important as the French and English translations described in the last two chapters. In only three cases was Engels involved in some way. We take these three up first: Italian, Polish, Yiddish.

Italian

Engels tried to promote an Italian edition in 1885. An Italian socialist named Pasquale Martignetti, a minor government official in Benevento, had translated Engels' Socialism, Utopian and Scientific in 1883. On June 13, 1885, Engels sent him a copy of the Manifesto (probably the latest edition of 1883), with the comment: "Old as it is, I think it still deserves to be read."[1]

Martignetti's immediate reply (June 27) did not pick up the hint that he might do a translation; but Andréas thinks he did accomplish it later the same year.[2] But it remained unpublished for lack of money.

This was not the only unpublished translation. In 1888, in Reggio Emilia, a socialist circle held a lecture series (January–February) based on a translation of the Manifesto that was never published and is not extant.

In 1889, a Cremona paper, *L'Eco del Popolo*, carried a ten-installment series, from August 30–31 to November 3–4, presenting Sections I and II of the Manifesto, with some passages deleted, many paraphrased, and the whole peppered with inaccurate translations. The translator may have been the paper's editor, Leonida Bissolati.

The first more or less complete Italian translation appeared in February 1891, as *Il Manifesto del Partito Comunista 1847*, Biblioteca Popolare Socialista, No. 1 (Milan). The erroneous 1847 date, we see, is here elevated into the title itself. The translation was based on the French version in Mermeix's book, i.e., on Laura-2; but it was quite defective and much criticized for its bad quality. The translator, Pietro Gori, and the publisher, Flaminio Fantuzzi, were anarchist sympathizers, and put out the translation without the knowledge of Engels, who was told about it by brother Romualdo Fantuzzi only on March 18. Gori's foreword pleased Engels no more than the circumstances of the pirated publication.

By this time, a better edition was under way. Filippo Turati, publisher and editor of Critica Sociale and Engels' correspondent, had been preparing such a publication since at least 1890. Its translator was Pompeo Bettini, and it was planned to be No. 1 of a new "Socialist Library" series. Perhaps this project was delayed because of the Fantuzzi-Gori edition; *Critica Sociale* announced the new version in its numbers of January 15 and February 20, 1891, but it did not then appear. It may have been delayed again by the revision which the Bettini draft received from the hands of Turati and his companion Anna Kuliscioff. It was announced again on July 30, 1892.

The Bettini translation was first published, in eleven installments, in the Italian socialist organ *Lotta di Classe* (Milan), also edited by Turati: from September 17/18 to December 24/25, 1892, titled "Il Manifesto del Partito Comunista di Marx ed Engels (1848)." Sales were heavy, and on December 31 Turati announced that a pamphlet edition would come out in January. But on January 4, Turati wrote Engels asking for a new preface, arguing that this would help to overshadow the Fantuzzi-Gori production. This was a motivation calculated to impress Engels, and he did indeed yield to it. Engels' preface, "To the Italian Reader," dated February 1, 1893, written in French, was translated by Turati.[3]

The pamphlet appeared in the second half of March:

Carlo Marx e Federico Engels. Il Manifesto del Partito Comunista. Con un nuovo proemio al lettore italiano di Federico Engels. Milano, Uffici della Critica Sociale ... 1893, in 8o, 46-[2] p. (Biblioteca della Critica Sociale [No. 1]).

Engels' preface mentioned the Manifesto itself only glancingly. Three other prefaces (1872, 1883, 1890) were included.

Polish

The first Polish translation, by W. Piekarski in 1883, was described in Chapter 23 above. A second edition of the Piekarski version was put out in 1892, with some misprints corrected; but some of the accompanying prefatory material was left out. The main feature of this new edition was a special preface contributed by Engels.

The preface had been requested by the editor of *Przedswit*, Stefan Mendelson, who probably translated it. Dated February 10, 1892, the preface dealt notably with the role of the Polish national struggle against Russia, but it began by commenting on the "barometer" function of the Manifesto.

> ...[I]t is noteworthy that of late the Manifesto has become an index, as it were, of the development of largescale industry on the European continent. In proportion as large-scale industry expands in a given country, the demand grows among the workers of that country for enlightenment regarding their position as the working class in relation to the possessing classes, the socialist movement spreads among them, and the demand for the Manifesto increases. Thus, not only the state of the labor movement but also the degree of development of large-scale industry can be measured with fair accuracy in every country by the number of copies of the Manifesto circulated in the language of that country.

Yiddish

No complete Yiddish translation appeared until 1899, when it was put out by the Jewish Bund. But in 1897, when Abraham Cahan published the preamble and Section I in his New York monthly *Di Zukunft*, Cahan's introduction told of an earlier project that had involved Engels.

In August 1891, in connection with attending the Brussels international socialist congress, Cahan met Engels in London, through Eleanor Marx. Engels was very favorably impressed by the American *Judenapostel* (so he wrote Sorge in America); and it was probably at, or as a result of, this meeting that Engels promised Cahan to write a special preface for a Yiddish edition of the Manifesto.

Engels fulfilled this promise, and sent a preface to Cahan in New York. But, related Cahan in 1897, "it subsequently went astray." I assume this impersonal expression meant that Cahan or his staff lost the manuscript. As for the contents:

It was only very brief and expressed this idea: translation of the Manifesto into the Yiddish language—that is an excellent reply to the anti-Semitic lie that the Jews engender only exploiters, never workers.[5]

Cahan's 1897 introduction hinted that he tried to get another preface from Engels, and even that he postponed doing a complete translation until Engels came through with it. (This implies that he would refuse to publish a translation unless he was favored by getting the preface he demanded.) But it was not likely that Engels would once again do a preface for a *nonexistent* translation; and in any case Cahan was not especially clever in apparently blaming Engels for the fact that he, Cahan, failed to complete a translation.

Scandinavian

Danish. The first known Danish translation was published in seven installments in the party daily *Social-Demokraten* (Copenhagen), January 12 to 23, 1884: "Det Kommunistiske Manifest. Med Forfatternes Forord. (Efter den tredje avtoriserede tyske Udgave.)." As this indicates, it was based on the German edition of 1883. The unnamed translator was probably Edvard E. Wiinblad, who had become editor in chief of the paper in May 1881. Born of a German mother, he knew German.

This translation lacked some passages of Sections I and II. In his 1890 German preface, reviewing Manifesto translations, Engels noted:

Unfortunately it is not quite complete; certain essential passages, which seem to have presented difficulties to the translator, have been omitted, and in addition there are signs of carelessness here and there...[6]

Engels intended to revise the translation himself some day.

This translation was published as a brochure dated 1885 (although it probably came off the press before the end of 1884), labeled Volume 1 of a "Socialist Library" edited by Wiinblad for the Social-Democratic Party. New editions came out in 1898 and 1907, but there was no new translation until 1918.

Swedish. As we saw, the very first translation of the Manifesto had appeared in this language in 1848; but then there was nothing for thirty-eight years. In 1886, a new translation was published in the Social-Demokraten of Stockholm, appearing in ten installments from September 3 to November 12: "Det Kommunistiska Manifestet af Karl Marx och Friedrich Engels. Øfversatt af A. D-n." Based on the 1883 German edition, it contained the prefaces of 1872 and 1883.

Here, notes Andréas (A#207), "the translation follows the original very faithfully." This fact was not unrelated to its political background. A split in the Social-Democratic movement had taken place in Stockholm in January of 1886; the left-wing group took over the editorship of the party organ. As director of the paper, Axel Danielsson (the "A.D-n" credited on the title page) moved it toward a Marxist standpoint. Danielsson knew the 1848 Swedish version of the Manifesto, and made some use of it for his own translation.

The paper announced that the new translation would appear as a brochure, but this was not done—at any rate, not until 1903. It was only in 1919 that a complete Swedish translation came out that rectified some errors in the Danielsson version.

Norwegian. The *Social-Demokraten* of Christiana (the capital, now called Oslo) published its own version of the Manifesto in eight installments from November 13, 1886 to May 1887: "Det Kommunistiske Partis Manifest." Actually this was a reprint of the Danish translation of 1884 with the orthographical changes necessary to "translate" (or transpose) it into Norwegian. Although no separate pamphlet edition was issued, the installments were so printed that, cut out, they formed pamphlet pages.

The *Social-Demokraten* was the organ of the first Norwegian Social-Democratic association, at this time edited by Carl Jeppesen, the president and intellectual leader of the group.

It was only in 1918 that the Manifesto, in a new translation, was published in Norway as a pamphlet.

Other Western European Languages

Spanish. No translation of the Manifesto based mainly on the German original appeared in Spanish at all—not only before Engels' death, but up to 1918, the end of Andréas' survey.

As we saw, Mesa's translation of 1872 had been based mostly on French versions.[8] No other edition appeared for the next fourteen years. In 1886, *El Socialista* (Madrid) republished the Mesa translation in eight installments (June 11 to August 6); and in the autumn the text came out as Volume 1 in the paper's pamphlet series Biblioteca de El Socialista, preceded by an editorial introduction dated October 30. As in 1872, all of these reprints of the Mesa version omitted the subsection on "German or True Socialism"; but in the last-mentioned pamphlet edition, the note explaining the omission was now itself omitted.

Even in 1906, when a new translation by Rafael Garcia Ormaechea was published, it was based on Andler's French version, not on the German original.

Portuguese. Andréas has no record of any edition of the Manifesto published in Portugal after the 1873 version.[9] The first pamphlet edition in Portuguese came out in 1924 in Brazil—not in its capital or its chief city, but in Porto Alegre, a seaport where many foreigners lived. (See A#183.)

Dutch. The first edition in this language came out in 1892, translated by Christiaan Cornelissen:
Het Kommunistische Manifest van Karl Marx en Friedrich Engels. Naar de vierde geautoriseerde Duitsche uitgave bewerkt door C. Cornelissen. 's Gravenhage, B. Liebers & Co., 1892. XXII–106 p. (Volksbibliotheek. Zesde Aflevering.)

The gray-covered pamphlet contained a short foreword by the translator. As the title page indicated, it was based on the 1890 German edition. The Hague publisher-printer Bruno Liebers had been a militant in the First International, where he supported Marx in the fight against the Bakuninists.

No other Dutch translation came out until 1904.

Eastern European Languages

Russian. The Plekhanov translation of 1882 thoroughly monopolized the field. Andréas has much data on clandestine editions put out in various parts of the czarist domain by primitive methods, throughout the rump end of the century. This is more closely related to the history of the Russian movement than it is to the history of the Manifesto.

New translations were hardly needed. Yet, during his stay in Samara in 1889–1893, Lenin (reports Andréas) translated the Manifesto into Russian for the Samara Marxist circle, using a German edition in the circle's library. One would assume that the translation by Plekhanov was not available there. Typically, the manuscript translation circulated hand to hand, was loaned out to other circles, and was eventually destroyed in face of a threatened police search; it is not extant.

Andréas notes no other Russian translation, until a hectographed edition appeared about the end of the century in St. Petersburg, translated from a French edition by a V. Zabrezhnev; not extant. The first new translation that is extant came in 1903.

Bulgarian. A translation by Ivan Todorov Kutev was published in 1891 as a brochure:

> Manifest't' na Kommunisticheskata Partija ot Karla Marksa i Fridrikha Engelsa. Ruse, Skoro-pechjatnicata na Spiro Gulabchev, 1891, in 8°, [l]-V-[l]-91 p.

Ruse is a town on the Danube in northeastern Bulgaria. Gulabchev was the only publisher in the country who had relations with the socialists. The pamphlet itself did not name the translator. In its contents, the pamphlet in most respects followed the example of the Russian edition of 1882.

Kutev had finished his draft in 1890 but could not immediately line up a publisher. When the brochure was published (in January or February), the edition of 3000 "sold out like hot cakes," especially among students—according to Kutev. Only one other work by Marx or Engels had previously been published in Bulgaria, namely, Marx's *Wage-Labor and Capital*, in June 1886. The Kutev translation was superseded in 1900 by the publication of a version by Gueorgui Bakalov.

Czech. The first extant translation came out in 1893. Previously there had been an edition published in New York in 1882 by a translator who used the pen name "Vive la Liberté" (thought to be the Czech poet Leopold Kochmann); but no copy is known. In 1892 another manuscript translation circulated in Prague.

In 1893, the periodical *Delnické Listy* (Vienna) published a translation by August Radimsky, a Czech Social-Democrat who was an editor of the Vienna *Arbeiter-Zeitung*. This translation ran in seven installments, from January 10 to April 12, titled "Komunisticky Manifest," based on the German edition of 1890. Since the police refrained from confiscating the paper when it ran these installments, the editors put out the text as a brochure. Now the police did pounce; the entire edition was seized; no copy is now known. The Radimský translation came out in pamphlet form in 1898.

Rumanian. A translation by Panait Musoiu* came out in 1892, as a 64-page pamphlet: "Manifestul Comunist. Traducere de P. Musoiu. Jassy, 1892." This translation was mainly based on the French version in Mermeix's book (i.e., Laura-2), with the 1890 German edition used supplementarily. Later in 1892, the Manifesto brochure came out enlarged to eighty pages with other writings by Musoiu, all under the title *Manifest Comunist*, from the same publisher in Jassy, Stabilimentul Grafic "Miron Costin."

No copy is extant of a new translation published in 1893 by Ioan Nadejde,** with the title changed to *Socialist Manifesto* but with the word 'communist' (etc.) intact in the text-"Manifestul Socialist. Jassy. Biblioteca Partidei Social-Democratice e Muncitorilor din Rominia, Nr. 1."

Following the text of the Manifesto was an essay by Nadejde on "The Revolution and the Revolutionary Tactic," which we briefly discussed in Chapter 6 above. No new translation came out in Roumania until 1913.

Serbo-Croatian. The 1871 translation (see Chapter 18) was unrivaled until 1902.

Non-European Languages

Although we have had occasion to mention places of publication outside of Europe (New York, Brazil), the only non-European language we have to report on—within our time frame—is Armenian.

An Armenian translation of the Manifesto may have been published in 1894 by an Armenian student in Stuttgart, Jossif Atabekjanc, who was in touch with Karl Kautsky in that city. He had earlier published a translation of *Socialism, Utopian and Scientific*. In November 1894 he sent his Manifesto translation to Engels via Kautsky, but it is not known whether this was a manuscript or a printed publication. At any rate, no such publication is known. In his

---

* Musoiu (1864–1944) was an editor of the paper Munca and a contributor to other Roumanian socialist organs; he had published a translation of *Socialism, Utopian and Scientific* in 1891.

** Nadejde (1854–1928) was an early socialist in Rumania; corresponded with Engels during the 1880s; published his organ Contemporanul in Jassy (1881–1890); in the 1890s, edited *Lumea Nova;* and in 1893 helped to found the Social democratic Party. In 1899 he went over to the antisocialist side.

1888 preface to the Manifesto, Engels told of another manuscript translation in Armenian that he had heard about.

28. ENGLISH TRANSLATIONS: SURVEY FROM 1888 TO THE PRESENT

he foregoing chapters cover only the lifetime of Marx and Engels. But in the case of English translations, we will leave this time frame, and go on to survey whatever independent translations are available, that is, any translations providing later alternatives to the Authorized English Translation (A.E.T.) of 1888. To be sure, the A.E.T. pre-empted the field as far as the English-speaking public was concerned, and has never been in danger of being replaced. Since 1888, there have been four publications that offered some sort of alternative to the A.E.T.*

(1) The Aitken-Budgen translation.

The first new English translation after the A.E.T. came out in 1909, but the motive was not a felt need for a better version. It was published, admittedly, to answer the organizational need of the British sect, the Socialist Labour Party.

This group had split off from Hyndman's Social Democratic Federation in 1903, under the influence of its namesake (the American SLP) and the system of sectified "Marxism" called De Leonism. Its membership lay mainly in the big cities of Scotland, long the heartland of British sectism. Like its American equivalent, its dogma was that it alone "represented" the proletariat, all other alleged socialists being imposters and enemies of humanity. In 1921 it merged into the new Communist Party.

By putting the A.E.T. into the hands of the publisher Reeves, Engels had erected a juridical bar against pirated and distorted editions, at least in Britain. The SLP felt aggrieved that, despite being the only "Marxist" group on earth, it could not put out its own printing of the Manifesto in English. Therefore, it explained, it had to work up its own translation:

> We offer the workers of Great Britain a new translation of the "Communist Manifesto," not because we claim to have improved upon previous translations, but because these previous translations are the property of private firms and individuals.

So said the preface; it does not seem to have occurred to these people that they could use an edition of the Manifesto not published by their own "private firm." The result was a pink-covered pamphlet:

---

* Not discussed here is my own close translation of the Manifesto which, is included in the second part of this book and is the comparative basis of the annotation that comprises the third part; but as is emphasized in the preface to the second part of this work, this translation is *not* presented as an alternative to or substitute for the A.E.T.

Manifesto of the Communist Party. By Karl Marx & Friedrich Engels. Translated from the original for the Socialist Labour Party by Lily G. Aitken and Frank C. Budgen. Edinburgh, Printed and published by the Socialist Labour Party ... 1908, in 8o, III-29 p.

The translators, Aitken and Budgen, were—to judge from their preface—religious De Leonites, who argued that everything in the Manifesto was identical in every respect with every tenet held by their own sect.* The preface was dated September 1909; for this and other reasons, Andréas believes that the pamphlet was in fact published in 1909, not 1908. The first edition included new translations of the prefaces of 1872 and 1883 (both misdated) and of 1890.

"This translation," wrote Aitken and Budgen, "is accurate, and we believe that it renders the original at least more literally than previous English versions." In some places it *is* more literal; but the translation as a whole is not a competent one. A check of the first two full pages (pages 8-9 of the pamphlet) shows four omissions and seven other points of error. Although this translation is usually based on the original German, it occasionally yields to the A.E.T.'s reformulations, as when it follows the latter in changing "large-scale industry" to "modern industry" (one of the idiosyncrasies of the A.E.T.).

The SLP stereotyped the pages of this edition, and from the plates ran off a number of undated reprintings, up until 1942 or 1950 (Andréas gives both dates). The copy of this pamphlet which I possess was published by the "Socialist Labour Press" in Glasgow rather than Edinburgh, and it lacks the 1883 preface; but otherwise it is unchanged from the 1908/1909 edition described by Andréas. This edition was published soon after 1913.

(2) *The Pauls' translation.*

In 1928 the prolific translators Eden and Cedar Paul made a new translation of the Manifesto for publication by Martin Lawrence, the British publisher of Communist literature (later named Lawrence & Wishart). In 1930 this translation was used for the Manifesto text in the first English edition of a work by D. Ryazanov which presented a detailed commentary on, and much documentation related to, the Manifesto:

The Communist Manifesto of Karl Marx and Friedrich Engels, with an introduction and explanatory notes by D. Ryazanoff ... London, Martin Lawrence, 1930. 365 p.

---

* This claim was supported by a rather flagrant bit of prestidigitation. They quoted the first four sentences of Section II of the Manifesto, which of course negated the very idea of a sect organization like the SLP, and then asserted that the Marx-Engels preface of 1872 contained the "definite and unequivocal statement" that these sentences *are now quite obsolete.* But the 1872 preface referred (unequivocally) to "the revolutionary measures proposed at the *end* of Section II." Although self-refuted, this transparent claim by the translators remained even in later editions.

92

This publication was based on the second Russian edition of Ryazanov's study, published in 1922 (the smaller first edition having appeared in 1921). Besides the text of the Manifesto itself, Ryazanov presented an introduction, long explanatory notes section by section, and an appendix of related documents and prefaces. In its time this was a valuable contribution to the field of Marx studies, not because of Ryazanov's introduction but because of the documentation and historical expositions.

The translation by the Pauls based itself on the original German for the most part, though now and then it accepted one or another of the A.E.T.'s reformulations. Its literary qualities are superior to the A.E.T.'s, but unfortunately it often sacrifices close accuracy to the interests of stylistic felicity. The more it rises superior to the A.E.T. in its literary finish, the less reliable it is as a guide to the meaning of the original in detail. The Manifesto, or any such work, cannot be translated like a novel.

One reason for the defects in this version is that the Pauls evidently followed a theory of translation which teaches that the original must be rewritten with the same freedom, or abandon, as a copy editor feels as he revises the language of a freshman reporter. The result is that, in sentence after sentence, we get a good deal of Eden and Cedar substituted for Karl and Friedrich; and sometimes there are departures so substantial as to constitute outright mistakes. Using this translation is risky; and no conclusions about Marx's ideas can be based on its language.

(3) *The revised A.E.T. of about 1932.*

In the early 1930s, Lawrence & Wishart in London and International Publishers in New York put out editions which presented a lightly revised version of the A.E.T. Surprisingly, Andréas (page 376) does not list a certain 1932 edition put out by the Communist publishing houses in the United States and England in hundreds of thousands of copies—perhaps the largest mass edition of the Manifesto (or any other socialist work) ever issued in English. And this edition offered not the A.E.T. but a revision of the A.E.T.—without indicating this fact by a word!

Manifesto of the Communist Party... Authorized English translation. Edited and annotated by Friedrich Engels. New York, International Publishers, 1932. 47 + 1 p.

So says the imprint on my copy of this edition. While this copy gives 1932 as the publication date, "it is the sixth and seventh printing, 1935, 100,000 [copies]." Although "printed in the U.S.A.," the spellings throughout are British, indicating that primary publication and printing took place in Britain.

This edition gives no hint that the text has been revised. Yet it is peppered with changes—by my count, about fifty-six in addition to numerous editorial changes in punctuation, spelling, capitalization, and hyphenation.

This revision is an odd business. A number of the changes make slight improvements in the flow of sentences or modernize the style; a large number are niggling alterations of no account; some are altogether pointless; some introduce literary bungles; and there are a couple of unfortunate changes that look like typographical mistakes. Probably the worst correction is the rewriting of a famous passage so as to change the A.E.T.'s "win the battle of democracy" to "establish democracy." (This change copies the Pauls' version; this is done also in some other places.)

There are enough changes scattered around the pages to make it risky to quote as the A.E.T., and not enough changes to give the whole thing point. There is no attempt whatever to get behind the A.E.T. to the German original. The operation is quite anonymous; there is no indication of who perpetrated this bungling revision, aside from the sponsorship of the two Communist publishing houses.

The sad tale does not end here. Since the pamphlet had no warning statement, even in small print, it was inevitable that it would be used for the text of the Manifesto by one of the many commercial editions of the classic put out by publishers for college Great Books courses and sociology classes. Sure enough, this happened to an unfortunate Harvard professor:

> *The Communist Manifesto*. With selections from *The Eighteenth Brumaire of Louis Bonaparte* and *Capital*. ... Edited by Samuel H. Beer, Harvard University. New York, Appleton-CenturyCrofts, Inc., n.d. (c1955). 96p.

Neither Professor Beer's introduction nor any other page of the edition shows awareness of the fact that the Manifesto's text here is *not* that of the A.E.T. as claimed. It was simply shoveled in from the 1932 mass edition.

Although, as mentioned, the International Publishers edition in my possession uses British spelling, I have not myself seen a Lawrence & Wishart edition with this pseudo-A.E.T. text. But Andréas lists a 1948 L&W edition of 64 pages with the following description: "text revised, with about fifty changes in the text, and with a detailed list of the expressions and phrases changed." (A#495, page 273.) This certainly sounds as if it might be the same as the revised A.E.T. of the 1932 mass edition (which did not have the "detailed list"). I have already indicated the conjecture that L&W had issued the same A.E.T. revision (pseudo-A.E.T.) in the early 1930s.

(4) Joseph Katz's revision.

Another light revision of the A.E.T. was offered by one of the commercial editions of the Manifesto that was referred to above, this time with a warning:

> *The Communist Manifesto*... Introduction by Francis B. Randall. Translation by Samuel Moore. Edited by Joseph Katz. New York, Washington Square Press, 1964. 144 p.

A publisher's statement says that "This edition is a revised and modernized translation." A back-page blurb makes clear that the revision was made by Joseph Katz.

This revision in no respect goes back to the German original. All of the A.E.T.'s reformulations have been retained. Most of the changes are of the sort made by English instructors on freshman compositions: 'that' for 'which,' and so on; yet, in at least one place the antiquated "economical" for "economic" is retained. In the few cases where more substantive changes are introduced, the result is more disconcerting, as when "barbarians" is changed to "underdeveloped nations," or "peasants" changed to "farmers." In another passage, the insertion of "initiative" looks like a grosser type of blunder. But the main problem raised by an examination of the revision is the question why it was done at all, since the pointlessness of the large majority of the changes is extreme.

For the sake of an unreasonable completeness, we must mention that an independent translation of the Manifesto may be found in an unpublished Ph.D. dissertation by Elliot Erikson, *Karl Marx and the Communist Manifesto* (Stanford University, 1954). This translation weaves through the pages between 154 and 221, mostly through footnotes, some of which are five pages long; it valiantly ignores the A.E.T. completely. Unfortunately, it is crammed with egregious errors of translation, several per paragraph: for example, "customs boundary" becomes the "line of the Danube"; a mysterious reference to "other-worldly foretopmasts" shows up in another place. The English is semiliterate, sometimes turning into gibberish. Of the dissertation itself, the less said the better. The oddest thing about this Ph.D. thesis is that Mr. Erikson was granted his degree.

To sum up: none of the versions considered here has any claim to replace the A.E.T. for any purpose. Unquestionably the A.E.T. will continue unchallenged as the standard English version.

REFERENCE NOTES

Titles are given in abbreviated form; full titles and publication data are provided in the Bibliography. Book and articles titles are not distinguished in form. Page numbers apply to the edition cited in the Bibliography. Volume and page are usually separated by a colon: for example, 1:305 means Volume 1, page 305.

The first source cited is the actual source of the quotation or statement; it is sometimes followed by a [bracketed] reference that cites an extant translation (like MECW) if the first reference is to the original, or vice versa. This second reference is given for the reader's convenience only.

Some frequently used abbreviations are:

E = Engels
Ltr = Letter M = Marx
ME = Marx and Engels
MECW = Marx and Engels, *Collected Works*
MEGA = Marx and Engels, *Gesamtausgabe*
MESW = Marx and Engels, *Selected Works in Three Volumes* (1969-1970)
MEW = Marx and Engels, *Werke*
N.R.Z. = *Neue Rheinische Zeitung*
N.R.Z. Revue = *Neue Rheinische Zeitung, politisch-ökonomische Revue*

Chapter 1
The London-Brussels Connection
1. M: *Herr Vogt*, in MEW 14:439.
2. E: *On Hist. of the Communist League*, in MEW 21:214f.
3. Ibid., 215.

Chapter 2
The Comunist League
1. Ltr, E to M, Oct. 25-26, 1847, in MEW 27:98.
2. Ltr, E to M, Nov. 23-24, 1847, in MEW 27:107.
3. E: *On Hist. of the Communist League*, in MEW 21:215f.
4. Lessner: Before 1848 and After, in *Remin. of M & E*, 153.
5. ME: Pref. to the German ed. of 1872, in Struik, ed.: *Birth of the C.M.*, 129.

Chapter 3
Who Wrote the Manifesto?
1. Ltr, E to M, Jan. 14, 1848, in MEW 27:111.
2. *Bund der Kom.* 1:198, also p.1091, note 167.
3. This manuscript page is reproduced in MEW 4:610 or MECW 6:577. It was discovered by Engels among Marx's posthumous papers; first published in 1908.

For the outline, see MECW 6:576; it was written on the cover of a notebook dated Dec. 1847.

hapter 4
A Dark-Green Pamphlet
1. Lessner: Before 1848 and After, in *Remin. of M & E*, 153.
2. After the facsimile in Andréas, 433.
3. *London Landmarks*, 3.

Chapter 5
Whose Manifesto was It?
1. E: *Marx & the N.R.Z.*, in MEW 21:16.
2. ME: Pref. to the German ed. of 1872, in Struik, ed.: *Birth of the C.M.*, 129.
3. See above, Chap. 2, p..
4. M: *Herr Vogt*, in MEW 14:439.

Chapter 6
Some Historical Controversies
1. See A#308.
2. M: *Herr Vogt*, in MEW 14:90,88.
3. Laski: *Karl Marx, an Essay*, 17.
4. Considérant: *Manifeste de la Démocratie*, 171-77.

5. Andler: *Introduction Historique et Commentaire*, in his edition of *Le Manifeste Communiste*, tome II; tome I contains the translation. Mehring took up Andler's claim in *Neue Zeit*, Jan. 8, 1902, Jg.20, Bd.1, No.15. *Le Mouvement Socialiste* in 1902 carried a French translation of Mehring's article with a reply by Andler.

6. Arnold Winkler: *Die Entstehung des "Kommunistischen Manifests"* (Vienna, 1936). A refutation was offered by Hermann Bollnow, in *Göttinger Universitäts-Zeitung*, 1948, Jg. III, No.6, p.8. (These references are from Andréas, p.6 fn.)

Chapter 7
The Misdating Problem

1. ME: *Alliance of the Soc. Dem. & IWMA*, Chap.8, Sec.1. Repeated in the German edition of this brochure (translation revised by Engels), published 1874, in MEW 18:425.

2. See A#81.

3. See A#94.

4. Hyndman: *Record of an Adventurous Life*, 205.

5. See A#145.

6. ME: *Corrisp. con Ital.*, 308 [MEW 36:326]. Andréas(A#196) gives the quote a little differently (source not mentioned), but this does not affect the error about 1847.

7. MEW 21:342 gives Engels' own German translation of the preface; MEW 2:635 gives a new German translation. In the latter version, the year 1847 is actually italicized as if for emphasis. This raises the question whether it was italicized in the original publication.

8. For example, in the collection ME: *On Britain*; also in the Henderson & Chaloner translation of the work, p.359.

9. Kautsky: *Der Weg zur Macht*, 22; in the 1909 English translation *The Road to Power*, p.14.

10. Bernstein: *Voraussetzungen des Sozialismus [etc.]*, Chap.2, p.22. The English translation, *Evolutionary Socialism*, silently omits this chapter.

Chapter 8
The Manifesto in the Revolution of 1848

1. E: *Movements of 1847*, in MEW 4:494 [MECW 6:520].

2. E: *The Beginning of the End in Austria*, in MEW 4:504 [MECW 6:530].

3. E: *Three New Constitutions*, in MEW 4:514 [MECW 6: 540].

4. For this activity, see my account in *KMTR* 2, Special Note J.

5. The March issues were March 13, 15, 17; Section I appeared on Apr. 28, May 3, May 5; see A#16.

Chapter 9
The Phantom Translations of Forty-Eight

1. Ltr, E to M, Apr. 25, 1848, in MEW 27:126.

2. See A#23, 24.

3. For 1886, see A#207.

Chapter 10
The Manifesto After the Revolution

1. Andréas, p.29–30.

2. For Marx's letter, see MECW 10:387f or MEW 7:323.

3. Ltr, E to Liebknecht, Feb. 4, 1885, in MEW 36:279.

Chapter 11
Helen Macfarlane and the First English Translation

1. Ltr, M to E, Feb. 23, 1851, in MEW 27:196 [MECW 38: 296].

2. Ltr, Mrs. Marx to E, Dec. 19, 1850, in MEW 27:612 [MECW 38:560].

3. Black & Black, eds.: *The Harney Papers*. Sec. IV is "Letters from Harney to Marx and Engels, 1846 to 1895." It contains five letters written to Engels in 1850.

4. Ltr, E to M, Jan. 8, 1851, in MEW 27:164 [MECW 38: 264].

5. Ltr, M to Weydemeyer, Oct. 16, 1851, in MEW 27:581f [MECW 38:481].

Chapter 12
Fade-Out in the Fifties

1. E: *On the History of the CL*, in MESW 3:173.

2. Ltr, M to Mrs. Marx, June 21, 1856, in MEW 29:536.

3. See A#36.

4. E: Pref. to German ed. of 1890, in MESW 1:102.

Chapter 13
The Sixties: Lassalle and Hirschfeld

1. For this passage, see MECW 17:78–80 or MEW 14:438f; also Struik, ed.: *Birth of the C.M.*, 147–49.

2. For Marx's discussion of, and quotes from, the Manifesto in his *Herr Vogt*, see MEW 14:448–50 or MECW 17:88–91.

3. Ltr, M to E, Jan. 28, 1863, in MEW 30:322.

4. Ltr, Mrs. Marx to S. Meyer, beginning of Feb. 1866, in MEW 31:588.

5. See Andréas, p.38, for his arguments.

6. Andréas, p.38;6.

Chapter 14
The Meyer Edition of 1866
1. This is the editorial estimate given in MEW 31:492, followed by Andréas, p.38.
2. In letters of Nov. 13 and Dec. 4, 1865, they asked Marx for advice; Marx responded in late November 1865 and Jan. 15 and 24, 1866. (See *Karl Marx, Chronik seines Lebens*, 247, 249.)
3. Ltr, Mrs. Marx to S. Meyer, beginning of Feb. 1866, in MEW 31:588.
4. ME: Pref. to the German ed. of 1872, in Struik, ed.: *Birth of the C.M.*, 130.
5. Hermann Schlüter: *Die Internationale in Amerika*, 82.

Chapter 15
The Late Sixties: Liebknecht's Modest Proposal
1. See above, Chap.7, p..
2. Ltr, E to Kugelmann, July 10, 1869, in MEW 32:620.
3. Ltr, E to M, July 1, 1869, in MEW 32:329.
4. Ltr, M to E, July 3, 1869, in MEW 32:331.
5. Quoted in MEW 32:768f, note 363.
6. Ltr, M to E, July 3, 1869, in MEW 32:331.

Chapter 16
English Sideshow
1. Ltr, M to Lafargues, Feb. 15, 1869, in MEW 32:593; retranslated.
2. For Marx's comments on Cowell Stepney, see the preceding and the following note, and also: Ltr, M to Meyer & Vogt, Apr. 9, 1870, in MEW 32:667, and Ltr, M to Mrs. Marx, Aug. 25, 1871, in MEW 33:272f.
3. Ltr, M to Kugelmann, Feb. 11, 1869, in MEW 32:589.
4. Ltr, M to Sorge, Dec. 15, 1881, in MEW 35:248.
5. *Gen. Council of the First Intl.* 3:230, meeting of May 3, 1870.
6. Freymond, ed.: *Prem. Intle.*, 1:251.

Chapter 17
Russian Sideshow
1. See A#42, also Aff38.
2. Andréas, p.49-50.
3. Ltr, M to E, Apr. 29, 1870, in MEW 32:492.
4. Ltr, M to E, Mar. 24, 1870, in MEW 32:467.
5. ME: Pref. to the German ed. of 1872, in Struik, ed.: *Birth of the C.M*, 129.
6. ME: *Alliance of the Soc. Dem. & IWMA*, 89.

7. ME: Pref. to Russian ed. of 1882, in MEW 19:295.
8. E: Pref. to the English ed. of 1888, in Struik, ed.: *Birth of the C.M.*, 135.
9. ME: Pref. to Russian ed. of 1882, in MEW 19:295.

Chapter 18
In the Wake of the Paris Commune: 1871-1873
1. S. Gompers: *Seventy Years of Life and Labor*, 1:381; quoted in A#59.
2. Ltr, E to Sorge, Nov. 16, 1872, in MEW 33:541.
3. E: Pref. to the English ed. of 1888, in Struik, ed.: *Birth of the C.M.*, 135.
4. Ltr, E to Sorge, Mar. 17, 1872, in MEW 33:432; the whole passage is quoted below.
5. Ltr, E to Sorge, Mar. 17, 1872, in MEW 33:432.
6. Ltr, E to Liebknecht, Feb. 15, 1872, in MEW 33:401.
7. Ltr, E to Sorge, Nov. 2, 1872, in MEW 33:536.
8. Ltr, E to Sorge, Nov. 16, 1872, in MEW 33:541.
9. ME: Pref. to the German ed. of 1872, in Struik, ed.: *Birth of the C.M.,* 129.

Chapter 19
Liebknecht's Fake Edition of 1872
1. Liebknecht, in the book *Leipziger Hochverrathsprozess [&c]*, 130, quoted by Andréas, p.62.
2. See, in retrospect, Ltr, E to Bebel, Apr. 30, 1883, in MEW 36:22.
3. As reported by Liebknecht in *Leipziger Hochverrathsprozess [&c]* (see note 1 above).
4. Quoted in MEW 33:745, n.242.
5. Ltr, M to Liebknecht, Apr. 13, 1871, in MEW 33:207.
6. Ltr, E to Sorge, Mar. 17, 1872, in MEW 33:432.
7. Quoted in MEW 33:745f, n.242.
8. Ltr, E to Liebknecht, Apr. 23, 1872, in MEW 33:451.
9. ME: Pref. to German ed. of 1872, in MEW 18:95f.
10. Ltr, E to M, May 1, 1851, in MEW 27:240.
11. Ltr, M to E, Apr. 15, 1869, in MEW 32:302.
12. Ltr, Bebel to Marx, May 19, 1873, quoted in Andréas, p.64.
13. Ltr, E to Hepner, Dec. 30, 1872, in MEW 33:554.
14. Ltr, E to Liebknecht, Feb. 12, 1873, in MEW 33:568.
15. Andréas, p.64.

Chapter 20
In the Wake of the Paris Commune: II
1. This article was mentioned above, Chap.18, p. fn.
2. Letter (not extant) to Carlo Cafiero; see Andréas A#67 .

Chapter 21
In the Wake of the Paris Commune: III
1. See above, Chap.20, p..
2. Ltr, E to Liebknecht, Jan. 27, 1874, in MEW 33:615.
3. Graham: *Socialism New and Old*, 129.
4. Details on these changes are given in an article by Franco Cagnetta; see reference in Andréas, p.172, note 15.
5. Based on Andréas, A#524, p.294.

Chapter 22
Editions and Proposed Editions of 1882
1. Letter from Sorge, quoted in MEW 34:580, n.291.
2. Ltr, M to Sorge, Apr. 4, 1876, in MEW 34:179.
3. See *Karl Marx, Chronik seines Lebens*, 355f; MEW 34:580, n.291.
4. Ltr, E to Sorge, June 20, 1882, in MEW 35:332.
5. Ltr, E to Hepner, June 25, 1882, in MEW 35:344.
6. Re Mehring, see above, Chap.20, p..
7. Ltr, M to Lavrov, Jan. 23, 1882, in MEW 35:262.
8. Ltr, E to Sorge, June 29, 1883, in MEW 36:45.

Chapter 23
Marx's Death. Editions of 1883.
Authorized German Edition
1. This is the subject of a collection containing much interesting material: Foner, ed.: *When Marx Died*.
2. For the alleged Polish edition of 1848, see Chap.9; for an early Polish mention of the Manifesto, see Chap.21, p. (*Rownosc* article of 1881).
3. Ltr, E to Sorge, June 3, 1885, in MEW 36:323.
4. For his periodical publication, see above, Chap.21, p..
5. Re Laveleye, see above, Chap.20, p..
6. See above, Chap.20, p..
7. E: Marx and the *N.R.Z.*, in MEW 21:17.
8. E: *On the History of the CL*, in MEW 21:216.
9. J. Most's edition is discussed in the next chapter, Chap.24.
10. E: Pref. to German ed. of 1883, in MEW 21:3.

Chapter 24
Johann Most Hijacks the Manifesto
1. For this 1869 edition, see Chap.17.
2. Foner, ed.: *When Marx Died*, 106.
3. Ibid., 87.
4. Ibid., 88.
5. Ltr, E to Van Patten, Apr. 18, 1883; in most collections of Marx-Engels letters [MEW 36:11f].
6. Kipnis: *American Socialist Movement*, 20.
7. Ltr, E to Sorge, June 29, 1883, in MEW 36:45.

8. Quoted in MEW 36:750, n.68.
9. Hepner wrote to Engels to tell him this, May 7–12, 1883; quoted in MEW 36:750, n.68.

Chapter 25
The Three Versions of Laura Marx Lafargue
1. Ltr, M to E, Oct. 13, 1851, in MEW 27:358 [MECW 38: 475.
2. See A#25.
3. Ltr, M to E, Apr. 15, 1869, in MEW 32:302.
4. Ltr, E to M, Apr. 19, 1869, in MEW 32:307.
5. Ltr, M to Sorge, May 23, 1872, in MEW 33:469.
6. Ltr, E to Sorge, Nov. 16, 1872, in MEW 33:541.
7. Ibid.
8. Ltr, E to Laura Marx Lafargue, Apr. 11, 1883, in *E/ Lafargues: Correspondence*, 1:125.
9. Ltr, P. Lafargue to Engels, Nov. 4, 1885, ibid., 1: 317.
10. This letter is printed in *E/Lafargues: Correspondence*, 2:162 under the date Nov. 5, 1888, but Andréas says the date should be 1885. This certainly makes sense, especially tying in with Engels' letter to Laura of Nov. 7, 1885 (in MEW 36:380), which however is not in the E/Lafargues correspondence collection at all.
11. Ltr, E to Laura, Nov. 7, 1885; retranslated.
12. See Ltr, P. Lafargue to Engels, Oct. 11, 1885, in *E/Lafargues: Correspondence*, 1:309.
13. Ltr, Laura Lafargue to Engels, Oct. 23, 1885, in *E/Lafargues: Correspondence*, 1:315. These two proposed changes by Engels (both concerning the seventh demand in the ten-point program) are the only ones we know of definitely, since they are the only ones mentioned by Laura.
14. Although writing in 1890, Engels refers only to Laura-l, not to Laura-2, which he had helped improve. No doubt the explanation is simply a memory lapse.

Chapter 26
The Authorized English Translation of 1888
1. Hyndman: *The Record of an Adventurous Life*, 205.
2. Ltr, Sorge to Engels, Feb. 20, 1887, in MEW 36:837, n.731.
3. Ltr, E to Sorge, Mar. 10, 1887, in MEW 36:624.
4. Ibid.
5. Quoted in ME: *Letters to Americans*, p.184 fn.
6. Ltr, E to Sorge, May 4, 1887, in MEW 36:648.
7. Ibid.
8. Ltr, E to Mrs. Wischnewetzky, Feb. 22, 1888, in MEW 37:27; retranslated.
9. Cf. p. above, and see preceding note 8.
10. Ltr, E to P. Lafargue, Feb.7, 1888, in

E/Lafargues: Correspondence, 2:92.

11. Ibid.

12. E: Pref. to English ed. of 1888, in Struik, ed.: *Birth of the C.M.*, 135f.

13. MEGA I, 6:685f.

14. Andréas, Table VII, p.370f.

Chapter 27
International Roundup 1883–1895

1. Ltr, E to Martignetti, June 13, 1885, in ME: Corr. con Ital., 308 [MEW 36:326].

2. Andréas, A#196, p.l22. This belief is based on a letter by Martignetti to Engels of much later, Apr. 13, 1891.

3. In Struik, ed.: *Birth of the C.M.*, the editor's note on the Italian edition is erroneous; he ascribes the translation to Martignetti.

4. E: Pref. to the Polish ed. of 1892, in Struik, ed.: *Birth of the C.M.*, 141.

5. Andréas, p.199.

6. E: Pref. to the German ed. of 1890, in Struik, ed.: *Birth of the C.M.*, 138.

7. See above, Chap.9.

8. See above, Chap.18, p. .

9. See above, Chap.18, p. .

Bibliography (*Works Cited*)

Adoratsky, V. *The History of the Communist Manifesto.* (New York: International Publishers, 1938).

Adler, Georg. *Die Geschichte der ersten sozialpolitischen Arbeiterbewegung in Deutschland.* (Breslau: E. Trewendt, 1885).

_____. *Die Grundlagen der Karl Marx'schen Kritik der bestehenden Volkwirtschaf.* (Tübigen: H. Laupp) 1887).

Andler, Charles. "Le Manifeste Communist: Introduction Historique et Commentaire," in *Marx et Engels: Le Manifeste Communiste,* II (Paris: Cornély, 1901).

Andréas, Bert. *Le Manifeste Communiste de Marx et Engels. Histoire et Bibliographie 1848–1918.* (Milan: Feltrinelli, 1963).

Bernstein, Eduard. *Die Voraussetzungen des Sozialismus und die Aufgaben der Sozialdemokratie.* (Stuttgart: Dietz Nachf., 1902)

_____. *Evolutionary Socialism: A Criticism and Affirmation.* (New York: Huebsch, 1909).

Bernstein, Samuel. *The First International in America.* (New York: A. M. Kelley, 1962).

Black, Frank Gees & Renee Metier. *The Harney Papers..* (Assen: Van Gorcum, 1969).

Brandes, Georg. *Ferdinand Lassalle.* (Berlin: Verlag von F. Duncker, 1877).

Carr, E. H. *Studies in Revolution.* (London: MacMillan, 1950).

Considérant, Victor. *Manifeste de la Démocratie.* (Paris: Libraire Phalantéresterie, 1843).

Correspondence/Friedrich Engels, Paul et Laura Lafargue.. (Paris: Editions Sociales, 1956–59).

Dawson, William H. *German Socialism and Ferdinand Lassalle.* (London: S. Sonnenschein, 1888).

Eisenhart, Hugo. *Geschichte der Nationalökonomie.* (Jena: G. Fischer, 1881).

Ely, Richard T. *French and German Socialism in Modern Times.* (New York: Harper & Bros., 1883).

Foner, Phillip. *When Marx Died.* (New York: International Publishers, 1973).

Friedlieb, L. *Die rothe und die schwartze Internationale.* (Munich, 1874).

Freymond, Jacques. *Le Prémiere Internationale.* (Genéve: E. Droz, 1962–71).

The General Council of the First International ... (Series: *Documents of the First International)* Five unnumbered volumes published, each beginning as above, followed by the years covered. (Moscow: Progress Publishers, n.d.).

Gompers, Samuel. *Seventy Years of Life and Labor.* (New York: E. P. Dutton, 1925).

Graham, William. *Socialism New and Old.* (London: K. Paul, Trench & Co.,1890).

Gross, Gustav. *Karl Marx. Eine Studie.* (Leipzig, 1885).

Held, Adolf. *Zwei Bücher zur socialen Geschichte Englands.* (Leipzig: Duncke & Humblot, 1881).

Henderson & Chaloner. *Marx & Engels on Britain.* (Moscow: Foreign Languages Publishing House, 1962).

Huber, Johannes. *Die Philospohie in der Sozialdemokratis.* (Munich: M. Ernst, 1885).

Huberman, Leo & Sweezy, Paul M. *The Communist Manifesto After 100 Years.* (New York: Monthly Review Press, 1964).

Hyndman, H. M. *The Record of an Adventurous Life.* (New York: Macmillan, 1911).

Institut Marksa-Engelsa-Lenina. *Karl Marx, Chronik seines Lebens in Einzeldaten.* (Moscow: Marx-Engels Verlag, 1934).

Institut für Marxismus-Leninismus beim ZK der SED *Der Bund der Kommunisten: Dokumente und Materialien.* Band I:1836-1849. (Berlin: Dietz, 1970).

Jäger, Eugen. *Der Moderne Socialismus. Karl Marx, die Internationale Arbeiter-Association, Lassalle und die deutschen Socialisten.* (Berlin: G. van Munden, 1873).

Kaufmann, Rev. Moritz. *Utopias, or Schemes of Social Improvement. From Sir Thomas More to Karl Marx.* (Lomdon: C. K. Paul & Co., 1879).

Kautsky, Karl. *Der Weg zur Macht.* (Berlin: Buchhandlung Vorwärts, 1909).

_____. *The Road to Power.* (Chicago: S. A. Block, 1909).

Kerdijk, A. *Mannen van Beketeekens in Onze Dagen,* Vol. X. ed. N. C. Balsem. (Haarlem, 1879).

Kipnis, Ira. *American Socialist Movement.* (New York:: Columbia University Press, 1952).

Kirkup, Thomas. *History of Socialism.* (London & Edinburgh: A. & C. Black, 1892).

Labriola, A. *Essays in the Materialist Conception of History.* (Chicago: Charles H. Kerr, 1904).

Laski, Harold. *The Communist Manifesto: A Socialist Landmark.* (London: G. Allen & Unwin, 1948).

Laveleye, Emile de. *Le Socialisme Contemporain.* (Bruxelles: C. Murquardt, 1881).

_____. *The Socialism of Today.* (London: Field & Tuer, 1885).

Lessner, Friedrich. "Before 1848 and After" in *Reminiscences of Marx and Engels.* (Moscow: Foreign Languages Publishing House, 1956?).

Liebknecht, Wilhelm. *Der Leipziger Hochverrathsprozess.*

Ausführlicher Bericht. (Berlin: Rutten & Loening, 1960).

M. B. (Moritz Busch ?) *Geschichte der Internationale.* (Leipzig, 1872).

Malon, Benoit. *Histoire de Socialisme.* (Lugano: F. Veladini, 1879).

Mehring, Franz. *Die Deutsche Socialdemokratie.* (Bremen: Weser Zeitung, 1879).

Mermeix (Gabriel Terrail). *La France Socialiste. Notes d'Histoire Contemporaine.*

(Paris: F. Fetscherin & Chuit, 1886).

Meyer, Rudolph. *Der Emancipationskampf des Vierten Standes.* (1874).

Padover, Saul K. *Karl Marx: An Intimate Biography.* (McGraw-Hill: New York, 1978).

Rae, John. *Contemporary Socialism.* (New York: C. Scribner's & Sons, 1884).

Resch, Peter. *Die Internationale.* (Leipzig: Graz, 1886).

Ryazonov, D. *The Communist Manifesto of Karl Marx and Friedrich Engels.* (London: Martin Lawrence, 1930).

Sachs, Emanie. *The Terrible Siren.* (New York:: Harper, 1928).

Schlütter, Hermann. *Die Internationale in Amerika.*

Schuster, Richard. *Die Social-Demokratie.* (1875).

Steccanella, Valentino. *Del Communismo.*(Rome: Della S. C. di Propaganda Fide, 1882).

Stieber, Wilhelm & Wermuth, K. G. L. *Die Communisten-Verschwörungen des neunzehnten Jahrhunderts.*

(Hildesheim: G. Olms, 1960).

Struik, Dirk J. *Birth of the Communist Manifesto.* (New York: International Publishers, 1971).

Testut, Oscar. *L'Internationale.* (Paris: E. Lachaud, 1871).

Villetard, Edmond. *Histoire de l'Internationale.* (Paris: Garnier Fréres, 1872).

Winkler, Arnold. *Die Entstehung des "Kommunistischen Manifests".*

(Vienna: Arbeiten der Wirtschaftsgeschichtlichen institutes der Hochschule für Welthandel, 1936).

Woolsey, Theodore. *Communism and Socialism in Their History and Theory.* (New York: C. Scribner's, 1880).

WHY A NEW TRANSLATION?

The Authorized English Translation of 1888 was put into shape by Engels himself, on the basis of a draft translation by his friend Samuel Moore; it was, indeed, the only translation of the Manifesto for which Engels took complete responsibility. When the A.E.T.'s title page said "edited by Frederick Engels," it meant in reality: translation revised and finalized by Engels. Moore's name did not even appear on the title page; his role was reported at the end of Engels' preface.

This reflected the real state of affairs. If you go through a sentence-by-sentence comparison of the A.E.T. with the German text, it becomes crystal-clear that there were two modes of writing embodied in the A.E.T.: a close, near-literal rendition of the original by a conscientious translator—which gives way from time to time to boldly revisionary rewriting of the words of the original. The first mode was that of Samuel Moore, who however would not have dreamed of taking such liberties with the original as we will have occasion to note. The second mode reflected the revisions in the language of the Manifesto made by Engels as he "edited" Moore's draft.

There is virtually no in-between style. I think that anyone who makes such a close textual comparison will be able to say with moral certainty: *I can see just where Engels did his rewriting of Moore's draft almost as plainly as if I were standing looking over his shoulder.*

The real translator of the A.E.T., then, must be taken to be Engels, using Moore's draft as a first approximation. And, as mentioned, this was exactly what Engels himself conveyed on the title page.

Now this fact would seem to give the A.E.T. such impregnable authority as to make a new translation a folly. It certainly explains why the A.E.T. immediately monopolized the field, continues to do so to this day, and can never be displaced in the future.*

In fact, any *replacement* of the A.E.T. by any other version is quite out of the question, even if the A.E.T. were not such a successful translation as, indeed, it was. For over a century now, the A.E.T. has been *the* manifesto itself for English-speaking people—and many others; and in its own right it is now a "historical document" (as Marx and Engels called the Manifesto).

And yet, despite all that, a new English version *is* needed—for a specific purpose. It is needed as a supplement to the A.E.T., in a didactic and reference role. Why is such an auxiliary version necessary?

The minor reason is that Engels was forced to do the work in a hurry. The facts indicate that he devoted only about a week or so to it. The circumstances are related in Section I; it is enough to repeat what he himself wrote about this rush in a letter to Paul Lafargue:

I look to Laura [Marx's daughter] for *improvements* to the translation—my revision had

---

* Part I of this work describes the two independent translations that were published after the A.E.T.—one by Aitken and Budgen, another by Eden and Cedar Paul—and explains why neither offered a useful alternative of any sort to the A.E.T.

to be done in some haste and it [Laura's criticism] would be of the greatest help to me for a reprint.

We see that he expected to revise the translation for a second printing. But he was unable to do this, since publisher William Reeves stereotyped the plates of the edition. In any case, no revision was ever made.

Certainly, then, Engels was not of the opinion that the A.E.T. as we know it was definitive. If it was finally written on brazen tablets, this was not done by Engels himself. This consideration should be kept in mind when we come to some passages in the A.E.T. which may be seen as betraying carelessness or haste—for example, the omission of whole sentences.

The major reason would hold even if Engels had been able to make the "improvements" in the translation that he intended. Engels deliberately revised—rewrote—the formulation of many a sentence in order to adapt the Manifesto for the workers of a nation other than the one it was originally written for: workers with different backgrounds, with less of a theoretical orientation, farther removed from the original by nearly a half century and two revolutions.

We know how uneasy Engels was about the capacity of the English and American workers of the time to understand and appreciate the Manifesto—this not only in general but in the period shortly before he did the A.E.T. He wrote about this concern in many letters. It is this consideration that guided his pen, in many a paragraph, as he worked on Moore's draft. In a few cases he exorcised this fear by means of explanatory footnotes; there is a cluster of three historical-explanatory footnotes right at the beginning of Section I. But the publication could not be turned into a mass of footnotery, without changing its hoped-for popular character. He must have been tempted to add many others, and indeed he yielded five more times.

In other cases he resorted to parenthetical insertions;, made little changes that could be brought off in a few words; added a few explanatory elaborations here and there. The difference in German between *Klasse* and *Stand* had to be ignored, of course. "Lumpenproletariat" was out of the question in English (and would remain so for about a half century). What would an Anglo-Saxon head make of a "national class" in the Manifesto's usage? What was a political *Katzenjammer*? In 1848, a reference to the new idea of cell system prisons was up to date; what do you do about it forty years later? ... and so on.

Marx and Engels had for decades resisted every proposal or suggestion that they revise or update the Manifesto in any way, and had insisted (wisely, I think) that the text should be considered a "historical document": *This is what it said in 1848.* Yet here was Engels doing a kind of limited revision or updating of the language, telling himself that it was all in aid of better communicating the 1848 document to contemporary Anglo-Saxon noggins.

He could not have foreseen that subsequent generations of English-speaking readers, favorable or hostile—searching through the holy writ of the Manifesto for evidence to support whatever they wanted to prove—treated the new English formulations as if they had been engraved on the brazen tablets *in 1848*. This pattern, alas, was an element in the intellectual-political history of Marxism (and anti-Marxism) for the next century.

In any case, the considerations that Engels had in mind as he worked hurriedly on the translation should not *now* continue weighing on all those who come to the Manifesto to inquire into its views. It is necessary to provide a way of getting behind the A.E.T.

The New English Version

The fact that the new English version (N.E.V.) offered here is intended to supplement the A.E.T., not replace it, determines a number of its features. If it were proposed as the only, or primary, translation, many passages or phrases would be done differently.

In doing any translation, you constantly run into situations where you can solve the problem in two or more equally correct ways. In many cases, the A.E.T. represents one possible choice; in such cases the N.E.V. often sets down another alternative —not necessarily because it is better, let alone more "correct" —but simply to show the possibilities. In these cases there is no special significance involved in the differences. For example, in Par.136 the word *raunen* may mean either "whisper" or "murmur"; the A.E.T. uses the first, the N.E.V. the second. The import is obviously the same, but in some cases the presentation of such alternatives may help the reader see the range of meaning involved. Of course, the meaning of a word is seldom a *point* in thought but rather an area, a range. I follow this pattern in the case only of alternatives that seem equally good, never just to be different. It follows that in these cases there is no implication that the A.E.T.'s version is wrong or inferior. Where a substantive difference is claimed, this point will be made explicitly in the Annotations.

The function of the N.E.V. as a supplement also conditions the fact that it is more often near-literal or very close than it would otherwise have been. It is no part of my aim to achieve a finer literary gloss than the A.E.T. In fact, there may be some places where the esthetic qualities of the N.E.V. have suffered for the sake of greater transparency in meaning.

While punctuation is an indication of meaning and is therefore significant in the translation process, it must be kept in mind that German conventions differ from English and, besides, have changed since 1848. Not only cannot the original German punctuation be followed, but the A.E.T.'s punctuation is partly nineteenth-century and partly Germanized. The N.E.V. modernizes punctuation in terms of the meaning.

The same goes for capitalization. Here, as for punctuation and especially for spelling, the N.E.V. follows modern American conventions. The rule for capitalizing political designations goes as follows. 'Communist' is capitalized only when it refers to an organization officially so called; lower-case 'communist', when it refers to the general ideology. Of course, the difference is sometimes uncertain, but in the present case 'Communist' is taken to refer to the Communist League, 'communist' to its general ideology and politics. Since German rules for capitalization are completely different, none of these decisions has anything to do with the original work.

Paragraph numbering has been added to the text of the Manifesto to provide a framework for annotation and reference. Like other features, paragraphing has changed from edition to edition. Here the paragraphing follows the first German edition of 1848, like the new translation in general. However, the first edition itself cannot be followed absolutely, since at Par.162 it made a typographical error which we cannot reproduce: it inserted a paragraph break in the middle of a sentence. This paragraph break has been ignored.

For ease of comparison, the A.E.T. and the N.E.V. are printed in parallel columns. Since the Annotations frequently refer to the formulations of the first German edition of 1848, this version is reproduced in a third column. This reproduction is, for ease of use by the modern reader, transliterated from the fraktur font of the original into a modern font. Typographical errors and misspellings are retained. Finally, a fourth column reproduces the first English translation of the Manifesto by Helen Macfarlane. The role Marx and Engels probably played in this translation was discussed in chapter 11 of part I of this book.

One problem this procedure presents is: what to do with the notes introduced by Engels in the 1888 A.E.T. and the introductory material introduced by the editor of the *Red Republican*? The simplest solution was the one chosen. Engels' notes and Harney's material are noted in the text in the usual way and the notes themselves are included at the end of the text.

Manifest

der

Kommunistischen Partei.

Veröffentlicht im Februar 1848

‚Proletarier aller Länder vereinigt Euch!'

London.

Gedruckt in der Office der „Bildungs-Gesellschaft für Arbeiter"
von J. E. Burghard
46, LIVERPOOL STREET, BISHOPSGATE

Manifest

der

Kommunistischen Partei.

---

¹Ein Gespenst geht um in Europa—das Gespenst des Kommunismus. Alle Mächte des alten Europa haben sich zu einer heiligen Hetzjagd gegen dies Gespenst verbündet, der Papst und der Czar, Metternich und Guizot, französische Radikale und deutsche Polizisten.

²Wo ist die Oppositionspartei, die nicht von ihren regierenden Gegnern als kommunistisch verschrieen worden wäre, wo die Oppositionspartei, die den fortgeschritteneren Oppositionsleuten sowohl, wie ihren reaktionären Gegnern den brandmarkenden Vorwurf des Kommunismus nicht zurückgeschleudert hätte?

³Zweierlei geht aus dieser Thatsache hervor.

⁴Der Kommunismus wird bereits von allen europäischen Mächten als eine Macht anerkannt.

⁵Es ist hohe Zeit daß die Kommunisten ihre Anschauungsweise, ihre Zwecke, ihre Tendenzen vor der ganzen Welt offen darlegen, und den Märchen vom Gespenst des Kommunismus ein Manifest der Partei selbst entgegenstellen.

⁶Zu diesem Zweck haben sich Kommunisten der verschiedensten Nationalität in London versammelt und das folgende Manifest entworfen, das in englischer, französischer, deutscher, italienischer, flämmischer und dänischer Sprache veröffentlicht wird.

I.

Bourgeois und Proletarier.

⁷Die Geschichte aller bisherigen Gesellschaft ist die Geschichte von Klassenkämpfen.

110

German Communism.

MANIFESTO OF THE GERMAN

COMMUNIST PARTY.

(Published in February, 1848.)

¹A frightful hobgoblin stalks throughout Europe. We are haunted by a ghost, the ghost of Communism. All the Powers of the Past have joined in a holy crusade to lay this ghost to rest,—the Pope and the Czar, Metternich and Guizot, French Radicals and German police agents. ²Where is the opposition which has not been accused of Communism by its enemies in Power? And where the opposition that has not hurled this blighting accusation at the heads of the more advanced oppositionists, as well as at those of its official enemies? ³Two things appear on considering these facts. ⁴I. The ruling Powers of Europe acknowledge Communism to be also a Power. ⁵II. It is time for the Communists to lay before the world an account of their aims and tendencies, and to oppose these silly fables about the bugbear of Communism, by a manifesto of the Communist Party.

CHAPTER I.

BOURGEOIS AND PROLETARIANS.

⁷HITHERTO the history of Society has been the history of the battles between the classes composing it.

𝕸𝖆𝖓𝖎𝖋𝖊𝖘𝖙𝖔 𝖔𝖋 𝖙𝖍𝖊 𝕮𝖔𝖒𝖒𝖚𝖓𝖎𝖘𝖙 𝕻𝖆𝖗𝖙𝖞

by

KARL MARX, and FREDERICK ENGELS

A SPECTRE is haunting Europe—the spectre of Communism. All the Powers of old Europe have entered into a holy alliance to exorcise this spectre; Pope and Czar, Metternich and Guizot, French Radicals and German police spies.

[2]Where is the party in opposition that has not been decried as communistic by its opponents in power? Where the Opposition that has not hurled back the branding reproach of Communism, against the more advanced opposition parties, as well as against its reactionary adversaries?

[3]Two things result from this fact.

[4]I. Communism is already acknowledged by all European Powers to be itself a Power.

[5]II. It is high time that Communists should openly, in the face of the whole world, publish their views, their aims, their tendencies, and meet this nursery tale of the Spectre of Communism with a Manifesto of the party itself.

[6]To this end, Communists of various nationalities have assembled in London, and sketched the following manifesto, to be published in the English, French, German, Italian, Flemish and Danish languages.

I

BOURGEOIS AND PROLETARIANS. (a)

[7]The history of all hitherto existing society () is the history of class struggles.

MANIFESTO

OF THE

COMMUNIST PARTY

[1]A specter is haunting Europe—the specter of communism. All the powers of old Europe have allied themselves in a holy witchhunt against this specter: the pope and the czar, Metternich and Guizot, French Radicals and German policemen.

[2] Where is the opposition party that has not been decried as communist by its opponents in power? Where the opposition party that has not hurled the branding reproach of communism back at the more progressive opposition elements as well as at its reactionary opponents?

[3] Two things emerge from this fact.

[4] Communism is already recognized as a power by all European powers.

[5] It is high time that the Communists openly laid before the whole world their point of view, their aim, their tendencies, and confront the fables about the specter of communism with a manifesto of the party itself.

[6] To this end Communists of the most various nationalities have assembled in London and drawn up the following manifesto, which will be published in English, French, German, Italian, Flemish, and Danish.

I

BOURGEOIS AND PROLETARIANS

[7] The history of all society up to now has been the history of class struggles.

[8]Freier und Sklave, Patrizier und Plebejer, Baron und Leibeigner, Zunftbürger und Gesell, kurz, Unterdrücker und Unterdrückte standen in stetem Gegensatz zu einander, führten einen ununterbrochenen, bald versteckten bald offenen Kampf, einen Kampf, der jedesmal mit einer revolutionären Umgestaltung der ganzen Gesellschaft endete, oder mit dem gemeinsamen Untergang der kämpfenden Klassen.

[9]In den früheren Epochen der Geschichte finden wir fast überall eine vollständige Gliederung der Gesellschaft in verschiedene Stände, eine mannichfaltige Abstufung der gesellschaftlichen Stellungen. Im alten Rom haben wir Patrizier, Ritter, Plebejer, Sklaven; im Mittelalter Feudalherren, Vasallen, Zunftbürger, Gesellen, Leibeigene, und noch dazu in fast jeder dieser Klassen wieder besondere Abstufungen.

[10]Die aus dem Untergange der feudalen Gesellschaft hervorgegangene moderne bürgerliche Gesellschaft hat die Klassengegensätze nicht aufgehoben. Sie hat nur neue Klassen, neue Bedingungen der Unterdrückung, neue Gestaltungen des Kampfes an die Stelle der alten gesetzt.

[11]Unsere Epoche, die Epoche der Bourgeoisie, zeichnet sich jedoch dadurch aus, daß sie die Klassengegensätze vereinfacht hat. Die ganze Gesellschaft spaltet sich mehr und mehr in zwei große feindliche Lager, in zwei große einander direkt gegenüberstehende Klassen—Bourgeoisie und Proletariat.

[12]Aus den Leibeigenen des Mittelalters gingen die Pfahlbürger der ersten Städte hervor; aus dieser Pfahlbürgerschaft entwickelten sich die ersten Elemente der Bourgeoisie.

[13]Die Entdeckung Amerika's, die Umschiffung Afrika's schufen der aufkommenden Bourgeoisie ein neues Terrain. Der ostindische und chinesische Markt, die Kolonisirung von Amerika, der Austausch mit den Kolonien, die Vermehrung der Tauschmittel und der Waaren überhaupt gaben dem Handel, der Schifffahrt, der Industrie einen niegekannten Aufschwung, und damit dem revolutionären Element in der zerfallenden feudalen Gesellschaft eine rasche Entwicklung.

[8]Freemen and Slaves, Patricians and Plebeians, Nobles and Serfs, Members of Guilds and journeymen,—in a word, the oppressors and the oppressed, have always stood in direct opposition to each other. The battle between them has sometimes been open, sometimes concealed, but always continuous. A never-ceasing battle, which has invariably ended, either in a revolutionary alteration of the social system, or in the common destruction of the hostile classes.

[9]In the earlier historical epochs we find almost everywhere a minute division of Society into classes or ranks, a variety of grades in social position. In ancient Rome we find Patricians, Knights, Plebeians, Slaves; in mediæval Europe, Feudal Lords, Vassals, Burghers, Journeymen, Serfs; and in each of these classes there were again grades and distinctions. [10]Modern Bourgeois Society, proceeded from the ruins of the feudal system, but the Bourgeois régime has not abolished the antagonism of classes.

New classes, new conditions of oppression, new forms and modes of carrying on the struggle, have been substituted for the old ones. [11]The characteristic of our Epoch, the Era of the Middle-class, or Bourgeoisie, is that the struggle between the various Social Classes, has been reduced to its simplest form. Society incessantly tends to be divided into two great camps, into two great hostile armies, the Bourgeoisie and the Proletariat.

[12]The burgesses of the early Communes sprang from the Serfs of the Middle Ages, and from this Municipal class were developed the primitive elements of the modern Bourgeoisie. [13]The discovery of the New World, the circumnavigation of Africa, gave the Middleclass—then coming into being—new fields of action. The colonization of America, the opening up of the East Indian and Chinese Markets, the Colonial Trade, the increase of commodities generally and of the means of exchange, gave an impetus, hitherto unknown, to Commerce, Shipping, and the revolutionary element in the old decaying, feudal form of Society.

[8]Freeman and slave patrician and plebeian, lord and serf, guildmaster(c) and journeyman, in a word, oppressor and oppressed, stood in constant opposition to one another carried on an uninterrupted, now hidden, now open fight a fight that each time ended, either in a revolutionary re-constitution of society at large, or in the common ruin of the contending classes.

[9]In the earlier epochs of history, we find almost everywhere a complicated arrangement of society into various orders, a manifold gradation of social rank. In ancient Rome we have patricians, knights, plebeians, slaves; in the middle ages feudal lords, vassals, guild-masters, journeymen, apprentices, serfs; in almost all of these classes, again, subordinate gradations.

[10]The modern bourgeois society that has sprouted from the ruins of feudal society, has not done away with class antagonisms. It has but established new classes, new conditions of oppression, new forms of struggle in place of the old ones.

[11]Our epoch, the epoch of the bourgeoisie, possesses, however this distinctive feature; it has simplified the class antagonisms. Society as a whole is more and more splitting up into two great hostile camps, into two great classes directly facing each other: Bourgeoisie and Proletariat.

[12]From the serfs of the middle ages sprang the chartered burghers of the earliest towns. From these burgesses the first elements of the bourgeoisie were developed.

[13]The discovery of America, the rounding of the Cape, opened up fresh ground for the rising bourgeoisie. The East-Indian and Chinese Markets, the colonisation of America, trade with the colonies, the increase in the means of exchange and in commodities generally, gave to commerce, to navigation, to industry, an impulse never before known, and thereby, to the revolutionary element in the tottering feudal society, a rapid development.

[8]Freeman and slave, patrician and plebeian, baron and serf, master guildsman and journeyman, in short, oppressor and oppressed, stood in constant opposition to each other, and carried on an uninterrupted struggle, now hidden, now open, a struggle that each time ended with a revolutionary remolding of the whole society or with the common ruin of the contending classes.

[9]In the earlier epochs of history we find almost everywhere a thorough going structuring of society into various orders, a multifarious gradation of social ranks. In ancient Rome we have patricians, knights, plebeians, slaves; in the Middle Ages, feudal lords, vassals, master guildsman, journeymen, serfs; and in addition there were distinct gradations in turn within almost all of these classes.

[10]The modern bourgeois society that arose out of the downfall of feudal society has not abolished class antagonism. It has only put new classes, new conditions of oppression, new forms of struggle in place of the old ones.

[11]Our epoch, the epoch of the bourgeoisie, is however distinguished by the fact that it has simplified the class antagonisms. The whole society is more and more splitting up into two great hostile camps, into two great classes directly confronting each other—bourgeoisie and proletariat.

[12]From the serfs of the Middle Ages arose the burgesses of the first towns; from this burgessdom developed the first elements of the bourgeoisie.

[13]The discovery of America and the circumnavigation of Africa established a new terrain for the rising bourgeoisie. The East Indian and Chinese markets, the colonization of America, trade with the colonies, the increase in the means of exchange and in commodities generally, these gave a previously unknown impetus to commerce, navigation, and industry, and thereby a rapid development to the revolutionary element in the crumbling feudal society.

[14]Die bisherige feudale oder zünftige Betriebs-
weise der Industrie reichte nicht mehr aus für den
mit den neuen Märkten anwachsenden Bedarf.
Die Manufaktur trat an ihre Stelle. Die Zunft-
meister wurden verdrängt durch den industriellen
Mittelstand; die Theilung der Arbeit zwischen
den verschiedenen Corporationen verschwand
vor der Theilung der Arbeit in der einzelnen
Werkstatt selbst.

[15]Aber immer wuchsen die Märkte, immer
stieg der Bedarf. Auch die Manufaktur reichte
nicht mehr aus. Da revolutionirten der Dampf
und die Maschinerie die industrielle Produktion.
An die Stelle der Manufaktur trat die moderne
große Industrie, an die Stelle des industriellen
Mittelstandes traten die industriellen Millionäre,
die Chefs ganzer industriellen Armeen, die
modernen Bourgeois.

[16]Die große Industrie hat den Weltmarkt
hergestellt, den die Entdekung Amerika's vorbe-
reitete. Der Weltmarkt hat dem Handel, der
Schifffahrt, den Landkommunikationen eine
unermeßliche Entwicklung gegeben. Diese hat
wieder auf die Ausdehnung der Industrie zurück-
gewirkt, und in demselben Maße, worin Industrie, Handel, Schifffahrt, Eisenbahnen sich
ausdehnten, in demselben Maße entwickelte sich
die Bourgeoisie, vermehrte sie ihre Kapitalien,
drängte sie alle vom Mittelalter her überlieferten
Klassen in den Hintergrund.

[17]Wir sehen also wie die moderne Bourgeoisie
selbst das Produkt eines langen Entwickl-
ungsganges, einer Reihe von Umwälzungen in
der Produktions- und Verkehrsweise ist.

[14]The old feudal way of managing the
industrial interest by means of guilds and
monopolies was not found sufficient for the
increased demand caused by the opening up of
these new markets. It was replaced by the
manufacturing system. Guilds vanished before
the industrial Middle-class, and the division of
labour between the different corporations was
succeeded by the division of labour between the
workmen of one and the same great workshop.

[15]But the demand always increased, new
markets came into play. The manufacturing
system, in its turn, was found to be inadequate.
At this point industrial Production was revolutionised by machinery and steam. The modern
industrial system was developed in all its
gigantic proportions; instead of the industrial
Middle-class we find industrial millionaires,
chiefs of whole industrial armies, the modern
Bourgeois, or Middle-class Capitalists. [16]The
discovery of America was the first step towards
the formation of a colossal market, embracing
the whole world; whereby an immense
developement of the Bourgeoisie, the increase
of their Capital, the superseding of all classes
handed down to modern times from the
Middle Ages, kept pace with the developement
of Production, Trade, and Steam
communication.

[17]We find, therefore, that the modern
Bourgeoisie are themselves the result of a long
process of developement, of a series of
revolutions in the modes of Production and Exchange.

114

[14]The feudal system of industry, under which industrial production was monopolised by closed guilds, now no longer sufficed for the growing wants of the new markets. The manufacturing system took its place. The guild-masters were pushed on one side by the manufacturing middle-class; division of labour between the different corporate guilds vanished in the face of division of labour in each single workshop.

[15]Meantime the markets kept ever growing, the demand ever rising. Even manufacture no longer sufficed. Thereupon, steam and machinery revolutionised industrial production. The place of manufacture was taken by the giant Modern Industry, the place of the industrial middle-class, by industrial millionaires, the leaders of whole industrial armies, the modern bourgeois.

[16]Modern Industry has established the world-market for which the discovery of America paved the way. This market has given an immense development to commerce, to navigation, to communication by land. This development has, in its turn, reacted on the extension of industry; and in proportion as industry, commerce, navigation, railways extended, in the same proportion the bourgeoisie developed, increased its capital and pushed into the background every class handed down from the Middle Ages.

[17]We see, therefore, how the modern bourgeoisie is itself the product of a long course of development of a series of revolutions in the modes of production and of exchange.

[14]The hitherto existing feudal or guild-system mode of carrying on industry no longer sufficed for the growing demand that came with the new markets. Manufacture took its place. The master guildsmen were crowded out by the industrial middle class; the division of labor between the different corporate guilds vanished in face of the division of labor inside the individual workshop itself.

[15]But the markets kept ever growing, the demand ever rising. Even manufacture no longer sufficed. Then steam and machinery revolutionized industrial production. In place of manufacture came modern large-scale industry; in place of the industrial middle class came industrial millionaires, the heads of whole industrial armies, the modern bourgeois.

[16]Large-scale industry has established the world market, for which the discovery of America prepared the way. The world market has given an immeasurably great development to commerce, navigation, and overland communication. This in turn has reacted on the expansion of industry; and in the same proportion as industry, commerce, navigation, and railways expanded, so too the bourgeoisie developed, increased its capital, and pushed into the background all classes handed down from the Middle Ages.

[17]We see, therefore, how the modern bourgeoisie is itself the product of a long course of development, of a series of transformations in the modes of production and intercourse.

[18]Jede dieser Entwicklungsstufen der Bourgeoisie war begleitet von einem entsprchenden politischen Fortschritt. Unterdrückter Stand unter der Herrschaft der Feudalherren, bewaffnete und sich selbst verwaltende Associationen in der Commune, hier unabhängige städtische Republik, dort dritter steuerpflichtiger Stand der Monarchie, dann zur Zeit der Manufaktur Gegengewicht gegen den Adel in der ständischen oder in der absoluten Monarchie und Hauptgrundlage der großen Monarchieen überhaupt, erkämpfte sie sich endlich seit der Herstellung der großen Industrie und des Weltmarktes im modernen Repräsentativstaat die ausschließliche politische Herrschaft. Die moderne Staatsgewalt ist nur ein Ausschuß, der die gemeinschaftlichen Geschäfte der ganzen Bourgeoisklasse verwaltet.

[19]Die Bourgeoisie hat in der Geschichte eine höchst revolutionäre Rolle gespielt.

[20]Die Bourgeoisie, wo sie zur Herrschaft gekommen, hat alle feudalen, patriarchalischen, idyllischen Verhältnisse zerstört. Sie hat die buntscheckigen Feudalbande, die den Menschen an seinen natürlichen Vorgesetzten knüpften, unbarmherzig zerrissen, und kein anderes Band zwischen Mensch und Mensch übrig gelassen, als das nackte Interesse, als die gefühllose „baare Zahlung.“ Sie hat die heiligen Schauer der frommen Schwärmerei, der ritterlichen Begeisterung, der spießbürgerlichen Wehmuth in dem eiskalten Wasser egoistischer Berechnung ertränkt. Sie hat die persönliche Würde in den Tauschwerth aufgelöst, und an die Stelle der zahllosen verbrieften und wohlerworbenen Freiheiten die Eine gewissenlose Handelsfreiheit gesetzt. Sie hat, mit einem Wort, und die Stelle der mit religiösen und politischen Illusionen verhüllten Ausbeutung die offene, unverschämte, direkte, dürre Ausbeutung gesetzt.

[21]Die Bourgeoisie hat alle bisher ehrwürdigen und mit frommer Scheu betrachteten Thätigkeiten ihres Heiligenscheins entkleidet. Sie hat den Arzt, den Juristen, den Pfaffen, den Poeten, den Mann der Wissenschaft in ihre bezahlten Lohnarbeiter verwandelt.

[18]Each of the degrees of industrial evolution, passed through by the modern Middle-class, was accompanied by a corresponding degree of political developement. This class was oppressed under the feudal régime, it then assumed the form of armed and self-regulating associations in the mediæval Municipalities; in one country we find it existing as a commercial republic, or free town; in another, as the third taxable Estate of the Monarchy; then during the prevalence of the manufacturing system (before the introduction of steam power) the Middle-class was a counterpoise to the Nobility in absolute Monarchies, and the groundwork of the powerful monarchical States generally. Finally, since the establishment of the modern industrial system, with its world-wide market, this class has gained the exclusive possession of political power in modern representative States. Modern Governments are merely Committees for managing the common affairs of the whole Bourgeoisie.

[19]This Bourgeoisie has occupied an extremely revolutionary position in History.

[20]As soon as the Bourgeois got the upper hand, they destroyed all feudal, patriarchal, idyllic relationships between men. They relentlessly tore asunder the many-sided links of that feudal chain which bound men to their "natural superiors," and they left no bond of union between man and man, save that of bare self-interest, of cash payments. They changed personal dignity into market value, and substituted the single unprincipled freedom of trade for the numerous, hardly earned, chartered liberties of the Middle Ages. Chivalrous enthusiasm, the emotions of piety, vanished before the icy breath of their selfish calculations. In a word, the Bourgeoisie substituted shameless, direct, open spoliation, for the previous system of spoliation concealed under religious and political illusions. [21]They stripped off that halo of sanctity which had surrounded the various modes of human activity, and had made them venerable, and venerated. They changed the physician, the jurisprudent, the priest, the poet, the philosopher, into their hired servants.

[18]Each step in the development of the bourgeoisie was accompanied by a corresponding political advance of that class. An oppressed Class under the sway of the feudal nobility, an armed and self-governing association in the mediæval commune (d), here independent urban republic (as in Italy and Germany), there taxable "third estate" of the monarchy (as in France), afterwards, in the period of manufacture proper, serving either the semi-feudal or the absolute monarchy as a counterpoise against the nobility, and, in fact, corner stone of the great monarchies in general, the bourgeoisie has at last, since the establishment of Modern Industry and of the world-market, conquered for itself, in the modern representative State, exclusive political sway. The executive of the modern State is but a committee for managing the common affairs of the whole bourgeoisie.

[19]The bourgeoisie, historically, has played a most revolutionary part.

[20]The bourgeoisie, wherever it has got the upper hand, has put an end to all feudal patriarchal idyllic relations. It has pitilessly torn asunder the motley feudal ties that bound man to his "natural superiors", and has left remaining no other nexus between man and man than naked self-interest, than callous "cash payment". It has drowned the most heavenly ecstacies of religious fervour of chivalrous enthusiasm of philistine sentimentalism, in the icy water of egotistical calculation. It has resolved personal worth into exchange value, and in place of the numberless indefeasible chartered freedoms, has set up that single, unconscionable freedom—Free Trade. In one word, for exploitation, veiled by religious and philosophical illusions, it has substituted naked, shameless, direct brutal exploitation.

[21]The bourgeoisie has stripped of its halo every occupation hitherto honoured and looked up to with reverent awe. It has converted the physician, the lawyer, the priest the poet the man of science, into its paid wage-labourers.

[18]Each of these steps in the development of the bourgeoisie was accompanied by a corresponding political advance. Oppressed social estate under the rule of the feudal lords, armed and self-governing associations in the commune, here independent urban republic, there taxable third estate of the monarchy, then during the period of manufacture a counterpoise against the nobility in the estates-based monarchy or in the absolute monarchy, and cornerstone of the great monarchies in general: the bourgeoisie has at last, since the establishment of large-scale industry and the world market, conquered for itself exclusive political power, in the modern representative state. The modern state power is only a committee that manages the common affairs of the whole bourgeois class.

[19]The bourgeoisie has played a most revolutionary role in history.

[20]Where the bourgeoisie has come to power, it has destroyed all feudal, patriarchal, idyllic relations. It has relentlessly burst the variegated feudal ties that bind a person to his natural superiors, and left no bond between people other than naked self-interest, than callous "cash payment." It has drowned the holy paroxysms of pious fervor, of chivalrous enthusiasm, of philistine sentimentality in the ice-cold water of egoistic calculation. It has dissolved personal dignity into exchange value, and in place of countless chartered freedoms dearly won, it has set up a single conscienceless one, freedom of trade. In short, in place of exploitation veiled with religious and political illusions, it has substituted open, unashamed, direct, blunt exploitation.

[21] The bourgeoisie has stripped the halo from all occupations hitherto considered respectable and regarded with pious awe. It has converted the physician, the lawyer, the priest, the poet, the man of learning into its paid wage-laborers.

[22]Die Bourgeoisie hat dem Familienverhälniß seinen rührend-sentimentalen Schleier abgerissen und es auf ein reines Geldverhältniß zurück-gefürt.

[23]Die Bourgeoise hat enthüllt wie die brutale Kraftäußerung, die die Reaktion so sehr am Mittelalter bewundert, in der trägsten Bärenhäut-erei ihre passende Ergänzung fand. Erst sie hat bewiesen was die Thätigkeit der Menschen zu Stande bringen kann. Sie hat ganz andere Wunderwerke vollbracht als egyptische Pyramid-en, römische Wasserleitungen und gothische Kathedralen, sie hat ganz andere Züge ausgefürt, als Völkerwanderungen nnd Kreuzzüge.

[24]Die Bourgeoisie kann nicht existiren ohne die Produktionsinstrumente, also die Produktions-verhältnisse, also sämmtliche gesellschaftlichen Verhältnisse fortwärend zu revolutioniren. Unveränderte Beibehaltung der alten Produktionsweise war dagegen die erste Existenzbedingung aller früheren industriellen Klassen. Die fortwärende Umwälzung der Produktion, die ununterbrochene Erschütterung aller gesellschaftlichen Zustände, die ewige Unsicherheit und Bewegung zeichnet die Bourgeois-Epoche vor allen früheren aus. Alle festen, eingerosteten Verhältnisse mit ihrem Gefolge von altehrwürdigen Vorstellungen und Anschauungen werden ausgelöst; alle neugebil-deten veralten, ehe sie verknöchern können. Alles Ständische und Stehende verdampft, alles Heilige wird entweiht, und die Menschen sind endlich gezwungen, ihre Lebensstellung, ihre gegenseitigen Beziehungen mit nüchternen Augen anzusehen.

[25]Das Bedürfniß nach einem stets ausgedeh-nteren Absatz für ihre Produkte jagt die Bourgeoisie über die ganze Erdkugel. Ueberall muß sie sich einnisten, überall anbauen, überall Verbindungen herstellen.

[22]They tore the touching veil of sentiment from domestic ties, and reduced family-relations to a mere question of hard cash. [23]The Middle-classes have shown how the brutal physical force of the Middle Ages, so much admired by Reactionists, found its befitting complement in the laziest ruffianism. They have also shown what human activity is capable of accomplishing. They have done quite other kinds of marvellous work than Egyptian pyramids, Roman aqueducts, or Gothic Cathedrals; and their expeditions have far surpassed all former Crusades, and Migrations of nations.

[24]The Bourgeoisie can exist only under the condition of continuously revolutionising machinery, or the instruments of Production. That is, perpetually changing the system of production, which again amounts to changing the whole system of social arrangements. Persistence in the old modes of Production was, on the contrary, the first condition of existence for all the preceding industrial Classes. A continual change in the modes of Production, a never ceasing state of agitation and social insecurity, distinguish the Bourgeois-Epoch from all preceding ones. The ancient ties between men, their opinions and beliefs—hoar with antiquity—are fast disappearing, and the new ones become worn out ere they can become firmly rooted. Every thing fixed and stable vanishes, everything holy and venerable is desecrated, and men are forced to look at their mutual relations, at the problem of Life, in the soberest, the most matter of fact way.

[25]The need of an ever-increasing market for their produce, drives the Bourgeoisie over the whole globe—they are forced to make settlements, to form connections, to set up means of communication everywhere.

[22]The bourgeoisie has torn away from the family its sentimental veil and has reduced the family relation to a mere money relation.

[23]The bourgeoisie has disclosed how it came to pass that the brutal display of vigour in the Middle Ages, which Reactionists so much admire, found its fitting complement in the most slothful indolence. It has been the first to show what man's activity can bring about. It has accomplished wonders far surpassing Egyptian pyramids, Roman aqueducts, and Gothic cathedrals; it has conducted expeditions that put in the shade all former Exoduses of nations and crusades.

[24]The bourgeoisie cannot ext without constantly revolutionising the instruments of production, and thereby the relations of production, and with them, the whole relations of society. Conservation of the old modes of production in unaltered form, was, on the contrary, the first condition of existence for all earlier industrial classes. Constant revolutionising of production, uninterrupted disturbance of all social conditions, everlasting uncertainty and agitation distinguish the bourgeois epoch from all earlier ones. All fixed, fast-frozen relations, with their chain of ancient and venerable prejudices and opinions, are swept away all new-formed ones become antiquated before they can ossify. Ah that is solid melts into air, all that is holy is profaned, and man is at last compelled to face with sober senses, his real conditions of life, and his relations with his kind

[25]The need of a constantly expanding market for its products chases the bourgeoisie over the whole surface of the globe. It must nestle everywhere, settle everywhere, establish connexions everywhere.

[22]The bourgeoisie has torn away from the family relationship its touchingly sentimental veil, and has reduced it to a purely money relationship.

[23]The bourgeoisie has revealed how the brutal display of energy which the Reaction so much admires about the Middle Ages found its fitting complement in the most sluggish indolence. It has been the first to show what people's activity can accomplish. It has performed wonders quite different from Egyptian pyramids, Roman aqueducts and Gothic cathedrals; it has carried out expeditions quite different from mass migrations and crusades.

[24]The bourgeoisie cannot exist without continually revolutionizing the instruments of production, hence the relations of production, hence social relations as a whole. In contrast, maintenance of the old mode of production unchanged was the first condition of existence of all earlier industrial classes. Continual transformation of production, uninterrupted upsetting of all social conditions, everlasting insecurity and movement distinguish the bourgeois epoch from all earlier ones. All fixed, rusted-in relations, with their train of old time-honored conceptions and opinions, become dissolved; all newly formed ones become antiquated before they can ossify. All that is established and stable evaporates away, all that is holy is profaned, and people are at last compelled to face their position in life and their mutual relations with sober eyes.

[25]The need for an ever-expanding outlet for its products drives the bourgeoisie over the entire globe. It must gain a footing everywhere, settle everywhere, establish connections everywhere.

[26]Die Bourgeoisie hat durch die Exploitation des Weltmarkts die Produktion und Konsumtion aller Länder kosmopolitisch gestaltet. Sie hat zum großen Bedauern der Reaktionäre den nationalen Boden der Industrie unter den Füßen weggezogen. Die uralten nationalen Industrieen sind vernichtet worden und werden noch täglich vernichtet. Sie werden verdrängt durch neue Industrieen, deren Einführung eine Lebensfrage für alle civilisirte Nationen wird, durch Industrieen, die nicht mehr einheimische Rohstoffe, sondern den entlegensten Zonen angehörige Rohstoffe verarbeiten, und deren Fabrikate nicht nur im Lande selbst, sondern in allen Welttheilen zugleich verbraucht werden. An die Stelle der alten, durch Landeserzeugnisse befriedigten Bedürfnisse treten neue, welche die Produkte der entferntesten Länder und Klimate zu ihrer Befriedigung erheischen. An die Stelle der alten lokalen und nationalen Selbstgenügsamkeit und Abgeschlossenheit tritt ein allseitiger Verkehr, eine allseitige Abhängigkeit der Nationen von einander. Und wie in der materiellen, so auch in der geistigen Produktion. Die geistigen Erzeugnisse der einzelnen Nationen werden Gemeingut. Die nationale Einseitigkeit und Beschränktheit wird mehr und mehr unmöglich, und aus den vielen nationalen und lokalen Literaturen bildet sich eine Weltliteratur.

[27]Die Bourgeoisie reißt durch die rasche Verbesserung aller Produktions-Instrumente, durch die unendlich erleichterten Kommunikationen alle, auch die barbarischten Nationen in die Civilisation. Die wohlfeilen Preise ihrer Waaren sind die schwere Artillerie, mit der sie alle chinesischen Mauern in den Grund schießt, mit der sie den hartnäckigsten Fremdenhaß der Barbaren zur Kapitulation zwingt. Sie zwingt alle Nationen die Produktionsweise der Bourgeoisie sich anzueignen, wenn sie nicht zu Grunde gehen wollen; sie zwingt sie die sogenannte Civilisation bei sich selst einzuführen, d. h. Bourgeois zu werden. Mit einem Wort, sie schafft sich eine Welt nach ihrem eigenen Bilde.

120

[26]Through their command of a universal market, they have given a cosmopolitan tendency to the production and consumption of all countries. To the great regret of the Reactionists, the Bourgeoisie have deprived the modern Industrial System of its national foundation. The old national manufactures have been, or are being, destroyed. They are superseded by new modes of industry, whose introduction is becoming a vital question for all civilized nations, whose raw materials are not indigenous, but are brought from the remotest countries, and whose products are not merely consumed in the home market, but throughout the whole world. Instead of the old national wants, supplied by indigenous products, we everywhere find new wants, which can be supplied only by the productions of the remotest lands and climes. Instead of the old local and national feeling of self-sufficingness and isolation, we find a universal intercourse, an inter-dependence, amongst nations. The same fact obtains in the intellectual world. The intellectual productions of individual nations tend to become common property. National one-sidedness and mental limitation are fast becoming impossible, and a universal literature is being formed from the numerous national and local literatures. [27]Through the incessant improvements in machinery and the means of locomotion, the Bourgeoisie draw the most barbarous savages into the magic circle of civilization. Cheap goods are their artillery for battering down Chinese walls, and their means of overcoming the obstinate hatred entertained towards strangers by semi-civilized nations. The Bourgeoisie, by their competition, compel, under penalty of inevitable ruin, the universal adoption of their system of production; they force all nations to accept what is called civilization—to become Bourgeois—and thus the middle class fashions the world anew after its own image.

[26]The bourgeoisie has through its exploitation of the world-market given a cosmopolitan character to production and consumption in every country. To the great chagrin of Re-actionists, it has drawn out from under the feet of industry the national ground on which it stood. All old-established national industries have been destroyed or are daily being destroyed. They are dislodged by new industries, whose introduction becomes a life and death question for all civilised nations, by industries that no longer work up indigenous raw material but raw material drawn from the remotest zones; industries whose products are consumed, not only at home, but in every quarter of the globe. In place of the old wants, satisfied by the productions of the country, we find new wants, requiring for their satisfaction the products of distant lands and climes. In place of the old local and national seclusion and self-sufficiency, we have intercourse in every direction, universal inter-dependence of nations. And as in material so also in intellectual production. The intellectual creations of individual nations become common property. National one-sidedness and narrow-mindedness become more and more impossible, and from the numerous national and local literatures, there arises a world literature.

[27]The bourgeoisie, by the rapid improvement of a instruments of production, by the immensely facilitated means of communication, draws all, even the most barbarian, nations into civilisation. The cheap prices of its commodities are the heavy artillery with which it batters down all Chinese walls, with which it forces the barbarians intensely obstinate hatred of foreigners to capitulate. It compels all nations, on pain of extinction, tn adopt the bourgeois mode of production; it compels them to introduce what it calls civilisation into their midst, i.e., to become bourgeois themselves. In one word, it creates a world after its own image.

[26]Through the exploitation of the world market the bourgeoisie has given a cosmopolitan form to the production and consumption of all countries. To the great regret of reactionaries, it has pulled industry's national ground from under its feet. The age-old national industries have been destroyed or are daily being destroyed. They are crowded out by new industries, whose introduction becomes a life-and-death question for all civilized nations—by industries that no longer work up domestic raw materials but raw materials from the remotest regions, industries whose products are consumed not only at home but in every part of the world as well. In place of the old wants, satisfied by home-country products, there appear new ones, whose satisfaction requires the products of the farthest lands and climes. In place of the old local and national self-sufficiency and isolation, a many-sided intercourse comes on the scene, a many-sided interdependence of nations. And as in material production, so also in intellectual production. The intellectual products of individual nations become common property. National onesidedness and narrowmindedness become more and more impossible, and out of the many national and local literatures a world literature takes shape.

[27]Through the rapid improvement of all instruments of production, through endlessly facilitating communication, the bourgeoisie drags all nations, even the most barbarian, into civilization. The cheap prices of its com-modities are the heavy artillery with which it levels all Chinese walls to the ground, with which it forces the barbarians' stubbornest anti-foreigner hatred to capitulate. It forces all nations to adopt the mode of production of the bourgeoisie if they do not want to go under; it forces them to introduce so-called civilization at home, i.e., to become bourgeois. In short, it creates a world after its own image.

[28]Die Bourgeoisie hat das Land der Herrschaft der Stadt unterworfen. Sie hat enorme Städte geschaffen, sie hat die Zahl der städtischen Bevölkerung gegenüber der ländlichen in hohem Grade vermehrt, und so einen bedeutenden Theil der Bevölkerung dem Idiotismus des Landlebens entrissen. Wie sie das Land von der Stadt, hat sie die barbarischen und halbbarbarischen Länder von den civilisirten, die Bauernvölker von den Bourgeoisvölkern, den Orient vom Occident abhängig gemacht.

[29]Die Bourgeoisie hebt mehr und mehr die Zersplitterung der Produktionsmittel, des Besitzes und der Bevölkerung auf. Sie hat die Bevölkerung agglomerirt, die Produktionsmittel centralisirt und das Eigenthum in wenigen Händen koncentrirt. Die nothwendige Folge hiervon war die politische Centralisation. Unabhängige, fast nur verbündete Provinzen mit verschiedenen Interessen, Gesetzen, Regierungen und Zöllen wurden zusammengedrängt in Eine Nation, Eine Regierung, Ein Gesetz, Ein nationales Klasseninteresse, Eine Douanenlinie.

[30]Die Bourgeoisie hat in ihrer kaum hundertjährigen Klassenherrschaft massenhaftere und kolossalere Produktionskräfte geschaffen als alle vergangenen Generationen zusammen. Unterjochung der Naturkräfte, Maschinerie, Anwendung der Chemie auf Industrie und Ackerbau, Dampfschiffahrt, Eisenbahnen, elektrische Telegraphen, Urbarmachung ganzer Welttheile, Schiffbarmachung der Flüsse, ganze aus dem Boden hervorgestampfte Bevölkerungen—welch früheres Jahrhundert ahnte, daß solche Produktionskräfte im Schooß der gesellschaftlichen Arbeit schlummerten.

[28]The Bourgeoisie has subjected the *country* to the ascendancy of the *town*; it has created enormous cities, and, by causing an immense increase of population in the manufacturing, as compared with the agricultural districts, has saved a great part of every people from the idiotism of country life. Not only have the Bourgeoisie made the country subordinate to the town, they have made barbarous and half-civilized tribes dependent on civilized nations, the agricultural on the manufacturing nations, the East on the West. [29]The division of property, of the means of production, and of population, vanish under the Bourgeois régime. It agglomerates population, it centralises the means of production, and concentrates property in the hands of a few individuals. Political centralization is the necessary consequence of this. Independent provinces, with different interests, each of them surrounded by a separate line of customs and under separate local governments, are brought together as one nation, under the same government, laws, line of customs, tariff, the same national class-interest. [30]The Bourgeois regime has only prevailed for about a century, but dnring that time it has called into being more gigantic powers of production than all preceding generations put together. The subjection of the elements of nature, the developement of machinery, the application of chemistry to agriculture and manufactures, railways, electric telegraphs, steam ships, the clearing and cultivation of whole continents, canalizing of thousands of rivers; large populations, whole industrial armies, springing up, as if by magic! What preceding generation ever dreamed of these productive powers slumbering within society?

[28]The bourgeoisie has subjected the country, to the rule of the towns ,It has created enormous cites, has greatly increased the urban population as compared with the rural, and has thus rescued a considerable part of the population from the idiocy of rural life. Just as it has made the country dependent on the towns,so it has made barbarian and semi-barbarian countries dependent on the civilised ones, nations of peasants on nations of bourgeois, the East on the West.

[29]The bourgeoisie keeps more and more doing away with the scattered state of the population, of the means of production, and of property. It has agglomerated population, centralised means of production, and has concentrated property in a few hands. The necessary consequence of this was political centralisation. Independent or but loosely connected provinces, with separate interests, laws, governments and systems of taxation, became lumped together into one nation, with one government one code of laws, one national class-interest, one frontier and one customs-tariff.

[30]The bourgeoisie, during its rule of scarce one hundred years, has created more massive and more colossal productive forces than have a preceding generations together. Subjection of Nature's forces to man, machinery, application of chemistry to industry and agriculture, steam-navigation, railways, electric telegraphs, clearing of whole continents for cultivation, canalization of rivers, whole populations conjured out of the ground--what earlier century had even a presentiment that such productive forces slumbered in the lap of social labour?

[28] The bourgeoisie has subjected the countryside to the rule of the town. It has created enormous cities;   it has greatly increased the size of the urban population as compared with the rural, and thus has rescued a significant part of the population from the privatized isolation of rural lide. Just as it has made the country dependent on the town, so it has made the barbarian and semibarbarian countries dependent on the civilized ones, the peasant nations on the bourgeois nations, the Orient on the Occident.

[29]The bourgeoisie more and more does away with the dispersal of the means of production, of ownership, and of the population. It has agglomerated the population, centralized the means of production, and concentrated property in a few hands. The necessary consequence of this was political centralization.   Independent provinces, provinces scarcely more than confederated together, provinces with different interests, laws, governments, and tariff system, were consolidated into one nation, one government, one law code, one national class interest, one customs boundary.

[30]During its class rule of scarcely a hundred years, the bourgeoisie has created more massive and more colossal productive forces than have all past generations together. Subjugation of nature's forces, machinery, application of chemistry to industry and agriculture, steam navigation, railways, electric telegraphs, clearing of whole continents for cultivation, making rivers navigable, whole populations conjured up out of the ground what earlier century suspected that such productive forces slumbered in the womb of social labor?

[31]Wir haben aber gesehen: Die Produktions-
und Verkehrsmittel, auf deren Grundlage sich die
Bourgeoisie heranbildete, wurden in der feudalen
Gesellschaft erzeugt. Auf einer gewissen Stufe
der Entwicklung dieser Produktions- und
Verkehrsmittel entsprachen die Verhältnisse,
worin die feudale Gesellschaft producirte und
austauschte, die feudale Organisation der Agrikultur und Manufaktur, mit einem Wort die
feudalen Eigenthums-Verhältnisse den schon
entwickelten Produktivkräften nich mehr. Sie
hemmten die Produktion statt sie zu fördern. Sie
verwandelten sich in eben so viele Fesseln. Sie
mußten gesprengt werden, sie wurden gesprengt.
[32]An ihre Stelle trat die freie Konkurreuz mit
der ihr angemessenen gesellschaftlichen und
politischen Konstitution, mit der ökonomischen
und politischen Herrschaft der Bourgeois-Klasse.
[33]Unter unsren Augen geht eine ähnliche
Bewegung vor. Die bürgerlichen Produktions-
und Verkehrs-Verhältnisse, die bürgerlichen
Eigenthums-Verhältnisse, die moderne bürgerliche Gesellschaft, die so gewaltige Produktions-
und Verkehrsmittel hervorgezaubert hat, gleicht
dem Hexenmeister, der die unterirdischen
Gewalten nicht mehr zu beherrschen vermag, die
er herauf beschwor. Seit Dezennien ist die
Geschichte der Industrie und des Handels nur
noch die Geschichte der Empörung der
modernen Produktivkräfte gegen die modernen
Produktions-Verhältnisse, gegen die Eigenthums-
Verhätnisse, welche die Lebens-Bedingungen der
Bourgeoisie und ihrer Herrschaft sind. Es genügt
die Handelskrisen zu nennen, welche in ihrer
periodischen Wiederkehr immer drohenden die
Existenz der ganzen bürgerlichen Gesellschaft in
Frage stellen. In den Handelskrisen wird ein
großer Theil nicht nur der erzeugten Produkte,
sondern sogar der bereits geschaffenen Produktivkräfte regelmäßig vernichtet. In der Krisen
bricht eine gesellschaftliche Epidemie aus, welche
allen früheren Epochen als ein Widersinn
erschienen wäre—die Epidemie der Ueberproduktion. Die Gesellschaft findet sich plötzlich
in einen Zustand momentaner Barbarei zurück-
versetzt;

[31]We have seen that these means of
production and traffic which served as the
foundation of middle-class developement,
originated in feudal times. At a certain point in
the evolution of these means, the arrangements
under which feudal society produced and
exchanged the feudal organization of
agriculture and industrial production,—in a
word, the feudal conditions of property—no
longer corresponded to the increased
productive power. These conditions now
became a hindrance to it,—they were turned
into fetters which had to be broken, and they
were broken. [32]They were superseded by
unlimited competition, with a suitable social
and political constitution, with the economical
and political supremacy of the middle class.
[33]At the present moment a similar movement is
going on before our eyes. Modern middle-class
society, which has revolutionised the conditions
of property, and called forth such colossal
means of production and traffic, resembles the
wizard who evoked the powers of darkness, but
could neither master them, nor yet get rid of
them when they had come at his bidding. The
history of manufactures and commerce has
been for many years the history of the revolts of
modern productive power against the modern
industrial system—against the modern
conditions of property—which are vital
conditions, not only of the supremacy of the
middle-class, but of its very existence. It
suffices to mention the commercial crises
which, in each of their periodical occurrences,
more and more endanger the existence of
middle-class society. In such a crisis, not only
is a quantity of industrial products destroyed,
but a large portion of the productive power
itself. A social epidemic breaks out, the
epidemic of over-production, which would
have appeared a contradiction in terms to all
previous generations. Society finds itself
suddenly thrown back into momentary
barbarism;

[31]We see then: the means of production and of exchange on whose foundation the bourgeoisie built itself up, were generated in feudal society. At a certain stage in the development of these means of production and of exchange, the conditions under which feudal society produced and exchanged, the feudal organisation of agriculture and manufacturing industry, in one word, the feudal relations of property became no longer compatible with the already developed productive forces; they became so many fetters. They had to be burst asunder; they were burst asunder.

[32]Into their place stepped free competition accompanied by a social and political constitution adapted to it and by the economical and political sway of the bourgeois class.

[33]A similar movement is going on before our own eyes. Modern bourgeois society with its relations of production, of exchange and of property, a society that has conjured up such gigantic means of production and of exchange, is like the sorcerer, who is no longer able to control the powers of the nether world whom he has called up by his spells. For many a decade past the history of industry and commerce is but the history of the revolt of modern productive forces against modern conditions of production against the property relations that are the conditions for the existence of the bourgeoisie and of its rule. It is enough to mention the commercial crises that by their periodical return put on its trial each time more threateningly, the existence of the entire bourgeois society. In these crises a great part not only of the existing products, but also of the previously created productive forces, are periodically destroyed. In these crises there breaks out an epidemic that in an earlier epochs, would have seemed an absurdity—the epidemic of over-production. Society suddenly finds itself put back into a state of momentary barbarism;

[31]We have, in any case, seen that the means of production and intercourse on whose basis the bourgeoisie was built up were generated in feudal society. At a certain stage in the development of these means of production and intercourse, the conditions under which feudal society produced and exchanged, the feudal organization of agriculture and manufacture, in short, the feudal relations of property, no longer corresponded with the already developed productive forces. They hampered production instead of furthering it. They turned into so many fetters. They had to be burst asunder; they were burst asunder.

[32]Into their place stepped free competition along with the social and political constitution appropriate to it, along with the economic and political rule of the bourgeois class.

[33]A similar movement is going on before our eyes. The bourgeois relations of production and intercourse, bourgeois property relations, the modern bourgeois society that has conjured up such mighty means of production and intercourse—this is like the sorcerer who is no longer able to control the subterranean powers that he has called up. For decades the history of industry and commerce has been only the history of the revolt of the modern productive forces against the modern relations of production, against the property relations that are the conditions of existence for the bourgeoisie and its rule. It is enough to mention the commercial crises which, in their periodic recurrence, always threateningly call into question the existence of the entire bourgeois society. In these commercial crises a large part not only of the products that had been made but even of the previously created productive forces are regularly destroyed. In these crises a societal epidemic breaks out that would have seemed an absurdity to all earlier epochs—the epidemic of overproduction. Society suddenly finds itself set back to a condition of temporary barbarism;

eine Hungersnoth, ein allgemeiner Verwüstungs-
krieg scheinen ihr alle Lebensmittel abgeschnitten
zu haben; die Industrie, der Handel scheinen
vernichtet, und warum? Weil sie zu viel Civilisation, zu viel Lebensmittel, zu viel Industrie, zu
viel Handel besitzt. Die Produktivkräfte, die ihr
zur Verfügung stehen, dienen nicht mehr zur
Beförderung der bürgerlichen Civlisation und der
bürgerlichen Eigenthums-Verhältnisse; im
Gegentheil, sie sind zu gewaltig für diese Verhältnisse geworden, sie werden von ihnen gehemmt,
und so bald sie dies Hemmniß überwinden,
bringen sie die ganze bürgerliche Gesellschaft in
Unordnung, gefährden sie die Existenz des
bürgerlichen Eigenthums. Die bürgerlichen
Verhältnisse sind zu eng geworden um den von
ihnen erzeugten Reichthum zu fassen.—
Wodurch überwindet die Bourgeoisie die Krisen?
Einerseits durch die erzwungene Vernichtung
einer Masse von Produktivkräften; andererseits
durch die Eroberung neuer Märkte, und die
gründlichere Ausbeutung der alten Märkte.
Wodurch also? Dadurch, daß sie allseitigere und
gwaltigere Krisen vorbereitet und die Mittel, den
Krisen vorzubeugen, vermindert.

[34]Die Waffen, womit die Bourgeoisie den
Feudalismus zu Boden geschlagen hat, richten
sich jetzt gegen die Bourgeoisie selbst.

[35]Aber die Bourgeoisie hat nicht nur die
Waffen geschmiedet, die ihr den Tod bringen;
sie hat auch die Männer gezeugt, die diese
Waffen führen werden — die modernen Arbeiter,
die Proletarier.

[36]In demselben Maße, worin sich die
Bourgeoisie, d. h. das Kapital entwickelt, in dem-
selben Maße entwickelt sich das Proletariat, die
Klasse der modernen Arbeiter, die nur so lange
leben als sie Arbeit finden, und die nur so lange
Arbeit finden, als ihre Arbeit das Kapital ver-
mehrt. Diese Arbeiter, die sich stückweis ver-
kaufen müssen, sind eine Waare wie jeder andre
Handelsartikel, und daher gleichmäßig allen
Wechselfällen der Konkurrenz, allen
Schwankungen des Marktes ausgesetzt.

126

a famine, a devastating war, seems to have
deprived it of the means of subsistence;
manufactures and commerce appear
annihilated,—and why? Because society
possesses too much civilization, too many of the
necessaries of life, too much industry, too much
commerce. The productive power possessed
by society no longer serves as the instrument of
middle-class civilization, of the middle-class
conditions of property; on the contrary, this
power has become too mighty for this system,
it is forcibly confined by these conditions; and
whenever it surpasses these artificial limitations,
it deranges the system of Bourgeois society, it
endangers the existence of Bourgeois property.
The social system of the middle-class has
become too small to contain the riches it has
called into being. How does the middle-class
try to withstand these commercial crises? On
the one hand, by destroying masses of
productive power; on the other, by opening up
new markets, and using up the old ones more
thoroughly. That is, they prepare the way for
still more universal and dangerous crises, and
reduce the means of withstanding them. [34]The
weapons with which the middle-class overcame
feudalism are now turned against the middle-
class itself. [35]And the Bourgeoisie have not only
prepared the weapons for their own
destruction, they have also called into existence
the men that are destined to wield these
weapons, namely, the modern working men,
the Proletarians.

[36]The developement of the Proletariat has
kept pace with the developement of the middle-
class— that is, with the development of capital;
for the modern working men can live only as
long as they find work, and they find it only as
long as their labour increases capital. These
workers, who must sell themselves by
piecemeal to the highest bidder, are a
commodity like other articles of commerce,
and, therefore, are equally subject to all the
variations of the market, and the effects of
competition.

it appears as if a famine, a universal war of devastation had cut off the supply of every means of subsistence; industry and commerce seem to be destroyed; and why? Because there is too much civilisation, too much means of subsistence, too much industry, too much commerce. The productive forces at the disposal of society no longer tend to further the development of the conditions of bourgeois property; on the contrary, they have become too powerful for these conditions, by which they are fettered, and so soon as they over-come these fetters, they bring disorder into the whole of bourgeois society, endanger the existence of bourgeois property. The conditions of bourgeois society are too narrow to comprise the wealth created by them. And how does the bourgeoisie get over these crises? On the one hand by enforced destruction of a mass of productive forces; on the other by the conquest of new markets, and by the more thorough exploitation of the old ones. That is to say, by paving the way for more extensive and more destructive crises, and by diminishing the means whereby crises are prevented.

[34]The weapons with which the bourgeoisie felled feudalism to the ground are now turned against the bourgeoisie itself.

[35]But not only has the bourgeoisie forged the weapons that bring death to itself; it has also called into existence the men who are to wield those weapons—the modern working-class—the proletarians.

[36]In proportion as the bourgeoisie, i.e. capital, is developed, in the same proportion is the proletariat the modern working-class, developed, a class of labourers, who live only so long as they find work, and who find work only so long as their labour increases capital. These labourers, who must sell themselves piecemeal are a commodity like every other article of commerce, and are consequently exposed to all the vicissitudes of competition, to all the fluctuations of the market.

a famine, a universal devastating war seem to have cut off all means of subsistence; industry and commerce seem to be destroyed. And why? Because society possesses too much civilization, too much of the means of subsistence, too much industry, too much commerce. The productive forces that are at its disposal no longer serve to further bourgeois civilization and bourgeois property relations. On the contrary, they have become too powerful for these relations, they are impeded by them; and as soon as they overcome this impediment, they bring the whole of bourgeois society into disorder, they endanger the existence of bourgeois property. Bourgeois relations have become too narrow to encompass the wealth created by them. —By what means does the bourgeoisie overcome these crises? On the one hand, by the enforced destruction of a mass of productive forces; on the other, by the conquest of new markets and the more thorough exploitation of the old markets. By what means, then? By preparing the way for more universal and more violent crises, and by diminishing the means of preventing crises.

[34]The weapons with which the bourgeoisie struck feudalism down are now directed against the bourgeoisie itself.

[35]But the bourgeoisie has not only forged the weapons that deal death to it; it has also brought into existence the men who will wield these weapons—the modern workers, the *proletarians*.

[36]In proportion as the bourgeoisie, i.e., capital, develops, so also does the proletariat, the class of modern workers, who live only so long as they find work and who find work only so long as their labor augments capital. These workers, who must sell themselves piecemeal, are a commodity like every other article of commerce and are consequently equally exposed to all vicissitudes of competition and to all fluctuations of the market.

[37]Die Arbeit der Proletarier hat durch die Ausdehnung der Maschinerie und die Theilung der Arbeit allen selbstständigen Charakter und damit allen Reiz für den Arbeiter verloren. Er wird ein bloßes Zubehör der Maschine, von dem nur der einfachste, eintönigste, am leichtesten erlernbare Handgriff verlangt wird. Die Kosten die der Arbeiter verursacht, beschränken sich daher fast nur auf die Lebensmittel, die er zu seinem Unterhalt und zur Fortpflanzung seiner Race bedarf. Der Preis einer Waare, also auch der Arbeit ist aber gleich ihren Produktionskosten. In demselben Maße, in dem die Widerwärtigkeit der Arbeit wächst, nimmt daher der Lohn ab. Noch mehr, in demselben Maße wie Maschinerie und Theilung der Arbeit zunehmen, in demselben Maße nimmt auch die Masse der Arbeit zu, sei es durch Vermehrung der Arbeitsstunden, sei es durch Vermehrung der in einer gegebenen Zeit geforderten Arbeit, beschleunigten Lauf der Maschinen u. s. w.

[38]Die Moderne Industrie hat die kleine Werkstube des patriarchalischen Meisters in die große Fabrik des industriellen Kapitalisten verwandelt. Arbeiter-Massen in der Fabrik zusammengedrängt, werden soldatisch organisirt. Sie werden als gemeine Industriesoldaten unter die Aufsicht einer vollständigen Hierarchie von Unteroffizieren und Offizieren gestellt. Sie sind nicht nur Knechte der Bourgeoisklasse, des Bourgeoisstaates, sie sind täglich und stündlich geknechtet von der Maschine, von dem Aufseher, und vor Allem von dem einzelnen fabrizirenden Bourgeois selst. Diese Despotie ist um so kleinlicher, gehässiger, erbitternder, je offener sie den Erwerb als ihren letzten Zweck proklamirt.

[39]Je weniger die Handarbeit Geschicklichkeit und Kraftäußerung erheischt, d. h. je mehr die moderne Industrie sich entwickelt, desto mehr wird die Arbeit der Männer durch die der Weiber und Kinder verdrängt. Geschlechts- und Alters-Unterschiede haben keine gesellschaftliche Geltung mehr für die Arbeiterklasse. Es gibt nur noch Arbeitinstrumente, die je nach Alter und Geschlecht verschiedene Kosten machen.

[37]Through the division of labour and the extension of machinery, work has lost its individual character, and therefore its interest for the operative. He has become merely an accessory to, or a part of the machine, and all that is required of him is a fatiguing, monotonous, and merely mechanical operation. The expense the wages-slave causes the capitalist is, therefore, equal to the cost of his keep and of the propagation of his race. The price of labour, like that of any other commodity, is equal to the cost of its production. Therefore wages decrease in proportion as the work to be performed becomes mechanical, monotonous, fatiguing, and repulsive. Further, in proportion as the application of machinery and the division of labour increase, the amount of work increases also, whether it be through an increase in the hours of work, or in the quantity of it demanded in a given time, or through an increased rate of velocity of the machinery employed.

[38]The modern industrial system has changed the little shop of the primitive patriarchal master into the large factory of the Bourgeois—capitalist. Masses of operatives are brought together in one establishment, and organized like a regiment of soldiers; they are placed under the superintendence of a complete hierarchy of officers and sub-officers. They are not only the slaves of the whole middle-class (as a body), of the Bourgeois political régime,—they are the daily and hourly slaves of the machinery, of the foreman, of each individual manufacturing Bourgeois. This despotism is the more hateful, contemptible, and aggravating, because gain is openly proclaimed to be its only object and aim. [39]In proportion as labour requires less physical force and less dexterity—that is, in proportion to the development of the modern industrial system—is the substitution of the labour of women and children for that of men. The distinctions of sex and age have no *social* meaning for the Proletarian class. Proletarians are merely so many instruments which cost more or less, according to their sex and age.

[37]Owing to the extensive use of machinery and to division of labour, the work of the proletarians has lost all individual character and, consequently, all charm for the workman. He becomes an appendage of the machine, and it is only the most simple, most monotonous, and most easily acquired knack, that is required of him. Hence, the cost of production of a workman is restricted, almost entirely, to the means of subsistence that he requires for his maintenance, and for the propagation of his race. But the price of a commodity, and therefore also of labour, is equal to its cost of production. In proportion, therefore, as the repulsiveness of the work increases, the wage decreases. Nay more, in proportion as the use of machinery and division of labour increases, in the same proportion the burden of toil also increases, whether by prolongation of the working hours, by increase of the work exacted in a given time, or by increased speed of the machinery, etc.

[38]Modern industry has converted the little workshop of the patriarchal master into the great factory of the industrial capitalist. Masses of labourers, crowded into the factory, are organised like soldiers. As privates of the industrial army they are placed under the command of a perfect hierarchy of officers and sergeants. Not only are they slaves of the bourgeois class, and of the bourgeois State, they are daily and hourly, enslaved by the machine, by the over-looker, and, above all, by the individual bourgeois manufacturer himself. The more openly this despotism proclaims gain to be its end and aim, the more petty, the more hateful and the more embittering it is.

[39]The less the skill and exertion of strength implied in manual labour, in other words, the more modern industry becomes developed, the more is the labour of men superseded by that of women. Differences of age and sex have no longer any distinctive social validity for the working class. All are instruments of labour, more or less expensive to use, according to their age and sex.

[37]Through the spread of machinery and the division of labor, the labor of the proletarians has lost all independent character and hence all attractiveness for the worker. He becomes a mere appendage of the machine; only the simplest, most monotonous, and most easily learned sort of manipulation is required of him. The costs that a worker involves are therefore restricted almost entirely to the means of subsistence needed for his maintenance and for the propagation of his kind. The price of a commodity, hence also the price of labor, is however equal to its cost of production. Consequently, in proportion as the work becomes more disagreeable, wages go down. More than that: in proportion as there is an increase in machinery and division of labor, there is also an increase in the amount of labor, whether by augmentation of the working hours, augmentation of the work exacted in a given time, speeded-up operation of the machines, etc.

[38]Modern industry has transformed the little workshop of the patriarchal master into the big factory of the industrial capitalist. Masses of workers, crowded together in the factory, are organized like soldiers. As common soldiers of industry, they are placed under the control of a complete hierarchy of commissioned and noncommissioned officers. They are not only thralls of the bourgeois class and of the bourgeois state, they are daily and hourly held in thralldom by the machine, by the overseer, and above all by the individual bourgeois manufacturer himself. This despotism is all the more petty, hateful, and embittering the more openly it proclaims that gain is its final aim.

[39]In proportion as manual labor requires less skill and exertion of strength, i.e., the more modern industry develops, the more is the labor of men displaced by that of women and children. Differences in sex and age no longer have any social validity for the working class. There are just instruments of labor that vary in expensiveness depending on age and sex.

[40]Ist die Ausbeutung des Arbeiters durch den Fabrikanten so weit beendigt, daß er seinen Arbeitslohn baar ausgezahlt erhält, so fallen die andern Theile der Bourgeoisie über ihn her, der Hausbesitzer, der Krämer, der Pfandverleiheru.s.w.

[41]Die bisherigen kleinen Mittelstände, die kleinen Industriellen, Kaufleute und Rentiers, die Handwerker und Bauern, alle diese Klassen fallen ins Proletariat hinab, theils dadurch, das ihr kleines Kapital für den Betrieb der großen Industrie nicht ausreicht, und der Konkurrenz mit den größeren Kapitalisten erliegt, theils dadurch, daß ihre Geschicklichkeit von neuen Produktionsweisen entwerthet wird. So rekrutirt sich das Proletariat aus allen Klassen der Bevölkerung.

[42]Das Proletariat macht verschiedene Entwicklungsstufen durch. Sein Kampf gegen die Bourgeoisie beginnt mit seiner Existenz.

[43]Im Anfang kämpfen die einzelnen Arbeiter, dann die Arbeiter einer Fabrik, dann die Arbeiter eines Arbeitszweiges an einen Ort gegen den einzelnen Bourgeois, der sie direkt ausbeutet. Sie richten ihre Angriffe nicht nur gegen die bürgerlichen Produktions-Verhältnisse, sie richten sie gegen die Produktions-Instrumente selbst; sie vernichten die fremden konkurrirenden Waaren, sie zerschlagen die Maschinen, sie stecken die Fabriken in Brand, sie suchen sich die untergegangene Stellung des mittelalterlichen Arbeiters wieder zu erringen.

[44]Auf dieser Stufe bilden die Arbeiter eine über das ganze Land zerstreute und durch die Konkurrenz zersplitterte Masse. Massenhafteres Zusammenhalten der Arbeiter ist noch nicht die Folge ihrer eigenen Vereinigung, sondern die Folge der Vereinigung der Bourgeoisie, die zur Erreichung ihrer eigenen politischen Zwecke das ganze Proletariat in Bewegung setzen muß und es einstweilen noch kann. Auf dieser Stufe bekämpfen die Proletarier also nicht ihre Feinde, sondern die Feinde ihrer Feinde, die Reste der absoluten Monarchie, die Grundeigenthümer, die nicht industriellen Bourgeois, die Kleinbürger. Die ganze geschichtliche Bewegung ist so in den Händen der Bourgeoisie konzentrirt; jeder Sieg, der so errungen wird, ist ein Sieg der Bourgeoisie.

[40]When the using-up of the operative has been so far accomplished by the mill-owner that the former has got his wages, the rest of the Bourgeoisie, householders, shopkeepers, pawnbrokers, &c., fall upon him like so many harpies.

[41]The petty Bourgeoisie, the inferior ranks of the middle-class, the small manufacturers, merchants, tradesmen, and farmers, tend to become Proletarians, partly because their small capital succumbs to the competition of the millionaire, and partly because the modes of production perpetually changing, their peculiar skill loses its value. Thus the Proletariat is recruited from various sections of the population. [42]This Proletarian class passes through many phases of development, but its struggle with the middle-class dates from its birth. [43]At first the struggle is carried on by individual workmen, then by those belonging to a single establishment, then by those of an entire trade in the same locality, against the individuals of the middle-class who directly use them up. They attack not only the middle-class system of production, but even the instruments of production; they destroy machinery and the foreign commodities which compete with their products; they burn down factories, and try to re-attain the position occupied by the producers of the middle ages. [44]At this moment of development, the Proletariat forms a disorganized mass, scattered throughout the country, and divided by competition. A more compact union is not the effect of their own development, but is the consequence of a middle-class union; for the Bourgeoisie requires, and for the moment are still enabled to set the whole Proletariat in motion, for the furtherance of their own political ends; developed in this degree, therefore, the Proletarians do not fight their own enemies, but the enemies of their enemies, the remains of absolute monarchy, the landowners, the non-manufacturing part of the Bourgeoisie and the petty shopocracy. The whole historical movement is thus, as yet, concentrated in the hands of the Bourgeoisie, every victory is won for them.

[40]No sooner is the exploitation of the labourer by the manufacturer, so far, at an end, that he receives his wages in cash, than he is set upon by the other portions of the bourgeoisie, the landlord, the shopkeeper, the pawnbroker, etc.

[41]The lower strata of the Middle class—the small tradespeople, shopkeepers, and retired tradesmen generally, the handicraftsmen and peasants—all these sink gradually into the proletariat, partly because their diminutive capital does not suffice for the scale on which Modern Industry is carried on, and is swamped in the competition with the large capitalists, partly because their specialised skill is rendered worthless by new methods of production. Thus the proletariat is recruited from all classes of the population.

[42]The proletariat goes through various stages of development. With its birth begins its struggle with the bourgeoisie.[43]At first the contest is carried on by individual labourers, then by the workpeople of a factory, then by the operatives of one trade, in one locality, against the individual bourgeois who directly exploits them. They direct their attacks not against the bourgeois conditions of production, but against the instruments of production themselves; they destroy imported wares that compete with their labour, they smash to pieces machinery they set factories ablaze, they seek to restore by force the vanished status of the workman of the Middle Ages.

[44]At this stage the labourers form an incoherent mass scattered over the whole country, and broken up by their mutual competition. If anywhere they unite to form more compact bodies, this is not yet the consequence of their own active union, but of the union of the bourgeoisie, which class, in order to attain its own political ends, is compelled to set the whole proletariat in motion, and is moreover yet, for a time able to do so. At this stage, therefore, the proletarians do not fight their enemies, but the enemies of their enemies, the remnants of absolute monarchy, the landowners, the non-industrial bourgeois, the petty bourgeoisie. Thus the whole historical movement is concentrated in the hands of the bourgeoisie; every victory so obtained is a victory for the bourgeoisie.

[40]When the exploitation of the worker by the manufacturer is so far at an end that he receives his wages in cash, then the other sections of the bourgeoisie set upon him: the landlord, the shopkeeper, the pawnbroker, etc.

[41]The small intermediate strata existing up to now—the small industrials, merchants, and rentiers, the artisans and peasants—all these classes sink down into the proletariat, partly because their small capital is not enough to carry on large-scale industry and succumbs in competition with the larger capitalists, partly because their skills are made worthless by new methods of production. Thus the proletariat is recruited from all classes of the population.

[42]The proletariat goes through various stages of development. Its struggle against the bourgeoisie begins with its own existence.

[43]In the beginning it is individual workers who carry on the struggle, then the workers of a factory, then the workers of a trade in one locality against the individual bourgeois who directly exploits them. They direct their attacks not only against the bourgeois relations of production, they direct them against the instruments of production themselves; they destroy competing foreign commodities, they smash machines, they set factories on fire, they seek to win back for themselves the departed status of the medieval worker.

[44]At this stage the workers form a mass dispersed over the whole country and splintered by competition. More massive amalgamation of the workers is not yet the consequence of their own unification but rather the consequence of the unification of the bourgeoisie, which has to set the whole proletariat in motion in order to attain its own political aims, and can still do so for the time being. At this stage, then, the proletarians are not fighting their own enemies but the enemies of their enemies, the remnants of absolute monarchy, the landowners, the nonindustrial bourgeois, the petty-bourgeois. The whole course of historical development is thus concentrated in the hands of the bourgeoisie; every victory that is so obtained is a victory for the bourgeoisie.

[45]Aber mit der Entwicklung der Industrie vermehrt sich nicht nur das Proletariat; es wird in größeren Massen zusammengedrängt, seine Kraft wächst und es fühlt sie mehr. Die Interessen, die Lebenslagen innerhalb des Proletariats gleichen sich immer mehr aus, indem die Maschinerie mehr und mehr die Unterschiedene der Arbeit verwischt und den Lohn fast überall auf ein gleich niedriges Niveau herabdrückt. Die wachsende Konkurrenz der Bourgeois unter sich und die daraus herhorgehenden Handelskrisen machen den Lohn der Arbeiter immer schwankender; die immer rascher sich entwickelnde, unaufhörliche Verbesserung der Maschinerie macht ihre ganze Lebensstellung immer unsicherer; immer mehr nehmen die Kollisionen zwischen dem einzelnen Arbeiter und dem einzelnen Bourgeois den Charakter von Kollisionen zweier Klassen an. Die Arbeiter beginnen damit, Coalitionen gegen die Bourgeois zu bilden; sie treten zusammen zur Behauptung ihres Arbeitslohns. Sie stiften selbst dauernde Associationen, um sich für diese gelegentlichen Empörungen zu verproviantiren. Stellenweis bricht der Kampf in Emeuten aus.

[46]Von Zeit zu Zeit siegen die Arbeiter, aber nur vorübergehend. Das eigentliche Resultat ihrer Kämpfe ist nicht der unmittelbare Erfolg, sondern die immer weiter um sich greifende Vereinigung der Arbeiter. Sie wird befördert durch die wachsenden Kommunikationsmittel, die von der großen Industrie erzeugt werden und die Arbeiter der verschiedenen Lokalitäten mit einander in Verbindung setzen. Es bedarf aber blos der Verbindung, um die vielen Lokalkämpfe von überall gleichem Charakter, zu einem nationalen, zu einem Klassenkampf zu centralisiren. Jeder Klassenkampf aber ist ein politischer Kampf. Und ide Vereinigung, zu der die Bürger des Mittelalters mit ihren Vicinalwegen Jahrhunderte bedurften, bringen die modernen Proletarier mit den Eisenbahnen in wenigen Jahren zu Stande.

[45]But the increase of the Proletariat keeps pace with the evolution of production; the working-class is brought together in masses, and learns its own strength. The interests and position of different trades become similar, because machinery tends to reduce wages to the same level, and to make less and less difference between the various kinds of labour. The increasing competition amongst the middle-class, and the commercial crises consequent thereupon, make wages always more variable, while the incessant improvements in machinery make the position of the Proletarians more and more uncertain, and the collisions betweeen the individual workmen and the individual masters, assume more and more the character of collisions between two classes. The workmen commence to form trades-unions against the masters; they turn out, to prevent threatened reductions in their wages. They form associations to help each other in, and to provision themselves for these occasional revolts. Here and there the struggle takes the form of riots. [46]From time to time the Proletarians are, for a moment, victorious, yet the result of their struggle is not an immediate advantage, but the ever increasing union amongst their class. This union is favoured by the facility of communication under the modern industrial system, whereby the Proletarians belonging to the remotest localities are placed in connection with each other. But connection is all that is wanting to change innumerable local struggles, having all the same character, into one national struggle—into a battle of classes. Every battle between different classes is a political battle, and the union, which it took the burghers of the middle ages centuries to bring about, by means of their few and awkward roads, can be accomplished in a few years by the modern Proletarians, by means of railways and steamships.

[45]But with the development of industry the proletariat not only increases in number; it becomes concentrated in greater masses, its strength grows, and it feels that strength more. The various interests and conditions of life within the ranks of the proletariat are more and more equalised, in proportion as machinery obliterates all distinctions of labour, and nearly everywhere reduces wages to the same low level. The growing competition among the bourgeois, and the resulting commercial crises, make the wages of the worker ever more fluctuating. The unceasing improvement of machinery, ever more rapidly developing, makes their livelihood more and more precarious; the collisions between individual workmen and individual bourgeois take more and more the character of collisions between two classes. Thereupon the workers begin to form combinations (Trades' Unions) against the bourgeois; they club together in order to keep up the rate of wages; they found permanent associations in order to make provision beforehand for these occasional revolts. Here and there the contest breaks out into riots.

[46]Now and then the workers are victorious, but only for a time. The real fruit of their battles lies, not in the immediate result, but in the ever expanding union of the workers. This union is helped on by the improved means of communication that are created by modern industry, and that place the workers of different localities in contact with one another. It was just this contact that was needed to centralise the numerous local struggles, all of the same character, into one national struggle between classes. But every class struggle is a political struggle. And that union, to attain which the burghers of the Middle Ages, with their miserable highways, required centuries, the modern proletarians, thanks to railways, achieve in a few years.

[45]But with the development of industry the proletariat not only increases in numbers, it is compacted into larger masses; its strength grows, and it feels its strength more. The interests and the conditions of life inside the proletariat are increasingly homogenized, as machinery more and more obliterates distinctions of labor and depresses wages nearly every where to similarly low levels. The growing competition among the bourgeois and the commercial crises resulting therefrom make the wages of the workers ever more fluctuating; the unceasing improvement of machinery, developing faster and faster, makes their whole position in life ever more insecure; more and more the collisions between individual workers and individual bourgeois take on the character of collisions between two classes. The workers thereupon begin to form combinations against the bourgeois; they get together in order to maintain their wages. They even set up ongoing associations in order to ensure supplies for these occasional revolts. Here and there the struggle breaks out into riots.

[46]From time to time the workers are victorious, but only transitorily. The real result of their struggles is not the immediate outcome but the ever-wider spreading unification of the workers. This unification is furthered by the growing means of communication that are created by large-scale industry and that place the workers of different localities in contact with one another. But it was simply this contact that was needed to centralize the many local struggles, everywhere similar in character, into a national struggle, a class struggle. Every class struggle, however, is a political struggle. And the unification which took centuries for the burghers of the Middle Ages with their poor local roads is brought about in a few years by the modern proletariat with railways.

[47]Diese Organisation der Proletarier zur Klasse, und damit zur politischen Partei, wird jeden Augenblick wieder gesprengt durch die Conkurrenz unter den Arbeitern selbst. Aber sie ersteht immer wieder, stärker, fester, mächtiger. Sie erzwingt die Anerkennung einzelner Interessen der Arbeiter in Gesetzesform, indem sie die Spaltungen der Bourgeoisie unter sich benutzt. So die Zehnstundenbill in England.

[48]Die Kollisionen der alten Gesellschaft überhaupt fördern mannichfach den Entwicklungsgang des Proletariats. Die Bourgeoisie befindet sich in fortwährendem Kampf; anfangs gegen die Aristokratie; später gegen die Theile der Bourgeoisie selbst, deren Interessen mit dem Fortschritt der Industrie in Widerspruch gerathen; stets gegen die Bourgeoisie aller auswärtigen Länder. In allen diesen Kämpfen sieht sie sich genöthigt an das Proletariat zu appelliren, seine Hülfe in Anspruch zu nehmen und es so in die politische Bewegung hineinzureißen. Sie selbst führt also dem Proletariat ihre eigenen Bildungselemente, d. h. Waffen gegen sich selbst zu.

[49]Es werden ferner, wie wir sahen, durch den Fortschritt der Industrie ganze Bestandtheile der herrschenden Klasse in's Proletariat hinabgeworfen oder wenigstens in ihren Lebensbedingungen bedroht. Auch sie führen dem Proletariat eine Masse Bildungselemente zu.

[50]In Zeiten endlich wo der Klassenkampf sich der Entscheidung nähert, nimmt der Auflösungsprozeß innerhalb der herrschenden Klasse, innerhalb der ganzen alten Gesellschaft, einen so heftigen, so grellen Charakter an, daß ein kleiner Theil der herrschenden Klasse sich von ihr lossagt und sich der revolutionären Klasse anschließt, der Klasse, welche die Zukunft in ihren Händen trägt. Wie daher früher ein Theil des Adels zur Bourgeoisie überging, so geht jetzt ein Theil der Bourgeoisie zum Proletariat über, und namentlich ein Theil der Bourgeois-Ideologen, welche zum theoretischen Verständniß der ganzen geschichtlichen Bewegung sich hinaufgearbeitet haben.

134

[47]This organisation of the Proletarians into a class, and therewith into a political party, is incessantly destroyed by the competitive principle. Yet it always reappears, and each time it is stronger and more extensive. It compels the legal acknowledgment of detached Proletarian rights, by profiting of the divisions in the *bourgeois* camp. For example, the Ten Hours' Bill in England. [48]The struggles of the ruling classes amongst themselves are favourable to the development of the Proletariat. The middle-class has always been in a state of perpetual warfare—first, against the aristocracy; and then against that part of itself whose interests are opposed to the further evolution of the industrial system; and, thirdly, against the *bourgeoisie* of other countries. During all of these battles, the middle-class has ever been obliged to appeal for help to the Proletarians, and so to draw the latter into the political movement. This class, therefore, has armed the Proletarians against itself, by letting them share in its own means of cultivation. [49]Further, as we have already seen, the evolution of the industrial system has thrown a large portion of the ruling class into the ranks of the Proletarians, or at least rendered the means of subsistence very precarious for this portion. A new element of progress for the Proletariat. [50]Finally, as the settlement of the class-struggle draws near, the process of dissolution goes on so rapidly within the ruling-class—within the worn-out body politic—that a small fraction of this class separates from it, and joins the revolutionary class, in whose hands lies the future. In the earlier revolutions a part of the *noblesse* joined the *bourgeoisie*; in the present one, a part of the *bourgeoisie* is joining the Proletariat, and particularly a part of the Bourgeois-ideologists, or middle-class thinkers, who have attained a theoretical knowledge of the whole historical movement.

[47]This organisation of the proletarians into a class, and consequently into a political party, is continually being upset again by the competition between the workers themselves. But it ever rises up again, stronger, firmer, mightier. It compels legislative recognition of particular interests of the workers, by taking advantage of the divisions among the bourgeoisie itself. Thus the ten-hours bill in England was carried.

[48]Altogether collisions between the classes of the old society further, in many ways, the course of development of the proletariat. The bourgeoisie finds itself involved in a constant battle. At first with the aristocracy; later on, with those portions of the bourgeoisie itself whose interests have become antagonistic to the progress of industry; at all times, with the bourgeoisie of foreign countries. In all these battles it sees itself compelled to appeal to the proletariat, to ask for its help, and thus, to drag it into the political arena. The bourgeoisie itself therefore, supplies the proletariat with its own elements of political and general education, in other words, it furnishes the proletariat with weapons for fighting the bourgeoisie.

[49]Further, as we have already seen, entire sections of the ruling classes are, by the advance of industry, precipitated into the proletariat or are at least threatened in their conditions of existence. These also supply the proletariat with fresh elements of enlightenment and progress.

[50]Finally, in times when the class-struggle nears the decisive hour, the process of dissolution going on within the ruling class, in fact within the whole range of old society, assumes such a violent, glaring character that a small section of the ruling class cuts itself adrift, and joins the revolutionary class, the class that holds the future in its hands. Just as, therefore, at an earlier period, a section of the nobility went over to the bourgeoisie, so now a portion of the bourgeoisie goes over to the proletariat and in particular, a portion of the bourgeois ideologists who have raised themselves to the level of comprehending theoretically the historical movement as a whole.

[47]This organization of the proletarians into a class, and thereby into a political party, is at every point ruptured again by the competition among the workers themselves. But it always rises up again, stronger, firmer, mightier. It compels the recognition of particular interests of the workers in the form of laws, by making use of divisions inside the bourgeoisie itself. Hence the Ten Hours Bill in England.

[48]Collisions inside the old society, on the whole, further the course of development of the proletariat in many ways. The bourgeoisie is involved in continual struggle: to begin with, against the aristocracy; later, against the sections of the bourgeoisie itself whose interests have come into contradiction with the progress of industry; always, against the bourgeoisie of every foreign country. In all these struggles it finds itself obliged to appeal to the proletariat, to enlist its help, and thus to thrust it into the political movement. The bourgeoisie itself thus supplies the proletariat with its own educational elements, i.e., with weapons against itself.

[49]Furthermore, as we saw, through the advance of industry whole sections of the ruling class are precipitated into the proletariat or at least are threatened in their conditions of existence. These also supply the proletariat with a quantity of educational elements.

[50]Finally, in times when the class struggle nears a decision, the process of dissolution inside the ruling class, inside the whole of the old society, assumes such an intense, glaring character that a small part of the ruling class cuts loose from it and joins the revolutionary class, the class that holds the future in its hands. Thus, just as previously a part of the nobility went over to the bourgeoisie, so now a part of the bourgeoisie goes over to the proletariat, and in particular a part of the bourgeois ideologists who have worked their way up to a theoretical comprehension of the course of historical development as a whole.

[51]Von allen Klassen welche heutzutage der Bourgeoisie gegenüber stehen, ist nur das Proletariat eine wirklich revolutionäre Klasse. Die übrigen Klassen verkommen und gehen unter mit der großen Industrie, das Proletariat ist ihr eigenstes Produkt.

[52]Die Mittelstände, der kleine Industrielle, der kleine Kaufmann, der Handwerker, der Bauer, sie Alle bekämpfen die Bourgeoisie, um ihre Existenz als Mittelstände, vor dem Untergang zu sichern. Sie sind also nicht revolutionär, sondern konservativ. Noch mehr, sie sind reaktionär, denn sie suchen das Rad der Geschichte zurückzudrehen. Sind sie revolutionör, so sind sie es im Hinblick auf den ihnen bevorstehenden Uebergang ins Proletariat, so vertheidigen sie nicht ihre gegenwärtigen, sondern ihre zukünftigen Interessen, so verlassen sie ihren eigenen Standpunkt um sich auf den des Proletariats zu stellen.

[53]Das Lumpenproletariat, diese passive Verfaulung der untersten Schichten der alten Gesellschaft, wird durch eine proletarische Revolution stellenweise in die Bewegung hineingeschleudert, seiner ganzen Lebenslage nach wird es bereitwilliger sein sich zu reaktionären Umtrieben erkaufen zu lassen.

[54]Die Lebensbedingungen der alten Gesellschaft sind schon vernichtet in den Lebensbedingungen des Proletariats. Der Proletarier ist eigenthumslos; sein Verhältniß zu Weib und Kindern hat nichts mehr gemein mit dem bürgerlichen Familienverhältniß; die moderne industrielle Arbeit, die moderne Unterjochung unter das Kapital, dieselbe in England wie in Frankreich, in Amerika wie in Deutschland, hat ihm allen nationalen Charakter abgestreift. Die Gesetze, die Moral, die Religion sind für ihn eben so viele bürgerliche Vorurtheile, hinter denen sich eben so viele bürgerliche Interessen verstecken.

[51]The Proletariat is the only truly revolutionary Class amongst the present enemies of the Bourgeoisie. All the other classes of Society are being destroyed by the modern Industrial system, the Proletariat is its peculiar product. [52]The small manufacturers, shopkeepers, proprietors, peasants, &c., all fight against the Bourgeoisie, in order to defend their position as small Capitalists. They are, therefore, not revolutionary, but conservative. They are even reactionary, for they attempt to turn backwards the chariot wheels of History. When these subordinate classes are revolutionary, they are so with reference to their necessary absorption into the Proletariat; they defend their future, not their present, interests,—they leave their own Class-point of view to take up that of the Proletariat.

[53]The Mob,—this product of the decomposition of the lowest substrata of the old Social system,—is partly forced into the revolutionary Proletarian movement. The social position of this portion of the people makes it, however, in general a ready and venal tool for Reactionist intrigues.

[54]The vital conditions of Society, as at present constituted, no longer exist for the Proletariat. Its very existence, is a flagrant contradiction to those conditions. The Proletarian has no property; the relation in which he stands to his family has nothing in common with Middle-class family relationships; the modern system of industrial labour, the modern slavery of Labour under Capital, which obtains in England as in France, in America as in Germany, has robbed him of his National Character. Law, Morality, Religion, are for him so many Middle-class prejudices, under which so many Middle-class interests are concealed.

[51]Of all the classes that stand face to face with the bourgeoisie to-day, the proletariat alone is a really revolutionary class. The other classes decay and finally disappear in the face of modern industry; the proletariat is its special and essential product.

[52]The lower middle-class the small manufacturer, the shopkeeper, the artisan, the peasant all these fight against the bourgeoisie, to save from extinction their existence as fractions of the middle class. They are therefore not revolutionary but conservative. Nay more, they are reactionary, for they try to roll back the wheel of history. If by chance they are revolutionary, they are so, only in view of their impending transfer into the proletariat, they thus defend not their present, but their future interests, they desert their own standpoint to place themselves at that of the proletariat.

[53]The "dangerous class", the social scum, that passively rotting mass thrown off by the lowest layer of old society, may here and there, be swept into the movement by a proletarian revolution; its conditions of life, however prepare it far more for the part of a bribed tool of reactionary intrigue.

[54]In the conditions of the proletariat those of old society at large are already virtually swamped. The proletarian is without property; his relation to his wife and children has no longer anything in common with the bourgeois family-relations; modern industrial labour, modern subjection to capital, the same in England as in France, in America as in Germany, has striped him of every trace of national character. Law, morality, religion, are to him so many bourgeois prejudices, behind which lurk in ambush just as many bourgeois interests.

[51]Of all the classes that nowadays confront the bourgeoisie, only the proletariat is a really revolutionary class. The other classes decay and go under, thanks to large-scale industry; the proletariat is its most characteristic product.

[52]The intermediate strata—the small industrial, the small merchant, the artisan, the peasant—all these fight against the bourgeoisie in order to safeguard from ruin their own existence as intermediate strata. They are therefore not revolutionary but conservative. More than that: they are reactionary, for they seek to turn back the wheel of history. When they are revolutionary, they are so in view of their impending passing-over into the proletariat; thus they defend not their present but their future interests, thus they give up their own standpoint to adopt the proletariat's.

[53]The lumpenproletariat, that passive putrefaction of the lowest strata of the old society, is here and there swept into the current of development by a proletarian revolution; in line with its whole life-situation it will more readily let itself be bought up for reactionary machinations.

[54]The conditions of existence of the old society are already nullified in the conditions of existence of the proletariat. The proletarian is propertyless; his relation to wife and children has nothing more in common with the bourgeois family relationship; modern industrial labor and modern subjection to capital, which are the same in England as in France and in America as in Germany, have stripped him of all national character. To him, laws, morality, religion are so many bourgeois prejudices, with bourgeois interests concealed behind each of them.

[55]Alle früheren Klassen, die sich die Herrschaft eroberten, suchten ihre schon erworbene Lebensstellung zu sichern, indem sie die ganze Gesellschaft den Bedingungen ihres Erwerbs unterwarfen. Die Proletarier können sich die gesellschaftlichen Produktivkräfte nur erobern, indem sie ihre eigene bisherige Aneignungsweise und damit die ganze bisherige Aneignungsweise abschaffen. Die Proletarier haben Nichts von dem Ihrigen zu sichern, sie haben alle bisherige Privatsicherheit und Privatversicherungen zu zerstören. [56]Alle bisherigen Bewegungen waren Bewegungen von Minoritäten oder im Interesse von Minoritäten. Die proletarische Bewegung ist die selbstständige Bewegung der ungeheuren Mehrzahl im Interesse der ungeheuren Mehrzahl. Das Proletariat, die unterste Schichte der jetzigen Gesellschaft, kann sich nicht erheben, nicht aufrichten, ohne daß der ganze Ueberbau der Schichten, die die offizielle Gesellschaft bilden, in die Luft gesprengt wird.

[57]Obgleich nicht dem Inhalt, ist der Form nach der Kampf des Proletariats gegen die Bourgeoise zu nächst ein nationaler. Das Proletariat eines jeden Landes muß natürlich zuerst mit seiner eigenen Bourgeoisie fertig werden.

[58]Indem wir die allgemeinsten Phasen der Entwicklung des Proletariats zeichneten, verfolgten wir den mehr oder minder versteckten Bürgerkrieg innerhalb der bestehenden Gesellschaft bis zu dem Punkt, wo er in eine offene Revolution ausbricht und durch den gewaltsamen Sturz der Bourgeoisie das Proletariat seine Herrschaft begründet.

[59]Alle bisherige Gesellschaft beruhte, wie wir gesehen haben, auf dem Gegensatz unterdrückender und unterdrückter Klassen. Um aber eine Klasse unterdrücken zu können, müssen ihr Bedingungen gesichert sein innerhalb deren sie wenigstens ihre knechtische Existenz fristen kann. Der Leibeigne hat sich zum Mitglied der Kommune in der Leibeigenschaft herangearbeitet, wie der Kleinbürger zum Bourgeois unter dem Joch des feudalistischen Absolotismus.

[55]All the hitherto dominant Classes, have tried to preserve the position they had already attained, by imposing the conditions under which they possessed and increased their possessions, upon the rest of Society. But the Proletarians can gain possession of the Productive power of Society,—of the instruments of Labour,—only by annihilating their own, hitherto acknowledged mode of appropriation. The Proletarians have nothing of their own to secure, their task is to destroy all previously existing private securities and possessions. [56]All the historical movements hitherto recorded were the movements of minorities, or movements in the interest of minorities. The Proletarian movement is the independent movement of the immense majority in favour of the immense majority. The Proletariat, the lowest stratum of existing society, cannot arouse, cannot rise without causing the complete disruption and dislocation of all the superincumbent classes.

[57]Though the struggle of the Proletariat against the Bourgeoisie is not a National struggle in its Content,—or Reality—it is so in its Form. The Proletarians of every country must settle accounts with the Bourgeoisie there.

[58]While we have thus sketched the general aspect presented by the development of the Proletariat, we have followed the more or less concealed Civil War pervading existing Society, to the point where it must break forth in an open Revolution, and where the Proletarians arrive at the supremacy of their own class through the violent fall of the Bourgeoisie. [59]We have seen, that all previous forms of Society have rested upon the antagonism of oppressing and oppressed Classes. But in order to oppress a Class, the conditions under which it can continue at least its enslaved existence must be secured. The Serf in the Middle Ages, even within his serfdom, could better his condition and become a member of the Comune; the burghers could become a Middle-class under the yoke of feudal Monarchy.

[55]All the preceding classes that got the upper hand, sought to fortify their already acquired status by subjecting society at large to their conditions of appropriation. The proletarians cannot become masters of the productive forces of society, except by abolishing their own previous mode of appropriation, and thereby also every other previous mode of appropriation. They have nothing of their own to secure and to fortify. Their mission is to destroy all previous securities for and insurances of individual property.

[56]All previous historical movements were movements of minorities, or in the interest of minorities. The proletarian movement is the self-conscious, independent movement of the immense majority, in the interest of the immense majority. The proletariat, the lowest stratum of our present society cannot stir, cannot raise itself up, without the whole superincumbent strata of official society being sprung into the air.

[57]Though not in substance, yet in form, the struggle of the proletariat with the bourgeoisie is at first a national struggle. The proletariat of each country must, of course first of all settle matters with its own bourgeoisie.

[58]In depicting the most general phases of the development of the proletariat, we traced the more or less veiled civil war, raging within existing society up to the point where that war breaks out into open revolution, and where the violent overthrow of the bourgeoisie, lays the foundation for the sway of the proletariat.

[59]Hitherto, every form of society has been based, as we have already seen, on the antagonism of oppressing and oppressed classes. But in order to oppress a class, certain conditions must be assured to it under which it can, at least, continue its slavish existence. The serf, in the period of serfdom, raised himself to membership in the commune, just as the petty bourgeois, under the yoke of feudal absolutism, managed to develop into a bourgeois.

[55]All previous classes that captured power sought to safeguard the status in life they had acquired by making the whole of society subject to the conditions under which they acquired it. The proletarians can conquer the social forces of production only by abolishing their own previous mode of appropriation and thereby the whole mode of appropriation hitherto existing. The proletarians have nothing of their own to safeguard; they have every hitherto existing private safeguard and private guarantee to destroy.

[56]All previous movements were movements of minorities or in the interest of minorities. The proletarian movement is the independent movement of the immense majority in the interest of the immense majority. The proletariat, the lowest stratum of present day society, cannot raise itself up, cannot stand erect, without bursting asunder the whole superstructure of strata that make up official society.

[57]In form, though not in content, the struggle of the proletariat against the bourgeoisie is at first a national one. The proletariat of each country must naturally first settle accounts with its own bourgeoisie.

[58]In sketching the most general phases of the development of the proletariat, we followed the more or less hidden civil war inside the existing society up to the point where it breaks out in an open revolution and the proletariat establishes its own rule through the forcible overthrow of the bourgeoisie.

[59]Every society so far has been based, as we have seen, on the antithesis of oppressing and oppressed classes. But to be able to oppress a class, one must assure it the conditions for at least eking out its servile existence. The serf worked up to becoming a member of the commune under serfdom; likewise, the petty-bourgeois to becoming a bourgeois under the yoke of feudal absolutism.

Der moderne Arbeiter degegen, statt sich mit
dem Fortschritt der Industrie zu heben, sinkt
immer tiefer unter die Bedingungen seiner eignen
Klasse herab. Der Arbeiter wird zum Pauper,
und der Pauperismus entwickelt sich noch rascher
als Bevölkerung und Reichthum. Es tritt hiermit
offen hervor, daß die Bourgeoisie unfähig ist noch
länger die herrschende Klasse der Gesellschaft zu
bleiben und die Lebensbedingungen ihrer Klasse
der Gesellschaft als regelndes Gesetz aufzuzwing-
en. Sie ist unfähig zu herrschen, weil sie unfähig
ist ihrem Sklaven die Existenz selbst innerhalb
seiner Sklaverei zu sichern, weil sie gezwungen ist
ihn in eine Lage herabsinken zu lassen, wo sie ihn
ernähren muß, statt von ihm ernährt zu werden.
Die Gesellschaft kann nicht mehr unter ihr leben,
d. h. ihr Leben ist nicht mehr verträglich mit der
Gesellschft.

[60]Die wesentlichste Bedingung für die Existenz
und für die Herrschaft der Bourgeoisklasse ist die
Anhäufung des Reichthums in den Händen von
Privaten, die Bildung und Vermehrung des
Kapitals. Die Bedingung des Kapitals ist die
Lohnarbeit. Die Lohnarbeit beruht aus-
schließlich auf der Konkurenz der Arbeiter unter
sich. Der Fortschritt der Industrie, dessen wil-
lenloser und wiederstandsloser Träger die
Bourgeoisie ist, setzt an die Stelle der Isolirung
der Arbeiter durch die Konkurenz ihre
revolutionäre Vereinigung durch die Association.
Mit der Entwicklung der großen Industrie wird
also unter den Füßen der Bourgeoisie die
Grundlage selbst weggezogen worauf sie
produzirt und die Produkte sich aneignet. Sie
produzirt vor Allem ihre eignen Todtengräber.
Ihr Untergang und der Sieg des Proletariats sind
gleich unvermeidlich.

But the modern Proletarian, instead of
improving his condition with the development
of modern Industry, is daily sinking deeper and
deeper even below the conditions of existence
of his own Class. The Proletarian tends to
become a pauper; and Pauperism is more
rapidly developed than population and Wealth.
From this it appears, that the Middle-class is
incapable of remaining any longer the ruling
Class of Society, and of compelling Society to
adopt the conditions of Middle-class existence
as its own vital conditions. This Class is
incapable of governing, because it is incapable
of ensuring the bare existence of its Slaves,
even within the limits of their slavery, because
it is obliged to keep them, instead of being kept
by them. Society can no longer exist under this
Class, that is, its existence is no longer
compatible with that of Society. [60]The most
indispensable condition for the existence and
supremacy of the Bourgeoisie, is the
accumulation of Wealth in the hands of private
individuals, the formation and increase of
Capital. The condition upon which Capital
depends is the Wages-system, and this system
again, is founded upon the Competition of the
Proletarians with each other. But the progress
of the modern industrial system, towards which
the Bourgeoisie lend an unconscious and
involuntary support, tends to supersede the
isolated position of Proletarians by the
revolutionary Union of their Class, and to
replace Competition by Association. The
progress of the modern industrial system,
therefore, cuts away, from under the feet of the
Middle-class, the very ground upon which they
produce and appropriate to themselves the
produce of Labour. Thus the Bourgeoisie
produce before all the men who dig their very
grave. Their destruction and the victory of the
Proletarians are alike unavoidable.

The modern labourer, on the contrary, instead of rising with the progress of industry, sinks deeper and deeper below the conditions of existence of his own class. He becomes a pauper, and pauperism develops more rapidly than population and wealth. And here it becomes evident that the bourgeois is unfit any longer to be the ruling class in society, and to impose its conditions of existence upon society as an overiding law. It is unfit to rule because it is incompetent to assure an existence to its slave within his slavery, because it cannot help letting him sink into such a state, that it has to feed him, instead of being fed by him. Society can no longer live under this bourgeoisie in other words, its existence is no longer compatible with society.

[60]The essential condition for the existence, and for the sway of the bourgeois class, is the formation and augmentation of capital; the condition for capital is wage labour. Wage-labour rests exclusively on competition between the labourers. The advance of industry, whose involuntary promoter is the bourgeoisie, replaces the isolation of the labourers, due to competition, by their revolutionary combination, and to association. The development of Modern Industry, therefore, cuts from under its feet the very foundation on which the bourgeoisie produces and appropriates products. What the bourgeoisie therefore produces, above all, are its own grave-diggers. Its fall and the victory of the proletariat are equally inevitable.

In contrast the modern worker, instead of rising with the progress of industry, sinks deeper and deeper below the conditions of his own class. The worker turns into a pauper, and pauperism develops even more rapidly than population and wealth. It thereby comes out into the open that the bourgeoisie is incapable of any longer remaining the ruling class in society and of imposing the conditions of existence of its own class on society as the controlling law. It is incapable of ruling because it is incapable of assuring a livelihood to its slave even within the framework of his slavery, because it is forced to let him sink into a condition where it must feed him instead of being fed by him. Society can no longer live under it, i.e., its existence is no longer compatible with society.

[60]The most essential precondition for the existence of the bourgeois class and for its rule is the accumulation of wealth in the hands of private persons, the formation and augmentation of capital. The precondition for capital is wage-labor. Wage-labor is based exclusively on competition among workers. The progress of industry, whose involuntary and irresistible vehicle is the bourgeoisie, replaces the isolation of the workers due to competition by their revolutionary unification due to association. With the development of large-scale industry, therefore, the very foundation on which the bourgeoisie produces and appropriates the products is pulled from under its feet. Above all, it produces its own gravediggers. Its downfall and the victory of the proletariat are alike inevitable.

II.

Proletarier und Kommunisten.

CHAPTER II.

PROLETARIANS AND COMMUNISTS.

[61]In welchem Verhältniß stehen die Kommunisten zu den Proletariern überhaupt?

[62]Die Kommunisten sind keine besondere Partei gegenüber den andern Arbeiterparteien.

[63]Sie haben keine von den Interessen des ganzen Proletariats getrennten Interessen.

[64]Sie stellen keine besondern Prinzipien auf, wonach sie die proletarische Bewegung modeln wollen.

[65]Die Kommunisten unterscheiden sich von den übrigen proletarischen Parteien nur dadurch, daß einerseits sie in den verschiedenen nationalen Kämpfen der Proletarier die gemeinsamen, von der Nationalität unabhängigen Interessen des gesammten Proletariats hervorheben und zur Geltung bringen, andrerseits dadurch, daß sie in den verschiedenen Entwicklungs-Stufen, welche der Kampf zwischen Proletariat uud Bourgeosie durchläuft, stets das Interesse der Gesammt-Bewegung vertreten.

[66]Die Kommunisten sind also praktisch der entschiedenste immer weiter treibende Theil der Arbeiterparteien aller Länder, sie haben theoretisch vor der übrigen Masse des Proletariats die Einsicht in die Bedingungen, den Gang und die allgemeinen Resultate der Proletarischen Bewegung voraus.

[67]Der nächste Zweck der Kommunisten ist derselbe wie der aller übrigen proletarischen Parteien: Bildung des Proletariats zur Klasse, Sturz der Bourgeoisieherrschaft, Eroberung der politischen Macht durch das Proletariat.

[68]Die theoretischen Sätze der Kommunisten beruhen keineswegs auf Ideen, auf Prinzipien, die von diesem oder jenem Weltverbesserer erfunden oder entdeckt sind.

[61] **WHAT** relationship subsists between the Communists and the Proletarians?— [62]The Communists form no separate party in opposition to the other existing working-class parties. [63]They have no interest different from that of the whole Proletariat. [64]They lay down no particular principles according to which they wish to direct and to shape the Proletarian movement. [65]The Communists are distinguishable among the various sections of the Proletarian party on two accounts—namely, that in the different *national* Proletarian struggles, the Communists understand, and direct attention to, the common interest of the collective Proletariat, an interest independent of all nationality; and that, throughout the various phases of development assumed by the struggle between the Bourgeoisie and the Proletariat, the Communists always represent the interest of the Whole Movement. [66]In a word, the Communists are the most advanced, the most progressive section, among the Proletarian parties of all countries; and this section has a theoretical advantage, compared with the bulk of the Proletariat—it has obtained an insight into the historical conditions, the march, and the general results of the Proletarian Movement. [67]The more immediate aim of the Communists is that of all other Proletarian sections. *The organisation of the Proletariat as a class, the destruction of Middle-class supremacy, and the conquest of political power by the Proletarians.*

[68]The theoretical propositions of the Communists are not based upon Ideas, or Principles, discovered by this or that Universal Reformer.

II.

II

PROLETARIANS AND COMMUNISTS.

PROLETARIANS AND COMMUNISTS

[61]In what relation do the Communists stand to the proletarians as a whole?

[62]The Communists do not form a separate party opposed to other working-class parties.

[63] They have no interests separate and apart from those of the proletariat as a whole.

[64] They do not set up any sectarian principles of their own, by which to shape and mould the proletarian movement.

[65]The Communists are distinguished from the other working class parties by this only: 1.In the national struggles of the proletarians of the different countries, they point out and bring to the front the common interests of the entire proletariat independently of all nationality. 2. In the various stages of development which the struggle of the working class against the bourgeoisie has to pass through, they always and everywhere represent the interests of the movement as a whole.

[66]The Communists, therefore, are on the one hand, practically, the most advanced and resolute section of the working class parties of every country, that section which pushes forward all others; on the other hand, theoretically, they have over the great mass of the proletariat the advantage of clearly understanding the line of march, the conditions, and the ultimate general results of the proletarian movement.

[67]The immediate aim of the Communists is the same as that of all the other proletarian parties: formation of the proletariat into a class, overthrow of the bourgeois supremacy, conquest of political power by the proletariat.

[68] The theoretical conclusions of the Communists are in no way based on ideas or principles that have been invented, or discovered, by this or that would-be universal reformer.

[61]In what relation do the Communists stand to the proletarians in general?

[62]The Communists are not a special party vis-a-vis the other workers' parties.

[63]They have no interests separate from the interests of the whole proletariat.

[64]They do not lay down any special principles on which they want to model the proletarian movement.

[65]The Communists are distinguished from the rest of the proletarian parties only by the fact that, on the one hand, in the various national struggles of the proletarians they bring out and emphasize the common interests of the proletariat as a whole independent of nationality; and that, on the other hand, in the various stages of development which the struggle between proletariat and bourgeoisie passes through, they always represent the interests of the movement as a whole.

[66]In practice, the Communists are therefore the most resolute section of the workers' parties of every country, always pressing forward; as for theory, they are ahead of the rest of the mass of the proletariat in the understanding of the preconditions, the course, and the general results of the proletarian movement.

[67]The immediate aim of the Communists is the same as that of all the other proletarian parties: constitution of the proletariat into a class, overthrow of bourgeois rule, conquest of political power by the proletariat.

[68]The theoretical tenets of the Communists are by no means based on ideas, on principles, that have been invented or discovered by this or that panacea-monger.

[69]Sie sind nur allgemeine Ausdrücke thatsächlicher Verhältnisse eines existirenden Klassenkampfes, einer unter unsern Augen vor sich gehenden geschichtlichen Bewegung. Die Abschaffung bisheriger Eigenthumsverhältnisse ist nichts den Kommunismus eigenthümlich Bezeichnendes.

[70]Alle Eigenthumsverhältnisse waren einem beständigen geschichtlichen Wechsel, einer beständigen geschichtlichen Veränderung unterworfen.

[71]Die französische Revolution z. B. schaffte das Feudal-Eigenthum zu Gunsten des bürgerlichen ab.

[72]Was den Kommunismus auszeichnet, ist nicht die Abschaffung des Eigenthums überhaupt, sondern die Abschaffung des bürgerlichen Eigenthums.

[73]Aber das moderne bürgerliche Privateigenthum ist der letzte und vollendeteste Ausdruck der Erzeugung un Aneignung der Producte, die auf Klassengegensätzen, die auf der Ausbeutung der Einen durch die Andern beruht.

[74]In diesem Sinn können die Kommunisten ihre Theorie in dem einen Ausdruck: Aufhebung des Privat-Eigenthums zusammenfassen.

[75]Man hat uns Kommunisten vorgeworfen, wir wollten das persönlich erworbene, selbsterarbeitete Eigenthum abschaffen; das Eigenthum, welches die Grundlage aller persönlichen Freiheit, Thätigkeit und Selbstständigkeit bilde.

[76]Erarbeitetes, erworbenes, selbstverdientes Eigenthum! Sprecht Ihr von dem kleinbürgerlichen, kleinbäuerlichen Eigenthum, welches dem bürgerlichen Eigenthum vorherging? Wir brauchen es nicht abzuschaffen, die Entwicklung der Industrie hat es abgeschafft und schafft es täglich ab.

[77]Oder sprecht Ihr vom modernen bürgerlichen Privateigenthum?

[69]Their propositions are merely general expressions for the actual conditions, causes, &c., of an existing battle between certain classes, the conditions of an historical Movement which is going on before our very eyes.

The abolition of existing conditions of Property does not form a distinguishing characteristic of Communism. [70]All such conditions have been subject to a continual change, to the operation of many historical Movements. [71]The French Revolution, for example, destroyed the feudal conditions of property, and replaced them by Bourgeois ones. [72]It is not, therefore, the *abolition of property generally* which distinguishes Communism; it is the *abolition of Bourgeois property*. [73]But Modern Middle-class private property is the last and most perfect expression for that mode of Production and Distribution which rests on the antagonism of classes, on the using up of the many by the few. [74]In this sense, indeed, the Communists might resume their whole Theory in that single expression—*The abolition of private property*.

[75]It has been reproached to us, the Communists, that we wish to destroy the property which is the product of a man's own labour; self-acquired property, the basis of all personal freedom, activity, and independence. [76]Self-acquired property! Do you mean the property of the small shopkeeper, small tradesman, small peasant, which precedes the present system of Middle-class property? We do not need to abolish that, the progress of industrial development is daily destroying it. [77]Or do you mean modern Middle-class property?

[68]They merely express,in general terms, actual relations springing from an existing class struggle, from a historical movement going on under our very eyes. The abolition of existing property-relations is not at all a distinctive feature of Communism.

[70]All property relations in the past have continually been subject to historical change consequent upon the change in historical conditions.

[71]The French Revolution, for example, abolished feudal property in favour of bourgeois property.

[72]The distinguishing feature of Communism is not the abolition of property generally, but the abolition of bourgeois property.

[73]But modern bourgeois private property is the final and most complete expression of the system of producing and appropriating products, that is based on class antagonisms, on the exploitation of the many by the few.

[74]In this sense,the theory of the Communists may be summed up in the single sentence: Abolition of private property.

[75]We Communists have been reproached with the desire of abolishing the right of personally acquiring property as the fruit of a man's own labour, which property is alleged to be the ground work of all personal freedom, activity and independence.

[76]Hard-won, self-acquired, self-earned property! Do you mean the property of the petty artisan and of the small peasant, a form of property that preceded the bourgeois form? There is no need to abolish that; the development of industry has to a great extent already destroyed it and is still destroying it daily.

[77]Or do you mean modern bourgeois private property?

[69] They are merely general expressions of actual relations in an existing class struggle, in a course of historical development going on before our eyes. The abolition of existing property relations is nothing peculiarly characteristic of communism.

[70]All property relations have been subject to a continual historical changeover, a continual historical alteration.

[71]The French Revolution, for example, abolished feudal property in favor of bourgeois property.

[72]What distinguishes communism is not the abolition of property in general, but the abolition of bourgeois property.

[73]But modern bourgeois private property is the last and most finished expression of the creation and appropriation of products based on class antagonisms, on the exploitation of some people by other people.

[74] In this sense the Communists can summarize their theory in this one phrase: abolition of private property.

[75] Communists have been taxed with wanting to abolish property that has been individually acquired by hard work—property which is said to form the foundation of all personal freedom, activity, and independence.

[76] Hard-won, self-acquired, self-earned property! Are you speaking of the petty-bourgeois property or small-peasant property that came before bourgeois property? We do not need to abolish it; the development of industry has abolished it and is daily abolishing it.

[77]Or are you speaking of modern bourgeois private property?

[78]Schafft aber die Lohnarbeit, die Arbeit des Proletariers ihm Eigenthum? Keineswegs. Sie schafft das Kapital, d. h. das Eigenthum, welches die Lohnarbeit ausbeutet, welches sich nur unter der Bedingung vermehren kann, daß es neue Lohnarbeit erzeugt, um sie von Neuem auszubeuten. Das Eigenthum in seiner heutigen Gestalt bewegt sich in dem Gegensatz von Kapital und Lohnarbeit. Betrachten wir die beiden Seiten dieses Gegensatzes. Kapitalist sein heißt nicht nur eine reinpersönliche, sondern eine gesellschaftliche Stellung in der Produktion einnehmen.

[79]Das Kapital ist ein gemeinschaftliches Produkt und kann nur durch eine gemeinsame Thätigkeit vieler Mitglieder, ja in letzter Instanz nur durch die gemeinsame Thätigkeit aller Mitglieder der Gesellschaft in Bewegung gesetzt werden.

[80]Das Kapital ist also keine persönliche, es ist eine gesellschaftliche Macht.

[81]Wenn also das Kapital in gemein-schaftliches, allen Mitgliedern der Gesellschaft angehöriges Eigenthum verwandelt wird, so verwandelt sich nicht persönliches Eigenthum in gesellschaftliches. Nur der gesellschaftliche Charakter des Eigenthums verwandelt sich. Es verliert seinen Klassen-Charakter.

[82]Kommen wir zur Lohnarbeit.

[83]Der Durchschnittspreis der Lohnarbeit ist das Minimum des Arbeitslohnes, d. h. die Summe der Lebensmittel, die nothwendig sind, um den Arbeiter als Arbeiter am Leben zu erhalten. Was also der Lohnarbeiter durch seine Thätigkeit sich aneignet, reicht blos dazu hin, um sein nacktes Leben wieder zu erzeugen. Wir wollen diese persönliche Aneignung der Arbeitsprodukte zur Wiedererzeugung des unmittelbaren Lebens keineswegs abschaffen, eine Aneignung, die keinen Reinertrag übrig läßt, der Macht über fremde Arbeit geben könnte. Wir wollen nur den elenden Charakter dieser Aneignung aufheben, worin der Arbeiter nur lebt, um das Kapital zu vermehren, nur so weit lebt, wie es das Interesse der herrschenden Klasse erheischt.

146

[78]Does labour under the Wages-system create property for the Wages-slave, for the Proletarian? No. It creates Capital, that is, a species of property which plunders Wages-labour; for Capital can only increase on condition of creating a new supply of Wages-labour, in order to use it up anew.

Property, in its present form, rests upon the antagonism of Capital and Wages-labour. Let us look at both sides of this antithesis. To be a Capitalist means to occupy not only a personal, but a social position in the system of production. [79]Capital is a collective product, and can be used and set in motion only by the common activity of many, or, to speak exactly, only by the united exertions of all the members of society. [80]Capital is thus not an individual, it is a social, power. [81]Therefore, when Capital is changed into property belonging in common to all the members of society, personal property is not thereby changed into social property. It was social property before. The social character only of property, in such a case, is changed. Property loses its class character. [82]—Let us now turn to Wages-labour. [83]The minimum rate of wages is the average price of Proletarian labour. And what is the minimum rate of wages? It is that quantity of produce which is necessary to conserve the working capacities of the labourer. What the Wages-slave can gain by his activity is merely what is requisite for the bare reproduction of his existence. We by no means wish to abolish this personal appropriation of the products of labour; an appropriation leaving no net profit, no surplus, to be applied to command the labour of others. We only wish to change the miserably insufficient character of this appropriation, whereby the producer lives only to increase Capital; that is, whereby he is kept alive only so far as it may be the interest of the ruling class.

[78]But does wage labour create any property for the labourer? Not a bit. It creates capital, *i.e.*, that kind of property which exploits wage-labour, and which cannot increase except upon condition of begetting a new supply of wage labour for fresh exploitation. Property, in its present form, is based on the antagonism of capital and wage labour. Let us examine both sides of this antagonism.

To be a capitalist is to have not only a purely personal but a social *status* in production. [79]Capital is a collective product, and only by the combined action of many members, nay, in the last resort, only by the united action of all members of society, can it be set in motion.

[80]Capital is therefore not a personal, it is a social power.

[81]When, therefore, capital is converted into common property, into the property of all members of society, personal property is not thereby transformed into social property. It is only the social character of the property that is changed. It loses its class character.

[82]Let us now take wage-labour.

[83]The average price of wage-labour is the minimum wage, *i.e.*, that quantum of the means of subsistence, which is absolutely requisite to keep the labourer in bare existence as a labourer. What, therefore, the wage-labourer appropriates by means of his labour, merely suffices to prolong and reproduce a bare existence. We by no means intend to abolish this personal appropriation of the products of labour, an appropriation that is made for the maintenance and reproduction of human life, and that leaves no surplus wherewith to command the labour of others. All that we want to do away with, is the miserable character of this appropriation, under which the labourer lives merely to increase capital and is allowed to live only in so far as the interest of the ruling class requires it.

[78]But does wage-labor, the proletarian's labor, create property for him? By no means. It creates capital, i.e., property which exploits wage-labor, which can increase only on condition of generating new wage-labor in order to exploit it anew. Property in its present-day form revolves around the antagonism of capital and wage-labor. Let us look at both sides of this antagonism. To be a capitalist means to occupy not only a purely personal but a social position in production.

[79]Capital is a collective product and can be put in operation only by the joint activity of many members of society—indeed, in the last instance, only by the joint activity of all members of society.

[80]Capital, therefore, is not a personal Power, it is a social power.

[81]Therefore, when capital is changed into collective property belonging to all members of society, personal property is not changed into social property. Only the social character of property is changed. It loses its class character.

[82]Let us turn to wage-labor.

[83]The average price of wage-labor is the minimum wage, i.e., the quantity of means of existence that is necessary to maintain the existence of the worker as a worker. Therefore, what the wage-worker appropriates by means of his activity is merely sufficient to reproduce his bare existence. We by no means wish to abolish this personal appropriation of the products of labor for the purpose of reproducing direct subsistence—an appropriation which leaves no net surplus that can confer power over another's labor. We wish only to abolish the miserable character of this appropriation, whereby the worker lives only to augment capital and lives only insofar as the interests of the ruling class require it.

[84]In der bürgerlichen Gesellschaft ist die lebendige Arbeit nur ein Mittel, die aufgehäufte Arbeit zu vermehren. In der kommunistischen Gesellschaft ist die aufgehäufte Arbeit nur ein Mittel, um den Lebensprozeß der Arbeiter zu erweitern, zu bereichern, zu befördern.

[85]In der bürgerlichen Gesellschaft herrscht also die Vergangenheit über die Gegenwart, in der kommunistischen die Gegenwart über die Vergangenheit. In der bürgerlichen Gesellschaft ist das Kapital selbstständig und persönlich, während das thätige Individuum unselbstständig und unpersönlich ist.

[86]Und die Aufhebung dieses Verhältnisses nennt die Bourgeoisie Aufhebung der Persönlichkeit und Freiheit! Und mit Recht. Es handelt sich allerdings um die Aufhebung der Bourgeois-Persönlichkeit, Selbstständigkeit und Freiheit.

[87]Unter Freiheit versteht man innerhalb der jetzigen bürgerlichen Produktions-Verhältnisse den freien Handel, den freien Kauf und Verkauf.

[88]Fällt aber der Schacher, so fällt auch der freie Schacher. Die Redensarten vom freien Schacher, wie alle übrigen Freiheitsbravaden unserer Bourgeois haben überhaupt nur einen Sinn gegenüber dem gebundenen Schacher, gegenüber dem geknechteten Bürger des Mittelalters, nicht aber gegenüber der kommunistischen Aufhebung des Schachers, der bürgerlichen Produktions-Verhältnisse und der Bourgeoisie selbst.

[89]Ihr entsetzt Euch darüber, daß wir das Privateigenthum aufheben wollen. Aber in Eurer bestehenden Gesellschaft ist das Privateigenthum für 9 Zehntel ihrer Mitglieder aufgehoben; es existirt gerade dadurch, daß es für 9 Zehntel nicht existirt. Ihr werft uns also vor, daß wir ein Eigenthum aufheben wollen, welches die Eigenthumslosigkeit der ungeheuren Mehrzahl der Gesellschaft als nothwendige Bedingung voraussetzt.

[90]Ihr werft uns mit Einem Wort vor, daß wir Euer Eigenthum aufheben wollen. Allerdings das wollen wir.

[84]In Middle-class society, actual living labour is nothing but a means of increasing accumulated labour. In Communistic society, accumulated labour is only a means of enlarging, increasing, and varifying the vital process of the producers. [85]In Middle-class society, the Past reigns over the Present. In Communistic society, the Present reigns over the Past. In Middle-class society, Capital is independent and personal, while the active individual is dependent and deprived of personality. [86]And the destruction of such a system is called by Middle-class advocates, the destruction of personality and freedom. They are so far right, that the question in hand is the destruction of Middle-class personality, independence, and freedom. [87]Within the present Middle-class conditions of production, freedom means free trade, freedom of buying and selling. [88]But if trade, altogether, is to fall, so will free trade fall with the rest. The declamations about free trade, as all the remaining Bourgeois declamations upon the subject of freedom generally, have a meaning only when opposed to fettered trade, and to the enslaved tradesmen of the Middle Ages; they have no meaning whatever in reference to the Communistic destruction of profit-mongering, of the Middle-class conditions of production, and of the Middle-class itself. [89]You are horrified that we aim at the abolition of private property. But under your present system of society, private property has no existence for nine-tenths of its members; its existence is based upon the very fact that it exists not at all for nine-tenths of the population. You reproach us, then, that we aim at the abolition of a species of property which involves, as a necessary condition, the absence of all property for the immense majority of society. [90]In a word, you reproach us that we aim at the destruction of YOUR property. That is precisely what we aim at.

[84]In bourgeois society, living labour is but a means to increase accumulated labour. In Communist society, accumulated labour but a means to widen, to enrich, to promote the existence of the labourer.

[85]In bourgeois society, therefore, the past dominates the present; in communist society, the present dominates the past. In bourgeois society capital is independent and has individuality, while the human person is dependent and has no individuality.

[86]And the abolition of this state of things is called by the bourgeois, abolition of individuality and freedom! And rightly so. The abolition of bourgeois individuality bourgeois independence, and bourgeois freedom is undoubtedly aimed at.

[87]By freedom is meant under the present bourgeois conditions of production, free trade, free selling and buying.

[88]But if selling and buying disappears, free selling and buying disappears also. This talk about free selling and buying, and all the other "brave words" of our bourgeoisie about freedom in general have a meaning, if any, only in contrast with restricted selling and buying, with the fettered traders of the Middle ages, but have no meaning when opposed to the Communistic abolition of buying and selling, of the bourgeois conditions of production, and of the bourgeoisie itself.

[89]You are horrified at our intending to do away with private property. But in your existing society, private property is already done away with for nine-tenths of the population; its existence for the few is solely due to its non-existence in the hands of those nine-tenths. You reproach us, therefore, with intending to do away with a form of property, the necessary condition for whose existence is, the non-existence of any property for the immense majority of society.

[90]In one word, you reproach us with intending to do away with your property. Precisely so: that is just what we intend.

[84]In bourgeois society, living labor is only a means of augmenting accumulated labor. In communist society, accumulated labor is only a means of expanding, enriching, and fostering the workers' way of life.

[85]In bourgeois society, the past therefore holds sway over the present; in communist society, the present over the past. In bourgeois society, capital is independent and individual, while the active individual is dependent and deindividualized.

[86]And the abolition of these conditions the bourgeoisie calls the abolition of individuality and freedom! And with justice. What is involved, to be sure, is the abolition of bourgeois individuality, independence, and freedom.

[87]By freedom, under the present bourgeois relations of production, is understood free trade, free buying and selling.

[88]But if huckstering goes, then free huckstering goes too. The phrases about free huckstering, like all the rest of our bourgeoisie's bluster about freedom, have a meaning in general only as against the trammeled huckstering and enserfed burghers of the Middle Ages, but not as against the communist abolition of huckstering, of the bourgeois relations of production and of the bourgeoisie itself.

[89]You are horrified because we wish to abolish private property. But in your existing society private property is abolished for nine-tenths of its members; it exists at all thanks to the fact that for nine-tenths it does not exist. You tax us, therefore, with wanting to abolish a form of property which presupposes the propertylessness of the immense majority of society as its necessary precondition.

[90]You tax us, in short, with wishing to abolish your property. To be sure, that is what we wish to do.

[91]Von dem Augenblick an, wo die Arbeit nicht mehr in Kapital, Geld, Grundrente, kurz, in eine monopolisirbare gesellschaftliche Macht verwandelt werden kann, d. h. von dem Augenblick, wo das persönliche Eigenthum nicht mehr in bürgerliches umschlagen kann, von dem Augenblick an erklärt Ihr die Person sei aufgehoben.

[92]Ihr gesteht also, daß Ihr unter der Person Niemanden anders versteht, als den Bourgeois, den bürgerlichen Eigenthümer. Und diese Person soll allerdings aufgehoben werden.

[93]Der Kommunismus nimmt keinem die Macht sich gesellschaftliche Produkte anzueignen, er nimmt nur die Macht sich durch diese Aneignung fremde Arbeit zu unterjochen.

[94]Man hat eingwendet, mit der Aufhebung des Privateigenthums werde alle Thätigkeit aufhören und eine allgemeine Faulheit einreißen.

[95]Hiernach müßte die bürgerliche Gesellschaft längst an der Trägheit zu Grunde gegangen sein; denn die in ihr arbeiten, erwerben nicht, und die in ihr erwerben, arbeiten nicht. Das ganze Bedenken läuft auf die Tautologie hinaus, daß es keine Lohnarbeit mehr gibt, sobald es kein Kapital mehr gibt.

[96]Alle Einwürfe die gegen die kommunistische Aneignungs- und Produktionsweise der materiellen Produkte gerichtet werden, sind eben so auf die Aneignung und Produktion der geistigen Produkte ausgedehnt worden. Wie für den Bourgeois das Aufhören des Klasseneigenthums das Aufhören der Produktion selbst ist, so ist für ihn das Aufhören der Klassenbildung identisch mit dem Aufhören der Bildung überhaupt.

[97]Die Bildung, deren Verlust er bedauert, ist für die enorme Mehrzahl die Heranbildung zur Maschine.

[91]From the moment when Labour can no longer be changed into Capital,—into money, or rent,—into a social power capable of being *monopolised*; that is, from the moment when personal property can no longer constitute itself as Middle-class property, from that moment you declare that human personality is abolished. [92]You acknowledge, then, that for you personality generally means the personality of the Bourgeois, the Middle-class proprietor. It is precisely this kind of personality which is to be destroyed. [93]Communism deprives no one of the right of appropriating social products; it only takes away from him the power of appropriating the command over the labour of others. [94]It has been objected that activity will cease, and a universal laziness pervade society, were the abolition of private property once accomplished. [95]According to this view of the matter, Middle-class society ought, long since, to have been ruined through idleness; for under the present system, those who do work acquire no property, and those who acquire property do no work. This objection rests upon the tautological proposition, that there will be no Wages-labour whenever there is no Capital. [96]All the objections made to the Communistic mode of producing and distributing physical products, have also been directed against the production and distribution of intellectual products. As, in the opinion of the Bourgeois, the destruction of class property involves the cessation of appropriation, in like manner the cessation of class-civilisation, in his opinion, is identical with the cessation of civilisation generally. [97]The civilisation whose loss he deplores, is the system of civilising men into machines.

150

[91]"From the moment when labour can no longer be converted into capital, money, or rent, into a social power capable of being monopolised, from the moment when individual property can no longer be transformed into bourgeois property, into capital, from that moment, you say, individuality vanishes.

[92]You must therefore, confess that by "individual" you mean no other person than the bourgeois, than the middle-class owner of property. This person must, indeed, be swept out of the way, and made impossible.

[93]Communism deprives no man of the power to appropriate the products of society: all that it does is to deprive him of the power to subjugate the labour of others by means of such appropriation.

[94]It has been objected, that upon the abolition of private property all work will cease, and universal laziness will overtake us.

[95]According to this, society ought long ago to have gone to the dogs through sheer idleness; for those of its, members who work, acquire nothing, and those who acquire anything, do not work. The whole of this objection is but another expression of the tautology: that there can no longer be any wage-labour when there is no longer any capital.

[96]All objections urged against the Communistic mode of producing and appropriating material products, have, in the same way, been urged against the Communistic modes of producing and appropriating intellectual products. Just as, to the bourgeois, the disappearance of class property is the disappearance of production itself so the disappearance of class culture is to him: identical with the disappearance of all culture.

[97]That culture, the loss of which he laments, is, for the enormous majority, a mere training to act as a machine.

[91]"From the moment when labor can no longer be converted into capital, money, ground rent, in short, into a monopolizable social power. i.e., from the moment when individual property can no longer be changed over into bourgeois property—from that moment, you assert, the individual is abrogated.

[92]You thereby confess that by individual you understand none other than the bourgeois, the bourgeois property owner. And indeed, this individual is to be abrogated.

[93]Communism takes away from no one the power to appropriate social products; it only takes away the power to subjugate others' labor by means of such appropriation.

[94]It has been objected that with the abolition of private property all activity will cease and universal laziness will spread.

[95]According to this, bourgeois society would long ago have had to go under through slothfulness; for in it those who work do not acquire anything and those who do acquire do not work. This whole consideration amounts to the tautology that wage-labor ceases to exist as soon as capital ceases to exist.

[96]All objections that have been raised against the communist mode of production and appropriation of material products have likewise been extended to the appropriation and production of intellectual products. Just as for the bourgeois an end to class property is an end to production itself, so for him an end to class culture is identical with an end to culture in general.

[97]The culture whose loss he deplores means, for the enormous majority, their upbringing as machines.

[98]Aber streitet nicht mit uns, indem Ihr an Euren bürgerlichen Vorstellungen von Freiheit, Bildung, Recht u. s. w. die Abschaffung des bürgerlichen Eigenthums meßt. Eure Ideen selbst sind Erzeugnisse der bürgerlichen Produktions- und Eigenthums-Verhältnisse, wie Euer Recht nur der zum Gesetz erhobene Wille Eurer Klasse ist, ein Wille, dessen Inhalt gegeben ist in den materiellen Lebensbedingungen Eurer Klasse.

[99]Die interessirte Vorstellung, worin Ihr Eure Produktions- und Eigenthumsverhältnisse aus geschichtlichen, in dem Lauf der Produktion vorübergehenden Verhältnissen in ewige Natur und Vernunftgesetze verwandelt, theilt Ihr mit allen untergegangenen herrschenden Klassen. Was Ihr für das antike Eigenthum begreift, was Ihr für das feudale Eigenthum begreift, dürft Ihr nicht mehr begreifen für das bürgerliche Eigenthum.

[100]Aufhebung der Familie! Selbst die Radikalsten ereifern sich über diese schändliche Absicht der Kommunisten.

[101]Worauf beruht die gegenwärtige, die bürgerliche Familie? Auf dem Kapital, auf dem Privaterwerb. Vollständig entwickelt existirt sie nur für die Bourgeoisie; aber sie findet ihre Ergänzung in der erzwungenen Familienlosigkeit der Proletarier und der öffentlichen Prostitution.

[102]Die Familie des Bourgeois fällt natürlich weg, mit dem Wegfallen dieser ihrer Ergänzung und beide verschwinden mit dem Verschwinden des Kapitals.

[103]Werft Ihr uns vor, daß wir die Ausbeutung der Kinder durch ihre Eltern aufheben wollen? Wir gestehen dies Verbrechen ein. Aber sagt Ihr, wir heben die trautesten Verhältnisse auf, indem wir an die Stelle der häuslichen Erziehung die gesellschaftliche setzen.

[104]Und ist nicht auch Eure Erziehung durch die Gesellschaft bestimmt? Durch die gesellschaftlichen Verhältnisse, innerhalb deren Ihr erzieht, durch die direktere oder indirektere Einmischung der Gesellschaft vermittelst der Schule u. s. w. ? Die Kommunisten erfinden nicht die Einwirkung der Gesellschaft auf die Erziehung; sie verändern nur ihren Charakter, sie entreißen die Erziehung dem Einfluß einer herrschenden Klasse.

[98]But do not dispute with us, while you measure the proposed abolition of Middle-class property, by your Middle-class ideas of freedom, civilisation, jurisprudence, and the like. Your ideas are the necessary consequences of the Middle-class conditions of property and production, as your jurisprudence is the Will of your class raised to the dignity of Law, a Will whose subject is given in the economical conditions of your class. [99]The selfish mode of viewing the question, whereby you confound your transitory conditions of production and property with the eternal laws of Reason and Nature, is common to all ruling classes. What you understand with regard to Antique and Feudal property, you cannot understand with regard to modern Middle-class property. [100]—The destruction of domestic ties! Even the greatest Radicals are shocked at this scandalous intention of the Communists. [101]Upon what rests the present system, the Bourgeois system of family relationships? Upon Capital, upon private gains, on profit-mongering. In its most perfect form it exists only for the Bourgeoisie, and it finds a befitting compliment in the compulsory celibacy of the Proletarians, and in public prostitution. [102]The Bourgeois family system naturally disappears with the disappearance of its complement, and the destruction of both is involved in the destruction of Capital. [103]Do you reproach us that we intend abolishing the using up of children by their parents? We acknowledge this crime. Or that we will abolish the most endearing relationships, by substituting a public and social system of education for the existing private one? [104]And is not your system of education also determined by society? By the social conditions, within the limits of which you educate? by the more or less direct influence of society, through the medium of your schools, and so forth? The Communists do not invent the influence of society upon education; they only seek to change its character, to rescue education from the influence of a ruling class.

[98]But don't wrangle with us so long as you apply to our intended abolition of bourgeois property, the standard of your bourgeois notions of freedom, culture, law, &c. Your very ideas are but the outgrowth of the conditions of your bourgeois production and bourgeois property, just as your jurisprudence is but the will of your class made into a law for all, a will, whose essential character and direction are determined by the economical conditions of existence of your class.

[99]The selfish misconception that induces you to transform into eternal laws of nature and of reason, the social forms springing from your present mode of production and form of property -- historical relations that rise and disappear in the progress of production -- this misconception you share with every ruling class that has preceded you. What you see clearly in the case of ancient property, what you admit in the case of feudal property you are of course forbidden to admit in the case of your own bourgeois form of property.

[100]Abolition of the family! Even the most radical flare up at this infamous proposal of the Communists.

[101]On what foundation is the present family, the bourgeois family, based on capital, on private gain. In its completely developed form this family exists only among the bourgeoisie. But this state of things finds its complement in the practical absence of the family among the proletarians, and prostitution.

[102]The bourgeois family will vanish as a matter of course when its complement vanishes, and both will vanish with the vanishing of capital.

[103]Do you charge us with wanting to stop the exploitation of children by their parents? To this crime we plead guilty.

But, you will say, we destroy the most hallowed of relations, when we replace home education by social.

[104]And your education! Is not that also social, and determined by the social conditions under which you educate, by the intervention, direct or indirect, of society by means of schools, &c?

[98]But do not quarrel with us by gauging the abolition of bourgeois property in accordance with your bourgeois conceptions of freedom, culture, justice, etc. Your ideas are themselves products of bourgeois relations of production and property, just as your justice is only the will of your class elevated into law, a will whose content is set by the material conditions of existence of your class.

[99]The self-serving conception by which you convert your relations of production and property from historical relations, transitory in the course of production, into eternal laws of nature and reason -- this conception you share with all defunct ruling classes. What you perceive about the property of antiquity, what you perceive about feudal property, this you must not allow yourselves to perceive also about bourgeois property.

[100]Abolition of the family! Even the most radical get angry at this shameful intention of the Communists.

[101]What is the present-day family, the bourgeois family, based on? On capital, on private gain. In completely developed form it exists only for the bourgeoisie; but it finds its complement in the enforced familylessness of proletarians and in public prostitution.

[102]The family of the bourgeois will naturally cease to exist when this its complement ceases to exist, and both will disappear with the disappearance of capital.

[103]Do you tax us with wanting to abolish the exploitation of children by their parents? We confess this crime. But, you say, we abrogate the most intimate of relationships by replacing home education with social education.

[104]And is not your education also determined by society? by the social conditions under which you educate, by the direct or indirect intervention of society, through schools, etc.? The Communists have not invented society's impact on education; they merely change its character, they wrest education from the influence of a ruling class.

[105]Die bürgerlichen Redensarten über Familie und Erziehung über das traute Verhältniß von Eltern und Kindern werden um so ekelhafter, je mehr in Folge der großen Industrie alle Familienbande für die Proletarier zerrissen und die Kinder in einfache Handelsartikel und Arbeitsinstrumente verwandelt werden.

[106]Aber Ihr Kommunisten wollt die Weibergemeinschaft einführen, schreit uns die ganze Bourgeoisie im Chor entgegen.

[107]Der Bourgeois sieht in seiner Frau ein bloßes Produktions-Instrument. Er hört, daß die Produktions-Instrumente gemeinschaftlich ausgebeutet werden sollen und kann sich natürlich nicht anders denken, als daß das Loos der Gemeinschaftlichkeit die Weiber gleichfalls treffen wird.

[108]Er ahnt nicht, daß es sich eben darum handelt, die Stellung der Weiber als bloßer Produktions-Instrumente aufzuheben.

[109]Uebrigens ist nichts lächerlicher als das hochmoralische Entsetzen unsrer Bourgeois über die angebliche officielle Weibergemeinschaft der Kommunisten. Die Kommunisten brauchen die Weibergemeinschaft nicht einzuführen, sie hat fast immer existirt.

[110]Unsre Bourgeois nicht zufrieden damit, daß ihnen die Weiber und Töchter ihrer Proletarier zur Verfügung stehen, von der officiellen Prostitution gar nicht zu sprechen, finden ein Hauptvergnügen darin ihre Ehefrauen wechselseitig zu verführen.

[111]Die bürgerliche Ehe ist in Wirklichkeit die Gemeinschaft der Ehefrauen. Man könnte höchstens den Kommunisten vorwerfen, daß sie an der Stelle einer heuchlerisch versteckten, eine officielle, offenherzige Weibergemeinschaft einführeu wollen. Es versteht sich übrigens von selbst, daß mit Aufhebung der jetzigen Produktions-Verhältnisse auch die aus ihnen hervorgehende Weibergemeinschaft, d. h. die officielle und nicht officielle Prostitution verschwindet.

[112]Den Kommunisten ist ferner vorgeworfen worden, sie wollten das Vaterland, die Nationalität abschaffen.

[105]Middle-class talk about domestic ties and education, about the endearing connection of parent and child, becomes more and more disgusting in proportion as the family ties of the Proletarians are torn asunder, and their children changed into machines, into articles of commerce, by the extension of the modern industrial system. [106]But you intend introducing a community of women, shrieks the whole Middle-class like a tragic chorus. [107]The Bourgeois looks upon his wife as a mere instrument of production; he is told that the instruments of production are to be used up in common, and thus he naturally supposes that women will share the common fate of other machines. [108]He does not even dream that it is intended, on the contrary, to abolish the position of woman as a mere instrument of production. [109]For the rest, nothing can be more ludicrous than the highly moral and religious horror entertained by the Bourgeoisie towards the pretended official community of women among the Communists. We do not require to introduce community of women, it has always existed. [110]Your Middle-class gentry are not satisfied with having the wives and daughters of their Wages-slaves at their disposal,—not to mention the innumerable public prostitutes,—but they take a particular pleasure in seducing each other's wives. [111]Middle-class marriage is in reality a community of wives. At the most, then, we could only be reproached for wishing to substitute an open, above-board community of women, for the present mean, hypocritical, sneaking kind of community. But it is evident enough that with the disappearance of the present conditions of production, the community of women occasioned by them,—namely, official and non-official prostitution will also disappear.

[112]The Communists are further reproached with desiring to destroy patriotism, the feeling of Nationality.

[105]The bourgeois clap-trap about the family and education, about the hallowed co-relation of parent and child, become all the more disgusting, the more, by the action of Modern Industry, all family ties among the proletarians are torn asunder, and their children transformed, into simple articles of commerce and instruments of labour.

[106]But you Communists would introduce community of women, screams the whole bourgeoisie in chorus.

[107]The bourgeois sees in his wife a mere instrument of production. He hears that the instruments of production are to be exploited in common, and, naturally, can come to no other conclusion, than that the lot of being common to all will likewise fall to the women.

[108]He has not even a suspicion that the real point aimed at is to do away with the status of women as mere instruments of production.

[109]For the rest, nothing is more ridiculous than the virtuous indignation of our bourgeois at the community of women which, they pretend, is to be openly and officially established by the Communists. The Communists have no need to introduce community of women; It has existed almost from time immemorial.

[110]Our bourgeois, not content with having the wives and daughters of the proletarians at their disposal not to speak of common prostitutes, take the greatest pleasure in seducing each others' wives.

[111]Bourgeois marriage is in reality a system of wives in common and thus, at the most, what the Communists might possibly be reproached with, is that they desire to introduce,in substitution for a hypocritically concealed, an openly legalised community of women. For the rest, it is self-evident that the abolition of the present system of production must bring with it the abolition of the community of women springing from that system, i.e., of prostitution both public and private.

[112]The Communists are further reproached with desiring to abolish countries and nationality:

[105]The bourgeois phrases about family and education, about the intimate relations of parents and children, become all the mora disgusting the more all family ties for proletarians are severed as a result of large-scale industry, and the children are converted into simple articles of commerce and instruments of labor.

[106]But you Communists wish to introduce community of women, the whole bourgeoisie screams at us in chorus.

[107]The bourgeois sees in his wife a mere instrument of production. He hears that instruments of production are to be exploited in common, and naturally can only imagine that women will likewise share the fate of being held in common.

[108]He does not suspect that it is precisely a question of abrogating the position of women as mere instruments of production.

[109]Anyway, nothing is more ridiculous than the highly moral horror displayed by our bourgeois at the Communists' alleged official community of women. The Communists have no need to introduce community of women; it has almost always existed.

[110]Our bourgeois, not content with having the wives and daughters of their proletarians at their disposal, not to speak of official prostitution, take great pleasure in seducing each others' wives. [111]Bourgeois marriage is in reality a community of wives. At the most, Communists can be taxed with wanting to introduce an official and frank community of women in place of a hypocritically concealed one. Moreover, it is self-evident that with abolition of the present relations of production there also disappears the community of women arising out of them, i.e., official and unofficial prostitution.

[112]The Communists are further taxed with wanting to abolish the fatherland, to abolish nationality.

[113]Die Arbeiter haben kein Vaterland. Man kann ihnen nicht nehmen, was sie nicht haben. Indem das Proletariat zunächst sich die politische Herrschaft erobern, sich zur nationalen Klasse erheben, sich selbst als Nation konstituiren muß, ist es selbst noch national, wenn auch keineswegs im Sinne der Bourgeoisie.

[114]Die nationalen Absonderungen und Gegensätze der Völker verschwinden mehr und mehr schon mit der Entwicklung der Bourgeoisie, mit der Handelsfreiheit, dem Welmarkt, der Gleichförmigkeit der industriellen Produktion und der ihr entsprechenden Lebensverhältnisse.

[115]Die Herrschaft des Proletariats wird sie noch mehr verschwinden machen. Vereinigte Aktion wenigstens der civilisirten Länder ist eine der ersten Bedingungen seiner Befreiung.

[116]In dem Maße wie die Exploitation des einen Induviduums durch das andere aufgehoben wird, wird die Exploitation einer Nation durch die andre aufgehoben.

[117]Mit dem Gegensatz der Klassen im Innern der Nationen fällt die feindliche Stellung der Nationen gegen einander.

[118]Die Anklagen gegen den Kommunismus, die von religiösen, philosophischen und ideologischen Gesichtspunkten überhaupt erhoben werden, verdienen keine ausführlichere Erörterung.

[119]Bedarf es tiefer Einsicht um zu begreifen, daß mit den Lebensverhältnissen der Menschen, mit ihren gesellschaftlichen Beziehungen, mit ihrem gesellschaftlichen Dasein auch ihre Vorstellungen, Anschauungen und Begriffe, mit einem Worte auch ihr Bewußtsein sich ändert?

[120]Was beweist die Geschichte der Ideen anders, als daß die geistige Produktion sich mit der materiellen umgestaltet. Die herrschenden Ideen einer Zeit waren stets nur die Ideen der herrschenden Klasse.

[121]Man spricht von Ideen, welche eine ganze Gesellschaft revolutioniren; man spricht damit nur die Thatsache aus, daß sich innerhalb der alten Gesellschaft die Elemente einer neuen gebildet haben, daß mit der Auflösung der alten Lebensverhältnisse die Auflösung der alten Ideen gleichen Schritt hält.

156

[113]The Proletarian has no Fatherland. You cannot deprive him of that which he has not got. When the Proletariat obtains political supremacy, becomes the National Class, and constitutes itself as the Nation,—it will, indeed, be national, though not in the middleclass sense of the word. [114]The National divisions and antagonisms presented by the European Nations, already tend towards obliteration through the development of the Bourgeoisie, through the influence of free-trade, a worldwide market, the uniformity of the modern modes of Production and the conditions of modern life arising out of the present industrial system.

[115]The supremacy of the Proletariat will hasten this obliteration of national pecularities, for the united action of—at least—all civilized countries is one of the first conditions of Proletarian emancipation. [116]In proportion to the cessation of the using up of one individual by another, will be the cessation of the using up of one nation by another. [117]The hostile attitude assumed by nations towards each other, will cease with the antagonisms of the classes into which each nation is divided.

[118]The accusations against communism, which have been made from the Theological, Philosophical, and Ideological, points of view, deserve no further notice. [119]Does it require any great degree of intellect to perceive that changes occur in our ideas, conceptions, and opinions, in a word, that the *consciousness* of man alters with every change in the conditions of his physical existence, in his social relations and position? [120]Does not the history of Ideas show, that intellectual production has always changed with the changes in material production? The ruling ideas of any age have always been the ideas of the then ruling class. [121]You talk of ideas which have revolutionised society; but you merely express the fact, that within the old form of society, the elements of a new one were being formed, and that the dissolution of the old ideas was keeping pace with the dissolution of the old conditions of social life.

[113]The workingmen have no country. We cannot take from them what they have not got. Since the proletariat must first of all acquire political supremacy, must rise to be the leading class of the nation, must constitute itself <u>the</u> nation, it is, so far, itself national, though not in the bourgeois sense of the word.

[114]National differences, and antagonisms between peoples, are daily more and more vanishing, owing to the development of the bourgeoisie, to freedom of commerce, to the world-market, to uniformity in the mode of production and in the conditions of life corresponding thereto.

[115]The supremacy of the proletariat will cause them to vanish still faster. United action, of the leading civilised countries at least is one of the conditions for the emancipation of the proletariat.

[116]In proportion as the exploitation of one individual by another is put an end to, the exploitation of one nation by another will also be put an end to.

[117]In proportion as the antagonism between classes within the nation vanishes, the hostility of one nation to another will come to an end.

[118]The charges against Communism made from a religious, a philosophical and, generally, from an ideological standpoint are not deserving of serious examination.

[119]Does it require deep intuition to comprehend that man's ideas, views, and conceptions, in one word, man's consciousness changes with every change in the conditions of his material existence, in his social relations and in his social life?

[120]What else does the history of ideas prove, than that intellectual production changes its character in proportion as material production is changed? The ruling ideas of each age have ever been the ideas of its ruling class.

[121]When people speak of ideas that revolutionise society, they do but express the fact that within the old society, the elements of a new one have been created, and that the dissolution of the old ideas keeps even pace with the dissolution of the old conditions of existence.

[113]The workers have no fatherland. One cannot take from them what they do not have. In that the proletariat must first conquer political rule, raise itself to be the national class, and constitute itself as the nation, it is itself still national, though by no means in the bourgeoisie's sense.

[114]National divisions and antagonisms among peoples are already disappearing more and more along with the development of the bourgeoisie, with freedom of trade, the world market, uniformity of industrial production, and the corresponding condition of existence.

[115]The rule of the proletariat will make them disappear even more. United action at least of the civilized countries is one of the first conditions of the proletariat's emancipation.

[116]In proportion as the exploitation of one individual by another is abolished, the exploitation of one nation by another is abolished.

[117]Together with the antagonism between classes inside the nation, the hostile attitude of the nations to each other comes to an end.

[118]The charges against communism that are raised from religious, philosophical, and in general ideological standpoints do not deserve a detailed discussion.

[119]Does it require deep discernment to comprehend that people's conceptions, views, and ideas—in short, their consciousness—change along with their conditions of life, their social relations, and their social existence?

[120]What does the history of ideas show but that intellectual production is remolded along with material production? The ruling ideas of an age have always been but the ideas of the ruling class.

[121]People speak of ideas that revolutionize a whole society; they thereby merely express the fact that within the old society the elements of a new one have been formed, that the dissolution of the old ideas keeps pace with the dissolution of the old conditions of life.

[122]Als die alte Welt im Untergehen begriffen war, wurden die alten Religionen von der christlichen Religion besiegt. Als die christlichen Ideen im 18. Jahrhundert den Aufklärungs-Ideen unterlagen, rang die feudale Gesellschaft ihren Todeskampf mit der damals revolutionären Bourgeoisie. Die Ideen der Gewissens- und Religionsfreiheit sprachen nur die Herrschaft der freien Konkurrenz auf dem Gebiet des Gewissens aus.

[123]Aber wird man sagen, religiöse, moralische, philosophische, politische, rechtliche Ideen n. s. w. modificirten sich allerdings im Lauf der geschichtlichen Entwicklung. Die Religion, die Moral, die Philosophie, die Politik, das Recht, erhielten sich stets in diesem Wechsel.

[124]Es gibt zudem ewige Wahrheiten wie Freiheit, Gerechtigkeit u. s. w., die allen gesellschaftlichen Zuständen gemeinsam sind. Der Kommunismus aber schafft die ewigen Wahrheiten ab, er schafft die Religion ab, die Moral, statt sie neu zu gestalten, er widerspricht also allen bisherigen geschichtlichen Entwickelungen.

[125]Worauf reducirt sich diese Anklage? Die Geschichte der ganzen bisherigen Gesellschaft bewegte sich in Klassengegensätzen, die in den verschiedenen Epochen verschieden gestaltet waren.

[126]Welche Form sie aber auch immer angenommen, die Ausbeutung des einen Theils der Gesellschaft durch den andern ist eine allen vergangenen Jahrhunderten gemeinsame Thatsache. Kein Wunder daher, daß das gesellschaftliche Bewußtsein aller Jahrhunderte aller Mannigfaltigkeit und Verschiedenheit zum Trotz, in gewissen gemeinsamen Formen sich bewegt, Formen, Bewußtseinsformen, die nur mit dem gänzlichen Verschwinden des Klassengegensatzes sich vollständig auflösen.

[127]Die kommunistische Revolution ist das radikalste Brechen mit den überlieferten Eigenthums-Verhältnissen, kein Wunder, daß in ihrem Entwicklungsgange am radikalsten mit den überlieferten Ideen gebrochen wird.

[128]Doch lassen wir die Einwürfe der Bourgeoisie gegen den Kommunismus.

[122]When the antique world was in its last agony, Christianity triumphed over the antique religion. When the dogmas of Christianity were superseded by the enlightenment of the eighteenth century, feudal society was concentrating its last efforts against the then revolutionary Bourgeoisie. The ideas of religious liberty and freedom of thought were the expressions of unlimited competition in the affairs and free trade in the sphere of intellect and religion. [123]But you say, theological, moral, philosophical, political and legal ideas, are subject to be modified by the progress of historical developement. Religion, ethics, philosophy, politics, and jurisprudence are, however, of all times. [124]And we find, besides certain eternal ideas, for example, Freedom, Justice, and the like,—which are common to all the various social phases and states. But communism destroys these eternal truths; it pretends to abolish religion and Ethics, instead of merely giving them a new form; Communism, therefore, contradicts all preceding modes of historical development. [125]To what does this accusation amount? The history of all preceding states of society is simply the history of class antagonisms, which were fought under different conditions, and assumed different forms during the different historical epochs. [126]Whatever form these antagonisms may have assumed, the using up of one part of society by another part, is a fact, common to the whole past. No wonder then, that the social consciousness of past ages should have a common ground, in spite of the multiplicity and diversity of social arrangements: that it should move in certain common forms of thinking, which will completely disappear with the disappearance of class antagonism. [127]The communistic revolution is the most thorough-going rupture, with the traditionary conditions of property, no wonder then, that its progress will involve the completest rupture with traditionary ideas.

[128]But we must have done with the middle-class accusations against communism.

[122]When the ancient world was in its last throes, the ancient religions were overcome by Christianity. When Christian ideas succumbed in the 18th century to rationalist ideas, feudal society fought its death-battle with the then revolutionary bourgeoisie. The ideas of religious liberty and freedom of conscience, merely gave expression to the sway of free competition within the domain of knowledge.

[123]"Undoubtedly," it will be said, "religious, moral philosophical and juridical ideas have been modified in the course of historical development. But religion, morality, philosophy, political science, and law, constantly survived this change."

[124]"There are besides, eternal truths, such as Freedom, Justice, etc., that are common to all states of society. But Communism abolishes eternal truths, it abolishes all religion, and all morality, instead of constituting them on a new basis; it therefore acts in contradiction to all past historical experience."

[125]What does this accusation reduce itself to? The history of a past society has consisted in the development of class antagonisms, antagonisms that assumed different forms at different epochs.

[126]But whatever form they may have taken, one fact is common to all past ages, viz., the exploitation of one part of society by the other. No wonder, then, that the social consciousness of past ages, despite all the multiplicity and variety it displays, moves within certain common forms, or general ideas, which cannot completely vanish except with the total disappearance of class antagonisms.

[127]The Communist revolution is the most radical rupture with traditional property-relations; no wonder that its development involves the most radical rupture with traditional ideas.

[128]But let us have done with the bourgeois objections to Communism.

[122]When the ancient world was in course of going under, the old religions were vanquished by the Christian religion. When Christian ideas succumbed to the ideas of the Enlightenment in the eighteenth century, feudal society was in the throes of a struggle to the death with the then revolutionary bourgeoisie. The ideas of freedom of conscience and freedom of religion merely expressed the dominance of free competition in the sphere of conscience.

[123]"But," it will be said, "religious, moral, philosophical, political, juridical ideas, etc., have been modified in the course of historical development, to be sure. Religion, morality, philosophy, politics, jurisprudence always survived these vicissitudes.

[124]"There are, moreover, eternal truths like freedom, justice, etc, that are common to all social situations. Communism, however, abolishes eternal truths, it abolishes religion and morality, instead of recasting them anew; it therefore contradicts all historical development seen up to now."

[125]What does this charge amount to? The history of all society up to now has developed in class antagonisms that took different form in different epochs.

[126]But whatever form these antagonisms took, the exploitation of one part of society by the other is a fact common to all past centuries. No wonder, therefore, that the social consciousness of all centuries, despite all the multiplicity and diversity, moves in certain common forms--forms, forms of consciousness, which pass away completely only with the total disappearance of class antagonisms.

[127]The communist revolution is the most radical break with the traditional property relations; no wonder that in the course of its development there is the most radical break with the traditional ideas.

[128]However, let us leave behind the bourgeoisie's objections to communism.

[129]Wir sahen schon oben, daß der erste Schritt in der Arbeiter-Revolution die Erhebung des Proletariats zur herrschenden Klasse, die Erkämpfung der Demokratie ist.

[130]Das Proletariat wird seine politische Herrschaft dazu benutzen der Bourgeoisie nach und nach alles Kapital zu entreißen, alle Produktions-Instrumente in den Händen des Staats, d. h. des als herrschende Klasse organisirten Proletariats zu centralisiren und die Masse der Produktionskräfte möglichst rasch zu vermehren.

[131]Es kann dies natürlich zunächst nur geschehen vermittelst despotischer Eingriffe in das Eigenthumsrecht und in die bürgerlichen Produktions-Verhältnisse, durch Maaßregeln also, die ökonomisch unzureichend und unhaltbar erscheinen, die aber im Lauf der Bewegung über sich selbst hinaus treiben und als Mittel zur Umwälzung der ganzen Produktionsweise unvermeidlich sind.

[132]Diese Maaßregeln werden natürlich je nach den verschiedenen Ländern verschieden sein.

[133]Für die fortgeschrittensten Länder werden jedoch die folgenden ziemlich allgemein in Anwendung kommen können:

1) Expropriation des Grundeigenthums und Verwendung der Grundrente zu Staatsausgaben.

2) Starke Progressiv-Steuer.

3) Abschaffung des Erbrechts.

4) Konfiskation des Eigenthums aller Emigranten und Rebellen.

5) Centralisation des Kredits in den Händen des Staats durch eine Nationalbank mit Staatskapital und ausschließlichem Monopol.

6) Centralisation alles Transportwesens in den Händen des Staats.

7) Vermehrung der Nationalfabriken, Produktions-Instrumente, Urbarmachung und Verbesserung der Ländereien nach einem gemeinschaftlichen Plan.

8) Gleicher Arbeitzwang für Alle, Errichtung industrieller Armeen besonders für den Ackerbau.

[129]We have seen that the first step in the proletarian revolution, will be the conquest of Democracy, *the elevation of the Proletariat to the state of the ruling class.* [130]The Proletarians will use their political supremacy in order to deprive the middle-class of the command of capital; to centralise all the instruments of production in the hands of the State, that is, in those of the whole proletariat organized as the ruling class, and to increase the mass of productive power with the utmost possible rapidity. [131]It is a matter of course that this can be done, at first, only by despotic interference with the rights of property, and middle-class conditions of production. By regulations, in fact, which —economically considered—appear insufficient and untenable; which, therefore, in the course of the revolution, necessitate ulterior and more radical measures, and are unavoidable as a means towards a thorough change in the modes of production. [132]These regulations will, of course, be different in different countries. [133]But for the most advanced countries, the following will be pretty generally applicable:—

1. The national appropriation of the land, and the application of rent to the public revenue.

2. A heavy progressive tax.

3. Abolition of the right of inheritance.

4. Confiscation of the property of all emigrants and rebels.

5. Centralization of credit in the hands of the State, by means of a national bank, with an exclusive monopoly and a state-capital.

6. Centralization of all the means of communication in the hands of the state.

7. Increase of the national manufactories; of the instruments of production; the cultivation of waste lands and the improvement of the land generally according to a common plan.

8. Labour made compulsory for all; and the organization of industrial armies, especially for agriculture.

[129]We have seen above, that the first step in the revolution by the working class, is to raise the proletariat to the position of ruling class, to win the battle of democracy.

[130]The proletariat will use it political supremacy, to wrest by degrees, all capital from the bourgeoisie, to centralise all instruments of production in the hands of the State, *i.e.*, of the proletariat organised as the ruling class; and to increase the total of productive forces as rapidly as possible.

[131]Of course, in the beginning, this cannot be effected except by means of despotic inroads on the rights of property, and on the conditions of bourgeois production; by means of measures, therefore, which appear economically insufficient and untenable, but which, in the course of the movement, outstrip themselves, necessitate further inroads upon the old social order, and are unavoidable as a means of entirely revolutionising the mode of production.

[132]These measures will of course be different in different countries.

[133]Nevertheless in the most advanced countries, the following will be pretty generally applicable.

1. Abolition of property in land and application of all rents of land to public purposes.

2. A heavy progressive or graduated income tax.

3. Abolition of all right of inheritance.

4. Confiscation of the property of all emigrants and rebels.

5. Centralisation of credit in the hands of the State, by means of a national bank with State capital and an exclusive monopoly.

6. Centralisation of the means of communication and transport in the hands of the State.

7. Extension of factories and instruments of production owned by the State: the bringing into cultivation of waste lands, and the improvement of the soil generally in accordance with a common plan.

8. Equal liability of all to labour. Establishment of industrial armies, especially for agriculture.

[129]We have already seen, above, that the first step in the workers' revolution is the elevation of the proletariat to the ruling class, the winning of democracy.

[130]The proletariat will use its political rule to wrest bit by bit all capital from the bourgeoisie, to centralize all instruments of production in the hands of the state, i.e., of the proletariat organized as ruling class, and to augment the mass of productive forces as rapidly as possible.

[131]Of course, to begin with, this can be done only by means of despotic encroachments on the right of property and on the bourgeois relations of production, hence by measures which seem economically inadequate and untenable but which in the course of operation drive beyond their own limits, and are unavoidable as a means of transforming the whole mode of production.

[132]These measures will naturally be different depending on the different countries .

[133]For the most advanced countries, however, the following can be put into effect fairly generally:

1. Expropriation of landed property and use of ground rent to pay state expenses.

2. Heavy progressive tax.

3. Abolition of the right of inheritance.

4. Confiscation of the property of all émigrés and rebels.

5. Centralization of credit in the hands of the state through a national bank with state capital and an exclusive monopoly.

6. Centralization of the whole transportation system in the hands of the state.

7. Increase in national factories and instruments of production, reclamation and improvement of land in accordance with a common plan.

8. Equal obligation to work for everybody; establishment of industrial armies especially for agriculture.

9) Vereinigung des Betriebs von Ackerbau und Industrie, Hinwirken auf die allmählige Beseitigung des Gegensatzes von Stadt und Land.

10) Oeffentliche und unentgeldliche Erziehung aller Kinder. Beseitigung der Fabrikarbeit der Kinder in ihrer heutigen Form. Vereinigung der Erziehung mit materiellen Produktion u. s. w., u. s. w.

[134]Sind im Laufe der Entwicklung die Klassenunterschiede verschwunden, und ist alle Produktion in den Händen der associrten Individuen koncentrirt, so verliert die öffentliche Gewalt den politschen Charakter. Die Politische Gewalt im eigent lichen Sinn ist die organisirte Gewalt einer Klasse zur Unterdrückung einer andern. Wenn das Proletariat im Kampfe gegen die Bourgeoisie sich nothwendig zur Klasse vereint, durch eine Revolution sich zur herrschenden Klasse macht, und als herrschende Klasse gewaltsam die alten Produktions-Verhältnisse aufhebt, so hebt es mit diesen Produktions-Verhältnissen die Existenz-Bedingungen des Klassengegensatzes der Klassen überhaupt, und damit seine eigene Herrschaft als Klasse auf.

[135]An die Stelle der alten bürgerlichen Gesellschaft mit ihren Klassen und Klassen-Gegensätzen tritt eine Association, worin die freie Entwicklung eines Jeden, die Bedingung für die freie Entwicklung Aller ist.

9. The union of manufacturing and agricultural industry; with a view of gradually abolishing the antagonism between town and country.

10. The public and gratuitous education of all children; the abolition of the present system of factory labour for children; the conjunction of education and material production with other regulations of a similar nature.

[134]When Class distinctions will have finally disappeared, and production will have been concentrated in the hands of this Association which comprises the whole nation, the public power will lose its political character. Political power in the exact sense of the word, being the organised power of one class, which enables it to oppress another. When the proletariat has been forced to unite as a class during its struggle with the Bourgeoisie, when it has become the ruling class by a revolution, and as such has destroyed, by force, the old conditions of production, it destroys, necessarily, with these conditions of production, the conditions of existence of all class antagonism, of classes generally, and thus it destroys, also, its own supremacy as a class.

[135]The old Bourgeois Society, with its classes, and class antagonisms, will be replaced by an association, *wherein the free development of EACH is the condition of the free development of ALL.*

10. Free education for all children in public schools. Abolition of children's factory labour in its present form. Combination of education with industrial production, &c. &c.

[134]When, in the course of development, class distinctions have disappeared, and all production has been concentrated in the hands of a vast association of the whole nation, the public power will lose its political character. Political power properly so called, is merely the organised power of one class for oppressing another. If the proletariat during its contest with the bourgeoisie is compelled, by the force of circumstances, to organise itself as a class, if, by means of a revolution, it makes itself the ruling class, and, as such, sweeps way by force the old conditions of production, then it will, along with these conditions, have swept away the conditions for the existence of class antagonisms, and of classes generally, and will thereby have abolished its own supremacy as a class.

[135]In place of the old bourgeois society, with its classes and class antagonisms, we shall have an association, in which the free development of each is the condition for the free development of all.

9. Combined operations in running agriculture and industry, making for the gradual elimination of the antithesis of town and country.

10. Public education of all children free of charge. Elimination of children's factory labor in its present form. Combination of education with material production, etc., etc

[134]When, in the course of development, class distinctions have disappeared and all production is concentrated in the hands of associated individuals, the public power loses its political character. Political power in its proper sense is the organized power of one class for the oppression of another. When in the struggle against the bourgeoisie the proletariat necessarily unifies itself as a class, makes itself the ruling class through a revolution, and as ruling class forcibly abolishes the old relations of production, then along with these relations of production it abolishes the preconditions of existence of class antagonism and of classes in general, and therewith its own rule as a class.

[135]In place of the old bourgeois society with its classes and class antagonisms there comes an association in which the free development of each is the precondition for the free development of all.

CHAPTER III.

III.

Socialistische und kommunistische Literatur.

1) Der reaktionaire Socialismus.

a) Der feudale Socialismus.

SOCIALIST AND COMMUNIST

LITERATURE.

I.—REACTIONARY SOCIALISM.

a.—FEUDAL SOCIALISM.

[136]Die französische und englische Aristokratie war ihrer geschichtlichen Stellung nach dazu berufen, Pamphlete gegen die moderne bürgerliche Gesellschaft zu schreiben. In der französischen Julirevoluion von 1830, in der englischen Reformbewegung war sie noch einmal dem verhaßten Emporkömmling erlegen. Von einem ernsten politischen Kampfe konnte nicht mehr die Rede sein. Nur der literarische Kampf blieb ihr übrig. Aber auch auf dem Gebiete der Literatur waren die alten Redensarten der Restaurationszeit unmöglich geworden. Um Sympathie zu erregen, mußte die Aristokratie scheinbar ihre Interessen aus den Augen verlieren und nur noch im Interesse der exploitirten Arbeiterklasse ihren Anklageakt gegen die Bourgeoisie formuliren. Sie bereitete sich so die Genugthuung vor, Schmählieder auf ihren neuen Herrscher singen und mehr oder minder unheilschwangere Prophezeihungen ihm in's Ohr raunen zu dürfen.

[137]Auf diese Art entstand der feudalistische Socialismus, halb Klagelied, halb Pasquill, halb Rückhall der Vergangenheit, halb Dräuen der Zukunft, mitunter die Bourgeoisie in's Herz treffend durch bittres, geistreich zerreißendes Urtheil, stets komisch wirkend durch gänzliche Unfähigkeit den Gang der modernen Geschichte zu begreifen.

[138]Den proletarischen Bettlersack schwenkten sie als Fahne in der Hand, um das Volk hinter sich her zu versammeln. So oft es ihnen aber folgte, erblickte es auf ihrem Hintern die alten feudalen Wappen und verlief sich mit lautem und unehrerbeitigem Gelächter.

[139]Ein Theil der französischen Legitimisten und das junge England gaben dies Schauspiel zum Besten.

[136]THE historical position of the French and English Aristocracy devolved upon them, at a certain period, the task of writing pamphlets against the social system of the modern Bourgeoisie. These Aristocracies were again beaten by a set of detestable parvenus and nobodies in the July days of 1830, and in the English Reform Bill movement. There could be no longer any question about a serious political struggle. There remained only the possibility of conducting a literary combat. But even in the territory of Literature, the old modes of speech, current during the Restoration, had become impossible. In order to excite sympathy, the Aristocracy had to assume the semblance of disinterestedness, and to draw up their accusation of the Bourgeoisie, apparently as advocates for the used-up Proletarians. The Aristocracy thus revenged themselves on their new masters,—by lampoons and fearful prophecies of coming woe. [137]In this way feudal socialism arose—half lamentation, half libel, half echo of the Past, half prophecy of a threatening Future;—sometimes striking the very heart of the Bourgeoisie by its sarcastic, bitter judgments, but always accompanied by a certain tinge of the ludicrous, from its complete inability to comprehend the march of modern history. [138]The Feudal Socialists waved the Proletarian alms-bag aloft, to assemble the people around them. But as often as the people came, they perceived upon the hind parts of these worthies, the old feudal arms and quarterings, and abandoned them with noisy and irreverent hilarity. [139]A part of the French Legitimists and the party of Young England played this farce.

III.

SOCIALIST AND COMMUNIST LITERATURE.
I. Reactionary Socialism.
***a*. Feudal Socialism.**

[136]"Owing to their historical position, it became the vocation of the aristocracies of France and England to write pamphlets against modern bourgeois society. In the French revolution of July 1830, and in the English reform agitation, these aristocracies again succumbed to the hateful upstart. Thenceforth, a serious political contest was altogether out of question. A literary battle alone remained possible. But even in the domain of literature the old cries of the restoration period(*a*) had become impossible. In order to arouse sympathy, the aristocracy were obliged to lose sight apparently, of their own interests, and to formulate their indictment against the bourgeoisie in the interest of the exploited workingclass alone. Thus the aristocracy took their revenge by singing lampoons on their new master, and whispering in his ears sinister prophecies of coming catastrophe.

[137]In this way arose feudal socialism: half lamentation, half lampoon; half echo of the past, half menace of the future; at times, by its bitter, witty and incisive criticism, striking the bourgeoisie to the very hearts' core, but always ludicrous in its effect through total incapacity to comprehend the march of modern history.

[138]The aristocracy, in order to rally the people to them, waved the proletarian alms-bag in front for a banner. But the people, so often as it joined them, saw on their hindquarters the old feudal coats of arms, and deserted with loud and irreverent laughter.

[139]One section of the French Legitimists, and "Young England," exhibited this spectacle.

III

SOCIALIST AND COMMUNIST LITERATURE

1. Reactionary Socialism

(a) Feudal Socialism

[136]In line with their historical positions, the French and English aristocracies were called upon to write pamphlets against modern bourgeois society. In the French July Revolution of 1830 and in the English reform movement, they once again succumbed to the hated upstart. There could no longer be any question of a serious political struggle. Only a literary struggle remained for them. But even in the sphere of literature the old phrases of the Restoration period had become impossible. In order to arouse sympathy, the aristocracy had to apparently lose sight of its own interests and formulate its bill of indictment against the bourgeoisie only in the interest of the exploited working class. It thus prepared to get redress by singing lampoons on its new ruler and allowing itself to murmur more or less ill-boding prophecies in his ear.

[137]In this way arose feudal socialism, half song of lament and half pasquinade, half echo of the past and half menace of the future, now and then striking the bourgeoisie to the heart by bitter and wittingly cutting comment, always producing a comic effect through total incapacity to comprehend the course of modern history.

[138]They flourished the proletarian alms-bag in their hands as a banner, in order to rally the people behind them. But whenever the people followed them, they saw on their backsides the old feudal coats of arms and scattered away with loud and irreverent laughter.

[139]This spectacle was best exhibited by a part of the French Legitimists and by Young England.

[140]Wenn die Feudalen beweisen, daß ihre Weise der Ausbeutung anders gestaltet war als die bürgerliche Ausbeutung, so vergessen sie nur, daß sie unter gänzlich verschiedenen und jetzt überlebten Umständen und Bedingungen ausbeuteten. Wenn sie nachweisen, daß unter ihrer Herrschaft nicht das moderne Proleteriat existirt hat, so vergessen sie nur, daß eben die moderne Bourgeoisie ein nothwendiger Spröß-ling ihrer Gesellschaftsordnung war.

[141]Uebrigens verheimlichen sie den reaktionären Charakter ihrer Kritk so wenig, daß ihre Hauptanklage gegen die Bourgeoisie eben darin besteht, unter ihrem Regime entwickele sich eine Klasse, welche die ganze alte Gesellschaftsordnung in die Luft sprengen werde.

[142]Sie werfen der Bourgeoisie mehr noch vor, daß sie ein revolutionares Proletariat, als daß sie überhaupt ein Proletariat erzeugt.

[143]In der politischen Praxis nehmen sie daher an allen Gewaltmaßregeln gegen die Arbeiter-klasse Theil, und im gewöhnlichen Leben be-quemen sie sich, allen ihren aufgeblähten Re-densarten zum Trotz, die goldenen Aepfel aufzulesen, und Treue, Liebe, Ehre mit dem Schacher in Schaafswolle, Runkelrüben und Schnapps zu vertauschen.

[144]Wie der Pfaffe immer Hand in Hand ging mit dem Feudalen, so der pfäffische Socialismus mit dem feudalistischen.

[145]Nichts leichter als dem christlichen Ascetismus einen socialistischen Anstrich zu geben. Hat das Christenthum nicht auch gegen das Privateigenthum, gegen die Ehe, gegen den Staat geeifert? Hat es nicht die Wohlthätigkeit und den Bettel, das Cölibat und die Fleisch-esertödtung, das Zellenleben und die Kirche an ihre Stelle gepredigt? Der heitige Socialismus ist nur das Weihwasser, womit der Pfaffe den Aerger des Aristokraten einsegnet.

[140]When the Feudalists show that their mode of exploitation (*using up one class by another*) was different from the Bourgeois mode, they forget that their mode was practicable only under circumstances and conditions which have passed away—never to return. When they show that the modern Proletariat never existed under their supremacy, they simply forget, that the modern Bourgeoisie is the necessary offspring of their own social order. [141]For the rest, they so little conceal the reactionary nature of their criticism, that their chief reproach against the Bourgeoise-régime is, that of having created a class which is destined to annihilate the old social forms and arrangements altogether. [142]It is not so much that the Bourgeoisie having created a Proletariat, but that this Proletariat is revolutionary. [143]Hence, in their political practice, they take part in all reactionary measures against the working classes; and in ordinary life, despite their grandiloquent phrases, they condescend to gather the golden apples, and to give up chivalry, true love, and honour for the traffic in wool, butcher's meat, and corn. [144]As the parson has always gone hand-in-hand with the landlord, so has Priestly Socialism with Feudal Socialism. [145]Nothing is easier than to give Christian ascetism a tinge of Socialism. Has not Christianity itself vociferated against private property, marriage, and the powers that be? Have not charity, and mendi-city, celibacy and mortification of the flesh, monastic life, and the supremacy of the Church been held up in the place of these things? Sacred Socialism is merely the holy water, with which the priest besprinkles the impotent wrath of the Aristocracy.

[140]In pointing out that their mode of exploitation was different to that of the bourgeoisie, the feudalists forget that they exploited under circumstances and conditions that were quite different and that are now antiquated. In showing that under their rule, the modern proletariat never existed, they forget that the modern bourgeoisie is the necessary offspring of their own form of society.

[141]For the rest so little do they conceal the reactionary character of their criticism, that their chief accusation against the bourgeoisie amounts to this that under the bourgeois *régime* a class is being developed, which is destined to cut up root and branch the old order of society.

[142]What they upbraid the bourgeoisie with is not so much that it creates a proletariat as that it creates a *revolutionary* proletariat.

[143]In political practice, therefore, they join in all coercive measures against the working-class; and in ordinary life, despite their high falutin phrases,they stoop to pick up the golden apples dropped from the tree of industry, and to barter truth, love, and honour for traffic in wool,beetroot-sugar, and potato spirit.(*b*)

[144]As the parson has ever gone hand in hand with the landlord, so has Clerical Socialism with Feudal Socialism.

[145]Nothing is easier than to give Christian asceticism a socialist tinge.

[146]Has not Christianity declared against private property, against marriage, against the State? Has it not preached in the place of these, charity and poverty, celibacy and mortification of the flesh, monastic life and Mother Church? Christian Socialism is but the Holy Water with which the priest consecrates the heart-burnings of the aristocracy.

[140]When the feudalists show that their mode of exploitation was framed differently from bourgeois exploitation, they simply forget that they exploited under entirely different and now outlived circumstances and conditions. When they point out that under their rule the modern proletariat did not exist, they simply forget that it was precisely the modern bourgeoisie that was a necessary offspring of their social order.

[141]In any case, they conceal the reactionary character of their critique so little that their main charge against the bourgeoisie is precisely that under its regime a class develops which will blow up the whole of the old social order.

[142]They blame the bourgeoisie more for creating a revolutionary proletariat than for just creating a proletariat at all.

[143]In political practice they therefore take part in all forcible measures against the working class, and in everyday life, despite all their puffed-up phrases, they deign to pick up the golden apples and to trade fidelity, love, and honor for huckstering in wool, sugar beets, and schnapps.

[144]Just as the priest always went hand in hand with the feudalist, so has clerical socialism with feudal socialism.

[145]There is nothing easier than to give Christian asceticism a socialistic veneer. Has not Christianity even inveighed against private property, against marriage, against the state? Has it not preached charity and beggary, celibacy and mortification of the flesh, monastic life and the church, in their stead? Religious socialism is merely the holy water with which the priest consecrates the anger of the aristocrat.

b) Kleinbürgerlicher Socialismus.

[146]Die feudale Aristokratie ist nicht die einzige Klasse, welche durch die Bourgeoisie gestürzt wurde, deren Lebensbedingungen in der modernen bürgerlichen Gesellschaft verkümmerten und abstarben. Das mittelalterliche Pfahlbürgerthum und der kleine Bauernstand waren die Vorläufer der modernen Bourgeoisie. In den weniger industriell und kommerciell entwickelten Ländern vegetirt diese Klasse noch fort neben der aufkommenden Bourgeoisie.

[147]In den Ländern, wo sich die moderne Civilisation entwickelt hat, hat sich eine neue Kleinbürgerschaft gebildet, die zwischen dem Proletariat und der Bourgeoisie schwebt und als ergänzender Theil der bürgerlichen Gesellschaft stets von Neuem sich bildet, deren Mitglieder aber beständig durch die Konkurrenz in's Proletariat hinabgeschleudert werden, ja selbst mit der Entwicklung der großen Industrie einen Zeitpunkt herannahen sehen, wo sie als selbstständiger Theil der modernen Gesellschaft gänzlich verschwinden, und im Handel, in der Manufaktur, in der Agrikultur durch Arbeitsaufseher und Domestiken ersetzt werden.

[148]In Ländern wie in Frankreich, wo die Bauernklasse weit mehr als die Hälfte der Bevölkerung ausmacht, war es natürlich, daß Schriftsteller, die für das Proletariat gegen die Bourgeoisie auftraten, an ihre Kritik des Bourgeoisregime's den kleinbürgerlichen und kleinbäuerlichen Maaßstab anlegten und die Partei der Arbeiter vom Standpunkt des Kleinbürgerthums ergriffen. Es bildete sich so der kleinbürgerliiche Socialismus. Sismondi ist das Haupt dieser Literatur nicht nur für Frankreich sondern auch für England.

b.—SHOPOCRAT* SOCIALISM.

[146]The Feudal Aristocracy are not the only class who are, or will be, destroyed by the Bourgeoisie. Not the only class, the conditions of whose existence become exhausted and disappear, under the modern middle-class system. The mediæval burgesses and yeoman were the precursors of the modern middle-class. In countries possessing a small degree of industrial and commercial development, this intermediate class still vegetates side by side with the flourishing Bourgeoisie. [147]In countries where modern civilization has been developed, a new intermediate class has been formed; floating as it were, between the Bourgeoisie and the Proletariat; and always renewing itself as a component part of Bourgeois society. Yet, the persons belonging to this class are constantly forced by competition downwards into the Proletariat, and the development of the modern industrial system will bring about the time when this small capitalist class will entirely disappear, and be replaced by managers and stewards, in commerce, manufactures, and agriculture. [148]In countries like France, where far more than one half of the population are small freeholders, it was natural, that writers who took part with the Proletariat against the Bourgeoisie, should measure the Bourgeois-régime by the small-capitalist standard; and should envisage the Proletarian question from the small-capitalist point of view. In this way arose the system of Shopocrat Socialism. Sismondi is the head of this school, in England as well as in France.

b. Petty Bourgeois Socialism.

(b) Petty-Bourgeois Socialism

[146]The feudal aristocracy was not the only class that was ruined by the bourgeoisie, not the only class whose conditions of existence pined and perished in the atmosphere of modern bourgeois society. The mediaeval burgesses and the small peasant proprietors were the precursors of the modern bourgeoisie. In those countries which are but little developed, industrially and commercially, these two classes vegetate side by side with the rising bourgeoisie.

[147]In countries where modern civilisation has become fully developed a new class of petty bourgeois has been formed, fluctuating between proletariat and bourgeoisie, and ever renewing itself as a supplementary part of bourgeois society. The individual members of this class, however, are being constantly hurled down into the proletariat by the action of competition, and, as modern industry develops, they even see the moment approaching when they will completely disappear as an independent section of modern society, to be replaced, in manufactures, agriculture and commerce, by overlookers, bailiffs and shopmen.

[148]In countries, like France, where the peasants constitute far more than half of the population, it was natural that writers who sided with the proletariat against the bourgeoisie, should use, in their criticism of the bourgeois *regime*, the standard of the peasant and petty bourgeois, and from the standpoint of these intermediate classes should take up the cudgels for the working-class. Thus arose petty bourgeois Socialism. Sismondi was the head of this school not only in France but also in England.

[146]The feudal aristocracy is not the only class that was overthrown by the bourgeoisie and whose conditions of existence faded away and died out in modern bourgeois society. The medieval burgesses and the small peasantry were the forerunners of the modern bourgeoisie. In countries that are little developed industrially and commercially, this class still continues to vegetate alongside the rising bourgeoisie.

[147]In countries where modern civilization has developed, a new petty-bourgeoisie has been formed, which hovers between the proletariat and the bourgeoisie and continually reforms itself afresh as a supplementary part of bourgeois society but whose members are constantly hurled down into the proletariat on account of competition; indeed, with the development of large-scale industry, they even see a time approaching when they disappear altogether as an independent part of modern society and are replaced in commerce, manufacturing, and agriculture by labor overseers and stewards.

[148]In countries like France, where the peasant class makes up far more than half the population, it was natural that writers who came out for the proletariat against the bourgeoisie applied the petty-bourgeois and small-peasant measuring rod to their critique of the bourgeois regime and took the side of the workers from the standpoint of the petty-bourgeoisie. This is how petty-bourgeois socialism took shape. Sismondi is the chief figure in this literature not only for France but also for England.

[149]Dieser Socialismus zergliederte höchst scharfsinnig die Widersprüche in den modernen Produktionsverhältnissen. Er enthüllte die gleißnerischen Beschönigungen der Oekonomen. Er wies unwiderleglich die zerstörenden Wirkungen der Maschinerie und der Theilung der Arbeit nach, die Koncentration der Kapitalien und des Grundbesitzes, die Ueberproduktion, die Krisen, den nothwendigen Untergang der kleinen Bürger und Bauern, das Elend des Proletariats, die Anarchie in der Produktion, die schreienden Mißverhältnisse in der Vertheilung des Reichthums, den industriellen Vernichtungskrieg der Nationen unter einander, die Auflösung der alten Sitten, der alten Familien-Verhältnisse, der alten Nationalitäten.

[150]Seinem positiven Gehalte nach will jedoch dieser Socialismus entweder die alten Produktions- und Verkehrsmittel wiederherstellen und mit ihnen die alten Eigenthumsverhältnisse und die alte Gesellschaft, oder er will die modernen Produktions- und Verkehrsmittel in den Rahmen der alten Eigenthumsverhältnisse, die von ihnen gesprengt werden, gesprengt werden mußten, gewaltsam wieder einsperren. In beiden Fällen ist er reaktionär und utopistisch zugleich.

[151]Zunftwesen in der Manufaktur und patriarchalische Wirthschaft auf dem Lande, das sind seine letzten Worte.

[152]In ihrer weitern Entwicklung hat sich diese Richtung in einen feigen Katzenjammer verlaufen.

c) Der deutsche oder der wahre Socialismus.

[153]Die socialistische und kommunistische Literatur Frankreichs, die unter dem Druck einer herrschenden Bourgeoisie entstand und der literarische Ausdruck des Kampfs gegen diese Herrschaft ist, wurde nach Deutschland eingeführt zu einer Zeit, wo die Bourgeoisie so eben ihren Kampf gegen den feudalen Absolutismus begann.

[149]This school of socialism has dissected with great acuteness the modern system of production, and exposed the fallacies contained therein. It unveiled the hypocritical evasions of the political economists. It irrefutably demonstrated the destructive effects of machinery, and the division of labour; the concentration of capital and land in a few hands; over production; commercial crisis; the necessary destruction of the small capitalist; the misery of the Proletariat; anarchy in production, and scandalous inequality in the distribution of wealth; the destructive industrial wars of one nation with another; and the disappearance of old manners and customs, of patriarchal family arrangements, and of old nationalities. [150]But in its practical application, this Shopocrat, or Small-Capitalist Socialism, wish either to re-establish the old modes of production and traffic, and with these, the old condtions of property, and old society altogether—or forcibly to confine the modern means of production and traffic within the limits of these antique conditions of property, which were actually destroyed, necessarily so, by these very means. In both cases, Shopocrat Socialism is, at the same time reactionary and Utopian. [151]Corporations and guilds in manufactures, patriarchal idyllic arrangements in agriculture, are its beau ideal. [152]This kind of Socialism has run to seed, and exhausted itself in silly lamentations over the past.

c.—GERMAN OR "TRUE" SOCIALISM.

[153]The Socialist and Commnnist literature of France originated under the Bourgeois-régime, and was the literary expression of the struggle against middle-class supremacy. It was introduced into Germany at a time when the Bourgeoisie there had began their battle against Feudal despotism.

[149]This school of Socialism dissected with great acuteness the contradictions in the conditions of modern production. It laid bare the hypocritical apologies of economists. It proved, incontrovertibly, the disastrous effects of machinery and division of labour; the concentration of capital and land in a few hands; overproduction and crises; it pointed out the inevitable ruin of the petty bourgeois and peasant the misery of the proletariat, the anarchy in production, the crying inequalities in the distribution of wealth, the industrial war of extermination between nations, the dissolution of old moral bonds, of the old family relations, of the old nationalities.

[150]In its positive aims, however, this form of Socialism aspires either to restoring the old means of production and of exchange, and with them the old property relations, and the old society, or to cramping the modern means of production and of exchange, within the framework of the old property relations that have been, and were bound to be, exploded by those means. In either case, it is both reactionary and Utopian.

[151]Its last words are: corporate guilds for manufacture; patriarchal relations in agriculture.

[152]Ultimately, when stubborn historical facts had dispersed all intoxicating effects of self-deception, this form of Socialism ended in a miserable fit of the blues.

German or "True" Socialism.

[153]The Socialist and Communist literature of France, a literature that originated under the pressure of a bourgeoisie in power, and that was the expression of the struggle against this power, was introduced into Germany at a time when the bourgeoisie, in that country, had just begun its contest with feudal absolutism.

[149]This socialism dissected most acutely the contradictions in the modern relations of production. It laid bare the hypocritical apologetics of the economists. It irrefutably demonstrated the destructive effects of machinery and the division of labor, the concentration of capital and landed property, overproduction, crises, the necessary ruin of the small burghers and peasants, the misery of the proletariat, anarchy in production, the glaring disproportions in the distribution of wealth, the industrial war to the knife among nations, the dissolution of the old mores, old family relationships, and old nationalities.

[150]In terms of its positive content, however, this socialism wishes either to re-establish the old means of production and exchange and along with them the old property relations and the old society, or else it wishes to forcibly reimprison the modern means of production and exchange within the framework of the old property relations which they burst asunder, and had to burst asunder. In both cases it is reactionary and utopian at the same time.

[151]The guild system in manufacturing and a patriarchal economy on the land: these are its last words.

[152]In its further development this tendency expired in the blue funk of a hangover.

(c) German or True Socialism

[153]The socialist and communist literature of France, which arose under the impress of a ruling bourgeoisie and is the literary expression of the struggle against this rule, was introduced into Germany at a time when the bourgeoisie had just begun its struggle against feudal absolutism.

[154]Deutsche Philosophen, Halbphilosophen und Schöngeister bemächtigten sich gierig dieser Literatur und vergassen nur, daß bei der Einwanderung jener Schriften aus Frankreich die französischen Lebensverhältnisse nicht gleichzeitig nach Deutschland eingewandert waren. Den deutschen Verhältnissen gegenüber verlor die französische Literatur alle unmittelbar praktische Bedeutung und nahm ein rein literarisches Aussehen an. Als müßige Spekulation über die wahre Gesellschaft, über die Verwirklichung des menschlichen Wesens mußte sie erscheinen. So hatten für die deutschen Philosophen des 18. Jahrhunderts die Forderungen der ersten französischen Revolution nur den Sinn, Forderungen der „praktischen Vernunft" im Allgemeinen zu sein und die Willensäußerung der revolutionären französischen Bourgeoisie bedeuteten in ihren Augen die Gesetze des reinen Willens, des Willens wie er sein muß, des wahrhaft menschlichen Willens.

[155]Die ausschließliche Arbeit der deutschen Literaten bestand darin, die neuen französischen Ideen mit ihrem alten philosophischen Gewissen in Einklang zu setzen, oder vielmehr von ihrem philosophischen Stankpunkt aus die französischen Ideen sich anzueignen.

[156]Diese Aneignung geschah in derselben Weise, wodurch man sich überhaupt eine fremde Sprache aneignet, durch die Uebersetzung.

[157]Es ist bekannt wie die Mönche Manuscripte, worauf die klassischen Werke der alten Heidenzeit verzeichnet waren, mit abgeschmackten katholischen Heiligengeschichten überschrieben. Die deutschen Literaten gingen umgekehrt mit der profanen französischen Literatur um. Sie schrieben ihren philosophischen Unsinn hinter das französische Original. Z. B. hinter die französische Kritik der Geldverhältnisse schrieben sie „Entäußerung des menschlichen Wesens", hinter die französische Kritik des Bourgeoisstaats schrieben sie „Aufhebung der Herrschaft des abstrakt Allgemeinen" u. s. w.

[154]German Philosophers—half-philosophers, and would-be literati—eagerly seized on this literature, and forgot that with the immigration of these French writings into Germany, the advanced state of French society, and of French class-struggles, had not, as a matter of course, immigrated along with them. This French literature, when brought into contact with the German phasis of social development, lost all its immediate practical significance, and assumed a purely literary aspect. It could appear in no other way than as an idle speculation upon the best possible state of society, upon the realization of the true nature of man. In a similar manner, the German philosophers of the 18th century, considered the demands of the first French Revolution as the demands of "Practical Reason" in its general sense, and the will of the revolutionary French bourgeoisie, was for them the law of the pure will, of volition as it ought to be; the law of man's inward nature. [155]The all-engrossing problem for the German literati was to bring the new French ideas into accordance with their old philosophic conscience; or rather, to appropriate the French ideas without leaving the philosophic point of view. [156]This appropriation took place in the same way as one masters a foreign language; namely, by translation. [157]It is known how the Monks of the middle-ages treated the manuscripts of the Greek and Roman classics. They wrote silly Catholic legends over the original text. The German literati did the very reverse, with respect to the profane French literature. They wrote their philosophical nonsense behind the French original. For example, behind the French critique of the modern money-system, they wrote "Estrangement of Human Nature;" behind the French critique of the bourgeois-régime, they wrote, "Destruction of the Supremacy of the Absolute," and so forth.

172

[154]German philosophers, would be philosophers, and *beaux esprits*, eagerly seized on this literature, only forgetting that when these writings immigrated from France into Germany, French social conditions had not immigrated along with them. In contact with German social conditions, this French literature lost all its immediate practical significance, and assumed a purely literary aspect. Thus, to the German philosophers of the Eighteenth Century, the demands of the first French Revolution were nothing more than the demands of "Practical Reason" in general, and the utterance of the will of the revolutionary French bourgeoisie signified in their eyes the laws of pure Will, of Will as it was bound to be, of true human Will generally.

[155]The work of the German *literati* consisted solely in bringing the new French ideas into harmony with their ancient philosophical conscience, or rather, in annexing the French ideas without deserting their own philosophic point of view.

[156]This annexation took place in the same way in which a foreign language is appropriated, namely by translation.

[157]It is well known how the monks wrote silly lives of Catholic Saints *over* the manuscripts on which the classical works of ancient heathendom had been written. The German *literati* reversed this process with the profane French literature. They wrote their philosophical nonsense beneath the French original. For instance, beneath the French criticism of the economic functions of money, they wrote "Alienation of Humanity" and beneath the French criticism of the bourgeois State they wrote, "Dethronement of the Category of the General" and so forth.

[154]German philosophers, semi-philosophers, and beaux-esprits eagerly seized on this literature, and only forgot that when these writings emigrated from France the French conditions of existence did not migrate to Germany at the same time. Vis-à-vis German conditions, this French literature lost all immediate practical significance and assumed a purely literary complexion. It was bound to appear to be idle speculation about the True Society, about the realization of Human Nature. Thus, for the German philosophers of the eighteenth century, the demands of the first French Revolution meant only demands of "practical reason" in general, and the expression of the will of the revolutionary French bourgeoisie signified in their eyes the laws of pure will, of will as it had to be, of truly human will.

[155]The sole job done by the German litterateurs consisted in bringing the new French ideas into conformity with their old philosophic conscience, or, rather, in appropriating the French ideas on the basis of their own philosophic standpoint.

[156]This appropriation was carried out in the same way a foreign language is generally appropriated—by translation.

[157]We know how the monks wrote vapid tales of Catholic saints over manuscripts recording the classical works of ancient pagan days. The German litterateurs did just the opposite with the profane French literature. They wrote their philosophic nonsense underneath the French original. For example, underneath the French critique of money relations they wrote "alienation of human nature"; underneath the French critique of the bourgeois state they wrote "abolition of the supremacy of the abstractly universal," etc.

[158]Diese Unterschiebung ihrer philosophischen Redensarten unter die französischen
Entwicklungen taufte sie "Philosophie der
That," "wahrer Socialismus," "Deutsche
Wissenschaft des Socialismus," "Philosophische
Begründung des Socialismus" u. s. w.
[159]Die französisch-socialistisch kommunistische Literatur wurde so förmlich entmannt.
Und da sie in der Hand des Deutschen aufhörte,
den Kampf einer Klasse gegen die andere
auszudrücken, so war der Deutsche sich bewußt,
die französische Einseitigkeit überwunden, statt
wahrer Bedürfnisse, das Bedürfniß der
Wahrheit, und statt die Interessen des
Proletariers die Interessen des menschlichen
Wesens, des Menschen überhaupt vertreten zu
haben, des Menschen, der keiner Klasse, der
überhaupt nicht der Wirklichkeit, der nur dem
Dunsthimmel der philosophischen Phantasie
angehört.
[160]Dieser deutsche Socialismus, der seine
unbeholfene Schulübungen so ernst und
feierlich nahm und so marktschreierisch
ausposaunte, verlor indeß nach und nach seine
pedantische Unschuld.
[161]Der Kampf der deutschen namentlich der
preußischen Bourgeoisie gegen die Feudalen
und das absolute Königthum, mit einem Wort,
die liberale Bewegung wurde ernsthafter.
[162]Dem wahren Socialismus war so
erwünschte Gelegenheit geboten, der politischen
Bewegung die socialistischen Forderungen
gegenüber zu stellen.
Die überlieferten Anatheme gegen den
Liberalismus, gegen den Repräsentativ-Staat,
gegen die bürgerliche Konkurrenz, bürgerliche
Preßfreiheit, bürgerliches Recht, bürgerliche
Freiheit und Gleichheit zu schleudern und der
Volksmasse vorzupredigen, wie sie bei dieser
bürgerlichen Bewegung nichts zu gewinnen,
vielmehr Alles zu verlieren habe. Der deutsche
Socialismus vergaß rechtzeitig, daß die
französische Kritik, deren geistloses Echo er
war, die moderne bürgerliche Gesellschaft mit
den entsprechenden materiellen
Lebensbedingungen und der angemessenen
politischen Konstitution voraussetzt, lauter
Voraussetzungen, um deren Erkämpfung es sich
erst in Deutschland handelte.

174

[158]They baptized this interpolation of their
philosophic modes of speech, with the French
ideas by various names; "Philosophy in Action,"
"True Socialism," "The German Philosophy of
Socialism," "Philosophical Foundation of
Socialism," and the like. [159]The socialist and
communist literature of France was completely
emasculated. And when it had ceased, in
German hands, to express the struggle of one
class against another, the Germans imagined
they had overcome French one-sidedness. They
imagined they represented, not true interests
and wants, but the interests and wants of
abstract truth; not the proletarian interest, but
the interest of human nature, as man as
belonging to no class, a native of no merely
terrestial countries,—of man, belonging of the
misty, remote region of philosophical
imagination. [160]This German socialism, which
composed its clumsy school themes with such
exemplary solemnity, and then cried them along
the street, gradually lost its pedantic and
primitive innocence. [161]The battle of the
German, particularly of the Prussian
bourgeoisie, against feudalism and absolute
monarchy, in a word, the liberal movement,
became more serious. [162]True socialism had now
the desired opportunity of placing socialist
demands in opposition to the actual political
movement; of hurling the traditionary second-
hand Anathemas against liberalism,
constitutional governments, bourgeois
competition and free trade, bourgeois freedom
of the press, bourgeois juries, bourgeois freedom
and equality; the opportunity of preaching to the
masses that they had nothing to gain and every
thing to lose by this middle-class movement.
German socialism forgot, very opportunely, that
the French polemics, whose unmeaning echo it
was,— presupposed the modern middle-class
system of society, with the corresponding
physical conditions of social existence, and a
suitable political constitution presupposed, in
fact, the very things which had no existence in
Germany, and which were the very things to be
obtained by the middle-class movement.

[158]The introduction of these philosophical phrases at the back of the French historical criticisms they dubbed "Philosophy of Action", "True Socialism," "German Science of Socialism," "Philosophical Foundation of Socialism" and so on.

[159]The French Socialist and Communist literature was thus completely emasculated. And, since it ceased, in the hands of the German to express the struggle of one class with the other, he felt conscious of having overcome "French one-sidedness," and of representing, not true requirements, but the requirements of Truth, not the interests of the proletariat, but the interests of Human Nature, of Man in general who belongs to no class, has no reality, who exists only in the misty realm of philosophical phantasy.

[160]This German Socialism, which took its school-boy task so seriously and solemnly, and extolled its poor stock-in-trade in such mountebank fashion, meanwhile gradually lost its pedantic innocence.

[161]The fight of the German, and, especially, of the Prussian bourgeoisie, against feudal aristocracy and absolute monarchy, in other words, the liberal movement, became more earnest.

[162]By this, the long wished-for opportunity was offered to "True Socialism" of confronting the political movement with the socialist demands, of hurling the traditional anathemas against liberalism, against representative government against bourgeois competition, bourgeois freedom of the press, bourgeois legislation, bourgeois liberty and equality, and of preaching to the masses that they had nothing to gain, and everything to lose, by this bourgeois movement. German Socialism forgot in the nick of time, that the French criticism, whose silly echo it was, presupposed the existence of modern bourgeois society, with its corresponding economic conditions of existence, and the political constitution adapted thereto, the very things whose attainment was the object of the pending struggle in Germany.

[158]This interpolation of their philosophic phrases underneath the French analyses they christened "philosophy of action," "true socialism," "German science of socialism," "philosophical foundation of socialism " etc,

[159]The French socialist-communist literature was thus veritably emasculated. And since in the German's hands it ceased to express the struggle of one class against the other, the German felt conscious of overcoming French onesidedness, of representing the Need for Truth rather than true needs, and the Interests of Human Nature, of Humanity in general, rather than the interests of the proletarian—representing a Humanity belonging to no class, belonging in general not to reality but only to the misty heaven of philosophic fantasy,

[160]This German socialism, which took its clumsy school exercises so seriously and solemnly, and cried them up so like a market peddler, meanwhile gradually lost its pedantic innocence.

[161]The struggle of the German and especially the Prussian bourgeoisie against the feudalists and the absolute monarchy, in short, the liberal movement, became more serious.

[162]True Socialism was thus offered its wished-for opportunity of counterposing the socialist demands to the actual course of politics, of hurling the traditional anathemas against liberalism, the representative state, bourgeois competition, bourgeois freedom of the press, bourgeois law, bourgeois freedom and equality, and of preaching to the masses of people how they had nothing to gain from this bourgeois movement and everything to lose instead. German socialism opportunely forgot that the French critique, whose banal echo it was, presupposed modern bourgeois society with the corresponding material conditions of existence and the appropriate political constitution—the very presuppositions whose attainment was only now at issue in Germany.

[163]Er diente den deutschen absoluten Regierungen mit ihrem Gefolge von Pfaffen, Schulmeistern, Krautjunkern und Büreaukraten als erwünschte Vogelscheuche gegen die drohend aufstrebende Bourgeoisie.

[164]Er bildete die süßliche Ergänzung zu den bittern Peitschenhieben und Flintenkugeln, womit dieselben Regierungen die deutschen Arbeiter-Aufstände bearbeiteten.

[165]Ward der wahre Socialismus dergestalt eine Waffe in der Hand der Regierungen gegen die deutsche Bourgeoisie, so vertrat er auch unmittelbar ein reactionäres Interesse, das Interesse der deutschen Pfahlbürgerschaft. In Deutschland bildet das vom sechzehnten Jahrhundert her überlieferte und seit der Zeit in verschiedener Form hier immer neu wieder auftauchende Kleinbürgerthum die eigentliche gesellschaftliche Grundlage der bestehenden Zustände.

[166]Seine Erhaltung ist die Erhaltung der bestehenden deutschen Zustände. Von der industriellen und politischen Herrschaft der Bourgeoisie fürchtet es den sichern Untergang, einer Seits in Folge der Koncentration des Kapitals, anderer Seits durch das Aufkommen eines revolutionären Proletariats. Der wahre Socialismus schien ihm beide Fliegen mit einer Klappe zu schlagen. Er verbreitete sich wie eine Epidemie.

[167]Das Gewand, gewirkt aus spekulativem Spinnweb, überstickt mit schöngeistigen Redeblumen, durchtränkt von liebesschwülem Gemüthsthau, dies überschwängliche Gewand, worin die deutschen Socialisten ihre paar knöchernen ewigen Wahrheiten einhüllten, vermehrte nur den Absatz ihrer Waare bei diesem Publikum.

[168]Seiner Seits erkannte der deutsche Socialismus immer mehr seinen Beruf, der hochtrabende Vertreter dieser Pfahlbürgerschaft zu sein.

[163]German socialism was used by the German despots and their followers,—priests, schoolmasters, bureaucrats and bullfrog country squires,—as a scarcrow to frighten the revolutionary middle-class. [164]It was the agreeable finish to the grape-shot, and cat o'nine tails, with which these Governments replied to the first proletarian insurrections of Germany. [165]While "true socialism" was thus employed in assisting the Governments against the German bourgeoisie, it also directly represented a reactionary interest, that of the German small capitalists and shopocracy. In Germany the real social foundation of the existing state of things, was this class, remaining since the 16th century, and always renewing itself under slightly different forms. [166]Its preservation was the preservation of the existing order of things in Germany. The industrial and political supremacy of the bourgeoisie involved the annihilation of this intermediate class; on the one hand, by the centralisation of capital; on the other, by the creation of a revolutionary proletariat. German, or "true" socialism, appeared to this shopocracy as a means of killing two birds with one stone. It spread like an epidemic. [167]The robe of speculative cobwebs, adorned with rhetorical flourishes and sickly sentimentalism,—in which the German socialists wrapped the dry bones of their eternal, absolute truths, increased the demand for their commodity among this public. [168]And the German socialists were not wanting in due appreciation of their mission, to be the grandiloquent representatives of the German shopocrats.

[163]To the absolute governments, with their following of parsons, professors, country squires and officials, it served as a welcome scarecrow against the threatening bourgeoisie.

[164]It was a sweet finish after the bitter pills of floggings and bullets, with which these same governments, just at that time, dosed the German working-class risings.

[165]While this "True" Socialism thus served the governments as a weapon for fighting the German bourgeoisie, it, at the same time, directly represented a reactionary interest, the interest of the German Philistines. In Germany the *petty bourgeois* class, a *relique* of the 16th century, and since then constantly cropping up again under various forms, is the real social basis of the existing state of things.

[166]To preserve this class, is to preserve the existing state of things in Germany. The industrial and political supremacy of the bourgeoisie threatens it with certain destruction; on the one hand, from the concentration of capital; on the other, from the rise of a revolutionary proletariat. "True" Socialism appeared to kill these two birds, with one stone. It spread like an epidemic.

[167]The robe of speculative cobwebs, embroidered with flowers of rhetoric, steeped in the dew of sickly sentiment, this transcendental robe in which the German Socialists wrapped their sorry "eternal truths" all skin and bone, served to wonderfully increase the sale of their goods amongst such a public.

[168]And on its part, German Socialism recognised, more and more, its own calling as the bombastic representative of the petty bourgeois Philistine.

[163]To the German absolute governments, with their retinues of priests, schoolmasters, cabbage-junkers, and bureaucrats, it served as a welcome scarecrow against the rising bourgeoisie that threatened them.

[164]It constituted a sugary supplement to the bitter floggings and shootings with which these same governments handled the German working-class uprisings.

[165]While in this way True Socialism became a weapon in the hands of the governments against the German bourgeoisie, it also directly represented a reactionary interest, the interest of German petty-bourgeois philistinedom. In Germany the petty-bourgeoisie, which had been handed down from the sixteenth century and since then kept cropping up here afresh in various forms, constitutes the actual social foundation of the existing state of things.

[166]Its preservation is the preservation of the existing state of things in Germany. From the industrial and political rule of the bourgeoisie it fears certain ruin, on the one hand as a result of the concentration of capital, and on the other hand through the rise of a revolutionary proletariat. In its eyes True Socialism seemed to kill two birds with one stone. It spread like an epidmic.

[167]The robe woven out of speculative cobwebs, embroidered with belletristic flowers of rhetoric, saturated in a dewy sentiment sweltry with Love— this rhapsodic robe, in which the German socialists wrapped a few of their fossilized Eternal Truths, merely increased the sale of their wares to this public.

[168]On its part, German socialism more and more recognized its calling to be the grandiloquent representative of this petty-bourgeois philistinedom.

[169]Er proklamirte die deutsche Nation als die normale Nation nnd den deutschen Spießbürger als den Normal-Menschen. Er gab jeder Niedertracht desselben einen verborgenen höheren socialistischen Sinn, worin sie ihr Gegentheil bedeutete. Er zog die letzte Konsequenz, indem er direkt gegen die rohdestruktive Richtung des Kommunismus auftrat, und seine unparteiische Erhabenheit über alle Klassenkämpfe verkündete. Mit sehr wenigen Ausnahmen gehören alles, was in Deutschland von angeblich socialistischen und kommunistischen Schriften cirkulirt, in den Bereich dieser schmutzigen entnervenden Literatur.

2) Der konservative oder Bourgeois-Socialismus.

[170]Ein Theil der Bourgeoisie wünscht den socialen Mißständen abzuhelfen, um den Bestand der bürgerlichen Gesellschaft zu sichern.
[171]Es gehören hierher, Oekonomisten, Philantropen, Humanitäre, Verbesserer der Lage der arbeitenden Klassen, Wohlthätigkeits-Organisirer, Abschaffer der Thierquälerei, Mäßigkeits-Vereinsstifter, Winkelreformer der buntscheckigsten Art. Und auch zu ganzen Systemen ist dieser Bourgeois-Socialismus ausgearbeitet worden.
[172]Als Beispiel führen wir Proudhon's Philosophie de la misere an.
[173]Die socialistischen Bourgeois wollen die Lebensbedingungen der modernen Gesellschaft ohne die nothwendig daraus hervorgehenden Kämpfe und Gefahren. Sie wollen die bestehende Gesellschaft mit Abzug der sie revolutionirenden und sie auflösenden Elemente. Sie wollen die Bourgeoisie ohne das Proletariat. Die Bourgeoisie stellt sich die Welt, worin sie herrscht, natürlich als die beste Welt vor. Der Bourgeois-Socialismus arbeitet diese tröstliche Vorstellung zu einem halben oder ganzen System aus. Wenn er das Proletariat auffordert seine Systeme zu verwirklichen, um in das neue Jerusalem einzugehen, so verlangt er im Grunde nur, daß es in der jetzigen Gesellschaft stehen bleibe, aber seine gehässigen Vorstellungen von derselben abstreife.

178

[169]They proclaimed the German nation to be the archetypal nation; the German cockneys, to be archetypal men. They gave every piece of cockney rascality a hidden socialist sense, whereby it was interpreted to mean the reverse of rascality. They reached the limits of their system, when they directly opposed the destructive tendency of communism, and proclaimed their own sublime indifference towards all class-antagonism. With very few exceptions, all the so-called socialist and communist publications which circulate in Germany emanate from this school, and are enervating filthy trash.

II.—CONSERVATIVE, OR BOURGEOIS SOCIALISM.

[170]A part of the Bourgeoisie desires to alleviate social dissonances, with a view of securing the existence of middle-class society.
[171]To this section belong economists, philanthropists, humanitarians, improvers of the condition of the working classes, patrons of charitable institutions, cruelty-to-animals-bill supporters, temperance advocates, in a word, hole and corner reformers of the most varied and piebald aspect. This middle-class Socialism has even been developed into complete systems.
[172]As an example, we may cite Proudhon's Philosophy of Poverty. [173]The socialist bourgeois wish to have the vital conditions of modern society without the accompanying struggles and dangers. They desire the existing order of things, *minus* the revolutionary and destructive element contained therein. They wish to have a bourgeoisie without a proletariat. The bourgeoisie, of course, consider the world wherein they reign, to be the best possible world. Bourgeois socialism developes this comfortable hypothesis into a complete system. When these socialists urge the proletariat to realise their system, to march towards the New Jerusalem, they ask in reality, that the proletariat should remain within the limits of existing society, and yet lay aside all bitter and unfavourable opinions concerning it.

[169]It proclaimed the German nation to be the model nation, and the German petty philistine to be the typical man. To every villanous meanness of this model man it gave a hidden, higher, socialistic interpretation, the exact contrary of its real character. It went to the extreme length of opposing the "brutally destructive" tendency of Communism, and of proclaiming its supreme and impartial contempt of all class struggles. With very few exceptions, all the so-called Socialist and Communist publications that now (1847) circulate in Germany belong to the domain of this foul and enervating literature.

[169]It proclaimed the German nation to be the standard nation and the German philistine to be the standard human being. To everything mean about him it gave a hidden, higher, socialistic sense in which it meant its opposite. It drew the final conclusion by coming out squarely against the crudely destructive tendency of communism and proclaiming its own impartial elevation above all class struggles. With very few exceptions, all the self-styled socialist and communist writings circulating in Germany belong to the domain of this foul, enervating literature.

2. Conservative or Bourgeois Socialism.

[170]A part of the bourgeoisie is desirous of redressing social grievances, in order to secure the continued existence of bourgeois society.

[171]To this section belong economists, philanthropists, humanitarians improvers of the condition of the working class, organisers of charity, members of societies for the prevention of cruelty to animals, temperance fanatics, hole and corner reformers of every imaginable kind. This form of Socialism has, moreover, been worked out into complete systems.

[172]We may cite Proudhon's *Philosophie de la Misère* as an example of this form.

[173]The socialistic bourgeois want all the advantages of modern social conditions without the struggles and dangers necessarily resulting therefrom. They desire the existing state of society minus its revolutionary and disintegrating elements. They wish for a bourgeoisie without a proletariat. The bourgeoisie naturally conceives the world in which it is supreme to be the best; and bourgeois socialism develops this comfortable conception into various more or less complete systems. In requiring the proletariat to carry out such a system, and thereby to march straightway into the social New Jerusalem, it but requires in reality, that the proletariat should remain within the bounds of existing society, but should cast away all its hateful ideas concerning the bourgeoisie.

2. Conservative or Bourgeois Socialism

[170]A part of the bourgeoisie wishes to remedy *social ills*, in order to safeguard the existence of bourgeois society.

[171]Under this head belong economists, philanthropists, humanitarians, improvers of the condition of the working classes, charity organizers, opponents of cruelty to animals, founders of temperance societies, hole-and-corner reformers of the most variegated kinds. And this bourgeois socialism has even been worked out in whole systems.

[172]As example we cite Proudhon's *Philosophie de la Misère*.

[173]The socialistic bourgeois want the conditions of existence of modern society without the struggles and dangers necessarily arising therefrom. They want the existing society minus the elements that revolutionize it and break it up, They want the bourgeoisie without the proletariat. The bourgeoisie conceives the world in which it rules as naturally the best of worlds. Bourgeois socialism works this comforting conception up into a partial or complete system. When it calls on the proletariat to put its system into effect in order to enter the New Jerusalem, at bottom it is merely asking the proletariat to remain inside present-day society but to cast off its hateful ideas about that society.

[174]Eine zweite, weniger systematische und mehr praktische Form des Socialismus suchte der Arbeiterklasse jede revolutionäre Bewegung zu verleiden, durch den Nachweis, wie nicht diese oder jene politische Veränderung, sondern nur eine Veränderung der materiellen Lebensverhältnisse, der ökonomischen Verhältnisse ihr von Nutzen sein könne. Unter Veränderung der materiellen Lebensverhältnisse versteht dieser Socialismus aber keineswegs Abschaffung der bürgerlichen Produktions-Verhältnisse, die nur auf revolutionärem Wege möglich ist, sondern administrative Verbesserungen, die auf dem Boden dieser Produktionsverhältnisse vor sich gehen; also an dem Verhältniß von Kapital und Lohnarbeit nichts ändern, sondern im besten Fall der Bourgeoisie die Kosten ihren Herrschaft vermindern und ihren Staatshaushalt vereinfachen.

[175]Seinen entsprechenden Ausdruck erreicht der Bourgeois-Socialismus erst da, wo er zur bloßen rednerischen Figur wird.

[176]Freier Handel! im Interesse der arbeitenden Klasse; Schutzzölle! im Interesse der arbeitenden Klasse; Zellengefängnisse! im Interesse der arbeitenden Klasse, das ist das letzte, das einzig ernst gemeinte Wort des Bourgeois-Socialismus.

[177]Ihr Socialismus besteht eben in der Behauptung, daß die Bourgeois Bourgeois sind—im Interesse der arbeitenden Klasse.

3) Der kritisch-utopistische Socialismus und Kommunismus.

[178]Wir reden hier nicht von der Literatur, die in allen großen modernen Revolutionen die Forderungen des Proletariats aussprach (Schriften Babeufs u. s. w.).

[174]A second, less systematic, and more practical school of middle-class socialists, try to hinder all revolutionary movements among the producers, by teaching them that their condition cannot be improved by this or that political change,—but only by a change in the material conditions of life, in the economical arrangements of society. Yet, by a change in the modern life-conditions, these socialists do not mean the abolition of the middle-class modes of production and distribution, attainable only in a revolutionary manner; they mean administrative reforms, to be made within the limits of the old system, which, therefore, will leave the relation of capital and wages-labour untouched,—and, at most, will merely simplify the details and diminish the cost of bourgeois government. [175]This kind of socialism finds its most fitting expression in empty rhetorical flourishes. [176]Free Trade! for the benefit of the working classes. A tariff! for the benefit of the working classes. Isolated imprisonment and the silent system! for the benefit of the working classes. This last phrase is the only sincere and earnest one, among the whole stock in trade of the middle-class socialists. [177]Their socialism consists in affirming, that the bourgeois is a bourgeois . . . for the benefit of the working classes!

III.—CRITICAL-UTOPIAN SOCIALISM & COMMUNISM.

[178]We do not speak here of the literature, which, in all the great revolutions of modern times, has expressed the demands of the proletariat: as leveller pamphleteers, the writings of Babeuf and others.

180

[174]A second and more practical, but less systematic form of this socialism sought to depreciate every revolutionary movement in the eyes of the working class, by showing that no mere political reform, but only a change in the material conditions of existence in economical relations, could be of any advantage to them. By changes in the material conditions of existence, this form of Socialism, however, by no means understands abolition of the bourgeois relations of production, an abolition that can be effected only by a revolution, but administrative reforms, based on the continued existence of these relations; reforms, therefore, that in no respect affect the relations between capital and labour, but, at the best lessen the cost, and simplify the administrative work, of bourgeois government.

[175]Bourgeois Socialism attains adequate expression, when, and only when, it becomes a mere figure of speech.

[176]Free trade:for the benefit of the working class. Protective duties: for the benefit of the working class. Prison Reform: for the benefit of the working class. This is the last word and the only seriously meant word of bourgeois Socialism.

[177]It is summed up in the phrase: the bourgeois is a bourgeois—for the benefit of the working class.

[174]A second, less systematic and more practical form of socialism tried to make the working class disgusted with any revolutionary movement by showing that not this or that political change but only a change in the material conditions of existence, in the economic conditions, could be of advantage to them. By change in the material conditions of existence, however, this socialism by no means understands abolition of the bourgeois relations of production, which is possible only in revolutionary ways, but rather administrative improvements that proceed on the basis of these relations of production, that therefore change nothing in the relationship of capital and wage-labor, but in the best case lessen for the bourgeoisie the cost of its rule and simplify governmental ways and means for it.

[175]Bourgeois socialism attains its appropriate expression only when it becomes simply a figure of speech.

[176]Free trade!—in the interests of the working class. Protective tariffs!—in the interests of the working class. Prisons on the cell system!—in the interests of the working class. This is the last word of bourgeois socialism, the only one it means seriously.

[177]Its socialism consists precisely in the assertion that the bourgeois are bourgeois—in the interests of the working class.

3. Critical-Utopian Socialism and Communism.

[178]We do not here refer to that literature which, in every great modern revolution, has always given voice to the demands of the proletariat: such as the writings of Babeuf and others.

3. Critical-Utopian Socialism and Communism

[178]We are not speaking here of the literature that in all great modern revolutions addressed the demands of the proletariat (writings of Babeuf, etc.).

181

[179]Die ersten Versuche des Proletariats in einer Zeit allgemeiner Aufregung, in der Periode des Umsturzes der feudalen Gesellschaft direkt sein eignes Klasseninteresse durchzusetzen, scheiterten nothwendig an der unentwickelten Gestalt des Proletariats selbst, wie an dem Mangel der materiellen Bedingungen seiner Befreiung, die eben erst das Produkt der bürgerlichen Epoche sind. Die revolutionäre Literatur, welche diese'ersten Bewegungen des Proletariats begleitete, ist dem Inhalt nach nothwendig reaktionär. Sie lehrt einen allgemeinen Ascetismus und eine rohe Gleichmacherei.

[180]Die eigentlich socialistischen und kommunistischen Systeme, die Systeme St. Simons, Fourriers, Owens u. s. w. tauchen auf in der ersten unentwickelten Periode des Kampfs zwischen Proletariat und Bourgeoisie, die wir oben dargestellt haben. (S. Bourgeoisie und Proletariat.)

[181]Die Erfinder dieser Systeme sehen zwar den Gegensatz der Klassen, wie die Wirksamkeit der auflösenden Elemente in der herrschenden Gesellschaft selbst. Aber sie erblicken auf der Seite der Proletariats keine geschichtliche Selbstthätigkeit, keine ihm eigenthümliche politische Bewegung.

[182]Da die Entwicklung des Klassengegensatzes gleichen Schritt hält mit der Entwicklung der Industrie, finden sie eben so wenig die materiellen Bedingungen zur Befreiung des Proletariats vor, und suchen nach einer socialen Wissenschaft, nach socialen Gesetzen, um diese Bedingungen zu schaffen.

[183]An die Stelle der gesellschaftlichen Thätigkeit muß ihre persönlich erfinderische Thätigkeit treten, an die Stelle der geschichtlichen Bedingungen der Befreiung phantastische, an die Stelle der allmählig vor sich gehenden Organisation des Proletariats zur Klasse eine eigens ausgeheckte Organisation der Gesellschaft. Die kommende Weltgeschichte löst sich für sie auf in die Propaganda und die praktische Ausführung ihrer Gesellschaftspläne.

182

[179]The first attempts of the proletariat towards directly forwarding its own class-interest, made during the general movement which overthrew feudal society, necessarily failed,—by reason of the crude, undeveloped form of the proletariat itself; as well as by the want of those material conditions for its emancipation, which are but the product of the bourgeois-epoch. The revolutionary literature, which accompanied this first movement of the proletariat, had necessarily a reactionary content. It taught a universal asceticism and a rude sort of equality.

[180]The Socialist and communist systems, properly so called, the systems of St. Simon, Owen, Fourier and others, originated in the early period of the struggle between the proletariat and the bourgeoisie, which we described in Chap. I. [181]The inventors of these systems perceived the fact of class-antagonism, and the activity of the dissolvent elements within the prevailing social system. But they did not see any spontaneous historical action, any characteristic political movement, on the part of the proletariat. [182]And because the development of class-antagonism keeps pace with the development of the industrial system, they could not find the material conditions for the emancipation of the proletariat; they were obliged to seek for a social science, for social laws, in order to create those conditions. [183]Their personal inventive activity took the place of social activity, imaginary conditions of proletarian emancipation were substituted for the historical ones, and a subjective, fantastic organisation of society, for the gradual and progressive organisation of the proletariat as a class. The approaching phasis of universal history resolved itself, for them, into the propagandism and practical realisation of their peculiar social plans.

[179]The first direct attempts of the proletariat to attain its own ends, made in times of universal excitement when feudal society was being overthrown, these attempts necessarily failed, owing to the then undeveloped state of the proletariat as well as to the absence of the economic conditions for its emancipation, conditions that had yet to be produced, and could be produced by the impending bourgeois epoch alone. The revolutionary literature that accompanied these first movements of the proletariat had necessarily a reactionary character. It inculcated universal asceticism and social levelling in its crudest form.

[180]The Socialist and Communist system properly so called, those of St. Simon, Fourier, Owen and others, spring into existence in the early undeveloped period, described above, of the struggle between proletariat and bourgeoisie, (see section I. Bourgeoisie and Proletariat)

[181]The founders of these systems see, indeed, the class antagonisms, as well as the action of the decomposing elements in the prevailing form of society. But the proletariat as yet in its infancy, offers to them the spectacle of a class without any historical initiative or any independent political movement.

[182]Since the development of class antagonism keeps even pace with the development of industry, the economic situation, as they find it, does not as yet offer to them the material conditions for the emancipation of the proletariat. They therefore search after a new social science, after new social laws, that are to create these conditions.

[183]Historical action is to yield to their personal inventive action, historically created conditions of emancipation to phantastic ones, and the gradual spontaneous class-organisation of the proletariat to an organisation of society specially contrived by these inventors. Future history resolves itself, in their eyes, into the propaganda and the practical carrying out of their social plans.

[179]The first attempts of the proletariat to directly push its own class interests, made at a time of general ferment, in the period of the overthrow of feudal society, necessarily came to grief owing to the undeveloped state of the proletariat itself as well as to the absence of material conditions for its emancipation, conditions that are in fact only the product of the bourgeois era. This revolutionary literature that accompanied these first movements of the proletariat is necessarily reactionary in content. It teaches a general asceticism and a crude leveling.

[180]The socialist and communist system proper, the systems of Saint-Simon, Fourier, Owen, etc., arise in the first, undeveloped period of the struggle between proletariat and bourgeoisie, which we have described above. (See "Bourgeoisie and Proletariat.")

[181]The inventors of these systems, to be sure, see the class antagonisms as well as the operation of the disintegrative elements in the dominant society itself. But they do not perceive any historical self-activity on the part of the proletariat, any political movement characteristic of it.

[182]Since the development of class antagonisms keeps pace with the development of industry, they accordingly do not find the material preconditions for the emancipation of the proletariat, and go searching for a social science, for social laws, in order to create these preconditions.

[183]Social activity has to be replaced by their personal inventive activity; historical preconditions of emancipation, by fanciful ones; the gradually advancing organization of the proletariat into a class, by an organization of society of their own concoction. To them, world history to come resolves itself into propaganda for their social plans and carrying them out in practice.

[184]Sie sind sich zwar bewußt in ihren Plänen hauptsachlich das Interesse der arbeitenden Klasse als der leidendsten Klasse zu vertreten. Nur unter diesem Gesichtspunkt der leidendsten Klasse existirt das Proletariat für sie.

[185]Die unentwickelte Form des Klassenkampfes, wie ihre eigene Lebenslage bringen es aber mit sich, daß sie weit über jenen Klassengegensatz erhaben zu sein glauben. Sie wollen die Lebenslage aller Gesellschaftsglieder, auch der bestgestellten verbessern. Sie appelliren daher fortwährend an die ganze Gesellschaft ohne Unterschied, ja vorzugsweise an die herrschende Klasse. Man braucht ihr System ja nur zu verstehen, um es als den bestmöglichen Plan der bestmöglichen Gesellschaft anzuerkennen.

[186]Sie verwerfen daher alle politische, namentlich alle revolutionäre Aktion, sie wollen ihr Ziel auf friedlichem Wege erreichen und versuchen durch kleine natürlich fehlschlagende Experimente, durch die Macht des Beispiels dem neuen gesellschaftlichen Evangelium Bahn zu brechen.

[187]Diese phantastische Schilderung der zukünftigen Gesellschaft entspricht in einer Zeit, wo das Proletariat noch höchst unentwickelt ist, also selbst noch phantastisch seine eigene Stellung auffaßt, seinem ersten ahnungsvollen Drängen nach einer allgemeinen Umgestaltung der Gesellschaft.

[188]Die socialistischen und kommunistischen Schriften bestehen aber auch aus kritischen Elementen. Sie greifen alle Grundlagen der bestehenden Gesellschaft an. Sie haben daher höchst werthvolles Material zur Aufklärung der Arbeiter geliefert. Ihre positiven Sätze über die zukünftige Gesellschaft, z. B., Aufhebung des Gegensatzes von Stadt und Land, der Familie, des Privaterwerbs, der Lohnarbeit, die Verkündung der gesellschaftlichen Harmonie, die Verwandlung des Staats in eine bloße Verwaltung der Produktion— alle diese ihre Sätze drücken blos das Wegfallen des Klassengegensatzes aus, der eben erst sich zu entwickeln beginnt, den sie nur noch in seiner ersten gestaltlosen Unbestimmtheit kennen. Diese Sätze selbst haben daher noch einen rein utopitstischen Sinn.

[184]They had, indeed, the consciousness of advocating the interest of the producers as the most suffering class of society. The proletariat existed for them, only under this point of view of the most oppressed class. [185]The undeveloped state of the class-struggle, and their own social position, induced these socialists to believe they were removed far above class-antagonism. They desired to improve the position of all the members of society, even of the most favoured. Hence, their continual appeals to the whole of society, even to the dominant class. You have only to understand their system, in order to see it is the best possible plan for the best possible state of society. [186]Hence too, they reject all political, and particularly all revolutionary action, they desire to attain their object in a peaceful manner, and try to prepare the way for the new social gospel, by the force of example, by small, isolated experiments, which, of course, cannot but turn out signal *failures*. [187]This fantastic representation of future society expressed the feeling of a time when the proletariat was quite undeveloped, and had quite an imaginary conception of its own position,—it was the expression of an instinctive want for a universal social revolution. [188]There are, however, critical elements contained in all these socialist and communist writings. They attack the foundation of existing society. Hence they contain a treasure of materials for the enlightenment of the Producers. Their positive propositions regarding a future state of society; e.g. abolition of the antgonism of town and country, of family institutions, of individual accumulation, of wages-labour, the proclamation of social harmony, the change of political power into a mere superintendence of production;—all these propositions expressed the abolition of class-antagonism, when this last was only commencing its evolution; and, therefore, they have, with these authors a purely Utopian sense.

[184]In the formation of their plans they are conscious of caring chiefly for the interests of the working-class, as being the most suffering class. Only from the point of view of being the most suffering class does the proletariat exist for them.

[185]The undeveloped state of the class struggle, as well as their own surroundings, cause Socialists of this kind to consider themselves far superior to all class antagonisms. They want to improve the condition of every member of society, even that of the most favoured. Hence, they habitually appeal to society at large, without distinction of class; nay, by preference, to the ruling class. For how can people, when once they understand their system, fail to see in it the best possible plan of the best possible state of society?

[186]Hence, they reject all political and especially a revolutionary action: they wish to attain their ends by peaceful means, and endeavour, by small experiments, necessary doomed to failure, and by the force of example, to pave the way for the new social Gospel.

[187]Such phantastic pictures of future society, painted at a time when the proletariat is still in a very undeveloped state, and has but a phantastic conception of its own position, correspond with the first instinctive yearnings of that class for a general reconstruction of society.

[188]But these Socialist and Communist publications contain also a critical element. They attack every principle of existing society. Hence they are full of the most valuable materials for the enlightenment of the working class. The practical measures proposed in them, such as the abolition of the distinction between town and country, of the family, of the carrying on of industries for the account of private individuals, and of the wage system, the proclamation of social harmony, the conversion of the functions of the State into a mere superintendence of production, all these proposals point solely to the disappearance of class-antagonisms which were, at that time, only just cropping up, and which, in these publications, are recognised under their earliest indistinct and undefined forms only. These proposals, therefore, are of a purely Utopian character.

[184]In their plans, to be sure, they are conscious of mainly representing the interests of the working class as the most suffering class. Only from this standpoint of being the most suffering class does the proletariat exist for them.

[185]The undeveloped force of the class struggle as well as their own position in life brings it about, however, that they believe themselves to be far superior to the aforementioned class antagonism. They want to improve the position in life of all members of society, even those who are most well-off. They therefore continually appeal to the whole of society without distinction, indeed preferably to the ruling class. Surely one need only understand their system to acknowledge it the best possible plan of the best possible society.

[186]They therefore reject all political and especially all revolutionary action; they want to attain their goal in peaceful ways, and try to clear the way for the new social gospel by small experiments that naturally fail, by the force of example.

[187]This fanciful depiction of the future society at a time when the proletariat is still extremely undeveloped, hence itself still has a fanciful conception of its own position, corresponds to its first presageful thrust toward a general reconstruction of society.

[188]The socialist and communist writings, however, contain critical elements too. They attack all the foundations of the existing society. They therefore have supplied extremely valuable material for the enlightenment of the workers. Their positive propositions on the future society—for example, abolition of the town-and-country antithesis, of the family, of private gain, of wage-labor; the proclamation of social harmony, the conversion of the state into a mere administration of production—all of these propositions of theirs simply express the disappearance of the class antagonism which is only just beginning to develop, which they still know of only in its first ill-defined amorphousness. These propositions themselves, therefore, still have a purely utopian sense.

[189]Die Bedeutung des kritischen utopistischen Socialismus und Kommunismus steht im umgekehrten Verhältniß zur geschichtlichen Entwicklung. In demselben Maaße, worin der Klassenkampf sich entwickelt und gestaltet, verliert diese phantastische Erhebung über denselben, diese phantastische Bekämpfung desselben, allen praktischen Werth, alle theoretische Berechtigung. Waren daher die Urheber dieser Systeme auch in vieler Beziehung revolutionär, so bilden ihre Schüler jedes Mal reaktionäre Sekten. Sie halten die alten Anschauungen der Meister fest gegenüber der geschichtlichen Fortentwicklung des Proletariats. Sie suchen daher konsequent den Klassenkampf wieder abzustumpfen nnd die Gegensätze zu vermitteln. Sie träumen noch immer die versuchsweise Verwirklichung ihrer gesellschaftlichen Utopien, Stiftung einzelner Phalanstere, Gründung von home-Colonien, Errichtung eines kleinen Icariens,—Duodez-Ausgabe des neuen Jerusalems—und zum Aufbau aller dieser spanischen Schlösser müssen sie an die Philantropie der bürgerlichen Herzen und Geldsäcke appelliren. Allmählig fallen sie in die Categorie der oben geschilderten reaktionären oder konservativen Socialisten, und unterscheiden sich nur mehr von ihnen durch mehr systematische Pedanterie, durch den fanatischen Aberglauben an die Wunderwirkungen ihrer socialen Wissenschaft.

[190]Sie treten daher mit Erbitterung aller politischen Bewegung der Arbeiter entgegen, die nur aus blindem Unglauben an das neue Evangelium hervorgehen konnte.

[191]Die Owenisten in England, die Fourieristen in Frankreich, reagiren dort gegen die Chartisten, hier gegen die Reformisten.

[189*]The importance of critical-utopian Socialism and Communism, stands in an inverted proportion to the progress of the historical movement. In proportion as the class-battle is evolved and assumes a definite form, so does this imaginary elevation over it, this fantastic resistance to it, lose all practical worth, all theoretical justification. Hence, it happens, that although the originators of these systems were revolutionary in various respects, yet their followers have invariably formed reactionary sects. They hold fast by their master's old dogmas and doctrines, in opposition to the progressive historical evolution of the Proletariat. They seek, therefore, logically enough, to deaden class opposition, to mediate between the extremes. They still dream of the experimental realization of their social Utopias through isolated efforts,—the founding of a few phalanteres, of a few home colonies, of a small Icaria,—a duodecimo edition of the New Jerusalem; and they appeal to the philanthropy of Bourgeois hearts and purses for the building expences of these air-castles and chimeras. They gradually fall back into the category of the above mentioned reactionary or conservative Socialists, and distinguish themselves from these only by their more systematic pedantry, by their fanatical faith in the miraculous powers of their Social panacea. [190]Hence, they violently oppose all political movements in the Proletariat, which indeed, can only be occasioned by a blind and wilful disbelief in the new Gospel. [191]In France, the Fourierists oppose the Reformists; in England, the Owenites react against the Chartists.*

[189]The significance of Critical-Utopian Socialism and Communism bears an inverse relation to historical development. In proportion as the modern class struggle develops and takes definite shape, this phantastic standing apart from the contest these phantastic attacks on it lose a practical value and all theoretical justification. Therefore, although the originators of these systems were, in many respects, revolutionary, their disciples have, in every case, formed mere reactionary sects. They hold fast by the original views of their masters, in opposition to the progressive historical development of the proletariat They, therefore, endeavour, and that consistently, to deaden the class struggle and to reconcile the class antagonisms. They still dream of experimental realisation of their Social Utopias, of founding isolated "phalanstries" of establishing "Home Colonies," of setting up a "Little Icaria" (c) duodecimo editions of the New Jerusalem, and to realise all these castles in the air they are compelled to appeal to the feelings and purses of the bourgeois. By degrees they sink into the category of the reactionary conservative Socialists depicted above, differing from these only by more systematic pedantry, and by their fanatic and superstitious belief in the miraculous effects of their social science.

[190]They, therefore, violently oppose all political action on the part of the working class; such action, according to them, can only result from blind unbelief in the new Gospel.

[191]The Owenites in England, and the Fourierists in France, respectively oppose the Chartists and the "Réformistes."

[189]The significance of critical utopian socialism and communism stands in inverse proportion to historical development. In proportion as the class struggle develops and takes shape, this fanciful elevation above the class struggle and this fanciful attack on it lose all practical value and all theoretical justification, Therefore, while the founders of these systems were indeed revolutionary in many respects, their disciples always form reactionary sects. They hold fast to the old views of the Masters as against the further historical development of the proletariat. Therefore they consistently seek to blunt the class struggle and to reconcile the antagonism. They still keep on dreaming of the experimental realization of their social utopias, of forming individual phalansteries, of establishing home colonies, of setting up a little Icaria—a duodecimo edition of the New Jerusalem; and to build all these castles in Spain they have to appeal to the philanthropy of bourgeois hearts and moneybags. Gradually they sink into the category of the above-described reactionary or conservative socialists and are differentiated from them only by more systematic pedantry, by fanatical superstitious belief in the miraculous effects of their social science.

[190]They therefore come out vehemently against all political activity by the workers, activity which could only arise from blind disbelief in the new gospel.

[191]The Owenites in England and the Fourierists in France came out against the Chartists and the *Réforme* tendency respectively.

IV.

Stellung der Kommunisten zu den verschiedenen oppositionellen Parteien.

[192]Nach Abschnitt 2 versteht sich das Verhältniß der Kommunisten zu den bereits konstituirten Arbeiterparteien von selbst, also ihr Verhältniß zu den Chartisten in England und den agrarischen Reformern in Nordamerika.

[193]Sie kämpfen für die Erreichung der unmittelbar vorliegenden Zwecke und Interessen der Arbeiterklasse, aber sie vertreten in der gegenwärtigen Bewegung zugleich die Zukunft der Bewegung. In Frankreich schließen sich die Kommunisten an die socialistisch-democratische Partei an gegen die konservative und radikale Bourgeoisie, ohne darum das Recht aufzugeben sich kritisch zu den aus der revolutionären Ueberlieferung herrührenden Phrasen und Illusionen zu verhalten.

[194]In der Schweiz unterstützen sie die Radikalen, ohne zu verkennen, daß diese Partei aus widersprechenden Elementen besteht, theils aus demokratischen Socialisten im französischen Sinn, theils aus radikalen Bourgeois.

[195]Unter den Polen unterstützen die Kommunisten die Partei, welche eine agrarische Revolution zur Bedingung der nationalen Befreiung macht. Dieselbe Partei, welche die Krakauer Insurrektion von 1846 in's Leben rief.

[196]In Deutschland kämpft die kommunistische Partei, sobald die Bourgeoisie revolutionär auftritt, gemeinsam mit der Bourgeoisie gegen die absolute Monarchie, das feudale Grundeigenthum und die Kleinbürgerei.

[197]Sie unterläßt aber keinen Augenblick bei den Arbeitern ein möglichst klares Bewußtsein über den feindlichen Gegensatz von Bourgeoisie und Proletariat herauszuarbeiten, damit die deutschen Arbeiter sogleich die gesellschaftlichen und politischen Bedingungen, welche die Bourgeoisie mit ihrer Herrschaft herbeiführen muß, als eben so viele Waffen gegen die Bourgeoisie kehren können, damit, nach dem Sturz der reaktionären Klassen in Deutschland, sofort der Kampf gegen die Bourgeoisie selbst beginnt.

IV

POSITION OF THE COMMUNISTS

IN RELATION TO THE

VARIOUS EXISTING OPPOSITION PARTIES.

[192]Section II has made clear the relations of the Communists to the existing working class parties, such as the Chartists in England and the Agrarian Reformers in America.

[193]The Communists fight for the attainment of the immediate aims, for the enforcement of the momentary interests of the working class; but in movement of the present they also represent and take care of the future of that movement. In France the Communists ally themselves with the Social Democrats (a) against the conservative and radical bourgeoisie, reserving, however, the right to take up a critical position in regard to phrases and illusions traditionally handed down from the great Revolution.

[194]In Switzerland they support the Radicals, without losing sight of the fact that this party consists of antagonistic elements, party of Democratic Socialists, in the French sense, partly of radical bourgeois.

[195]In Poland they support the party that insists on an agrarian revolution, as the prime condition for national emancipation, that party which fomented the insurrection of Cracow in 1846.

[196]In Germany they fight with the bourgeoisie whenever it acts in a revolutionary way, against the absolute monarchy, the feudal squirearchy, and the petty bourgeoisie.

[197]But they never cease, for a single instant to instil into the working class the clearest possible recognition of the hostile antagonism between bourgeoisie and proletariat in order that the German workers may straightway use, as so many weapons against the bourgeoisie, the social and political conditions that the bourgeoisie must necessarily introduce along with its supremacy, and in order that, after the fall of the reactionary classes in Germany, the fight against the bourgeoisie itself may immediately begin.

IV

POSITION OF THE COMMUNISTS

ON THE

VARIOUS   OPPOSITION PARTIES

[192]From Section II, the relationship of the Communists to the already constituted workers' parties is self-evident, hence their relationship to the Chartists in England and the agrarian reformers in North America.

[193]They fight for the attainment of the immediate aims and interests of the working class, but in the present-day movement they at the same time represent the future of the movement. In France the Communists align themselves with the socialist-democratic party against the conservative and radical bourgeoisie, without thereby giving up the right to take a critical attitude toward the phrases and illusions deriving from the revolutionary tradition.

[194]In Switzerland they support the Radicals, without forgetting that this party consists of contradictory elements, partly of democratic socialists in the French sense, partly of radical bourgeois.

[195]Among the Poles the Communists support the party that makes an agrarian revolution the precondition for national emancipation, the same party that called into being the Cracow insurrection of 1846.

[196]In Germany, as soon as the bourgeoisie acts in a revolutionary way the Communist party fights together with the bourgeoisie against the absolute monarchy, feudal landed property, and the petty-bourgeoisie.

[197]But they do not for a minute cease to forge among the workers the clearest possible consciousness of the hostile antagonism of bourgeoisie and proletariat, so that the German workers can straightway take the social and political preconditions which the bourgeoisie must bring about along with its rule and turn them into so many weapons against the bourgeoisie, so that after the overthrow of the reactionary classes in Germany the struggle against the bourgeoisie itself may immediately begin.

[198]Auf Deutschland richten die Kommunisten ihre Hauptaufmerksamkeit, weil Deutschland am Vorabend einer bürgerlichen Revolution steht, und weil es diese Umwälzung unter fortgeschritteneren Bedingungen der europäischen Civilisation überhaupt, und mit einem viel weiter entwickelten Proletariat vollbringt als England im siebenzehnten und Frankreich im achtzehnten Jahrhundert, die deutsche bürgerliche Revolution also nur das unmittelbare Vorspiel einer proletarischen Revolution sein kann.

[199]Mit einem Wort, die Kommunisten unterstützen überall jede revolutionäre Bewegung gegen die bestehenden gesellschaftlichen und politischen Zustände.

[200]In allen diesen Bewegungen haben sie auch angenommen haben möge, als die Grundfrage der Bewegung hervor.

[201]Die Kommunisten arbeiten endlich überall an der Verbindung und Verständigung der demokratischen Parteien aller Länder.

[202]Die Kommunisten verschmähen es, ihre Ansichten und Absichten zu verheimlichen. Sie erklären es offen, daß ihre Zwecke nur erreicht werden können durch den gewaltsamen Umsturz aller bisherigen Gesellschaftsordnung. Mögen die herrschenden Klassen vor einer Kommunistischen Revolution zittern. Die Proletarier haben nichts in ihr zu verlieren als ihre Ketten. Sie haben eine Welt zu gewinnen.

[203]Proletarier aller Lander vereinigt Euch !

[199]The Communists invariably support every revolutionary movement against the existing order of things, social and political. [200]But in all these movements, they endeavour to point out the property question, whatever degree of development, in every particular case, it may have obtained—as the leading question. [201]The Communists labour for the union and association of the revolutionary parties of all countries. [202]The Communists disdain to conceal their opinions and ends. They openly declare, that these ends can be attained only by the overthrow of all hitherto existing social arrangements. Let the ruling classes tremble at a Communist Revolution. The Proletarians have nothing to lose in it save their chains. They will gain a World. [203]Let the Proletarians of all countries unite!

[198]The Communists turn their attention chiefly to Germany, because that country is on the eve of a bourgeois revolution, that is bound to be carried out under more advanced conditions of European civilisation, and with a much more developed proletariat than that of England was in the seventeenth, and of France in the eighteenth century, and because the bourgeois revolution in Germany will be but the prelude to an immediately following proletarian revolution.

[199]In short, the Communists everywhere support every revolutionary movement against the existing social and political order of things.

[200]In all these movements they bring to the front, as the leading question in each, the property question, no matter what its degree of development at the time.

[201]Finally, they labour everywhere for the union and agreement of the democratic parties of all countries.

[202]The Communists disdain to conceal their views and aims. They openly declare that their ends can be attained only by the forcible, overthrow of all existing social conditions. Let the ruling classes tremble at a Communist revolution. The proletarians have nothing to lose but their chains. They have a world to win.

[203]Working men of all countries unite!

[198]It is to Germany that the Communists direct their main attention, since Germany stands on the eve of a bourgeois revolution; and since it is carrying out this upheaval under more advanced conditions of European civilization in general and with a much more developed proletariat than was true of England in the seventeenth and France in the eighteenth century, the German bourgeois revolution can therefore be only the immediate prelude to a proletarian revolution.

[199]In short, the Communists everywhere support every revolutionary movement against the existing social and political state of affairs.

[200]In all these movements they emphasize the property question as the basic question of the movement, no matter what more or less developed form it may have taken.

[201]Finally, the Communists work everywhere for the alliance and accord of the democratic parties of all countries.

[202]The Communists disdain to conceal their views and intentions. They openly declare that their aims can be attained only by the forcible overthrow of every existing social order. Let the ruling classes tremble at a communist revolution. In it the proletarians have nothing to lose but their chains. They have a world to win.

[203]*Proletarians of all countries, unite!*

Engels' Notes to the A.E.T.

Par. 7 (Title) (*a*)

By bourgeoisie is meant the class of modern Capitalists, owners of the means of social production and employers of wage-labour. By proletariat, the class of modern wage-labourers who, having no means of production of their own, are reduced to selling their labour-power in order to live.

Par. 7 (*b*)

That is, all *written* history. In 1847, the pre-history of society, the social organization existing previous to recorded history, was all but unknown. Since then, Haxthausen discovered common ownership of land in Russia, Maurer proved it to be the social foundation from which all Teutonic races started in history, and by and bye village communities were found to be, or have been the primitive form of society everywhere from India to Ireland. The inner organization of this primitive Communistic society was laid bare, in its typical form, by Morgan's crowning discovery of the true nature of the *gens* and its relation to the *tribe*. With the dissolution of these primaeval communities society begins to be differentiated into separate and finally antagonistic classes. I have attempted to retrace this process of dissolution in: "Der Ursprung der Familie des Privateigenthums und des Staats," 2nd edit., Stuttgart 1886.

Par. 8 (*c*)

Guild-master, that is a full member of a guild, a master within, not a head of a guild.

Par. 18 (*d*)

"Commune" was the name taken, in France, by the nascent towns even before they had conquered from their feudal lords and masters, local self-government and political rights as "the Third Estate." Generally speaking, for the economical development of the bourgeoisie, England is here taken as the typical country, for its political development, France.

Par. 136 (*a*)

Not the English Restoration 1660 to 1689, but the French Restoration 1814 to 1830.

Par. 136 (*b*)

This applies chiefly to Germany where the landed aristocracy and squirearchy have large portions of their estates cultivated for their own account by stewards, and are, moreover, extensive beetroot-sugar manufaturers and distillers of potato spirits. The wealthier British aristocracy are, as yet, rather above that; but they, too, know how to make up for declining rents by lending their names to floaters of more or less shady joint-stock companies.

Par. 189 (*a*)

Phalanstères were socialist colonies on the plan of Charles Fourier; Icaria was the name given by Cabet to his Utopia and, later on, to his American Communist colony.

The party then represented in parliament by Ledru-Rollin, in literature by Louis Blanc, in the daily press by the *Réforme*. The name of Social Democracy signified, with these its inventors, a section of the Democratic or Republican party more or less tinged with Socialism.

Par. 189 (*a*)

Harney's Introduction to Helen Macfarlane's 1850 Translation.

The following Manifesto, which has since been adopted by all fractions of German Communists, was drawn up in the German language, in January 1848, by Citizens *Charles Marx* and *Frederic Engels*. It was immediately printed in London, in the German language, and published a few days before the outbreak of the Revolution of February. The turmoil consequent upon that great event made it impossible to carry out, at that time, the intention of translating it into all the languages of civilized Europe. There exist two different French versions of it in manuscript, but under the present oppressive laws of France, the publication of either of them has been found impracticable. The English reader will be enabled, by the following excellent translation of this important document, to judge of the plans and principles of the most advanced party of the German Revolutionists.

It must not be forgotten, that the whole of this Manifesto was written and printed before the Revolution of February.

Macfarlane's Footnotes.

Par. 146 (Title)

The term in the original is *Kleinbürger*; meaning small burghers, or citizens. A class, comprising small capitalists generally, whether small farmers, small manufacturers, or retail shopkeepers. As thes last form the predominant element of this class in England. I have chosen the term *Shopocrat* to express the German term.

Par. 153 (Title)

It was the set of writers characterized in following chapter, who themselves called their theory "**TRUE SOCIALISM**;" if, therefore, after perusing this chapter, the reader should not agree with them as to the name, this is no fault of the authors of the Manifesto.

Par. 191

It is not to be forgotten that these lines were written before the revolution of February, and that the examples have, accordingly, reference to the state of parties of that time.

PART III: ANNOTATIONS

Introductory Note

These Annotations are intended solely to explain what the Manifesto said, especially as read in 1848, and in no way to provide an exposition or commentary or exegesis on the ideas or thought content of the work.

To be sure, the dividing line is not always clear. Explaining what the text is saying certainly does often throw light on the Manifesto's ideas. But in no case have I taken space to do the latter for its own sake. For example, a theoretical commentary on the Manifesto would naturally have to discuss the formation of Marx's theory of the state; but such an exposition is out of bounds here. On the other hand, anyone who undertakes this exposition should know what Marx meant by the famous phrase which the A.E.T. translated misleadingly as "win the battle of democracy"; and this is addressed in the Annotations on Par.129.

I can draw this line with some equanimity because I have written on the larger subject in another work, *Karl Marx's Theory of Revolution*, especially Volume 2. And the formation of Marx's theory of the state is rather extensively covered in several chapters of Volume I of that work. Similarly, many of the problems raised by the Manifesto are discussed at considerable length in KMTR, and at various points in these Annotations I have simply referred the reader to its pages. To take another example, I would have been tempted to devote a good deal more apace to the term "lumpenproletariat" If I had not already presented a great deal of material on the subject in KMTR.

The Annotations aim to cover the following kinds of material.

(1) Explanation of translation choices and formulations in the N.E.V., especially in relation to those in the A.E.T.

(2) Differences between the A.E.T. and the first German edition of 1848.

(3) Changes made in the successive German editions published during the lifetime of Marx and Engels.

(4) Explanations of words, terms and phrases, as needed. This refers particularly to German expressions in the original text, but, where necessary, also to the English.

(5) Explanations of names and historical allusions.

(6) In the course, it may be useful to refer to other translations of the Manifesto in which Marx or Engels had a hand. The publication history of the Manifesto was the subject of Part I of this work and reference to that material will be made when necessary.

Books about the Manifesto

This heading, if taken literally, would introduce a list several hundred pages long. Here I want to introduce a handful of books specially relevant to the present purposes.

The best-known work of annotation on the Manifesto is that by D. Ryazanov, first published in Russian in 1921, then in an enlarged edition in 1922. The second Russian edition was published in English in 1930:

The Communist Manifesto of Karl Marx and Friedrich Engels. With an introduction and explanatory notes by D. Ryazanov. London, Martin Lawrence, 1930. [Translation by Eden & Cedar Paul.]

It included a new translation of the Manifesto by the Pauls. (I have commented in Part I on why their version is unacceptable.) Ryazanov's "explanatory notes" are especially devoted to painting the economic and social background of the work and the biographical context. Much of it is still well worth reading; nowadays much of it has been better done by a good biography of Marx like McLellan's. It does not cover most of the topics taken up in the Annotations.

Ryazanov's book also presented a useful selection of documents relevant to the Manifesto: prefaces, other writings by Marx and Engels, the text of the *Kommunistische Zeitschrift* (1847 organ of the CL), etc. With the exception of the last, this material may also be found in a more recent collection:

Birth of the Communist Manifesto. With full text of the Manifesto, all prefaces by Marx and Engels, early drafts by Engels and other supplementary material. Edited and annotated, with an introduction by Dirk J. Struik. New York, International Publishers, 1971.

By and large, this collection is the most useful one of the kind now available. Struik's introduction provides a historical survey. The "Explanatory Notes" take only a few pages; this work is not devoted to annotation.

Other books or parts of books that are in some sense on the Manifesto are, for the most part, really discussions of Marxism in general. This is true, for example, of E. H. Carr's essay in his *Studies in Revolution*, A. Labriola's in his *Essays in the Materialistic Conception of History*, Sweezy and Huberman's essay "The Communist Manifesto After 100 Years" in an edition of the Manifesto itself, or H. J. Laski's much reprinted introduction to the Manifesto.

Charles Andler's work on the Manifesto, in French, offers essay-notes on the various parts of the document much like Ryazanov's in form, if not in content. His *Le Manifeste Communiste* appeared in two volumes, the first volume being a new French translation of the Manifesto, the second volume offering the commentary:

Le Manifeste Communiste. I. Traduction nouvelle par Charles Andler avec les articles de F. Engels dans *La Réforme* (1847-1848). Bibliothèque Socialiste, 8 1906. II. Introduction historique et commentaire. Bibliothèque Socialiste, 9-10.1910. Paris, E. Cornély

Form of the Annotations

(1) The Annotations are organized by paragraph number, in accordance with the paragraph numbering assigned to the N.E.V.

(2) *Titles* are assigned to the number of the first paragraph they head. For example, the title of Section III is under "Par. 136: Title, Section III." Since Section III has subsections, these titles are treated similarly. For example, the title "Conservative or Bourgeois Socialism" is dealt with under "Par. 170: Title, Subsection 2." As it happens, Section III, Subsection 1, has further subdivisions, but these titles are treated as a part of the first paragraph they head, not separately. The quick way to find the title annotations is to consult the table of contents.

(3) On each paragraph of the Manifesto, there are numbered *points*, each with a heading of its own. The headings are often composed of the words or expressions to be discussed. Sometimes they are general headings, such as "A.E.T. editing." This heading is used to point to more or less routine alterations made by the A.E.T., editorial changes which do not affect the meaning but which are noticeable enough to warrant mention. Some differences between the A.E.T. and the German text are not mentioned at all if they are plainly of no significance whatever. Thus, in Par. 188, the German text says "critical elements,"- while the A.E.T. makes it "a critical element."

(4) Under each paragraph, the numbered points are generally arranged in the order in which their subjects occur in the paragraph. More general points may be put first (if important) or last (if not).

(5) Reference to a point in a paragraph is made in the short form: paragraph/point. For example, Par.100/2 refers to Par.100, point 2. The number of a paragraph used alone refers to the text of the Manifesto itself. In references to titles, the paragraph number is followed by a parenthesis with 'T' (for title) followed by the number of the section or subsection so titled; for example, Par.136 (TIII)/2; Par. 136 (TI)/1.

(6) In general, it is inherent in the form of the Annotations that there are great differences in *level of importance* from one point to another. Some of the points, in my opinion, deal with problems of great moment for the understanding of the development of Marx's thought; and some deal with details of small importance. To be sure, the second category is tricky: some points of small importance have been blown up by enterprising marxologists to vast proportions in pursuit of their objectives. Perhaps, dear reader, you will attach historic significance to a point that I may think is trivial. In this work, my aim is simply to present the facts.

(7) The Annotations do *not* assume a knowledge of German; on the contrary I have sought to make them useful precisely to readers who have no German at all. If I have gone beyond this at some point or other, I plead only that some readers may find the additional information useful.

(8) Single quote marks are used when an English word is pointed to as a word; italics are used for foreign words in the same case. Words, phrases, or short passages quoted from the text of the Manifesto in English or German, and coming from the Manifesto paragraph under discussion, are distinguished by degree symbols (°like this°). Other quotations are in double quote marks as usual.

(9) References to citations from Marx's and Engels' writings are given in short form. Where possible, the reader is referred to a chapter or section in a work, without a page number to a specific edition. (The chapter divisions of *Capital*, Volume I, refer to the English edition only.) In other cases, the citation is made by a page reference to one of the following editions by abbreviation:.

MEW Marx-Engels *Werke*. Berlin, Dietz, 1956-68. (39 volumes plus supplements.)
MECW Marx & Engels. *Collected Works*. (New York, London, 1975-).
MESW Marx & Engels. *Selected Works in three volumes*. Moscow, Progress Pub., 1969-70. (The abbreviation refers to this edition only.)

Even where the reference is to MECW or MESW, the English translation used may reflect my own revision. Writings in these editions are identified by their initial page number.
References to other works are also in short form. Full bibliographical data will be found in the appendix, "Works Cited," under the author or other main entry.

(10) Throughout the Annotations comparisons are made between the formulations in the N.E.V. and the A.E.T. In all these comparisons the sentence is constructed so that the N.E.V., that is, the original formulation, is given first. In the point headings, a slash mark (/) indicates such a comparison, with the N.E.V.'s words or expression given before the slash mark, the A.E.T.'s after it.

(11) *Abbreviations*. Instead of a separate list of abbreviations used in this work, all abbreviations are identified in the Index.

MANIFESTO OF THE COMMUNIST PARTY

[PREAMBLE]

Main Title

(1) MANIFESTO. Programmatic statements were often called a credo or "confession of faith" (*confessio fidei*, *Glaubensbekenntnis*), especially if cast in the form of a catechism, the traditional form derived from the analogous practices of religious movements. Moses Hess had drafted one; Engels did two drafts in this form in 1847 (see Part I). Shortly before the second congress of the CL in November 1847, he wrote Marx: "I believe we would do best to drop the catechism form and entitle the thing: Communist Manifesto. Since a certain amount of history has to be related in it, the present form is quite unsuitable." (MEW 27:107 or *MECW* 38:149; see Part I, Chap. 3.) The question-and-answer form became unwieldy when long answers were given to short questions; but a manifesto was simply a straight-forward statement, an exposition, an "address" to the working-class public. "Address" (*Ansprache*) was a term attached to CL statements of a less basic character.

The term 'manifesto' itself was an old one. Even in English, though derived from Italian, it had been used at least since the mid-1600s in the sense of a public declaration. For example, Victor Considérant, the Fourierist leader, had published a *Manifeste de la Démocratie* (the name of which has persuaded some marxologists that he anticipated Marx's manifesto). Andréas has pointed to what may be the first use of "manifesto" coupled with "communist"--in the title of a series of articles in a French Fourierist journal in 1841--but this is merely a point of curiosity.* It was already standard terminology. Incidentally, it is amusing to note that in 1852 Marx lampooned a certain politician's "manifesto mania": "As soon as anyone hatched a new idea...he issued a manifesto," and indeed "brought this fabrication of manifestos, proclamations and pronunciamentos to an unbelievable level..." (MEW 8:274 or MECW 11:266).

(2) COMMUNIST. For the difference in usage in the 1840s between 'socialist' and 'communist', see the note on the former term, Par.136 (TIII)/3. To this we may add the following. The Communist League people had, in any case, long called themselves Communists, even before adopting the name of the group. They had been most heavily influenced, before coming under the impact of Marx and Engels, by Wilhelm Weitling and Etienne Cabet, both of whom used 'Communist' for self-designation. Cabet, indeed, was the only one of the founders of utopian sects who regularly used this label, no doubt because his "New Jerusalem" called for the abolition of private property in production, unlike the Saint--Simonians and Fourierists. Associated with this was the fact that the Cabetists ("Icarians") oriented toward a working-class clientele to a greater extent than the other two. Hence the

---

* The title was "Manifeste des Communistes," in *La Phalange*, May 19-June 11, 1841. It was mentioned by Hess in an article in the *Rheinische Zeitung* in April 1842, an article certainly read by Marx at the time.

two leading indicia of the "Communists" went together: abolition of private property in production and a working-class orientation.

(3) PARTY. From the standpoint of present-day usage, the most misleading word in the main title is 'party.' No organization called the 'Communist Party' existed, nor did the title claim otherwise. At this time, and until the rise of the modern party system in the course of the century, 'party' usually meant a tendency or current of opinion and not an organization. (See KMTR 1:153n, 2:212n.) Note that the organization actually sponsoring the Manifesto, the CL, was not mentioned in its pages. In other words, Marx viewed the document as expounding a point of view, not as laying down the organizational program of a sect. (For more about this, see Part I, Chap. 6.) Engels was not very enlightening when later, in 1884 and 1885, he tried to explain the term 'Communist Party' to the modern party. In one article he wrote: "On the outbreak of the February Revolution, the German 'Communist Party,' as we called it, consisted only of a small core, the Communist League..." In another, he referred to the League of the Just as "the Communist party in process of formation." (MESW 3:164,180.) In neither case would his readers have understood how the term was really used. (See also Par.62/1.)

(4) THE TWO FORMS OF THE TITLE. The short form *The Communist Manifesto* was affixed to the publication for the first time in the German edition of 1872 as mentioned in Part I. But it had already been informally used more than once by Marx and Engels in their correspondence; indeed, we have seen that Engels used it in his 1847 letter to Marx suggesting the term 'manifesto.' No doubt the short form was used by others too. Besides, by the last quarter of the century, 'party' was tending more and more to invite an organizational interpretation. The short form also had some advantages in situations of precarious legality. Immediately after the 1872 German edition, a Spanish edition done by José Mesa with Engels' help used the new short title; and the "authorized German editions" continued it. However, *Communist Manifesto* never supplanted the original title; both were used worldwide, and still are.

Par. 1

(1) SPECTER OF COMMUNISM. Various pre-Marx sources for this phrase have been found, enough to show that it was by no means a new one. In 1842, a then influential book by Lorenz Stein, on socialism and communism in France, referred to "communism, a dark, menacing specter, in whose reality nobody wants to believe, and whose existence however everyone acknowledges and fears..." (Page 4.) In 1846, an article by Wilhelm Schulz in a Rotteck and Welcker encyclopedia began with the sentence: "For the last few years there has been talk about communism in Germany, and it has now become a menacing specter, of which some take fright and which others use to inspire fright." In 1847, an anonymous brochure *Der Pauperismus und die Volksschule* said: "there is a growling of the thunder of discontent with the status quo, and...the flashing lightning illumines the pale specter of communism." Marx need not have been thinking of any one passage, but simply of the currency of the phrase. In any case, his statement was not an exaggeration: as Hammen avers: "When Marx spoke of a 'spectre of communism' haunting Europe in 1848, he was stating a verifiable fact, as far as France and the German world were concerned." (Page 418.)

204

(2) WITCHHUNT. The German *Hetzjagd* means a hunting down; but the stem also connotes baiting or hounding; and so the word has the flavor of 'witchhunt' even if the 'witch' analogy is not there. The A.E.T.'s term °holy alliance°, was no doubt intended to remind of the Holy Alliance erected in 1815 as the reactionary united front of Russia, Austria and Prussia, supported by most of Europe's crowned heads, initiated by the czar and dominated by Metternich.

(3) THE POPE. Giovanni Maria Mastai-Ferretti (1792—1878) became pope in 1846 as Pius IX. At the time Marx was writing the Manifesto, Mastai-Ferretti was still new in the papal chair, and widely regarded as a reformer and liberalizer. In 1847 he instituted some partial reforms to laicize the government of the Papal States--far from enough to satisfy the demands for self-government. In writing °the pope° Marx probably did not have this particular pontiff solely in mind, but rather the office and its history. The preceding pope, Gregory XVI, in office from 1831 to 1846, had reacted to the revolution of 1830 in France with a regime of repressive measures (propped on Austrian bayonets) which even Metternich found embarrassing, and was liberal only in his employment of spies and prisons. To be sure, Pius IX too became a bitter reactionary after he fled the 1848 Rome insurrection and was restored by French guns. His pontificate produced the dogma of the Immaculate Conception and of papal infallibility, also the Syllabus condemning modern science, tolerance, and other devilish modern inventions, not to speak of various denunciations of socialism and the loss in 1870 of the papacy's temporal power.

(4) THE CZAR. Nicholas I (1796-1855, crowned 1825) was the embodiment of Russian autocratic despotism. Where his predecessor, brother Alexander I, had muttered about liberalization and reforms, Nicholas trusted only the knout, barracks discipline, and the secret police. His reign was inaugurated with the crushing of the Decembrist officers' conspiracy (mildly proconstitutional); he continued with the straitjacketing of Europe in a renewed Holy Alliance, helped to suppress the 1848 revolution for the Hapsburgs, and died in the midst of the Crimean War, which would begin the process of dissolution of the old Russia.

(5) METTERNICH. Clemens Wenzel Nepomuk Lothar, Prince von Metternich (1773-1859), was a Rhinelander by birth who married into the upper circles of Austrian society, and became (after an initial dalliance with Napoleon) the chief architect of the Hapsburg Empire's policies. Within this empire, the "Metternich system" depended on censorship, espionage, police agents, and the forceful repression of all revolutionary, democratic, and national aspirations to extend Austrian sway over Italy and the German states. Externally, Metternich became the leading spirit of the European reaction inaugurated with the Congress of Vienna (1814-1815) and the establishment of the Holy Alliance--until in 1848 he had to flee to England. Marx was writing the Manifesto just as the "Age of Metternich" (1815-1848) was crumbling. In our day Metternich's chief distinction is as the ideological hero of Henry Kissinger.

(6) GUIZOT. François Guizot (1787-1874) was eminent in France both as historian and statesman. Of a Huguenot family, originally a lawyer, he became a professor of modern history at Paris, and went into politics as one of the so-called "Doctrinaires" (middle-of-the-road royalists) in 1816—1830. Taking part in the 1830 revolution which installed Louis Philippe, he prospered as an Orleanist champion in the July Monarchy, entering the cabinet in 1832. He then moved closer to conservatism, as a representative of

finance-capitalist interests, and became the leading force in the government (foreign minister 1840-1848). In 1847 he also became premier—the last one under the old French monarchy, thrown out of power by the 1848 revolution. He devoted his last years to the writing of history. Marx's phrase "Metternich and Guizot" sums up the official face of European power at both ends of the continent on the eve of the upheaval.

(7) FRENCH RADICALS. 'Radical' was the decorative label for the tendency of moderate bourgeois republicans around the organ *Le National*, as distinct (at least in Marx's usage) from the tendency around *La Réforme* (for which see Par.191/4). The director of *Le National* since 1841 was Armand Marrast (1801-1852). Other representative figures were Louis Antoine Garnier-Pagès (1803-1878) and Lazare Hippolyte Carnot (1801-1888), son of a famous Napoleonic general and father of a president of the Third Republic. Alphonse de Lamartine (1790-1867), a prominent poet and a sentimental politician, can be associated with this tendency, which was not defined by an organization. Many of these figures peopled the cabinet ministries of the government installed by the 1848 revolution, and provided one of the great historic examples of falling between two stools, as they fought against the aspirations of the people in movement while denouncing the monarchists.

(8) GERMAN POLICEMEN. The A.E.T. changed this to °police spies,° perhaps because the English could not be expected to react as negatively as Continentals to mere 'policemen' or 'police agents.' But °police-spies° does not really reflect the 1848 text, which had in mind the use of the state's whole police apparatus, not merely *mouchards* (Marx's usual term for police spies and stoolpigeons whatever language he was using).

Par. 2

(1) BRANDING REPROACH. That is, discrediting or searing accusation. As editor of the *Rheinische Zeitung* in Cologne in 1842, Marx himself had encountered precisely such an accusation, branding his paper as flirting with communism, for publishing an article by Weitling. The charge came from the leading German daily, the *Allgemeine Zeitung* of Augsburg. Marx was by no means a socialist or communist at this point, and defended the publication of Weitling's article on the ground that it raised the important social questions of the day for open discussion. (See KMTR 1:61f.) To be sure, he did not hurl the "branding reproach" back at its makers.

Par.5

(1) OPENLY. The decision to come out °openly...before the whole world,° discarding the practice and perspective of conspiratorialism, was one of the conditions which Marx and Engels laid down for joining the CL in 1847. Conspiratorialism was the tradition for the type of revolutionaries who had formed the organization; and this paragraph—which may sound today like an oratorical flourish—was in 1848 the declaration of an important turn. Engels had also written a repudiation of conspiratorialism into both of his drafts; his *Principles of Communism* stated that "The Communists know only too well that all conspiracies are not

only futile but even harmful. They know only too well that revolutions are not made deliberately and arbitrarily.." (MECW 6:349).

Par. 6

(1) COMMUNISTS...IN LONDON. This refers directly to a meeting in London, yet the organization that held the congress, that sponsored the Manifesto, is not named. Why the Communist League was not mentioned anywhere in the publication is a complex question which is discussed in Part I, Chapter 5.

(2) MOST VARIOUS NATIONALITIES. The A.E.T. tones down the superlative used in the original, but in any case the claim was somewhat exaggerated. The membership was largely German, plus a few English radicals who were members of the CL and a sprinkling of Scandinavians, Dutch, and some others. Besides, mere members could not attend the congress (Friedrich Lessner mentions this fact in his memoirs), no doubt because of a remnant of the older conspiratorial attitudes. Therefore it is doubly uncertain how many of the people °assembled in London° belonged to the °verschiedensten° nationalities. This paragraph sounds like a claim, but it was really a program—the aspiration of the CL to be, in principle, an international movement, not a German group. Every organizational initiative taken or supported by Marx was of this international sort, beginning with the Communist Correspondence Committee in Brussels and continuing later with the International itself. Even in later decades, Marx and Engels explicitly refused to take out membership in the German Social-Democratic Party.

(3) PROMISED TRANSLATIONS. Efforts were indeed made to produce the five translations listed: English, French, Italian, Flemish, and Danish; also Spanish, Polish, and (possibly) Hungarian. Translations were drafted in whole or part for at least French and English, perhaps others, but none was published. Engels himself did part of an English translation in April 1848; it was not finished, and is not extant. Only one translation actually came out before 1850: a Swedish version, issued in Stockholm at the end of 1848, probably done by Per Götrek. Subsequent prefaces by Marx and Engels spoke of some of these translations as if published in 1848, but they were probably relying on the statement made in this paragraph; in any case, no such translations are extant or even known for sure. (More details on this question can be found in Part I.)

(4) PREAMBLE. The first six paragraphs of the Manifesto are usually called its Preamble.

BOURGEOIS AND PROLETARIANS

Par. 7: Title, Section I

(1) ENGELS' NOTE. The first footnote is attached to the terms in the section title, °Bourgeois and Proletarians,° Observe that Engels thought it necessary to explain these terms to the English working-class public in 1888; but he did *not* include this note in his 1890 German edition. The content of the footnote is considered under the next two points. It

should be borne in mind that Engels' definitions were given in terms of Marx's mature theory; they would have been rather less accurate in 1848. Engels' two drafts for the Manifesto offered formal definitions of 'proletariat' and its differentiation from slaves, serfs, and medieval artisans as well as definitions of 'bourgeoisie.'

(2) BOURGEOIS. This word (here masculine plural), meaning the persons making up the bourgeoisie, was of course French, and even into the twentieth century it was felt to be a foreign word in English, hence often italicized in ordinary use. In 1848 it was still essentially a foreign word in German. All this shows where most of socialist terminology was coming from, namely, France. The German-language equivalent *Bürger* was sometimes used, even by socialists, but this word had, and has, various meanings: townsman (its original meaning), civilian, citizen, and others. A *Bürger* was a member of the *Bürgerschaft* or *Bürgertum*, but the latter term (the equivalent of 'bourgeoisie') was more often used in compounds—e.g., *Kleinbürgerschaft*, which we will see in the Manifesto. There are other complications, which have led not infrequently to mistranslations.

In French and English, 'bourgeois' is also an adjective, and can be so in German; but in German the adjective more often than not is *bürgerlich*, as in Par. 10. In that paragraph we meet a key phrase *bürgerlich Gesellschaft*: here it means 'bourgeois society' but especially around this time it was likely to mean 'civil society.' (See KMTR 1:32—34.) In short: when German uses 'bourgeois(ie),' the meaning is unequivocal, but all forms with *Bürger* need closer examination. The fact that the Manifesto uses 'bourgeois(ie)' without ado reflects its intended public.

Engels' note properly equates 'bourgeoisie' with 'capitalist class'; these two were regularly used interchangeably by Marx and Engels. For the relation of these terms to 'middle class,' see Pr. 14/5.

(3) PROLETARIANS. This word, with its cognate 'proletariat,' was quite new in 1848 in its present meaning. Its usual meaning at that time was quite different: the lowest stratum of poor and propertyless in town or country, or (especially by the nineteenth century) the Common People in the usual amorphous sense. This old meaning, which was broader than 'workers,' was still alive when, in the decade or two before the Manifesto, it began assuming its modern meaning, which is narrower than 'workers.' This modern meaning stemmed from modern conditions, the growth of wage-labor, of workers who lived by selling their labor power. The Chartists already used the new meaning; Blanqui used the old one. In using the modern term without explanation at this early date, the Manifesto reflected an advanced mode of thinking. It made clear, for example, that 'proletariat' was not simply a synonym for 'working class' that the proletariat was the working-class peculiar to capitalism, °the class of modern wage-laborers° (as Engels' note says). This is the distinction made in Par. 35, which see.

Par. 7

(1) PRIMITIVE CLASSLESS SOCIETY. Engels' footnote on the words °all hitherto existing society° was made necessary by the fact that he and Marx had developed the view, from the early 1850s on, that the first form of human society was a village community

208

without fixed class divisions. For this highly contentious subject, see KMTR 1, Chap. 21. Engels translated his 1888 note for the 1890 German edition with two changes: (a) He dropped the last sentence referring to his own work *Origin of the Family*. (b) The reference to °village communities° was expanded to °village communities with common property in land°. The next three notes are on the scientists mentioned in Engels' footnote.

(2) HAXTHAUSEN. Baron August von Haxthausen (1792—1866) was a German agrarian historian and economist who became a Prussian state official. On behalf of the Prussian government, he made a study of Prussian agrarian conditions (*Die ländliche Verfassung in der Provinz Preussen*, 1839), and was asked by the czar's government to do likewise in Russia (*Studien über die innern Zustände, das Volksleben und insbesondere die ländlichen Einrichtungen Russlands* 1847-1852). His material on the *obshchina* (Russian village community) led Narodnik theorists to "discover" it as the peculiarly Russian base for a noncapitalist road to socialism, though Haxthausen's own views were on the reactionary side.

(3) MAURER. Georg Ludwig von Maurer (1790-1872) was a German historian of law and early social institutions. His works sought to prove that the Mark community (out of which the medieval town arose) was a voluntary association of free men holding lands communally, under an elected chief. This view of the roots of German society as emerging out of institutions of primitive democracy and communality was violently attacked, particularly by the Right. Marx and Engels admired his work exceedingly. The continuing dispute over Maurer's views is partly involved with controversy over Marxist views—as is true of the next man too.

(4) MORGAN. Lewis Henry Morgan (1818-1881) was an American ethnologist best known for his contributions to social-evolutionary theory in anthropology. Originally a lawyer, he investigated Native American (especially Iroquois) culture, decried the spoliation of the Native Americans, and founded a society to study and aid the Native American population. His chief work *Ancient Society* (1877) presented his view of social-historical origins. Marx hailed Morgan's work as an application of historical materialism to primitive history; Engels made great use of Morgan in his *Origin of the Family*. While Morgan was recognized as an outstanding anthropologist (elected president of the American Association for the Advancement of Science in 1880), the later anti-evolutionary trend of this science has downgraded him, not least of all because Marx's utilization of his work caused it to be regarded as "Marxist" in some sense. The myth that Morgan's views are simply "obsolete" and of no interest now (as distinct from requiring updating, like Darwin's) is equivalent to the belief that the contemporary anti-evolutionary dogmas of anthropology are beyond debate. For the issues in this continuing controversy, one can begin with the references cited in Leslie A. White's article on Morgan in the *International Encyclopedia of the Social Sciences*.

Par. 8

(1) CLASSES. The four pairs of social strata here listed are by no means coordinate, and reflect popular historical terminology. In particular, they reflect juridical social orders (social estates, *Stände*) rather than social classes properly so called; see Par.9/1. For example, the counterposition of °freeman and slave° was juridical; in terms of polar classes (ruling class and

basic working class) the counterposition was *slave-owners and slaves*. The counterposition °master guildsman and journeyman° involved more or less fixed social classes only as it became harder for journeymen to become masters and as journeymen came to be paid regular wages. (Cf. the A.E.T.'s addition of °apprentices° to this constellation in Par. 9.) Above all, this is not a list of polar classes. The corresponding passage in Engels' draft *Principles of Communism* was in fact better—see his answer to Question 15.

(2) MASTER GUILDSMAN. Engels' footnote, explaining that this term does not necessarily mean the master or head of a guild, was made necessary by the translation he chose: °guild-master°. In any case, it meant a master artisan, master in his own workshop, one member among others of a guild.

(3) COMMON RUIN OF THE CONTENDING CLASSES. This phrase is so deservedly famous that I do not dare offer an alternative, such as "the joint downfall of the classes in struggle." Above all, this passage shows how mythical is the view that Marx believed in some sort of metaphysical "inevitability of socialism," according to which socialist victory is as fatefully predestined as, say, the salvation of Calvinist saints: a myth mostly based on a reading of Par. 60. On the contrary, society is faced with the alternatives later tagged "socialism or barbarism"—either a revolution that remakes society or the collapse of the old order to a lower level. Engels later repeated the alternative in *Anti-Duhring* (end of Pt. II, Chap. 2): the productive forces out of control, "are driving the whole of bourgeois society towards ruin, or revolution." Or (Pt. III, Chap. 2): the proletariat has to accomplish its revolution "under penalty of its own destruction" if it fails to do so. The great example in everyone's mind of the °common ruin of the contending classes° was the revolutionless disintegration of the society of the Roman Empire into "Caesarism" and a "dark" age. (See KMTR 1:465.) In contemporary Europe, "class struggle and rivalry in conquest have tuned up the public power to such a pitch that it threatens to swallow the whole of society and even the state," thought Engels (*Origin of the Family*, Chap. 9). The Manifesto makes clear that the fate of society will be decided as usual by social struggle, not metaphysics.

Par. 9

(1) SOCIAL ESTATE AND CLASS. This is the first paragraph illustrating the use of the German term for social estates, *Stände* (singular, *Stand*), used in English mainly in the phrase 'third estate.' Though often translatable as 'class,' it means, more exactly, a social stratum organized in a juridical relationship fixed by the state or tradition, not simply by economics. An *estates assembly* was a (consultative or legislative) body comprising delegates from social estates, or delegates elected on estate lines, rather than by general suffrage. *Stand* is also a general word for 'rank,' 'order,' 'position.' In Par.9, orders (*Stände*) and classes (*Klassen*) are used as synonyms, the former in the first sentence, the latter in the second; but often *Stand* smacks of prebourgeois society. "In modern society," Marx told a Cologne jury in 1849, "there are still *classes* but no longer *estates*." (MEW 6:253 or MECW 8:336.) For a more thorough discussion, see KMTR 1:505-509. Below, the difference between 'class' and 'estate' is involved in other cases; for example, see Par. 18.

(2) EARLIER EPOCHS. Specifically, prebourgeois epochs of history.

(3) ALMOST EVERYWHERE. The fast reader should note the word °almost°. Though qualifications are often neglected in generalizing, there is no suggestion that social patterns enjoy anything like complete uniformity.

(4) THOROUGHGOING / COMPLICATED. Where the original said °thoroughgoing (or complete) structuring of society° into various estates, the A.E.T. made this °complicated°. The change may have been simply literary; or perhaps Engels felt that the original was an exaggeration. Actually, the idea of °complicated° is already represented in this sentence by °multifarious° (or °manifold°).

(5) APPRENTICES. The A.E.T. added this to the list after °journeymen°, to fill out the ranks of workingmen below the master artisan, especially since apprentices who could not break into guild ranks might turn into wage-laborers (modern proletarians).

Par. 10

(1) THE INTENSIVE 'NUR.' This is the first paragraph in which we meet the word °nur° (only, merely) used as an intensive rather than literally: modern bourgeois society °has only put new classes° in place of old ones. To belabor the obvious: it does not mean that this is literally the "only" thing bourgeois society has done! My reason for belaboring the obvious is that in other passages the intensive *nur* has persuaded some marxologists to take it *literatim*, even in the teeth of common sense. This intensive use of 'only,' 'but,' or 'nothing but' is frequent enough. If I tell Jones, "You are nothing but a scoundrel!" it is unlikely to mean that scoundrelism is Jones's sole and exclusive characteristic. The form 'nothing but' represents not only emphasis but also an elliptical thought. In the present case we are no doubt breaking down an open door; but it is necessary to do this with other cases in mind.

Par. 11

(1) POLAR CLASSES. This paragraph illustrates Marx's view of the polar classes, though the term is not his. He called them the "fundamental classes of modern society" (MECW 11:472) or "the extremes of a relation of production" (*Grundrisse*, 204)—the basic counterposition of ruling class to working class around which a mode of production is socially structured. In his *Principles of Communism* Engels called them "the two decisive classes of society and the struggle between them the main struggle of the day." (Ques. 19.) See above, Par.8/1.

(2) TWO CAMPS, TWO CLASSES. The Manifesto does not say that capitalist society consists only of the polar classes; its emphasis is on a long-term tendency—the tendency toward polarization. It says that this simplification is happening °more and more°, not that it has reached or will reach its apex. The myth that the Manifesto predicts the "disappearance" of all intermediate strata is taken up in Par.51/2.

While the metaphor seems to be that of a *duel* of classes, it should be noted that the first reference is to two great °camps° confronting each other. The word °camps° suggests what indeed became Marx's approach later, though it is not clear to what extent he already held it before the experience of the 1848 revolution. The proletariat, wrote Engels in 1870, "is still far from being the majority of the German people. It is, therefore, also compelled to seek allies." (MESW 2:163.) In 1848 he conceived the revolutionary *camp* to comprise the proletariat, small peasantry and petty-bourgeoisie, and believed that the proletarian revolution meant the victory of this camp *under the vanguard leadership of the proletariat*. The problem before each of the polar classes was to attract and hold some class allies and neutralize others: the real pattern, then, was not the classic duel but the confrontation of *camps*.

Par. 12

(1) THE BURGESSES. Marx uses here the term °Pfahlbürger°, with its collective form °Pfahlbürgerschaft°, as his label for the early commercial elements who began (about the thirteenth century) collecting around or outside the urban centers whose charters freed them from some onerous obligations to the feudal lords and allowed them to develop independently. Literally, the prefix *Pfahl-* refers to elements who lived outside the walls but within the palings or palisade (*Pfähle*), under the protection of the given town's charter, even if they were not formally citizens of the town. It is unlikely that Marx had this etymological limitation in mind; in effect, he was using the term to label the early trading elements that accreted around the chartered towns, from whom °developed the first elements of the bourgeoisie°. (Let us leave aside the historical question whether this was the only road that the developing bourgeoisie took.)

There certainly is no English term exactly equivalent to *Pfahlbürger*, but, as mentioned, I doubt that it is needed here; and the English 'burgess' is good enough as a historical term for the early-developing urban commercial class. However, the A.E.T. introduces a needless complication by translating *Pfahlbürger* as °chartered burghers°, and *Pfahlbürgerschaft* as °burgesses°—as if there were two different terms here. Perhaps Moore and Engels could not decide which to use and compromised on both. The terminological problem is complicated by the fact that both the German and the English terms have other meanings. Americans may be familiar with the colonial House of Burgesses, 'burgess' being a parliamentary deputy. And in modern German, *Pfahlbürger* means something like a philistine or petty-bourgeois babbitt (like *Spiessbürger*, which we will meet later). And, alas, it had this other meaning in 1848 too. Already in 1848, the *Pfahlbürger* of this paragraph was a historical term, while the 'philistine' meaning was contemporaneously current. In fact, we are going to find this second meaning in the Manifesto itself—see Par.165/3, Par.168/2.

Par. 14

(1) HITHERTO EXISTING. The A.E.T. omits this (in German one word, °bisherige°, i.e., 'up to now' as an adjective). The reason must have been to mentally push the feudal stage farther back into the past. In 1848 the guild system was by no means dead in Germany; but by 1888 it was simply past history for England.

(2) GUILD-SYSTEM MODE. Whereas the original simply put °guild-system° (as

212

adjective) in synonymy with °feudal°, the A.E.T. expanded it into an explanation: °under which industrial production was monopolised by closed guilds.° This insertion took the place of a footnote. In medieval Europe, the merchants' guilds had arisen by the eleventh century, but Marx was undoubtedly thinking mainly of the craft (artisanal) guilds.

(3) MANUFACTURING. Marx regularly used 'manufacture' in its literal sense of production by hand labor as opposed to machine production (machinofacture). The next paragraph makes no sense unless this is understood. Engels explained that, in establishment economics:

> all industry, not agricultural or handicraft, is indiscriminately comprised in the term of manufacture, and thereby the distinction is obliterated between two great and essentially different periods of economic history: the period of manufacture proper, based on the division of manual labor, and the period of modern industry based on machinery. It is, however, self-evident that a theory which views modern capitalist production as a mere passing stage in the economic history of mankind must make use of terms different from those habitual to writers who look upon that form of production as imperishable and final. (Preface, English edition, *Capital*, I.)

(4) MASTER GUILDSMEN / GUILD-MASTERS. See Par.8/2.

(5) MIDDLE CLASS. The difference between °industrial° middle class in the original and °manufacturing° middle class in the A.E.T. is not significant; both denote the capitalist class or bourgeoisie. But in both English and German, 'middle class' is a slippery term, and we will have trouble with it. Let us take the English first. In the nineteenth century—and after it too—English writers used 'middle class' to *include* the bourgeoisie, often as a global term for bourgeoisie and upper petty-bourgeoisie. (For the strict meaning of 'petty-bourgeoisie,' see Par.44/3.) This usage conceived of the bourgeoisie as being in the middle between the aristocracy and the Lower Orders (proletariat and small petty-bourgeoisie). Especially in writing English language journalistic articles, Marx and Engels usually followed this usage even in later writings. This meaning of 'middle class' was naturalized in America despite the absence of an aristocracy, and indeed it still influences its meaning today. In another meaning, 'middle class' or 'middle classes' denotes intermediate strata (often undefined) between the bourgeoisie and the working classes. This meaning is quite different, even though some writers might hazily think of the two class areas as similar. Though there may be overlapping, the important difference is that in the first case 'middle class' is mainly a synonym for 'bourgeoisie.' It is evident that opportunities for misinterpretation and mis-translation are legion. The nature of the intermediate strata, in the second meaning, will come up later in more than one point (see index).

But in the paragraph before us, the Manifesto did not use *Mittelklasse* (the more sociological term); it used °Mittelstand°—the more popular tag for strata seen as in-between some upper and lower class. Besides involving the general difference between *Stand* and *Klasse* (see Par.9/1), this term lacks sharp definition. We will meet it again in Par.41/1, Par.52/1.

In the present paragraph, °Mittelstand° is modified by °industriellen° (which the A.E.T. made °manufacturing°), and so in this case there can be no doubt that the bourgeoisie is meant, indeed the industrial bourgeoisie. But we will discover in the next paragraph that Marx actually had *small* industrialists in mind here.

(6) CORPORATE GUILDS. The original said "corporations," but of course this does not denote the modern corporation (joint-stock company separating nominal ownership from management control). The medieval corporation was any body of persons operating as a legal entity: besides the guilds, there were universities, religious bodies, municipal authorities, etc. But here 'corporations' means guilds only, hence the translation °corporate guilds°.

Par. 15

(1) MANUFACTURE. For the term, see Par.14/3. Here counterposed to °manufacture° is °modern large-scale industry,° that is, machinofacture, machine production.

(2) MODERN LARGE-SCALE INDUSTRY. The A.E.T. makes this °the giant, Modern Industry°. From here on, beginning with the next paragraph, the A.E.T. systematically changed 'large-scale industry' to 'modern industry' (usually capitalized), and, as here, avoided using the term 'large-scale [or big] industry' (*grosse Industrie*) at all. This idiosyncrasy was not reflected in the Laura (French) versions. Perhaps the aim was a literary effect.

(3) INDUSTRIAL MIDDLE CLASS. This is the same term as in Par.14 (see Par.14/5); but now the A.E.T. translates it °industrial° rather than °manufacturing° middle class. This change of appellation may blur the fact that exactly the same stratum is denoted.

We now read that this °industrial middle class° is *replaced* by another stratum, labeled °industrial millionaires.° This shows that Marx must have used the first term to mean *small* industrialists in contrast to very big capitalists. The terminology is not thought-through, and may obscure the fact that under discussion is a class, the capitalist class, with different sectors. All this reflects the state of Marx's economic theory in 1848.

Par. 16

(1) LARGE-SCALE INDUSTRY. For the A.E.T.'s version °modern industry°, see Par.15/2.

(2) WORLD MARKET. From early on, Marx saw the growth of a °world market° as a prime economic factor in the development of the capitalist mode of production. For Marx's and Engels' first extensive discussion of the world market, see the *German Ideology*, Pt. I (MECW 5:69-73). Both stressed the world market in several writings of 1847. In his draft *Principles of Communism* Engels based an important passage on this concept, answering Question 19, "Will it be possible for this [communist] revolution to take place in one country alone?" His answer was no, because of the interdependence enforced by the world market. Marx's most extensive survey of the contemporary meaning of the world market, before *Capital*, came in 1850 in three "Reviews" of recent history written for his magazine *NRZ-Revue*. (See MECW 10:257, 338, 490.) The present paragraph in the Manifesto reads like a preview of this. In *Capital*, especially Volume III, Marx emphasized that the world

market is "the basis and the vital element of capitalist production." (Chap. 6; see also Chap. 20.) This subject is continued in Par.26/1.

(3) PUSHED INTO THE BACKGROUND. In anticipation of our discussion of the mythical "disappearance of the middle classes," let us note here that the development of the capitalist class does not cause the older classes to "disappear"; they are °pushed into the background°—a quite different fate. See Par.51/2. By the classes °handed down from the Middle Ages° was meant chiefly the old ruling class—the landed aristocracy, with its bureaucratic-state formation in charge—and the traditional petty-bourgeoisie (for which see Par.44/3).

Par. 17

(1) TRANSFORMATIONS / REVOLUTIONS. The German word here is °Umwälzungen°. The base meaning of *Umwälzung* is a turning-over, overturn. While 'revolution' is a frequent translation, I prefer, wherever possible, to use 'transformation,' in order to keep it distinct from another good German word, *Revolution*. I do not suggest that in this context there is a difference in meaning.

(2) MODE OF INTERCOURSE. In the mature Marx, we would expect °modes of production and of exchange,° and this indeed is what the A.E.T. supplies. But the Manifesto's terminology was still that of the *German Ideology*, throughout which one finds the term *Verkehr* (intercourse) as in the present context. This word—broader and more amorphous than 'exchange' (*Austauch*)—means trading, trafficking, communication, intercourse of all sorts commercial, material, intellectual, etc. For its use in the *German Ideology*, look up 'intercourse' in the MECW 5 index.

Par. 18

(1) OF THAT CLASS. The A.E.T. adds these words. The motive was perhaps to avoid the possible interpretation that the rise of the bourgeoisie was *itself* the °political advance°. To be sure, that was true in a sense, but it is not the present point.

(2) OPPRESSED SOCIAL ESTATE. I use 'estate' rather than the A.E.T.'s 'class' only to point up the fact that the original does use *Stand* in this context, where it is tracing the changes in *prebourgeois* society. See the comment on this in Par.9/1.

(3) ASSOCIATIONS. The change from plural to singular was first made in the German edition of 1883, and was followed by the A.E.T.

(4) COMMUNE. This term was spelled just this way in the original German; in the A.E.T. it was expanded explanatorily to °medieval commune° and further expounded in a footnote by Engels. Engels' explanation was all the more necessary since the Paris Commune had given the term a revolutionary aura (just as in a later age the innocent word 'soviet' acquired a special meaning). But, as the footnote makes clear, 'commune' did not mean some special form of revolutionary government or society, but simply a "free town," a more or less autonomous municipality not controlled from the top by a centralized national government

in the French tradition. To be sure, in the postmedieval world this fact gave the commune form a democratic-reform and even revolutionary thrust in bureaucratized France; and in the Great French Revolution, as later in 1871, the establishment of commune government for the Paris municipality coincided with a social-revolutionary movement. (On the historical background of "the conspiratorial and revolutionary character of the municipal movement" in Germany and France, see Marx's letter to Engels of July 27, 1854.) But in the present paragraph, Marx was using °commune° simply as a historical appellation.

(5) ENGELS' NOTE ON 'COMMUNE.' In the German edition of 1890, Engels' footnote was shorter than in the A.E.T. It went as follows:.

> This is what the townsmen of Italy and France called their urban communities after they had bought from their feudal lords, or wrung from them, the first rights of self-government.

(6) A.E.T. INSERTION. The A.E.T.'s parenthetical explanation—°(as in Italy and Germany)°—is, in effect, an incorporated footnote.

(7) A.E.T. INSERTION: FRANCE. The same goes for the parenthesis: °(as in France)°. Note in this connection that this explains the phrase °third estate,° which is furthermore put into quotation marks by the A.E.T., both in the translation and the footnote.

(8) MANUFACTURE PROPER. The A.E.T. added °proper° to recall the special meaning given to 'manufacture' (see Par. 14/3).

(9) ESTATES-BASED (SEMIFEUDAL) MONARCHY. The German term used here by Marx, *ständischen...Monarchie*, is difficult to translate because it uses the adjective form of *Stand* (social estate). Marx here distinguished an absolute monarchy plain-and-simple from one modified or conditioned by organized estates assemblies (delegated bodies representing the various social estates and forming a 'semifeudal' legislative assembly). In the 1840s, one of the first political issues which both Marx and Engels (separately) had tackled was opposition to the attempt by "moderate" monarchists to substitute the demand for estates assemblies in place of the demand for modern constitutional representative assemblies by individual vote. In the A.E.T., °semi-feudal° was an English-language approximate stab at the meaning of *ständisch*. In 1884 Engels had written that 'estates-based monarchy' was a more accurate term than 'absolute monarchy' for the actual historical development. (See MEW 21:402.)

(10) MODERN INDUSTRY. See Par.15/2.

(11) EXCLUSIVE POLITICAL RULE. The statement that in 1848 the bourgeoisie had already won °exclusive° political power in the °modern representative state° is one of the best examples of the type of pedagogic exaggeration characteristic of parts of the Manifesto: an exaggeration from the standpoint of immediate fact, but an essential insight from the long view of social evolution. The bourgeoisie could be said to rule (this according to a passage in Engels' *Principles of Communism*) only "in England, France, and Belgium" (and one should add the United States), but in no European country could it be claimed that the bourgeoisie held state power in °exclusive° fashion. Still, in the Manifesto's view, the industrially advanced world was already "in principle" bourgeoisified, though the world still had decades to go to catch up with the principle. The "long view" was the Manifesto's strength and the

source of its continued relevance; but the gap with backward practice led to difficulties when the Manifesto was taken as literal gospel.

(12) NATURE OF THE STATE. The last sentence—one of the most frequently quoted of the Manifesto—was significantly changed in the A.E.T.. The original was a statement about °the modern state power°; the A.E.T. changed this to °the executive of the modern State°. It is true that a case can be made out for the translation (*Gewalt* as 'executive'), but there can be no doubt that the A.E.T. put the spotlight strongly on the state Executive as distinct from other departments of the government. This emphasis reflects that aspect of Marx's view of the nature of the state which sees the Executive as playing the central role in the development of the state as a class instrument. (On this see KMTR I:314—319.)

This sentence is doubtless the most succinctly aphoristic statement by Marx of his theory of the state. It is also probably the source of that common misquotation, "The state is the executive committee of the ruling class," which does not occur in this form. In the present paragraph, Marx was concerned with the bourgeois state; but in Par.134 he generalized on the oppressive nature of state power: °Political power in its proper sense is the organized power of one class for the oppression of another°. This is the negative side of °the common affairs of the whole [ruling] class°. For the development of Marx's theory of the state see KMTR I, Chap. 8, 11.)

Par. 19

(1) BOURGEOISIE'S REVOLUTIONARY ROLE. In the light of Par.17/1 note that the word here is °revolutionäre°. This introduces a long section on the revolutionary and progressive consequences of the rise of bourgeois society and its capitalist mode of production, in some respects as eulogistic a paean of praise to the world historic role of capitalism as can be found. The statement in Par.24 below—that °the bourgeoisie cannot exist without continually revolutionizing the instruments of production ... hence social relations as a whole°—is echoed in *Capital* (Chap. 15, Sec. 9), which also quotes these words.

Par. 20

(1) PATRIARCHAL...RELATIONS. The term °patriarchal° is used descriptively. In the *German Ideology* Marx had apparently treated 'patriarchalism' as a stage in societal development, listing "patriarchalism, slavery, estates, classes" as the ways in which labor was historically organized, and alluding to "patriarchal chieftains" as characteristic of "tribal" society (MECW 5:32f). There existed a "patriarchal theory of society" described by Sir Henry Maine as "the theory of its (society's] origin in separate families, held together by the authority and protection of the eldest valid male ascendant." Prominent in Hegel's view of history was the concept of a patriarchal society prior to the political state and giving rise to monarchy. But elsewhere, even in the *German Ideology*, Marx used 'patriarchal' descriptively for (e.g.) certain relations between masters and journeymen in the guild system, or between lords and serfs; that is, relations in which the master or lord assumed rights analogous to the

tribal father-despot alongside normal feudal modes of exploitation. This seems also to be the context of the present paragraph.

(2) NATURAL SUPERIORS. The A.E.T. (like Macfarlane) added quote marks to tell the reader that the expression was used ironically. In his *Condition of the Working Class in England*, Engels had used this phrase in quote marks with a footnote: "Favorite expression of English manufacturers." (Chap. on Competition.)

(3) "CASH PAYMENT." The quote marks were in the original. The expression was a favorite of Thomas Carlyle's: "in epochs when cash payment has become the sole nexus of man with man" (*Chartism*, 1840), or "Cash-payment is not the sole nexus of man with man" (*Past and Present*, 1843). Marx and Engels were well acquainted with both writings. The A.E.T. rightly used °nexus° for *Band* in view of the source.

(4) DEARLY WON / INDEFEASIBLE. The A.E.T.'s °indefeasible° is rather off the mark for *wohlerworbenen* (lit., well acquired).

Par. 21

(1) PAID WAGE-LABORERS. At the risk of again breaking down an open door, it must be pointed out that the claim made here is a metaphor: the members of the professions listed are *not* proletarians, despite the plain (ironical) statement. Once again I stress that the Manifesto, because of its aphoristic style, is peppered with figures of speech and polemical exaggerations, which need not be treated as discoveries in Marxist theory.

Par. 22

(1) FAMILY. This subject is taken up in Par.100/2, which see.

Par. 23

(1) REACTIONISTS. This alternative to 'reactionaries,' used by the A.E.T., was in good use in English in the mid-nineteenth century.

(2) FAR SURPASSING. This phrase, accompanied by °put in the shade°, was an opinion added by the A.E.T.; the original merely said °quite different°.

Par. 24

(1) REVOLUTIONIZING. See Par.19/1. This paragraph was quoted in *Capital*.

(2) EARLIER CLASSES. At the end of the second sentence: beginning with the 1890 German edition, °earlier industrial classes° was changed to °other [anderen] industrial classes°, that is, other than the bourgeoisie. The point involved is slight: the artisanry (for instance), while older than the bourgeoisie, coexisted with it and indeed remained important

218

well into the nineteenth century; hence Engels presumably felt that °earlier° was misleading.

Par. 25

(1) WORLD MARKET. The theme of the internationalization of bourgeois society continues (see Par.16/2 and the next paragraph).

Par. 26

(1) WORLD MARKET. The theme continues from the preceding paragraph. The typically sweeping statement that °The age-old national industries have been destroyed° (etc.) was made even more sweeping by a revision (made from the 1866 German edition on) changing °The° to °All°: surely an ill-considered alteration.

(2) THE EXPLOITATION... In the A.E.T., the initial phrase °the exploitation of the world market° was slightly revised to °its exploitation° (that is, the bourgeoisie's).

(3) CIVILIZED NATIONS. This term is discussed in Par.27/1.

(4) INTELLECTUAL PRODUCTION. This is not the first passage in which a connection has been made between socioeconomic development and the ideological superstructure; it was touched on also in Par.24, and will be completed in Par. 119-121. For the meaning of 'intellectual' in this connection, see Par.96/1.

Par. 27

(1) SO-CALLED CIVILIZATION. While °civilized nations° had already been referred to in Par.26 this paragraph makes clear how it is used. The scientific (ethnological) orthodoxy of the nineteenth century used 'savagery,' 'barbarism,' and 'civilization' (with a modifier like 'modern' as needed) as the technical names of historical stages in the progress of humankind—progress as measured by criteria laid down by different theories. L. H. Morgan, whom Marx and Engels greeted with enthusiasm in the 1880s, reinforced this pattern by his own usage. Side by side with this generally accepted scientific terminology existed the centuries-old practice of using 'barbarian' as a pejorative term for foreigners; 'civilized,' for one's own social customs and prejudices. The latter problem, plus changes in ethnological theory, has put this terminology out of fashion in the present day. For the mid-nineteenth century, the noteworthy contribution of the Manifesto, in the present paragraph, was to link the connotations of 'civilization' to *bourgeois* conceptions of progress. J. S. Mill had already discussed the positive and negative attributes of civilization as a "mixed good" (see Williams, *Keywords*, 49); a skeptical attitude to the blessings of civilization was neither new nor peculiar to Marx. What the Manifesto added was the notion that °so-called civilization° (taken as a modernizing process) was *bourgeoisification* of the world. This equation—°civilized° countries = °bourgeois nations°—is repeated explicitly at the end of the next paragraph, Par.28. The same equation had been implicit as early as the *German Ideology*: "Labor *is* free in all civilized

countries" but it is a matter of abolishing *this* "free" wage-labor relationship (MECW 5:205).

(2) BARBARIAN NATIONS AND CHINESE WALLS. Already prominent in world politics were the potentially revolutionary consequences of Asian resistance to European imperialist penetration. The opening of °The East Indian and Chinese markets° was already mentioned in Par.13 above. Engels' *Principles of Communism* (Ques. 11) had already remarked that "even China is now marching towards a revolution"—in a passage analogous to the present paragraph. In his magazine *NRZ-Revue* in 1850 Marx echoed the Manifesto's words: "dragging the most reluctant barbarian nations into world trade, into civilization," as he hailed a report that China was on "the eve of a social upheaval" that might usher in a Chinese Republic (MECW 10:265, 267). His interest mounted by 1853, as explained in his article "Revolution in China and in Europe," which looked to "the effect the Chinese revolution seems likely to exercise upon the civilized world." In his well-known article on British rule in India, he rounded on the civilized/barbarian dichotomy:

> The profound hypocrisy and inherent barbarism of bourgeois civilization lies unveiled before our eyes, turning from its home, where it assumes respectable forms, to the colonies, where it goes naked. (MECW 12:221]

On the use of 'barbarian,' see also Par.28/2.

Par. 28

(1) 'IDIOCY OF RURAL LIFE.' This oft-quoted A.E.T. expression is a mistranslation. The German word *Idiotismus* did not, and does not, mean 'idiocy' (*Idiotie*); it usually means 'idiom,' like its French cognate *idiotisme*. But here it means neither. In the nineteenth century, German still retained the original Greek meaning of forms based on the word *idiotes*: a private person, withdrawn from public (communal) concerns, *apolitical* in the original sense of isolation from the larger community. In the Manifesto, it was being used by a scholar who had recently written his doctoral dissertation on Greek philosophy and liked to read Aeschylus in the original. (For a more detailed account of the philological background and evidence, see KMTR 2:344f.) What the rural population had to be saved from, then, was the *privatized apartness* of a life-style isolated from the larger society: the classic *stasis* of peasant life. To inject the English 'idiocy' into this thought is to muddle everything. The original Greek meaning (which in the 19th century was still alive in German alongside the 'idiom' meaning) had been lost in English centuries ago. Moore was probably not aware of this problem; Engels had probably known it forty years before. He was certainly familiar with the thought behind it: in his *Condition of the Working Class in England* (1845), he had written about the rural weavers as a class "which had remained sunk in apathetic indifference to the universal interests of mankind." (MECW 4:309.) In 1873 he made exactly the Manifesto's point without using the word 'idiocy': the abolition of the town-country antithesis "will be able to deliver the rural population from the isolation and stupor in which it has vegetated almost unchanged for thousands of years" (*Housing Question* Pt. III, Chap. 3.)

(2) BARBARIAN COUNTRIES. See Par.27/1,2 for the equation of 'civilized' =

bourgeoisified and 'barbarian' = prebourgeois. Here and elsewhere Marx spoke of the peasantry as "the class that represents barbarism within civilization" (this quote being actually from his later *Class Struggles in France*, Chap. 2). In the light of the preceding note (point 1 above), it should be remarked that 'barbarian' too retained an ancient Greek flavor, meaning 'standing outside the bounds of high civilization.' Just as, to the Greeks, this meant their own civilization, to Marx it meant the advanced bourgeois civilization discussed in Par.27/1. In Par.33, below, compare the metaphorical use of °barbarism° and °civilization°, describing commercial crises.

(3) PEASANTS. While the rural population included more than the peasantry, the latter class was the most numerous. One of the most distinctive characteristics of the Manifesto was its almost complete neglect of the peasantry. In the present paragraph, the first in which the peasants are mentioned, the view is wholly negative. This led to the myth—among people whose research into Marx was limited to a thorough reading of the Manifesto—that Marx never paid any attention to this class at all, except to call it names. In truth, the Manifesto marked the very end of Marx's inattention to the peasant class. The picture changed immediately after the outbreak of the revolution in 1848, with Marx's and Engels' issuance (from Paris) of their "Demands of the Communist Party in Germany," which contained a section of positive demands on behalf of the peasantry. Then as editor of the Cologne *NRZ* during the revolution, Marx not only wrote and published a mass of materials on peasant problems, but indeed his Cologne group set about organizing the regional peasantry for the first time. And this was only the beginning. (See KMTR 2, Chap. 12-14, for Marx's and Engels' views on the peasantry.) But while Marx had disregarded the peasantry by and large for the first five years of his socialist career, this was not true, or not so true, of Engels, who for about a year had been well ahead of Marx in understanding the need for a proletarian-led class alliance; see Par.11/2. By the autumn of 1847 at least, Engels began writing about the need for an alliance of "the proletarians, small peasants and petty-bourgeoisie" as a revolutionary front—called "the Democracy"—against the alliance of "the bureaucracy, nobility and bourgeoisie" (MECW 6:294). He also wrote this view into his draft *Principles of Communism* (Ques. 18). The proviso was that the victory of this Democracy (the coalition) depended on the vanguard role of the proletariat within it. While further discussion of peasant policy takes us beyond the Manifesto itself, we will have to come back to the question of the petty-bourgeoisie (see Par.44/3 and Par.52/3) and "the Democracy" (see Par.129/2).

(4) TOWN AND COUNTRY; URBANIZATION. We postpone this subject, with which the present paragraph begins, to Par.133, Point 9.

Par. 29

(1) POLITICAL CENTRALIZATION. In 1848 °political centralization° meant, to German radicals and indeed liberals and progressives, the need for national unification of the thirty-odd German principalities into a single modern state. The political issue was only: under whose hegemony—Prussia? Austria? a revolutionary government? National 'centralization' was counterposed to national fragmentation. The process described in the present paragraph (°provinces ...consolidated into one nation°, etc.) had not yet taken place

221

in Germany (or in Italy) but had been accomplished long ago in France and England. Most German radicals looked upon the unitary centralization of France with envy, seeing it as the alternative to German backwardness. This was the left and liberal orthodoxy. Marx departed from this consensus from about 1852 on: as he viewed the phenomenon of Bonapartism in France, he began to emphasize the other side of the centralization issue—the meaning of *bureaucratic centralization*. This question was notably dealt with in his *Eighteenth Brumaire of Louis Bonaparte*: the "extraordinary centralization" of the French state created by the absolute monarchy has given rise to a "parasitic" bureaucratic machine enmeshing all of society (Chap. 4); "this executive power with its enormous bureaucratic and military organization... this appalling parasitic body" is "centralized as in a factory" (Chap. 7)... (See KMTR 1:395-402.) Marx's formulation in the Manifesto was echoed in his 1850 *Address to the Communist League*, where the still medieval fragmentation of Germany was contrasted to the need for "the strictest centralization" with a reference to "France in 1793." When Engels reprinted this address in 1885, he felt obliged to repudiate this reference, on behalf of Marx and himself, arguing that it was not true—as they and all German leftists once believed—that French supercentralization had arisen as a revolutionary measure in the Great French Revolution; he now maintained that "political, national centralization" is not in necessary contradiction with local self-government. (See MECW 10:285.) This question deserves to be pursued further, but not here.

Par. 30

(1) A HUNDRED YEARS. In assigning the beginning of the bourgeoisie's °class rule° to about a hundred years before, that is, to about the middle of the eighteenth century, Marx must have been thinking mainly of France (as was often true on sociopolitical patterns)—specifically, to the period leading up to the Great French Revolution.

(2) SOCIAL LABOR. Labor expended not in individual isolation but in *social production*, in socially organized association with other laborers. Under capitalism, as Marx stressed in *Capital*, the capitalist, who does the organizing, also garners the extra value produced by the socially organized labor. The labor theory of value speaks of the incorporation of *social* labor in a commodity.

Par. 31

(1) IN ANY CASE. Here, at the beginning of the paragraph, the first edition of 1848 had °aber° (however, but). This does not make very good sense; my °in any case° is an effort to make the best of it. From the 1866 edition on, German editions replaced °aber° with °also° (which in German means 'hence,' 'then'); and the A.E.T. followed this revision, using 'then.'

(2) MEANS OF...INTERCOURSE. For the use of °Verkehr (intercourse)° instead of the later term °exchange° (used by the A.E.T.), see Par.17/2. But notice that in the second sentence, when a verb form was required, the original *did* use °exchanged° (°austauschte°).

(3) CORRESPONDED / COMPATIBLE. A nuance: the formulation in the A.E.T.

222

°became no longer compatible with° is somewhat stronger than the original, which said corresponded with.

(4) A.E.T.: OMITTED SENTENCE. The A.E.T. dropped an entire sentence: °They hampered production instead of furthering it.° This omission was peculiar to the A.E.T. and happened in no other version, as far as I know. While one can speculate that it might have been done on the ground that the sentence was otiose, this is such a bad reason that I tend to think the explanation was simple inadvertence, either in the manuscript or at the printshop, not caught in the proofreading.

(5) BURST ASUNDER. Not only this word (°gesprengt°) but the sense of the passage was repeated by Marx in his well-known Chapter 32 of *Capital* I on the "Historical Tendency of Capitalist Accumulation." Only, there it referred to the downfall of capitalism, here to the fall of feudalism.

Par. 32

(1) FREE COMPETITION. The peculiarity of this formulation, indicating its early-Marx character, is that °free competition° is used as a formal label for capitalism or 'bourgeois relations of production.' As Engels had noted in his very first article on economics, this term was "the keyword of our present-day economists" (MECW 3:441), but he immediately added that "Free competition...is an impossibility" and pointed to the interpenetration of competition and monopoly.

Par. 33

(1) A SIMILAR MOVEMENT. This statement applies not to the preceding paragraph but to the historical pattern summarized in Par.31-32.

(2) RELATIONS...INTERCOURSE. For the use of °intercourse° (°Verkehr°) instead of °exchange°, see Par.17/2.

(3) COMMERCIAL CRISES. Before the Manifesto, it was Engels who had written most about the new phenomenon, of economic crises, beginning with his first article on economics (1843): here he already had crises occurring regularly every five or seven years "for the last eighty years" (MECW 3:433). He had a considerable passage on crises in his *Condition of the Working Class in England* (chapter on Competition) and in his *Principles of Communism* (Ques. 12). Modern nationwide economic crises are usually reckoned as beginning with the 1825-1826 depression, followed by 1836-1837 and 1847-1848. The Manifesto was written as the third big slump hit European capitalism; of course, it was not yet distinctively Marxist in its treatment of the subject.

(4) SOCIETAL EPIDEMIC. The A.E.T. omits the adjective. There seems no evident reason for the omission, though of course it does not affect the meaning.

(5) DEVASTATING WAR. The A.E.T.'s translation is essentially the same, °war of devastation°. But it was only the first edition of 1848 that said °Verwüstungskrieg° here; in the second edition of 1848 and all subsequent editions, the word became °Vernichtungskrieg,° which one would expect to see translated as 'war of annihilation' or 'destructive war.' However, the nuance is so slight one can't tell whether Engels went back to the original

edition.

(6) BOURGEOIS CIVILIZATION. Where the 1848 editions referred to furthering °bourgeois civilization and bourgeois property relations°, the German editions from 1872 on changed these words to: °the development of the conditions of bourgeois property°. The A.E.T. adopted this change. There are two points involved here. (a) The change meant that the term °bourgeois civilization° was deleted. See the discussion in Par.27/1 and 2, also Par.28/2; the term might well have been considered increasingly ambiguous as the nineteenth century entered its last quarter. (b) °Conditions of bourgeois property° is an inadvisable translation. It is true that °Verhältnisse° can mean either 'conditions' or 'relations,' but in the present context the standard term uses 'relations.' (Note that the A.E.T. had to add the words °the development of°.) The same point applies to, and is confirmed by, the use of °Verhältnisse° in the next sentence. We will see other examples below.

Par. 35

(1) PROLETARIANS. The A.E.T. eliminated the original's emphasis on this word, besides changing °workers° to °working class°. See the point made in Par.7(T1)/3. The theme of this paragraph was given aphoristic form in the "gravediggers" metaphor of Par.60 below.

Par. 36

(1) WORKER AS COMMODITY. As we will see below (Par. 37/4), Marx had not yet made his vital distinction in economic theory between the nature of labor and labor power as a commodity. But even for 1848 the present formulation is loose. It is only under chattel-slavery that the workers themselves are commodities. At this time Marx would say that the worker's *labor* is the commodity, not the worker's person; later, that his *labor power* is the commodity.

Par. 37

(1) MERE: THE INTENSIVE 'NUR.' As a footnote to Par. 10, note that here, in the second sentence, the A.E.T. deleted the equivalent of the intensive *nur*; only here the word is not *nur* but °blosses° (mere, simple).

(2) APPENDAGE TO THE MACHINE. In this passage we have a preview of the detailed exposition in *Capital* (I, Part IV) of the distorting impact of factory labor on the worker. Aside from passing references in earlier writings, this was the first time that Marx stated the case.

(3) RACE / KIND. If the A.E.T. referred to the working class as a °race° (the German word here is also °Race°), one must keep in mind that this was good nineteenth-century English. °Race° here means, broadly, any sort of people taken globally, like the similar meaning of 'breed' still in use. Marx elsewhere referred to the "race of lawyers"; today this

224

could be done only jocularly.

(4) PRICE OF LABOR. Before the latter part of the 1850s Marx had not yet made his basic distinction between *labor* and *labor power*—a distinction basic to his theory of surplus value. What the proletarian sells (his commodity) is not his labor (that is, a certain amount of labor) but his capacity to labor, his labor power. It is the aim of the capitalist employer to extract as much labor as possible out of the labor power he purchases: this is the starting point of the analysis of surplus value. (See Engels' exposition in his introduction to Marx's *Wage-Labor and Capital*, which Marx based on lectures in Brussels given just before the writing of the Manifesto.) This is the most essential respect in which the Manifesto is early-Marx, destined to be superseded. The definition of the °price° of a commodity as °its cost of production° likewise shows the undeveloped state of the Manifesto's economic theory; see Par.82/1.

(5) BURDEN OF TOIL. The A.E.T. made a marked revision of the text in changing °amount [Masse] of labor° to °burden of toil°, a broader idea. This was a very good revision, given the fact (explained in the preceding point) that the economic theory of the Manifesto was inadequate—a clever rewording in that it did not go very far from the original.

Par. 38

(1) PATRIARCHAL MASTER. For °patriarchal°, see Par. 20/1. The °master° here is the master artisan; cf. the term 'master guildsman' in Par.8/2. This language has in mind the 'patriarchal' relations of the master with journeymen and apprentices.

(2) INDUSTRIAL ARMY; DESPOTISM. Although the phrase °industrial army°, used in the A.E.T., does not appear as such in the original, the idea is fully present (in °common soldiers of industry°, etc.), and the phrase had already been used in the Manifesto in Par.15. This is all the more interesting since the same term appears, in an entirely different context, in Par.133, Point 8, which see. The same metaphor is carried over to °despotism°, a word often used by Marx in a nonliteral way, so that this °despotism° may exist under a 'democratic' regime. See Par.131/1.

(3) THRALLS; THRALLDOM. The corresponding words in the A.E.T. are °slaves° and °enslaved°. The German words (°Knechte° and °geknechtet°) do not *literally* mean 'slaves,' etc., though they are translated this way often enough.

(4) BOURGEOIS MANUFACTURER. Literally: "the manufacturing bourgeois."

(5) FINAL AIM. In the A.E.T.: °end and aim°. In the German: °letzten Zweck°; but from the 1890 German edition on the adjective °letzten° (final, last) was dropped.

Par. 39

(1) LABOR...OF WOMEN AND CHILDREN. The words °and children° appeared only in the first edition of 1848; they vanished from the second edition of 1848, and remained out of all editions during Marx's and Engels' lifetime. (They were restored in the German edition of 1912 edited by Kautsky.) That they did not appear in the A.E.T. is an indication that

Moore and Engels did not check the first edition. The omission was doubtless made in error, since twice in the rest of the paragraph the text refers *both* to age and sex. It was the second edition of 1848 that became the basis for future editions; hence the omission was preserved.

(2) NO...SOCIAL VALIDITY. The second sentence (°Differences in sex and age no longer have any social validity for the working class°) was, unfortunately, historically untrue, in that the German working class had not reached the claimed state of development. It was not until 1875 (in part) and 1891 (more completely) that the more or less Marxist wing (Bebel-Liebknecht) of the German Social-Democracy defeated the Lassallean wing's opposition not only to women's equality but, more immediately, to encouraging rather than opposing the entrance of women into industry. It was this traditional attitude of conservative workingmen that the Manifesto was rejecting. (The A.E.T. thought it necessary to add °distinctive° to °social validity,° but I do not see how this helps.) For entirely different reasons, the labor of children was also a problem that could not simply be taken care of with the Manifesto's formula—so much so that the Manifesto itself proposed the partial abolition of child labor, in Par.133, Point 10. (Could this contradiction have been the reason why the words °and children° were dropped in the second edition?)

Par. 40

(1) BOURGEOISIE AND SHOPKEEPERS. An anticipatory point. We are going to see, below, a certain confusion about class labels, since Marx's social analysis was still in process of formation; and we must start here if we are going to keep the books straight on this matter. This paragraph lists three parts (°sections° or °portions°) °of the bourgeoisie°, and all three raise the question of how inclusive the term °bourgeoisie° is in the Manifesto. Elsewhere in Marx and Engels, the landlord is more usually treated as a part of or remnant of the old aristocratic ruling class—though much depends on what sort of 'landlord' is meant. At best, the reference is unclear. °The pawnbroker° was usually a shopkeeper (even if called the Poor Man's Banker); and the listing of °the shopkeeper° as a bourgeois is, again, highly dubious at best. The typical shopkeeper of the time did not live primarily by employing wage-labor; he was a *petty-bourgeois*, not a bourgeois—but we postpone discussion of this topic to Par.44/3. If landlords and shopkeepers are taken to be 'bourgeois,' then the term is being used very loosely; and such usages are indeed characteristic of many parts of the Manifesto, as we have seen.

It happens that in the very next paragraph, *in the A.E.T.*, the °shopkeeper° comes up again—but this time, presto-changeo, he is a member of °the lower strata of the middle class.° But in the original the term used here was not 'shopkeepers' but 'merchants.' (This confusion is examined below in Par.41/1d.)

Of course, the practical explanation for the listing of landlord, shopkeeper, pawnbroker in Par.40 was a thought about those exploitive elements who °set upon° the wage-workers to extract their pay envelopes, as auxiliary vultures. Whether they are 'bourgeois' scientifically speaking was a secondary matter, to be sure. We return to questions of terminology under the next paragraph.

(2) REVISED A.E.T. OF 1932. This version (see Part I, chapter 28, section 3.) changed the beginning of this paragraph to read as follows: "No sooner has the labourer received his

wages in cash, for the moment escaping exploitation by the manufacturer..."

Par. 41

(1) WHO EXACTLY SINK INTO THE PROLETARIAT? Engels subjected this paragraph to a considerable amount of "editing," that is, revising and rewriting. It is one of the passages used to claim that Marx had a theory, or made a prediction, about the "disappearance of the middle class(es)," but this question will be mainly taken up later (Par. 51/2). Here let us mention several points at which Engels revised the original's statements in the guise of translation.

(a) The most important one comes in the first line, for, to begin with, the A.E.T. completely omitted the qualifier °bisherigen° (°existing up to now°, former). In the original, this qualification emphatically made clear that the statement was about the *old* "middle ranks" ('*Mittelstände*' -see Par.14/5). The point was that the old class structure was breaking up; the subject was not any prediction about the future but a view of what *had been* happening.

(b) The A.E.T.'s translation of °kleinen Mittelstände° was °lower strata of the middle class°; but because of the pervasive ambiguity of 'middle class' (Par.14/5) I have preferred to use °intermediate strata° here. Besides, look at the list of 'strata' that follows! The A.E.T. rewrote this list thoroughly, no doubt because it would be hard to fit them all into 'lower strata of the middle class.'

(c) The °small industrials° of the original became °small tradespeople° in the A.E.T. To be sure, in the old days an 'industrial' did not necessarily mean an industrialist, and could once even have meant an industrial or manufacturing *worker*; but as a member of the 'small middle strata,' the term undoubtedly pointed (in the Manifesto) to the owner of a small manufactory or a master artisan who had a substantial industrial workshop. Engels' corresponding passage in the *Principles of Communism* did not use the vague substantive 'industrial'; he stressed that

> in almost all branches of labor, handicraft and manufacture have been ousted by large-scale industry.—As a result, the former middle classes [*bisherige Mittelstand*], especially the small master artisans, have been increasingly ruined...and two new classes which are gradually swallowing up all other classes have come into being... [viz., big capitalists, or bourgeoisie, and proletariat]. [MECW 6:342]

The context here suggests that Engels was using the term 'bourgeoisie' only for *big* capitalists, excluding small capitalists; and this sort of usage should be kept in mind in reading the Manifesto too. Let us remind again that the language here is not that of the mature Marx.

(d) As mentioned above, °merchants° (°Kaufleute°) became °shopkeepers° in the A.E.T.—an obvious effort to demote commercial capitalist elements down to the petty-bourgeoisie. For the second time Marx has listed a *small bourgeois* as the subject of this paragraph.

(e) °Rentiers° (the German original used the French word) meant persons living on (unearned) income from property or investments, hence perhaps not capitalists themselves but dependents on capital—certainly bourgeois elements. The A.E.T. rewrote this, rather wildly, as: °retired tradesmen generally°. The word °tradesmen° is thrown in gratuitously and repetitively simply to make a connection with those °lower strata of the middle class° with which the paragraph began. This is perhaps the oddest formulation in the A.E.T.

(f) Finally, °artisans and peasants° do fall into the °small intermediate strata°.

In short: while it is true that the paragraph (in the original) announced it was about the old middle ranks of society, it was also dealing with small bourgeois elements who were being squeezed out. What it wanted to say about all these elements was that they tended to become declassed, under the pressure of developing capitalist industry, and tended to fall into the ranks of the working classes: °Thus the proletariat is recruited from all classes of the population°. This conclusion has little to do with the belief that Marx was here predicting the total destruction of the 'middle class.' But we will return to this subject in Par.51/2.

(2) SINK GRADUALLY. The A.E.T. added the word °gradually°, presumably for very hurried readers.

(3) LARGER CAPITALISTS. The A.E.T. changed this to °large capitalists°. The original formulation neatly betrays what we explained in point 1 above: the beginning of the paragraph was concerned with *smaller capitalist* elements, not simply with the petty-bourgeois-ie or 'middle class.'

(4) SPECIALIZED SKILL. The modifier °specialized° was added by the A.E.T.

Par. 42

(1) PARAGRAPHING. The A.E.T. merged Par.42 with Par. 43; as far as I know, this was not done in any German edition. Incidentally, it strikes the eye that in general the Manifesto used unusually short paragraphs—unusual for German and for the times. See also Par.141/4.

Par. 43

(1) NOT ONLY. In the second sentence, the A.E.T. made what amounted to a historical correction. With the little word °only° (in °not only°) the original implied that Luddite workers directed attacks against the social system as well as against the machines; the A.E.T. deleted the °only°.

(2) CONDITIONS OF PRODUCTION. The German term, involving °Verhältnisse°, is usually translated °relations of production°, as an economic term in Marxism. Cf. the same point with regard to 'property relations' in Par.33/6. This translation is especially advisable when the meaning is systemic, as here. Engels must have thought that the translation using 'conditions' would be more accessible to the English public, but it is less accurate.

(3) COMPETING FOREIGN COMMODITIES. The A.E.T. inserted an explanation of the workers' motives by expanding this to: °imported wares that compete with their labor°. Incidentally, apropos of the preceding point 2, notice that Engels' translation used the "ordinary" word °wares° rather than the "technical" term °commodities°; in this case the motivation was hardly problematic.

228

(4) RESTORE BY FORCE. The words °by force° were added by the A.E.T.

Par. 44

(1) INCOHERENT MASS. The A.E.T. added the word °incoherent°, quite unnecessarily in view of the description.

(2) ENEMIES OF THEIR ENEMIES. In the pattern discussed here, the workers are fighting against the °enemies of their enemies°, that is, supporting the drive of the rising bourgeoisie for political power against the old ruling class. Later on in 1848, Marx pointed to a similar pattern about the February revolution against Louis Philippe, which was powered largely by working-class fighters but which handed power over to a bourgeois-republican regime that suppressed the same workers in a bloody massacre in June:

> What they [the people] instinctively hated in Louis Philippe was not Louis Philippe but the crowned rule of a class, capital on the throne. But, magnanimous as always, they fancied that they had destroyed their enemy after overthrowing the enemy of their enemies, the *common* enemy. [See this and more on the subject in KMTR 2:180f.]

Side by side with this pattern was another, in which workers supported, or were asked to support, the °enemies of their enemies° in order to overthrow the latter enemies, the immediate enemy. This was to be an important pattern for the future, but it was foreshadowed by Feudal Socialism and True Socialism; see Marx's discussion of these tendencies (Par. 136/2 and Par.153/1). Both patterns were united by the principle stated in the last sentence of this paragraph: as long as the workers' policies are based on those of the °enemies of their enemies°, the °course of historical development is thus concentrated in the hands of° an alien class.

(3) PETTY-BOURGEOISIE. This is the first time the term is used in the Manifesto (°Kleinbürger°) though some of these class elements have already been met. Let us start with a strictly scientific definition, without assuming that all usages in the Manifesto will follow it. The petty-bourgeoisie comprises persons who make their living primarily by the exercise of their own labor with their self-owned means of production (tools) or other property (like a shop)—typically, self-employed small producers and tradespeople. The two typical categories are (self-employed) artisans and shopkeepers. The interests and organization of this class are largely local; its perspectives are limited both in size and extent. What distinguishes the petty-bourgeoisie from the capitalist class (bourgeoisie) is that in principle its members are not employers living primarily by the extraction of surplus value from wage-workers; if they employ anyone, this relationship is a minor and subordinate element of their economic life. This means that the petty-bourgeoisie is not the same as the 'small bourgeoisie' (despite the similarity in label and etymology), although the one may shade into the other. (Therefore it is not helpful to omit the hyphen from 'petty-bourgeoisie' or to give it the Gallic spelling 'petit-bourgeoisie.') The petty-bourgeois earns his living primarily by his own labor; the bourgeois lives on surplus value extracted from others' labor, and the *small* bourgeois does so on a *small* scale. It is possible to regard the peasantry as the rural sector—or analogue, if

one prefers—of the petty-bourgeoisie (again, despite the urban etymology); this is often done inconsistently. The petty-bourgeoisie is certainly an intermediate stratum or group of strata, hence a sort of 'middle class'; but the term 'middle class(es)' has no specific meaning until one is assigned to it, and historically can be applied to a variety of social strata. In contrast, 'petty-bourgeoisie' is a rigorously definable class.

In French usage, the difference between *petit-bourgeoisie* and *petite bourgeoisie* is as unreliable as its English analogue; likewise in German, *Kleinbürgertum* and *kleine Bürgertum* waver back and forth. In all these languages, one must always ask what the writer really had in mind. (For a more extensive analysis of the petty-bourgeoisie, see KMTR 2, Chap. 11.) In the present paragraph, the petty-bourgeoisie is part of a list of class elements which the proletariat is said to fight. For a note on the Manifesto's attitude toward this class, thus hinted, see Par.52/3, which states it more strongly.

Par. 45

(1) COMBINATIONS (TRADES UNIONS). The parenthetical insertion of the term °trades' unions° (with an unnecessary apostrophe) was the contribution of the A.E.T. °Combination° (corresponding to the French *coalition*, German *Koalition*, as used in the Manifesto) was the name, originally almost equivalent to 'conspiracy,' under which workers' protective associations were banned in England and elsewhere since their beginnings in the seventeenth century. The repeal of this legislation, and the beginning of legal TU organization, took place in England only twenty-four years before the Manifesto. Six years before, there had been a general strike; and three years before, a new wave of TU action had begun. By about 1830 the term 'trade(s) union' had arisen alongside 'combination.'

Few people who now read the Manifesto realize that, outside of its authors, there was then not a single Continental socialist or would-be revolutionist who took a favorable attitude toward the class organization of the workers on the economic field—and only scattered exceptions even in England. The first prominent expression of the new conception was Engels' *Condition of the Working Class in England* (chapter on Labor Movements); in 1847 Marx's *Poverty of Philosophy* (last chapter) explained the new view against Proudhon, the "father of anarchism" who applauded the shooting of strikers by gendarmes. As Marx later averred: "in 1847, when all the political economists and all the Socialists concurred on one single point --the condemnation of *Trade-Unions*, I demonstrated their historical necessity." (For this, and more on Marx's views on trade unions, see KMTR 2, Chap. 4.) This was so because Marx's theory saw revolution in the first place as a matter of class dynamics, and not primarily as a vision of a certain New Social Order. Hence the TU, not the socialist sect, was "the real class organization of the proletariat" (ltr, Engels to Bebel, Mar. 18-28, 1875), and Marx's view of trade-unionism aimed to bridge the gap between "elementary" economic organization and social revolution.

(2) WAGES. The slight variation introduced by the A.E.T.—°rate of wages° instead of °wages°—does not affect the meaning. Marx's still limited analysis of wages at the time of the Manifesto can best be seen in lecture notes on the subject (MECW 6:415), including a section on trade unions. On Marx's theory of wages, see Par.82/1.

Par. 46

(1) CLASS STRUGGLE, POLITICAL STRUGGLE. The statement that °every class struggle is a political struggle° requires elucidation; for isn't an "elementary economic" strike also an act of class struggle?

(a) The Manifesto's meaning here is obscured by the A.E.T. In the original, the expression °a national struggle, a class struggle° equates one with the other, whereas the A.E.T. formulation suppresses this equation. The equation explains why a *classwide struggle* is a °political struggle° necessarily. A strike in (say) one factory is not yet a struggle of the whole class, the class as such. This aspect was perhaps expressed more clearly in the similar passage found in Marx's *Poverty of Philosophy*, which said that "the struggle of class against class is a political struggle," and explained that the "political struggle" level is reached on the eve of virtual civil war (MECW 6:211).

(b) There is also an element of still Hegelianized language in the Manifesto's formulation. For this, see Par. 47/1 below, and note that 'political' is used with the broader Hegelianizing meaning of 'societywide.' A struggle that puts control of society in question is 'political,' apart from the state of class-consciousness.

(c) For later explanations of a similar dictum given by Marx and Engels themselves see KMTR 2:125-127. In particular in 1881 (by which time the Hegelian content had completely dissolved out) Engels restated the idea as a *tendency*: "a struggle between two great classes of society necessarily becomes a political struggle. ... In every struggle of class against class, the next end fought for is political power..." (Article, "Trades Unions.")

(2) BURGHERS OF THE MIDDLE AGES. This passage illustrated a difference in usage between German and English. The German *Bürger* (here plural) covers townsmen (burghers), burgesses, bourgeois, not to speak of citizens. The reference to the *Bürger* of the Middle Ages reminds us that we met °Pfahlbürger° in Par.12 (there translated as °burgesses°). In English, one must make a choice; in this case I followed the A.E.T.'s °burghers°, but 'early bourgeois' would be possible too.

Par. 47

(1) CLASS, POLITICAL PARTY. First of all, the A.E.T.'s °consequently° may be misleading if it is taken to mean sequence in time. This statement *equates* °organization of the proletarians into a class° with their organization as °a political party°—bearing in mind that °party° here has the old broad meaning (see note 3 on Main Title). The note on Par.46/1 above gives part of the explanation. For the rest, this passage echoes a Hegelian distinction found in Marx in some early writings. According to this, an atomized, unorganized class is a "class in itself" (*an sich*) but becomes a "class for itself" (*für sich*) only when it is organized into a social entity and achieves consciousness of its social and political role. (The last time Marx used this mode of analysis was 1852, after which he fortunately seems to have dropped it in favor of plain German.) Aside from this, the following construction can be put on the statement under discussion, in the light of Par.46/1: when the proletariat actually achieves *classwide* organization (read this as *class* organization), this massive achievement necessarily

makes it a political power, that is, a social formation exercising influence over the whole community including the state. See also Par.67/3.

(2) TEN HOURS BILL. After a Short Time struggle lasting over decades, a Ten Hours Act was adopted by Parliament in 1847, limiting the labor of women and children to ten hours a day and 58 hours a week. The result of a complex interaction of political class forces, pushed on by the danger of working-class disaffection, this early example of "protective legislative for women" was the greatest advance in factory legislation in its time, though its enforcement was a continuing focus of class struggle. It had not yet gone into effect when the Manifesto was published. Engels published two articles on this act in 1850 (MECW 10:271, 288); Marx referred to it in his Inaugural Address of the International. The °divisions inside the bourgeoisie° were indeed notable, and were prominent at the time: "The discussions and divisions on the Factory Bill have been of the most confused and almost ludicrous kind" (*Leeds Times*); "...curious political state of things, such intermingling of parties, such a confusion of opposition..." (C. C. F. Greville). A leading supporter was the Tory landowner Lord Ashley; a leading opponent, the Radical leader John Bright, whose heart yearned to free black slaves, none of whom worked in Manchester mills. But the lines were even more twisted; in fact, not only °inside the bourgeoisie°. See below, Par. 48/1. Apropos of this bill: it happens that the sole extant manuscript page of a draft of the Manifesto starts with the following words (written in Mrs. Marx's hand): "...proletarians, for the Ten Hours Bill without sharing their illusions about the results of this measure."

Par. 48

(1) COLLISIONS INSIDE THE OLD SOCIETY. This paragraph can be partly read as generalizing on the experience of the fight over the Ten Hours Act (see Par.47/2). In fact, the A.E.T. unobtrusively changed °collisions inside [lit., of] the old society° into °collisions between the classes of the old society°. In making the class conflict central, Engels was no doubt thinking of the antagonism of aristocratic-Tory landowning elements to bourgeoisification in England. (There would long remain a current of antibourgeois feeling stemming from *pre*bourgeois modes of thought, later sometimes adopting a socialistic coloration—the British analogue of Feudal Socialism.) The Manifesto here speaks of struggle between the bourgeoisie and the aristocracy in the *beginning* (°to begin with°), but this tension was still a powerful political factor in 1848.

(2) EVERY FOREIGN COUNTRY. The A.E.T. deleted °every°, perhaps because of the development of the European system of war alliances. If so, this was not a good reason, since even inside such imperialist alliances the antagonisms among the national bourgeoisies went on.

(3) POLITICAL MOVEMENT. See the discussion of this phrase in Par.50/2 below.

(4) EDUCATIONAL ELEMENTS. The A.E.T. expanded this expression to °elements of political and general education°, and also added many words to an explanatory expansion of the last phrase, after the °i.e.° (or °in other words°). This introduces two paragraphs (Par.49-50) dealing primarily with the following question: How does the proletarian movement gain the help and services of *educated* persons, trained elements, people capable

232

of carrying on tasks requiring intellectual skills—such as editing a paper, writing manifestos, making effective speeches, etc.? This, remember, in an age when education, especially advanced education, tended to be the monopoly of the propertied classes (sometimes indeed called the 'educated classes'). Note that this question is *not* how the movement gains 'intellectuals' (whatever these are taken to be), though we will run into an allied question at the end of Par.50. 'Intellectual skills' does not mean the 'skills of intellectuals.'

We will see especially in Par.49 that changes made by the A.E.T. had the unintended effect of obscuring the original's emphasis on *education*. By adding °political° as well as °general° to °education°, the A.E.T. shifted attention a bit to a somewhat different question. Taken together with a similar change in Par.49, the implication might be seen that the bourgeois elements °precipitated into the proletariat° (Par.49), or which the bourgeoisie °supplies° (Par.48), were politically more advanced than the native proletarian elements; but for forty-odd years after the Manifesto, we know, Engels repeatedly and strongly proclaimed the opposite to be true. (See KMTR 2, Chap. 18, which describes Marx's and Engels' fight against intellectuals' influence in the movement.) Forty years after 1848, there was a real problem in understanding what the Manifesto was concerned with when it was published. In the first two Laura (French) versions, °educational elements° became "elements of its progress"; and in the third, the A.E.T. was obviously used as the model. See Par.49/2 below.

Par. 49

(1) AS WE SAW. In what previous paragraph did the Manifesto say that °whole sections of the ruling class° sink into the proletariat °or at least are threatened°...? This must refer to Par.47, where however the point was *not* made about °sections of the ruling class° but rather about °small intermediate strata° (or °lower strata of the middle class°). To be sure, that paragraph ended with the general statement that °the proletariat is recruited from all classes of the population°. Perhaps the present paragraph represents an afterthought, or a previous paragraph was not revised to suit.

(2) EDUCATIONAL ELEMENTS. While the original repeated this expression from Par.48, the A.E.T. again rewrote the formulation. It changed °a quantity of educational elements° to °fresh elements of enlightenment and progress°. This time, not even the word 'education(al)' was retained; see the discussion in Par.48/3. Note that the word 'progress' introduced here by the A.E.T. had been used in the Laura (French) versions from the first.

Par. 50

(1) BOURGEOIS RECRUITS. We now see the third in the list of answers to the question about °educational elements° (see Par.48/3). To summarize:

(a) In Par.48: Proletarians themselves are educated by being °thrust...into the political movement° by the bourgeoisie itself.

(b) In Par.49: Sections of the bourgeoisie (one may add: also of the middle classes) are proletarianized or declassed, bringing their educational and educated skills to the service of the proletarian movement.

(c) In the present paragraph: A °small part° of the bourgeoisie goes over to the proletarian revolutionary movement *politically*. There are three ideas here. (i) They do not become proletarians themselves but rather political or ideological supporters of the movement. (ii) Even for this small group, it happens (the Manifesto explains) only in a time of pre-revolutionary crisis—as was true in the period of the French Revolution, which is referred to as the historical model. (iii) Lastly, there is °in particular° a part of this °small part°, people whom the Manifesto calls °the bourgeois ideologists°, who have managed to grasp the historical dynamics of the situation.

It is in the third part of the third group that we finally meet persons who resemble what later came to be called 'intellectuals'—at least according to some definitions of that amorphous term. I mention this because many intellectuals who write books on Marx think that all these paragraphs are about themselves, that is, other intellectuals. Besides the Manifesto's view that even a °small part° can be won over only when the revolution already looms, not in "normal" times (when the pattern would presumably apply only to discrete individuals), there is no question about whom Marx was thinking of in the reference to °bourgeois ideologists°. Everyone knew of the prominent cases: in the first place, the great pioneers, Saint-Simon (an aristocrat), Fourier (a traveling salesman, no capitalist), and Owen (finally, a renegade capitalist). But as a matter of fact, no °small part° of the capitalists came over with Owen, no section of the aristocracy with Saint-Simon, no layers of 'intermediate strata' with Fourier. Anyway, *these* men were prodigies, and it is insulting to compare them with some writer or professor who joined the Social-Democracy after it had become respectable. The later problem, the real issue, about 'intellectuals' in the socialist movement had to do with people who did not °cut loose° from the bourgeois world but rather sought to cut the workers' party loose from its "antiquated" class foundations. (See KMTR, Chap. 17.)

(2) HISTORICAL MOVEMENT. This was the A.E.T.'s literal translation; I have used the translation °course of historical development° for the German phrase (historical °Bewegung°). My motive is to illustrate a certain usage of °movement° which is less common in English. 'Movement' here is not a current of people, but the 'movement' of history itself, the pattern or course or dynamics of historical change. For a previous example, see Par.48, where I used °political movement° in the latter sense. In this case it was the A.E.T. that chose not to be literal: it said °political arena° (which has the disadvantage of being a static term).

Par. 51

(1) THE "ONE REACTIONARY MASS" FORMULA. Under Lassallean influence, the party program adopted at the Gotha congress of 1875 unifying the Lassallean and "Eisenacher" organizations announced that relative to the working class, "all other classes form only one reactionary mass." In his *Critique of the Gotha Program*, Marx devoted a section (I, 4) to denouncing this idea. Aside from its scientific invalidity, its political meaning, taken at face value, was that the proletariat could not expect to gain class allies in the course of its social struggle. This was a disastrous acceptance of isolation, despite the very "revolutionary"

234

and uncompromising ring of the formula. (About how it fitted in with Lassallean politics, see KMTR 2:309f.) Marx's 1875 argument began by citing the present paragraph of the Manifesto, no doubt on the assumption that the Lassalleans would use it as justification. "Lassalle knew the *Communist Manifesto* by heart," Marx wrote, but he falsified its content for his own political purposes. Marx showed that, in the Manifesto's view, the bourgeoisie is still °a revolutionary class° with relation to the old society, and so cannot be said to form part of a single "reactionary mass." This certainly disposed of the Lassallean invention, and gave more careful form to the statement in the present paragraph that °only the proletariat is a really revolutionary class° (with a special emphasis on °really°). But Marx also asserted that the Manifesto's view of the 'middle strata' (*Mittelstände*) was similarly antithetical to the "one reactionary mass" formula; and this claim will be considered in Par.52/3 below. (For a lengthier account of the Lassalle formula, see KMTR 2, Chap. 11, Sec. 9-10.)

(2) "DISAPPEARANCE OF THE MIDDLE CLASSES." This paragraph—taken together with the next, and commonly with reference to Par.41 (which see)—has often been used to claim that Marx held a theory which predicted the "disappearance of the middle classes" under advanced capitalism. As explained in Par.41/1, the actual language of the Manifesto was not intended to be predictive, but rather to explain the *tendencies* of past and present. However, certain changes made by the A.E.T. had the unintended effect of seeming to bolster the claims, having been worded in 1888 without clairvoyant anticipation of the claims made after Bernstein's Revisionism was launched following Engels' death. Thus, the A.E.T. said that °the other classes°—other than bourgeoisie and proletariat—°decay and finally disappear°... Both words in the phrase °finally disappear° are artifacts of the translation process, the original merely saying that they °decay and go under° (°gehen unter°, fall to ruin, sink). Now it is true that *untergehen* has range enough to mean 'founder' or 'die ' but this is not really a philological dispute, like an exercise in Biblical exegesis. Marx expressed his views on the economic tendencies and fate of intermediate strata in other places, leaving no doubt that he held no theory about "disappeared" middle classes. (See KMTR, Special Note F.) The only question is whether the cited phrase in the Manifesto, °finally disappear°, is so decisive that the marxologists are justified in paying no attention to Marx's views on the matter in his mature economic writings. But this would be difficult, even if the words °finally disappear° had been present in the original. (This question is continued under Par. 147.)

(3) THE CASE OF 'MIT.' Bert Andréas, whose researches into the genesis and history of the Manifesto are pre-eminent, has raised a question about the word (°mit° = with) which the A.E.T. translates °in the face of° and which I have rendered °thanks to°. Andréas argues that the Manifesto's words °The other classes decay and go under with [*mit*] large-scale industry° literally means "along with large-scale industry"—as if large-scale industry also goes under. Of course, this could not have been the intended meaning. Andréas therefore conjectures that some words may have been inadvertently left out and never replaced—perhaps as follows: "gehen unter mit *der Entwicklung* der grossen Industrie" (the italicized words being inserted). This would read: "go under with [i.e., in line with] the development of large-scale industry." However, on the other hand, it is possible to believe that the use of *mit* was elliptical, even if poor style. As a matter of fact, very much the same construction with *mit* can be found in Par.114; it is not really a special problem.

(4) SPECIAL AND ESSENTIAL. The A.E.T. reformulated the original's °most characteristic product° to °special and essential product.°

(5) QUOTE IN 'CAPITAL.' Regarding the citation of this paragraph in *Capital*, see Par.60/5.

Par. 52

(1) INTERMEDIATE STRATA. Look back to Par.41, which begins in much the same way, only with °small intermediate strata° instead of °intermediate strata° (°Mittelstände°). Similarly to Par.41, the A.E.T. makes this °lower middle class°. In both cases, this is followed by a list of class elements—the same list, except that °rentiers° is now omitted:

(a) °Small industrial°: see my explanations in Par. 41/1c. Now the A.E.T. translates this °small manufacturer°, whereas previously it had been °small tradespeople°. Keep in mind the special meaning of 'manufacture' (Par.15/1).

(b) °Small merchant°: as before, the A.E.T. makes this °shopkeeper°.

(c) When °Mittelstände° recurs at the end of the first sentence, the A.E.T. turns it into °fractions of the middle class.°

I think these various terminological shifts were used by the A.E.T.—inconsistently, moreover—because Engels and Moore were taking into consideration the pervasive practice in English of using 'middle class' to mean the bourgeoisie, even the big bourgeoisie, in fact anyone who was not in the lord-and-lady class. (See Par.14/5.) And since it *was* done inconsistently, it was pervasively confusing. Certainly no conclusions should be drawn from the A.E.T.'s language without carefully going back to the original. Incidentally, all the Laura (French) versions turned °Mittelstände° (which is plural) into 'middle class' (singular), without qualification.

(2) RUIN / EXTINCTION. In the first sentence, the word which the A.E.T. translates as °extinction° is °Untergang°, which I render °ruin°. The point involved is exactly the same as was the case with its verb form *untergehen*—discussed in Par.51/2.

(3) REACTIONARY CLASSES (PETTY-BOURGEOISIE). Although this paragraph uses the broader term °intermediate strata° (°Mittelstände°, middle ranks of society), it will perhaps be clearer to link this discussion up with that of the *petty-bourgeoisie*, defined in Par.44/3. We will see in Par.165/1 that a similar point is made there, using the class term. Artisans and shopkeepers, masters of small workshops—these make up the urban petty-bourgeoisie, if we think of the peasantry as the rural petty-bourgeoisie. And these are primarily the elements listed at the beginning of this Manifesto paragraph. In using °Mittelstände°, the Manifesto was using an everyday German term; but since there is no everyday English equivalent, we have been forced to use 'intermediate strata ' which has the wrong reverberation or 'middle class(es) ' which has a somewhat different meaning.

This paragraph, above all, exemplifies the distinctive view of the Manifesto (soon abandoned by Marx) that the petty-bourgeoisie was simply a °reactionary° social force, flatly assigned to the other side of the barricades even as compared with the "revolutionary bourgeoisie" (cf. Par.51/1). Like the treatment of the peasantry (see Par.28/3), this purely negative view ended with the Manifesto, though there were echoes later on. This is one of the indications of Marx's sole authorship of the final Manifesto draft, for Engels had been writing quite differently for part of a year. Through 1847 Engels developed the programmatic conception of a bloc of Democratic classes (see Par.28/3). This class alliance would consist of the working classes exploited by the *new and old* ruling classes, bourgeoisie and aristocracy. These working classes were "the proletarians, small peasants and petty-bourgeoisie" (MECW 6:294). In his own draft for the Manifesto, he viewed the petty--bourgeoisie as a class which, under present conditions, "has in many respects the same interest as the proletariat" (ibid., 356). As soon as the revolution broke out in 1848, Marx swung over to Engels' view and followed it through the revolutionary period. The Manifesto therefore represented the end of the line, a dead end. The difference involved was great. In the new view, devised and pioneered by Engels, the revolutionary lineup was: the Democratic bloc (proletariat, small peasantry, petty-bourgeoisie) versus the bourgeoisie *and* the Old Regime. In the Manifesto's view, the lineup was: proletariat and bourgeoisie, as the two progressive-revolutionary classes, versus the classes of the Old Regime *including the petty-bourgeoisie*. (See the lineup adumbrated in Par.44, third sentence.) To be sure, there was still another change as a consequence of the experience of the revolution itself, but this is beyond our present purview. (For the entire pattern, see KMTR 2, Chap. 7-10.) It is important to understand, then, that the Manifesto is out of line: before its writing, Engels had developed different views, and Marx's, if any, are not on record; after its publication, Engels' views carried. The treatment of the petty-bourgeoisie in the Manifesto is an anomaly, but it plainly corresponded to a deeprooted antagonism in Marx to the petty-bourgeois role in society.

The present paragraph makes the flat statement that the °Mittelstände° are °reactionary°—not merely nonrevolutionary, not merely conservative, but reactionary in the most literal sense (°seek to turn back the wheel of history°). We will see this reiterated in Par.165. Yet in the present paragraph there is a fudging: "When [*or if*] they are revolutionary..." The same °Mittelstände°, or *individuals* in these middle ranks? It is only the latter that is consistent, but that is not what the words say. However, the only way to make sense of it is to assume that Marx was thinking of the elements (discussed in Par.41 and Par.49) that are proletarianized or declassed, not the °intermediate strata° as such. It certainly was not clear. Anyway, it is hardly an amendment of the original flat judgment of the petty-bourgeoisie (°reactionary°) to admit that elements dropping out of that class might be revolutionized.

Yet in Marx's aforementioned (Par.51/1) reference in 1875 to this passage of the Manifesto, we saw he sought to show that the Manifesto (contrary to the Lassalleans) did not treat the *Mittelstände* as "one reactionary mass." He did this by citing the Manifesto's words about their °impending passing-over into the proletariat°—without mentioning that the same passage stamped them as °reactionary°. Moreover, his citation was skewed: "the Manifesto," he claimed, "adds that the *Mittelstände*...(is becoming) revolutionary...in view of [its] impending" etc. But these are not the words of the Manifesto, which on the contrary posed a conditional thought. This was not a graceful way to repudiate the old language of the Manifesto. Strangest of all, in the preceding paragraph of this same passage, Marx yet once again treated the *Mittelstände* as lined up with the feudal lords, on one side of the barricades, against the proletariat-cum-bourgeoisie. This was precisely the outlived view of the Manifesto which he was trying to reject. All in all, one of the outstanding examples in Marx of utter confusion. (For the text of this passage in the *Critique of the Gotha Program*, see MEW 19:23; the *MESW* translation is bungled.)

(4) WHEN THEY ARE REVOLUTIONARY. For the sense of this codicil, see the preceding point (3). The A.E.T. made some changes. To be sure, the difference between the A.E.T.'s '*if*' and my '*when*' is not in the German, which uses a different locution now antiquated in English: "Be they revolutionary..." But besides using °if°, the A.E.T. inserts °by chance°. I am not sure why Engels did so (there is no question of literal 'chance') but certainly the effect is to limit the revolutionization to random *individuals* of the petty-bourgeoisie, not any class strata. The consequence is emphasis on the basic reactionary role of the class per se, and one wonders whether Engels really intended to do this in 1888. Along the same line, he inserted °only° in the next part of the sentence. The historical issue remains: can the proletariat hope to win at least significant strata of the 'intermediate classes' to its revolutionary cause, or should it cede these classes and strata to Reaction in advance? This historical issue applies to the small peasantry along with the urban petty-bourgeoisie, and the issue of a class alliance led by a proletarian vanguard is a fateful problem of social revolution.

(5) QUOTE IN 'CAPITAL.' Regarding the citation of this paragraph in *Capital*, see Par.60/5.

Par. 53

(1) LUMPENPROLETARIAT. Neither Marx nor Engels ever used this German term in English, nor did anyone else until recent times (lower-cased). Therefore, whenever they wished to refer to this social element, they cast around for an approximation: 'mob,' 'lazzaroni' (Neapolitan lumpens), etc. But there is no good substitute. The double attempt at one in the A.E.T. (°"dangerous class," the social scum°) is half a failure: °social scum° is certainly helpful, but °"dangerous class"° is misleading, especially since the quote marks show consciousness of its previous use. This use had usually been directed against the working class or against the Lower Classes generally, sinister forces whose instability was seen as a danger to "society," that is, to the upper classes. Or this misleading appellation was associated with the 'criminal classes,' or had other overtones that were no part of Marx's meaning of °lumpenproletariat°. In *Capital*, the substitute had been the plural form, "the 'dangerous' classes"—perhaps even worse. When the Manifesto was written, Marx was still unclear, or ambivalent, on an essential question about this social element: was this lumpenproletariat a section of the proletariat, or a social element outside it? As with other basic economic questions, it was only later that Marx clarified his own view, which was made clear in *Capital*. Here the lumpenproletariat was carefully differentiated not only from the unemployed (industrial reserve army) but from the lowest sedimentary layers of the pauperized proletariat (the "lazarus layers"). The "lumpenproletariat proper" consisted of elements precipitated out of the proletariat, elements like "vagabonds, criminals, prostitutes" and such. Elsewhere Marx made clear that by lumpenproletariat he meant the "refuse of all classes" (not only of the proletariat), the social detritus and offscourings from all parts of society, the common sewer: this from 1852 on. However, note that Engels' efforts at an English term in the A.E.T. did not make the most common translation mistake, one still encountered: namely, a term

viewing the lumpenproletariat as a poor or "ragged" section of the proletariat. The translations "tatterdemalion proletariat," "slum proletariat," and the like are erroneous, being based on an etymological misapprehension. (For details on the history and meaning of the term, see KMTR 2, Chap. 15, and Special Note G.)

(2) THROWN OFF BY; MAY. There were two very small changes made by the A.E.T. that reflect the later evolution of Marx's views. Where the original spoke of the °putrefaction° of the lowest strata, the A.E.T. changed °of° into °thrown off by°, thereby stressing that this social element *separates* itself from the working class. And in the statement about the possible role of the lumpenproletariat in revolution, °is swept° is weakened into °may...be swept°. In addition, the last few words of the paragraph are somewhat rewritten, but without any evident difference in meaning.

(3) MOVEMENT. As in Par.50/2 (which see), the German °Bewegung° (lit., °movement°, so used in the A.E.T.) here means the movement of social forces, the °current of development°. It does not have the organizational implication of a term like 'revolutionary movement.'

Par. 54

(1) THE "OLD SOCIETY." The first sentence, which is further examined in point 2 below, was already ambiguous in the German original. What °old society° was meant—the Old Regime of prebourgeois society or bourgeois society itself? In the Manifesto, this language usually means the former; but the context argues that Marx meant the latter. Perhaps this ambiguity is the reason the A.E.T. expanded it to °old society at large°, in order to embrace both.

(2) SWAMPED / NULLIFIED. What the A.E.T. translated as °virtually swamped° was the German word °vernichtet° (annihilated, nullified, negated). It can be read as 'negated' with a Hegelian accent; interpreted more concretely, 'annihilated' or 'destroyed ' which indeed was the version in the Laura (French) translations. I have compromised on °nullified°. But it seems to me that if this sentence is completely stripped of Hegelian connotations, it ceases to have much point. Engels' solution, °virtually swamped°, was not a happy one; but of course we know that he assumed that any Hegelianized meaning would be incomprehensible to Anglo-Saxon skulls. This was his typical dilemma.

(3) FAMILY RELATIONS. The fate of the family, which was touched on in Par.22 as here, will be taken up in Par. 100/2.

(4) NATIONAL CHARACTER. This likewise adumbrates a question later taken up at greater length: see under Par. 112-115; see also Par.57.

(5) LAWS, MORALITY, RELIGION. These problems of the ideological superstructure come up at greater length in Par.118-124; see e.g. Par.118/2.

(6) EXAGGERATIONS. See Par.18/11 regarding extrapolatory exaggerations in the Manifesto. Virtually all the statements in this paragraph, dealing with the level of consciousness of the proletariat (in which countries?), are obvious exaggerations in terms of the 1848 situation. Their positive content is to stress *tendencies*.

(7) REVISED A.E.T. OF 1932. In this version (see Part I, chapter 28, section 3) the first

sentence of the paragraph reads as follows: "The social conditions of the old society no longer exist for the proletariat."

Par. 55

(1) PROLETARIAT'S MODE OF APPROPRIATION. The language in the second sentence is confusing. What is meant by the proletariat's °own previous mode of appropriation°, which it has to abolish? Presumably, the Manifesto means the system of wage-labor.

(2) INDIVIDUAL PROPERTY. Much of the language of the last sentence was rewritten by the A.E.T. Besides replacing °to safeguard° with °to secure and to fortify°, and inserting a °mission°, the A.E.T. aimed the statement at °individual property°, whose °securities° and °insurances° it wanted to destroy. But this insertion of °individual property° was a tactical blunder, since it is precisely °individual° or °personal° property which socialists want to differentiate from private-business property or corporate property that is used to produce surplus value. This sort of careless translation—moreover an inaccurate one—was the kind of thing that bourgeois propagandists seized on to claim that the socialists' state would deprive hard-working people of everything they owned. (The usual socialist distinction is made in Par. 72-74.) To be sure, the Manifesto spoke of destroying every °private safeguard and private guarantee°, but at least the word 'private' (as in 'private property') was recognizable shorthand for 'private-capitalist.'

Par. 56

(1) A.E.T. ADDITION: HISTORICAL. The A.E.T. added the word °historical° in the first sentence. It would be assumed in any case. The Laura (French) versions added this word from the first.

(2) A.E.T. ADDITION: SELF-CONSCIOUS. The A.E.T. added the word °self-conscious° alongside °independent° etc. It has the effect of backing up and rounding out the intent of °independent°. Engels was no doubt seeking to emphasize—as he wrote in his 1888 preface to the A.E.T.—that "our notion from the very beginning was that 'the emancipation of the working class must be the act of the working class itself.'" (The quoted expression was approximately Marx's 1864 formulation of the principle of self-emancipation in the Rules of the International.) For the development of this principle in Marx and Engels, see KMTR 1, Chap. 10, and KMTR 2, Chap. 6. The idea will come to the fore again in the Manifesto in Par.181-184.

(3) MOVEMENT OF THE IMMENSE MAJORITY. One of the best examples of the *anticipatory exaggerations* of the Manifesto (see Par.54/6), this paragraph may give the impression it says that the proletariat already constitutes the "immense majority" of the population. Of course, Marx knew this was not so: it was beginning to be true in England, but certainly not in any other country. If many socialists of the time made this assertion, it was because they still held the old definition of the word 'proletariat': workingpeople, the Common People in an amorphous way comprising the entire peasantry and much of the

240

petty-bourgeoisie. But the modern class of wage-laborers was generally a distinct minority even in the 'working classes.' Even later in 1870, Engels wrote: "The class exclusively dependent on wages all its life is still far from being a majority of the German people. It is, therefore, also compelled to seek allies." (MECW 2: 163.) This offers a key to the Manifesto's statement: the 'proletarian movement' should be conceived as the movement *led* by a vanguard proletariat, leading other allied class elements behind its own program of social revolution. The focus here is not on whether the proletariat is (or will be) a majority by itself but on the fact that the movement it leads must be a °movement of the immense majority, in the interest of the immense majority°. The crux of this sentence is that it repudiated in the most definite way the prevalent concept of Jacobin or "Blanquist" revolutionism, which saw the Revolution as the coup of a determined band of revolutionists who would seize power one fine day and institute an educational dictatorship to bring the backward people up to the revolutionary level. In this conception the proletariat was not °independent° but rather totally dependent on revolutionary saviors and messiahs. The alternative was a view of the revolutionary movement as a class alliance led by a proletarian revolutionary vanguard—for which see also Par. 11/2 and Par.28/3; in general, see KMTR 2:38f.

(4) SPRUNG INTO THE AIR. This A.E.T. expression was, possibly, overinfluenced by the German term (°in die Luft gesprengt°); in the sense of 'explode,' it is rather antiquated. The same German verb is translated °burst asunder° in most similar loci in the Manifesto and in *Capital*. But, this aside, the metaphor in this sentence is surely one of the most striking in all of Marx. See also Par.141-142/3.

Par. 57

(1) NATIONAL FORM OF THE CLASS STRUGGLE. This paragraph gives the impression of being displaced. In content, it is a very important accompaniment of Par.112-117, which see. Perhaps it was placed here as a codicil to Par.54, which claimed that the proletarian has been °stripped...of all national character°.

Par. 58

(1) PROLETARIAN RULE. Although this paragraph is worded as if it were a summary of previous passages, this is in fact the first mention of the aim of the proletariat as °rule° in society—political rule, political power. The German word *Herrschaft* is variously translated as 'sway,' 'power,' 'dominion,' 'mastery,' 'ascendancy,' etc., but while the English translations tend to vary, Marx's usage sticks with *Herrschaft* pretty steadily. See also Par.67.

(2) FORCIBLE OVERTHROW. See the preceding note; this too is a first mention—of the view that the coming revolution must be based on the use of force, a view that is reinforced by the idea that there is a °hidden civil war° in society. The A.E.T.'s choice of °violent° (°gewaltsamen°) to describe the °overthrow of the bourgeoisie° had nothing to do with later efforts to distinguish between 'force' and 'violence'—the sort of distinction that defines an act as forcible if it is based on the threat of force, whether or not force is actually

used, the latter case defining 'violence.' While Marx later made clear that he left the door open for nonviolent conquests of power, in countries like England and the United States where suitable governmental machinery existed, he added that this supposition did not end the question of force. "Yet the 'peaceful' movement could turn into a 'forcible' one through the rebellion of those interested in the old status quo; if the latter are defeated by *force* (as in the American Civil War and the French Revolution), then it will be as rebels against 'legal' force." (MEW 34:498f.) See also Engels' preface to *Capital*, I, English edition. Engels' drafts of the Manifesto had also taken the question up. In his *Principles of Communism*, although repudiating conspiratorialism (see Par.5/1), he opined that victory through peaceful methods was desirable but it was the Communists' adversaries that were working to make a revolution necessary. "Should the oppressed proletariat in the end be goaded into a revolution, we Communists will then defend the cause of the proletarians by deed just as well as we do now by word." (MECW 6:349f) This is what came to be called the "defensive" formulation.

Par. 59

(1) SERF AND COMMUNE. For the medieval °commune°, see Par.18/4. A serf who succeeded in becoming °a member of the commune°` did so insofar as he became (say) an independent merchant, i.e., a member of the nascent bourgeoisie, as also °the petty-bourgeois° who figures in the second part of this sentence. This could hardly have been intended to serve as a summary of the genesis of the bourgeoisie, which is a good deal more complicated; it must be taken as a couple of illustrations. The contrast is with the relative inability of the proletarian to become a capitalist (except for rare exceptions, which are not to the point).

(2) WORKER TURNS INTO A PAUPER. This may sound as if the class of proletarians,.as such, is inevitably pauperized. This language reflected the socialistic propaganda of the day; later, in *Capital* I (Chap. 25), Marx made clear that the pauper layer is "the lowest sediment of the relative surplus population."

Par.60

(1) A.E.T. DELETION: A PRECONDITION FOR CAPITALISM. The A.E.T. made a correction in the form of a deletion. The original said that the precondition for the existence and rule of the bourgeoisie °is the accumulation of wealth in the hands of private persons°. This, as Marx later ascertained, is incorrect; for accumulation in the hands of °private persons° is by no means distinctive of capitalism—it is found in all exploitive societies before capitalism. The A.E.T. dropped the above-quoted words. The original went on to put another condition in apposition with this one, °the formation and augmentation of capital°—and this the A.E.T. kept in.

(2) WAGE-LABOR AND COMPETITION. The assertion that °Wage-labor is based exclusively on competition among workers° is either elliptical or overstated. In the first place, the meaning is that the *wage-labor system* is so based, i.e., capitalist relations. In the second

place, the statement was probably intended, and anyway should be taken, as a political one rather than simply socioeconomic: that is, bourgeois rule can be overcome insofar as the workers' °revolutionary unification° replaces their °isolation°.

(3) GRAVEDIGGERS. For the first echo of this metaphor, see Par.35/1.

(4) INEVITABILITY. Upon the shaky foundation of this paragraph's last sentence has been built a whole theory, repeated from tome to tome, according to which Marx held a metaphysical theory about the "inevitability of socialism." But--

(a) This alleged theory flies in the face of the strong statement earlier about the alternatives before society: social revolution or else "the common ruin of the contending classes." (See Par.8/3, which cites further evidence.)

(b) The phrase °equally inevitable° (used by the A.E.T. in all innocence) is nonsense if it is taken literally, like "equally perfect." My translation °alike inevitable° is just as literal. The word used here for °inevitable° (°unvermeidlich°) is the ordinary German word (unavoidable,' 'necessitated') which often, as in English, conveys nothing more than high hope and confidence in a hortatory context. The same applies to the use of 'inevitably' in the Marx-Engels preface to the Russian edition of the Manifesto. If a philosophic Theory of Inevitability were to be assigned to every writer who has used *unvermeidlich* in the same way, the history of thought would have to be rewritten. In practice, the *unvermeidlich* is counterposed to the accidental, in order to stress that a phenomenon obeys definite laws and is the outcome of causes that can be examined; it implies a scientific attitude to causation, not a metaphysical one.

(5) QUOTE IN 'CAPITAL.' The first volume of *Capital* (Chap. 32) carried a quotation from the Manifesto which is actually a portmanteau affair. In the form of a single passage, with suspension points, it packs together the latter part of Par.60 followed by all of Par.51 and the beginning of Par.52. Incidentally, in this note the Manifesto was misdated 1847—an error that reverberated through a remarkably large number of subsequent publications, and is still doing so.

(6) QUOTE IN 'HERR VOGT.' We have to unravel a very tangled textual issue, not because it will turn out to be important but in order to forestall anyone from thinking that it is. In his 1860 polemic *Herr Vogt* (see Part I, chapter 13), Marx seemed to be quoting from Par.60, as follows:

> In the first section of the Manifesto, titled "Bourgeois and Proletarians" (see Manifesto, p. 11), it is brought out in detail that the economic and, hence also in one form or another, the political *rule of the bourgeoisie* is the basic precondition both for the existence of the modern proletariat and for the creation of the "material (pre)conditions for its emancipation." [MEW 14:449 or MECW 17:90]

The words cited at the end are "materiellen Bedingungen seiner Befreiung." In this book Marx quoted the Manifesto from its first edition of 1848; in this edition, page 11 started with Par.60 (minus its first line) and went on to begin Section II. Unless he made an error, Marx must then have referred to Par.60. Unfortunately Par.60 scarcely answers his description of a discussion "in detail," and in particular it does not contain the four words cited. True, the entire Section I does answer the description very handily, but the reference to page 11 remains unexplained. Besides, as Andréas points out (page 36), the four words do not appear anywhere in Section I. Rather, says Andréas, those words are to be found in the second installment of Marx's 1847 article against Heinzen, "Moralizing Criticism and Critical Morality." The first complication is that Andréas' claim is inaccurate: the four words are *not* to be found in the source he cites; it offers only the words "material conditions"—which of course can be found in the Manifesto in several places. The second complication is that these four words do appear in the Manifesto—not in Section I but in Section III, Par.179. (The expression is virtually repeated, in similar but not exact form, in Par.182.) Moreover, Par.179 presents the very content that Marx referred to in *Herr Vogt*, not "in detail" but only in summary.

Now even if Andréas' facts were accurate, it would not do to hypothesize (as Andréas does) that Marx was really quoting from his unpublished revision of the Manifesto, for in this passage he refers with apparent exactness to page 11 of the published brochure. The reader of *Herr Vogt* would expect to find on page 11 what Marx said was there. There are two possible explanations: (i) Marx was being incredibly sloppy and careless in quoting his own work. (ii) The page reference in *Herr Vogt* was a misprint, for indeed Par.179 appeared on page 21 of the Manifesto's first edition. This error would still not account for Marx's reference to the first section instead of the third; hence both explanations may be true (or both untrue).

II

PROLETARIANS AND COMMUNISTS

Par. 61

(1) SECTISM. In asking the question that inaugurates Section II, Marx raised the question of *sectism*. By 'sectism' I mean the adoption of the *sect form of organization*, whether the sect be called a party, movement, league, or International. (The usual term is 'sectarianism,' which I prefer to use to denote certain *policies*.) A sect is a group whose reason for being revolves around its own political credo, its distinctive beliefs, which it takes as an ideological imprimatur establishing the defining wall between its membership and the outside unanointed world. The sectist counterposes his "correct" line against the very unsatisfactory class movement. "The development of socialist sectarianism and that of the real working-class movement always stand in inverse ratio to each other," Marx wrote to a friend (Nov. 23, 1871). "The sect," he told another, "sees the justification for its existence and its point of honor not in what it has in common with the class movement but in the *particular shibboleth* which *distinguishes* it from the movement" (Oct. 13, 1868). From the beginning of his movement activity (about 1845-1846 in Brussels) Marx rejected the sect form of organization, and in the course of time changed only in the direction of becoming more violently denun-

ciatory of socialist sects and sectists, particularly "Marxist" ones. He and Engels wrote more than once of the need to actually smash the pseudo-Marxist sects in England and the United States that had turned Marxism into the ossified dogma of a "salvation-bringing church." The formation of a *real* class movement, even if on a defective program, was more important than any number of sects with "correct" Marxist principles (letter to Bracke, May 5, 1875). Marx and Engels saw the task of revolutionists as bringing their "correct" ideas *into* the more backward class movement, not counterposed to it. These paragraphs Par.61-66 of the Manifesto emphasized this view as vigorously as anything they ever wrote later; as late as 1884 Engels quoted these very paragraphs didactically, to the membership of the German movement, as having "full validity" (MESW 3:164f).

Par. 62

(1) PARTY. For the meaning of 'party,' see note 3 on the Main Title. Here °other workers' parties° refers not only to tendencies and currents, but also to other 'arms' of the working-class movement, such as the trade-union movement. Ryazanov has made the point that Marx, along with the CL generally, must have been particularly concerned about seeming to set up an organizational rival to the Chartist movement in England—a movement which Marx regarded as the only 'working-class party' then existing. When G. J. Harney had organized the Fraternal Democrats, he had to combat Chartist suspicions that this group was intended as a party within a party, instead of a supplemental arm of the movement. (This discussion is continued in the next point.)

(2) SPECIAL / SEPARATE PARTY. The words of the original, °besondere Partei°, can be translated either way; but note that in the next paragraph the word °separate° occurs as a translation of the stronger word °getrennten°. (This is the past participle of the verb for 'separate,' 'divide.') This second usage *must* be translated as °separate°, and so it seems advisable to use °special party° in the present paragraph. It also has the right flavor. This problem is closely related to the next point.

(3) VIS-À-VIS / OPPOSED TO. In view of the misunderstandings surrounding Marx's rejection of a °separate° or °special party°, it is unfortunate that the A.E.T. used the formulation °opposed to° for the German °gegenüber°. The milder meaning of this word ('in relation to') creates fewer difficulties. For was it really true that the Communists did not 'oppose' other tendencies? Of course, they did oppose them, that is, they argued their opposing views; the original does not really aim to deny *this*. What the Manifesto is concerned with here is something else: organizational policy. In this connection the A.E.T. made another change, which seems very tiny yet affects the way the passage reads today. Where the original said °The Communists are not°..., the A.E.T. said that °The Communists do not form°... In English, that verb (°form°) may be interpreted actively (as 'establish,' 'set up') instead of as the intransitive verb that it is in the original (meaning 'constitute' or 'are'). Again: was it really true that the Communists did not °set up° a °separate° organization? Why, they had just done so, in establishing the Communist League! The A.E.T. sounds like a denial of this obvious fact, whereas the original was making a statement about the nonsectist character of the 'special' organization just established. In sum: in the course of a

few words, this A.E.T. sentence makes three tactical errors in translation, conveying a plainly misleading idea to most readers.

Par. 63

(1) SEPARATE. For this usage, see Par.62/2 above. Note that the A.E.T. expanded it to °separate and apart°—to make it stronger, since °separate° had also been used in Par. 62.

Par. 64

(1) SPECIAL PRINCIPLES. The A.E.T.'s alteration of this phrase to °sectarian principles° is taken up in point 2 below; here we discuss what the original actually said. It did *not* say that the Communists °do not lay down any special principles° of their own. This would obviously be false, since they were publishing a manifesto to do precisely that. It said: they did not lay down any special principles °on which they want to model the proletarian movement°. (In English this is called a 'restrictive clause' and eschews a comma; some of the comma punctuation in the A.E.T. is strictly Germanic.) This basic idea—refusal to present advanced ideas ultimatistically to the real social movement—had been set forth at greater length in Marx's very first organizational-programmatic discussions in letters published in his 1844 magazine (see KMTR 1:100-103). As before, if we keep eyes on the original, we see that what the Manifesto is rejecting is not the idea of °special principles° but rather a sectist conception of their role. (This line of thought is continued in Par.67-69.)

From another aspect, what Marx was rejecting under the head of °special principles° etc. was what he called a 'system' or 'system-mongering'—one of the dirtiest words in Marx's vocabulary. This meant: pulling and hauling on a set of ideas to force them willy-nilly into the prefabricated framework of a big ideological construction guaranteed to explain everything in the world, that is, the specialty of German idealist philosophers. This was the point Marx made, precisely in connection with this section of the Manifesto, in his book *Herr Vogt*. There he replied to a critic, who (he says) "'imagines' that I have 'tailored' a 'system,' whereas on the contrary...I rejected all systems..." (MEW 14:449 or MECW 17:90). Marx then quoted from Par.66 (see Par.66/3 below).

(2) SECTARIAN PRINCIPLES. The A.E.T.'s substitution of this term in place of °special principles° was, then, an attempt to underline the antisectist message of the Manifesto. True enough; but by making this substitution the A.E.T. shifted the spotlight. The point made by the original was washed out by the glare directed on the word °sectarian°. A reader could nod ("Yes, we should not be sectarian" or otherwise sinful) while losing sight of the original attack on °any special principles° that are laid down ultimatistically. Note that the A.E.T. also sought to gain emphasis by expanding °model° to °shape and mould.°

Par. 65

(1) DISTINGUISHED...ONLY. To present-day readers this must be the most surprising

statement in the Manifesto: the Communists differ from other °proletarian parties° *only* by two characteristics neither of which seems to specifically refer to communism or socialism! Leaving aside the internationalist emphasis (noted in point 2 below), both characteristics boil down to one: representation of the common interests of the whole proletarian movement. The thought may become clearer if we restate it as follows: Communists are peculiar in that they aim to organize a *class* movement, not a movement representing some social *or ideological* sector of the class. But note that this is what we already explained in Par.61/1, which rejected the organization of a sect—including the type of sect that calls itself communist *because it limits its membership to Communists*. Behind Marx's rejection of this organizational policy was his confident belief that a real class movement would necessarily move in the direction of communist programmatic views in the course of its class struggle; *but it would not begin with them ultimatistically*. We have already referred (see Par.64/1) to Marx's first exposition of this approach, in 1844. When this view is restated in the Manifesto, it should not be surprising, provided that Marx's total rejection of sectism has been taken seriously; but this seldom happens since the overwhelming majority of would-be Marxists have been, and are, organized in sects themselves. The following paragraphs Par.66—69 continue to point out what is *not* distinctive of the Communists.

(2) INDEPENDENT OF NATIONALITY. This is the third remark emphasizing the Manifesto's internationalist viewpoint (see Par.54/4, Par.57/1) even before getting to the main passage expounding the question of national and international approaches (see Par.112—117). It is also emphasized by a minor addition made by the A.E.T.: °always° is expanded to °always and everywhere°.

(3) THE MOVEMENT AS A WHOLE. The main message of this paragraph is repeated later in Par.193, in perhaps better-known words, about the 'present-day' and the 'future' movements.

Par. 66

(1) A.E.T. ADDITION: MOST ADVANCED. The A.E.T. inserted °most advanced° in addition to °[most] resolute'°, despite the fact that this idea was already covered in the second part of the sentence. It has the effect of immediately emphasizing the Communists *views* whereas the original began by emphasizing something else. Incidentally, this addition had been made already in the first of the Laura (French) versions, before it appeared in the A.E.T.

(2) PUSHES...ALL OTHERS. Instead of describing the Communists as °always pressing forward°, the A.E.T. says this is the section °which pushes forward all others°. This reformulation puts greater emphasis on the Communists' vanguard role.

(3) QUOTE IN 'HERR VOGT.' On the Manifesto quotes in Marx's *Herr Vogt* see Part I, chapter 13. In the context mentioned above (Par.64/1), Marx quoted the second part of Par.66 with two alterations. Instead of °the understanding of° etc., his citation went as follows (the changes being put in italics):

...the *critical* understanding of the preconditions, the course, and the general results of the *real social* movement.

The changes are relevant to the point being made in *Herr Vogt* (rejection of 'system'-mongering) but do not affect the Manifesto context. (This speaks against the view that Marx was quoting from the manuscript of a revised text; these changes look like ad-hoc explanatory changes.)

(4) A.E.T. ADDITION: ULTIMATE. In the last clause of the paragraph, the A.E.T. changed °general results° into °ultimate general results°. Obviously, in 1888 the motive for this one-word addition was to point to the communist (or socialist) social order as the 'ultimate' aim of the movement—*precisely because the original had not done this.* (See Par.65/1.) This was also the effect of another change so slight as to be nearly invisible: the °course° of the movement (in the A.E.T., °line of march°) is moved from second position to first mention, in the same clause.

Par. 67

(1) IMMEDIATE AIM. The presence of this phrase highlights the fact that there is no mention of an 'ultimate' aim in the preceding paragraph—not in the original (see Par. 66/4 above). If the conquest of power is an *immediate* aim, then the contrast must be with the communist transformation of society, the long-term societal revolution—which however has not yet been stated. As has often been said, Marx's reluctance to discuss the "music of the future" was extreme, never so much as in these early years, in reaction against the prevalent utopianism.

(2) SAME AS ALL THE OTHERS. This paragraph sees no °special principles° held by the Communists even regarding the conquest of power—an extreme example of the idea expressed in Par.64/1. It must be remembered that the socialist wing of Chartism (Harney's left wing) likewise spoke of "proletarian ascendancy" as the aim. As for the reformist utopian-socialist sects, Marx did not regard them as °proletarian parties°, as we will see in Section III. In any case, to him the aim of proletarian rule was simply a minimum program for any real proletarian socialists. In his 1872 *Housing Question*, Engels echoed the Manifesto:

> ...every real proletarian party, from the English Chartists onward, has put forward a class policy, the organization of the proletariat as an independent political party, as the primary condition of its struggle, and the dictatorship of the proletariat as the immediate aim of the struggle. [MESW 2:356]

(3) CONSTITUTION...INTO A CLASS. The formulation here is in the Hegelian mode discussed in Par.47/1: the proletariat is a class "in itself" from the beginning, but still has to 'constitute itself' as a class (a class "for itself") by becoming conscious of its class interests and by organizing.

Par. 68

(1) THEORETICAL TENETS. This and Par.69, which really should be united into a single paragraph, continue the strong emphasis of this section on the absence of °special principles° on the part of the Communists (see Par.64/1), especially in reaction against the claims of utopian sects.

(2) PANACEA-MONGER. This phrase, which the A.E.T. renders °would-be universal reformer°, is °Weltverbesserer° in the original—lit., world improver. While the closest translation might be 'universal reformer,' this does not capture the contemptuously pejorative connotation.

Par. 69

(1) HISTORICAL MOVEMENT. Same as in Par.50/2, which see.
(2) TENETS OF COMMUNISM. See Par.68/1 above.

Par. 70

(1) HISTORICAL CHANGE. In the A.E.T., Engels in effect rewrote this sentence explanatorily to add the statement that social change is the consequence of °the change in historical conditions°. In the course he added °in the past°—quite unnecessarily.

(2) PARAGRAPHING. As noted in Par.68/1, the paragraph breaks in this part of the Manifesto seem choppy. Not only Par.68-69 but especially Par.70-74 seem to be unnecessarily fragmented by breaks. This is not only un-German (see Par. 70 42/1) but disconcerting. Note that the A.E.T. at least consolidated Par.72-73.

Par. 72-74

(1) BOURGEOIS PRIVATE PROPERTY. These three paragraphs, taken together, correct the false impression given in Par.55 (see Par.55/2). The present use of the term °private property°, as in Par.74, became standard in the socialist movement, to differentiate *capitalist* property (surplus-value-producing property) from personal property. (See Par. 80/1.)

(2) PARAGRAPHING. See Par.70/2.

(3) SOME PEOPLE BY OTHER PEOPLE. In Par.73: the A.E.T.'s alteration of this phrase to °the many by the few° no doubt rested on the currency of the latter phrase in the English socialist movement, which in turn stemmed from the popularity of Shelley's poem "The Mask of Anarchy" ("Ye are many—they are few").

Par. 75

(1) PROPERTY AND HARD WORK. See the remarks in Par. 72-74/1 and Par.55/2.

Par. 76

(1) PETTY-BOURGEOIS PROPERTY. In the A.E.T., this phrase is replaced by °property of the petty artisan°, no doubt in order to be more comprehensible to the English public. To be sure, the term °petty-bourgeois° is more inclusive; see Par.44/3.

(2) ABOLISH / DESTROY. The A.E.T. replaced °abolish° with °destroy°, even though the German verb remains the same. Perhaps the reason was that 'destroy' is more objective in connotation.

(3) TO A GREAT EXTENT. The A.E.T. added this saving phrase for the sake of accuracy.

Par. 77

(1) PARAGRAPHING. It would be well to consider this lone sentence as the introduction to Par.78. That there is a paragraphing problem here is indicated by the change noted in Par.78/1.

Par. 78

(1) PARAGRAPHING. Beginning with the 1866 German edition, the next paragraph break (before °Capital is a collective product°...) was shifted one sentence up, that is, to before °To be a capitalist°... The A.E.T. naturally followed this change. The N.E.V. and these Annotations, however, as usual follow the original arrangement, that is, the first edition.

(2) A.E.T. EDITING. There is more than one case of rewording in this paragraph, as a comparison will show; but none affects the meaning.

(3) POSITION / STATUS. The A.E.T. italicized °status° (°Stellung°, position) even though the contrast is between °personal° and °social°; but this may have reflected not emphasis but the use of italics for a foreign (Latin) term.

Par. 79

(1) PARAGRAPHING. As the paragraphing correction (see Par.78/1) indicated, this sentence must be taken together with the last sentence of the preceding paragraph, and the thought is completed with Par.80-81.

(2) COLLECTIVE PRODUCT. The word for °collective° here is °gemeinschaftliches° (common, communal). When it recurs in Par.81 in the phrase °collective° property, the A.E.T. renders it °common° (property). I simply wish to point out that the same word is involved.

Par. 80

(1) PERSONAL PROPERTY. This paragraph, taken together with the next one, explains why the distinction is insisted on between 'private property' and 'personal property,' as in Par.72—74, which see.

Par.81

(1) COLLECTIVE PROPERTY. For the word °collective° or °common°, see Par.79/2.

Par.82

(1) WAGE-LABOR. The ensuing paragraphs on wage-labor, we must remind (see Par.36/1 and Par.37/4), reflect Marx's undeveloped economic theory of 1848, which in this area was still essentially based on Ricardo's political economy. In none of the prefaces which the authors wrote for the Manifesto (1872 on) did they think it necessary to comment on *this* superseded aspect of the document, though other (political) aspects were pointed to as needing revision; nor did Engels attach any footnote on the matter in the A.E.T. or 1890 German edition. The Manifesto did not completely reflect Marx's views on this question even in 1848. There are three writings by Marx in this period that do present his economic views as of the time of writing the Manifesto: *The Poverty of Philosophy* (1847); an 1847 manuscript titled "Wages" (MECW 6,415); and *Wage-Labor and Capital* (based on 1847 lectures, published 1849). In the case of the last-named work, a revised edition was issued by Engels 1891, and it is this revised edition that is usually read; for the original form, see MECW 9:197. Marx began developing his mature theory of wages about a decade after the Manifesto; the best place to read it is in his 1865 lecture *Wages (or Value), Price and Profit.*

Par. 83

(1) PRICE OF WAGE-LABOR. Later, Marx would say "price of labor power"; see Par.37/4.
(2) MINIMUM...SUBSISTENCE. See Par.82/1 above. As the present paragraph shows, Marx at this time accepted Ricardo's view that wages tended to fall absolutely to a subsistence minimum which is *interpreted purely in physiological terms*, that is, as just enough to keep the worker alive. It was this view which, ossified into a crude formula, became Lassalle's so-called Iron Law of Wages (enunciated 1863, after Marx had revised his own views). The ascription of a special Iron Law of Wages to Marx is anachronistic, since the minimum-subsistence theory held by Marx in 1848 was the then orthodox view of the bourgeois economists.
(3) A.E.T. ALTERATIONS. The A.E.T. makes two small changes in the first sentence which seem to be connected with the sense; it adds a couple of words which intensify what is outlived in the Manifesto's economic theory. Instead of merely °necessary° to maintain the

worker's existence, the A.E.T. redoubles the emphasis with °absolutely requisite°. This addition reinforces precisely what was wrong about the minimum-subsistence theory. And instead of °the existence of the worker°, the A.E.T. makes it °bare existence°. Perhaps Engels made these additions quite deliberately to deepen the difference between the 1848 theory and the mature theory, to show where the error lay.

(4) A.E.T. EDITING. In the rest of the paragraph, there are three changes that look like mere editing revisions. (i) In the second sentence, instead of °re-produce°, the A.E.T. expands to °prolong and reproduce°. (ii) In the third sentence, instead of °re-producing°, the A.E.T. expands to °maintenance and reproduction°. (iii) In the fourth sentence, instead of °lives only°, the A.E.T. says °is allowed to live only°. By the way, I have hyphenated °re-produce° only to emphasize that this ('produce again') is the very literal meaning of the German word.

Par. 84

(1) WORKERS' WAY OF LIFE. In the A.E.T.: °the existence of the labourer°. This is an attempt to translate the term in the original, the workers' °Lebensprozess°. The dictionary definition of *Lebensprozess* is 'vital functions,' physiologically speaking; the Manifesto's use is metaphorical. Maybe the current Jargon for it would be 'lifestyle.'

Par. 85—86

(1) INDIVIDUAL, INDIVIDUALITY. The German terms used here are based on the root *person* (°persönlich°, °unpersönlich°, °Persönlichkeit°), except for °active individual° (in the A.E.T.: °living person°), which is °thätige individuum°. It must be understood that in this period terms like 'individualism' were quite pejorative in European languages, especially French (which was *the* language of politics on the Continent); they implied something like egoism or at least the subordination of social to individual interests. Everywhere and always, the meaning of terms with the roots 'individual' and 'person' have been slippery, filled with ideological assumptions. 'Individualism' was a dirty word, the opposite of 'association,' for the Saint-Simonians and for Owen, and all through the nineteenth century popular punditry counterposed 'individualism' to 'socialism,' virtually making the former identical with capitalism. However, the Manifesto makes the following view plain: the bourgeoisie *claims* that its system lets individuality (or 'personalism,' if you wish) flourish, but this is not true, and it is really communism that brings about this good. This argument, then, is not over a pejorative, but over some meaning of 'individuality' (°Persönlichkeit°) that stresses the positive: the flowering of the human persona. This viewpoint was generally alien to the socialisms of the 1840s, though it had been developing in Marx with his *Economic and Philosophic Manuscripts of 1844*. Above all, what the Manifesto stresses is that the bourgeois conception of individualism is a classbound conception, and it implicitly counterposes the individualism made possible by communist society. (This question is taken up again in Par. 91-92; see Par.91/2, Par.92/1 below.)

(2) DEINDIVIDUALIZED. In bourgeois society, said the Manifesto, the °active° [or living] individual' is *unpersönlich*. This last adjective, of course, cannot be carried over literally

252

('impersonal'). I have rendered it °deindividualized°; the A.E.T. says that the °living person...has no individuality.°

Par. 87

(1) FREEDOM. In Par.86 Marx made plain he proposed to criticize not 'freedom' but only *bourgeois* freedom; and the A.E.T. repeated the adjective in order (I suppose) to make this clear. In Par.87 the indictment is leveled: by 'freedom' the bourgeoisie means only its own freedom to exploit untrammeled. About the time Marx started work on the Manifesto, he published an essay on Free Trade explaining that in present-day society that catchword meant "freedom of capital."

> Gentlemen! Do not be deluded by the abstract word Freedom! Whose freedom? Not the freedom of one individual in relation to another, but the freedom of Capital to crush the worker. [MECW 6:463]

The Manifesto did not take up a related subject that Marx devoted much attention to later: the meaning of "free" labor—that is, juridical freedom to sell one's labor power, unlike slave or serf, and "freedom" from ownership of the means of production. (This subject is continued in Par.88/2.) .

Par. 88

(1) HUCKSTERING. While the preceding paragraph spoke of °buying and selling°, this paragraph substitutes a pejorative term (°Schacher°), which I render °huckstering°. The A.E.T. ignored this stratagem.

(2) FREEDOM. See Par.87/1. The present paragraph points to the *historical* roots of the bourgeoisie's self-consciousness as exponent of a sort of freedom. It underlines that bourgeois talk of 'freedom' is not mere demagogy or hypocrisy but real—insofar as it really does free the productive forces from medieval trammels and restrictions, only to impose its own fetters. This is also the point about 'bourgeois freedom' and 'free competition' that Marx will later make in his *Grundrisse* manuscripts:

> This [bourgeois] kind of individual freedom is therefore at the same time the most complete abolition of all individual freedom and the complete subjugation of individuality to social conditions which take the form of objective forces... [*Grundrisse*, 545]

(3) A.E.T. EDITING. The A.E.T.'s editing of the original can be seen at the following points. (i) Where the original said °a meaning in general°, the A.E.T. (which added °in general° to the *preceding* clause) renders it °a meaning, if any°. (ii) The word which I have rendered °burghers° (of the Middle Ages) is °traders° in the A.E.T.; the German here °Bürger° on which see Par.7 (TI)/2 and Par.46/2. (iii) For the A.E.T.'s use of °conditions of

production°, see Par. 33/6b and Par.43/2.

Par. 89

(1) SECOND PERSON. For rhetorical effect, the Manifesto now addresses itself directly to the bourgeoisie. This goes on through Par.99, and then switches back to the third-person form.

(2) PRIVATE PROPERTY. In the present paragraph, it is especially the last sentence that makes clear the subject is exclusively the capitalist form of private property, not simply property in the form of personal possessions. See Par. 72—74/1.

(3) A.E.T. EDITING. Where the original said that private property °exists at all° ("thanks to" etc.), the A.E.T. altered this to °its existence for the few°—a change which makes the thought clearer.

Par. 91

(1) POLITICAL ECONOMY. The formulation in this paragraph is early-Marx; that is, it still reflects the language of the bourgeois economists whom Marx is now studying. For example, the idea that labor is °converted° into °money°, etc. would require some explanation in terms of Marx's later political economy. Also vague is the reference to the bourgeoisie's desire to change °individual property° into 'bourgeois property.' At this point, in apposition to °bourgeois property° the A.E.T. inserted °capital° in a partial effort to bridge the gap.

(2) INDIVIDUAL PROPERTY AND THE INDIVIDUAL. The German original says °persönliche Eigenthum°, but it would be misleading to translate this literally as 'personal property,' which in English suggests a distinction not intended here (cf. Par.55/2, Par.72—74/1). Here °individual property° simply means 'an individual's property.' The term ties up with the statement at the end: the bourgeois thinks that when an individual's property can no longer be used to "confer power over another's labor" (cf. Par.83), then °the individual is abrogated°. The German for °individual° here is °die Person°, not *Individuum*. The word for °abrogated° (°aufgehoben°) is one that is usually rendered 'abolished,' and indeed this suggests that the A.E.T. had good reason for saying °individuality° rather than °the individual°. I have chosen to be more literal simply to suggest alternatives. The bourgeois complains not that the individual person °vanishes° (the A.E.T.'s word) but that the °social power° inhering in his (bourgeois) individuality is done away with. See also Par.93/1.

Par. 92

(1) INDIVIDUAL. Regarding the rendering °individual° for °die Person°, see preceding

254

Par.91/2.

(2) BOURGEOIS / MIDDLE-CLASS. This is a clear case in which the A.E.T. uses °middle-class° (adjective) as a simple synonym for °bourgeois°; see Par.14/5.

(3) ABROGATED. This is the same word noted above, Par.91/2. The A.E.T. rewrote and expanded, doubtless to forestall the idea that the bourgeois would be eliminated physically or bodily; hence °abrogated° swelled up to °swept out of the way, and made impossible°.

Par. 93

(1) PROPERTY. Although this paragraph does not mention the word 'property,' it restates a little more explicitly an idea that has cropped up more than once already: the idea that was later represented by the distinction between 'private property' and 'personal property.' See Par.91/2 and the references given there. Note in particular that °the power to subjugate others' labor°, which plays such a basic role in defining types of property, had been mentioned earlier (Par.83).

(2) SOCIAL PRODUCTS. This means products created socially, by social labor (cf. Par.30/2).

Par. 94—95

(1) BOURGEOIS OBJECTION. The Manifesto replies to the bourgeois argument which assigns the driving force in society to 'private property' by making a point calculated to appeal to workers. But here it does not address itself to the real bourgeois claim behind the objection: that all dynamism in society rests on individual profit-seeking. Of course, refutations of this idea have been one of the major occupations of socialist propaganda. When the Manifesto says that, under capitalism, °those who do acquire do not work°, it is reflecting one of the earliest ideas of the socialist movement, heavily emphasized by Saint-Simon. The crux is what is meant by 'work,' since a typical capitalist especially in Marx's day might well claim to work harder than his employees—at his own job of extracting as much surplus value out of their labor as possible, as well as at the labors of superintendence. Marx's political economy would later explore the categories of 'useful' labor, 'productive' labor, etc.

Par. 96

(1) INTELLECTUAL PRODUCTS. That is, the products of mental labor, insofar as this labor can be disentangled from physical labor. The German word used here, °geistig°, means 'mental,' 'psychological,' 'intellectual,' 'spiritual,' etc.—pertaining to the mind rather than the body. But all this has nothing to do with what are called 'intellectuals' in English: 'intellectual labor' does not mean 'the labor of intellectuals,' and so on. Furthermore, let us note that °intellectual products° may be commodities just like material products; Marx's

political economy applies to intellectual labor as to physical or manual labor, and in fact does not assume that the two are easily separable. (For all this, see KMTR 2, Chap. 16.)

(2) CULTURE. The German word here is °Bildung°, which also means 'education' but is wider in range than any English word. At this point, MECW 6:501 has an editorial footnote which treats the A.E.T.'s rendering °culture° as an alteration from the original. This is an error. In the A.E.T. Engels merely took account of the fact that °Bildung° is used here with a broad meaning. It is quite true that *Bildung* is often translated 'education,' but when we come to the Manifesto's use of 'education' in the specific sense of 'school training' we will find the German word *Erziehung* (see Par. 103—105, Par.133, Pt. 10). Part of the problem is the fact that a word like *Bildung*, in actual use, may waver back and forth within its range of meaning; thus in Par.97 its meaning flows into the idea of 'training'—see Par.97/1.

(3) CLASS CULTURE. The relation of °intellectual products° to °class culture° had been raised glancingly before; cf. Par.26/4, Par.54/5. This problem, the socioeconomic roots of the ideological superstructure in class society, will be pursued in the paragraphs that follow.

Par. 97

(1) CULTURE. See the discussion above, Par.96/2. In passing, there is a play on words perpetrated in this paragraph. °Bildung°, which we have rendered °culture°, is played against °Heranbildung°, which means °upbringing° (in the A.E.T.: °training°). To preserve the word-play, I suppose that °Heranbildung° could be rendered 'acculturation' if sociological jargon were piled on paronomasia.

Par. 98

(1) MANUSCRIPT PAGE. There is a single manuscript page extant of a draft of the Manifesto (see MEW 4:610 or MECW 6:577). It contains an early version of this paragraph, almost identical with the final text. With Marx's deletions given in brackets, here it is:

> But do not quarrel with us by [counterposing] gauging the abolition of bourgeois property in accordance with your bourgeois ideas of freedom, culture, etc.! Your ideas themselves [are what] [prod] [are] [correspond] are products of the [existing] bourgeois relations of production and property, Just as your justice is only the will of your class elevated into law. [A] A will whose content is determined by the material conditions of existence of your class.

(2) SO LONG AS. The A.E.T.'s use of this conjunction (for the German *indem* construction) added a time element which is not in the original, and should have been avoided.

(3) OUR INTENDED. The A.E.T. added °our intended° to °abolition of bourgeois property°—unnecessarily, as far as I can see.

(4) JUSTICE / LAW. In the first sentence, the reference is to bourgeois conceptions of °Recht°. This inclusive German word (lit., right) is variously rendered: justice (system of), law

256

(system or theory of), jurisprudence, legal system, etc. No English term covers exactly the same territory. Here the reference is more to the 'theory of...' than to the 'system of...'

(5) INTENSIVE 'NUR.' In the original, in the second sentence, the use of °only° (°nur°) as an intensive—see the discussion in Par.10/1—occurs only in the second part of the sentence. For good measure the A.E.T. added it also to the first part (using the word °but° in both cases); thus it doubled the possibility of misunderstanding. The claim that Marx viewed bourgeois ideas as only, merely, exclusively, and solely excrescences of class interests, without any autonomous content, later had to be rebutted by Engels in a number of letters to puzzled correspondents. It is not impossible that the later prevalence of this claim rested partly on the intensive *nur* in this paragraph, since so many authorities on Marxism achieved their expertise by a careful reading of the Manifesto.

(6) CONDITIONS OF...PRODUCTION, ETC. For the A.E.T.'s use of °conditions° instead of °relations° see Par.33/6b and Par.43/2.

(7) A.E.T. EXPANSION. Where the original spoke of the °content° of the bourgeoisie's class °will°, the A.E.T. expanded °content° into °essential character and direction°. This amounts to an explanatory interpolation.

(8) MATERIAL / ECONOMIC. Referring to the °conditions of existence'° of the bourgeoisie, the originals adjective °material° was changed by the A.E.T. to °economical° (antiquated form of 'economic'). This is not accurate, strictly speaking, since 'material' is more inclusive than 'economic.' Perhaps the motive was to avoid the bad connotation, especially to English ears, of 'material' or 'materialistic,' etc.; but then one must wonder why the A.E.T. did not make the change consistently. In any case, this change was inadvisable.

Par. 99

(1) MANUSCRIPT PAGE. See Par.98/1. This draft of the Manifesto has an early version of Par.99. With Marx's deletions given in brackets, here it is, comprising two paragraphs :

> [Your] The self-serving conception of transforming [the] your [bourgeois] relations of production and property from historical [and merely] transitory relations corresponding to a certain [maturity of the] stage in the development of production [corresponding to the forces of] into eternal laws of nature and reason—this conception you share with all defunct ruling classes! What you perceive about feudal property you no longer perceive about bourgeois property.*

This passage is followed by a sentence fragment that has been entirely stricken:

---

* The translation in MECW 6:577f indicates that a somewhat revised decipherment of the manuscript is being used as compared with the text in MEW 4:610; but the differences are in details that need not concern us. This remark applies to the other citations from the manuscript page.

And yet you cannot deny the fact that [in the course of bourgeois] with the course of development of industry the onesided, on

There is a final paragraph on this page, about which see Par.150/3.

(2) SELF-SERVING CONCEPTION. The German adjective is °interessirte° (affected by self-interest). The A.E.T.'s °selfish°, a common rendering, was perhaps a shade more moralistic. The A.E.T.'s °misconception° (instead of °conception°) made explicit what is implied.

(3) A.E.T. EXPANSION. The A.E.T. rewrote and expanded a great deal of the first sentence. Its assumption, once again, must have been that the English public would not understand the term 'relations of production [etc.]'; it regularly substituted 'conditions of production (etc.],' as in Par.33/6b, Par.43/2 and elsewhere. In the present paragraph it used not 'conditions' but °social forms springing from° etc. It also expanded °transitory° into a whole clause, in which the word °relations° was inserted in a rewritten context.

(4) DEFUNCT. Where the original referred to past ruling classes as °defunct° (°untergegangenen°, perished or ruined), the A.E.T. merely said they °preceded you° (the bourgeoisie). I suppose this correction was introduced with the consideration that the ruling class preceding the bourgeoisie in (say) England was not yet defunct at all, especially in the governmental machinery, even though it had yielded dominant socioeconomic power to the bourgeoisie. Nor was the prebourgeois ruling class defunct in Germany in 1848, where the bourgeoisie had not won political power at all.

(5) ANTIQUITY. The A.E.T.'s °ancient property° may be misunderstood. The original was not referring to ancient or primitive times in general but to the classical antiquity of Greek and Roman society.

(6) A.E.T. EDITING. In the last sentence the A.E.T. introduced some flourishes not in the original, including °clearly°; °admit°; °forbidden°.

Par. 100

(1) SECOND PERSON. With this paragraph the Manifesto drops the second-person form of address begun in Par.89; see Par.89/1.

(2) FAMILY. In Par.100-102, the 'abolition' of the family is viewed in two different ways: in Par.100, as an °intention° (A.E.T.: °proposal°) of the Communists; in Par. 102, as a prediction. Back in Par.22 the family had been °reduced...to a purely money relationship°; in Par.54 the proletarian family had "nothing" in common with the bourgeois family. Moreover, more than once in this period Marx and Engels had already spoken of the abolition or dissolution of the family as an accomplished fact or an ongoing process. These different formulations of a critical attitude toward the family institution had been common among socialists from the beginning, or even before the beginning (for Plato and Campanella, see Par.106-111/1). Rejection of the family institution had already reached a high point in Fourier, who advocated a "new family" in the form of a compulsory amalgamation of families into a communal living group. Involved is a swirl of issues, with some confusion

258

among the following questions: sexual morality, status of women, forms of marriage (and divorce), and various kinds of family problems. In Marx's first period (1843-1848) he wrote freely about 'abolition' and 'dissolution' in this connection: for example, in his fourth Thesis on Feuerbach, which opines that the family "must be destroyed in theory and in practice"; in the *German Ideology*, which saw the family as one of the primary bases of private property and "slavery," since "wife and children are the slaves of the husband." Here too he (or Engels) recognized a basic gulf between the 'bourgeois family' (which was being dissolved) and the family among the proletariat, "where the family is *actually* abolished" (MECW 5:180). Engels too had written in broad terms about the "dissolution of the family" by the English factory system as early as 1843 (see MECW 3:424); and in his book *Condition of the Working Class in England* he had repeatedly announced the same dissolution not only among the proletariat but in general terms—a sentiment he could have found among the Owenites. But it is of interest that in his two drafts for the Manifesto he inserted not a word proposing, predicting, or positing the 'abolition of the family'—nothing like what Marx put in. What Marx was advocating in the Manifesto is not altogether clear from a reading of Par.100-102. The 'proposal' in Par.100 was put in the form of a bourgeois accusation or claim; in Par.101, the alleged nonexistence of the proletarian family was hedged by the vague qualifier 'in completely developed form'; and while the prediction in Par.102 of the vanishment of both bourgeois and proletarian family is brash enough, there is no hint of what is supposed to replace it. In any case, all of this rhetoric about the 'abolition (or dissolution) of the family,' which was rife among socialists, was characteristic only of early Marx and was obviously not thought through to a conclusion. For Marx's later view, see the summary passage in *Capital* (Chap. 15, Sec. 9): modern industry, by drawing women into productive life "outside the domestic sphere" "creates a new economic foundation for a higher form of the family and of the relations between the sexes"; the "Teutonic-Christian form of the family" is not final; and so on—a viewpoint further expounded by Engels in his *Origin of the Family*.

Par. 101

(1) FAMILY. See the discussion in Par.100/2.

(2) COMPLETELY DEVELOPED FORM. See Par.100/2 for my opinion that this qualifier is essentially a way of hedging. The statement actually says that the 'bourgeois family' exists only for the bourgeoisie—which is so much a tautology that it scarcely needs the qualification. What is the °completely developed form° of the bourgeois family? Since this formulation does not recur in Marx, it is hard to say what content it had, if any. My opinion is that the Manifesto's formulations about the family mainly reflect the contemporaneous swirl of the socialistic ferment of ideas on the issue-complex of sex/marriage/family/women—a set of problems which Marx and Engels thought through only later.

(3) PROLETARIAN FAMILYLESSNESS. Where the original referred to the °enforced familylessness° of proletarians, the A.E.T. made this the °practical absence of the family° among proletarians. The insertion of °practical° did a bit to soften and weaken the obviously exaggerated claim. Of course, as mentioned, it had been Engels' *Condition of the Working Class in England* that had encouraged such claims, but (as mentioned in Par.100/2) by 1847 Engels

did not repeat this language in his drafts for the Manifesto. For another reference to the proletarian family along the lines of the present paragraph, see Par.105; see also Par.188.

Par. 102

(1) FAMILY. See Par.100/2, which points out that the 'abolition' or 'dissolution' of the family is here presented as a prediction. What the prediction is, exactly, is not very clear. The "complement" of the bourgeois family, according to the preceding paragraph, is proletarian familylessness: is it this that is predicted to vanish, or is it the proletarian family? In either case, why is this vanishment the necessary precedent (or cause? or precondition?) of the vanishment of the bourgeois family? Or should this relationship be ignored in favor of the second statement, that °both will disappear with the disappearance of capital°? But for the reason given in Par.101/2 I do not think these are serious problems.

Par. 103

(1) EXPLOITATION OF CHILDREN BY PARENTS. This subject was further developed by Marx in *Capital*, I (Chap. 15, Sec. 9). It was indeed this subject that led to the passage mentioned in Par.100/2 above.

(2) PARAGRAPHING. From the German edition of 1866 on, a paragraph break was introduced before °But, you say.° The A.E.T. followed this revision.

(3) EDUCATION OF CHILDREN. By °social education° was meant the assumption by society of the responsibility for educating every child, as against the view that this task belonged exclusively to the parents (and their church). °Social education° did not *necessarily* mean state-controlled education, though it usually implied at least state-financed education; there were differences on these points among leftists and others. Engels probably absorbed his 1845 views of the question from the English working-class movement, which (as he reported in his book on England) "has repeatedly demanded of Parliament a system of strictly secular public education" (MECW 4:408; see also 253f). In his first draft for the Manifesto, he said that a democratic government would take care of "educating all children at the expense of the state" and "in state establishments" (MECW 6:102). In his *Principles of Communism*, this education would take place "in national institutions and at the expense of the nation," and would be "combined with production" (MECW 6:351). At this time (1847) Marx may have taken a more suspicious attitude toward this common socialist demand (see MECW 6:427). In any case, he does not raise this demand in the present paragraph, which mainly defends the right of "society" to supplant the parents as educator. However, he will return to the demand in Par.133, Pt. 10, which see.

Par. 104

(1) A.E.T. EDITING. In the first sentence, the differences between original and A.E.T. seem to be purely verbal. In the second sentence, the original's °impact° is replaced by the A.E.T.'s °intervention°, and the A.E.T. adds °seek to°: all changes that do not affect the

meaning.

(2) ITS CHARACTER. The A.E.T. makes clear that the antecedent of °its° is °impact° (or °intervention,° in the A.E.T. version).

(3) 'A RULING CLASS' OR 'THE RULING CLASS'? The first edition of 1848 said that the Communists wanted to °wrest education from the influence of a ruling class°—which means: from the influence of any ruling class, including presumably the victorious proletariat. The second edition of that year, the so-called thirty-page edition, changed this formulation to °influence of the ruling class°—which, in the context, is likely to be interpreted as referring to the existing ruling class. According to Andréas' table, the 1866 edition went back to the wording of the first edition, but he does not record what happened in the subsequent editions published during Marx's and Engels' lifetime. The text in MEW presents only the version of the second edition, without even an editorial note. The A.E.T. also used this formulation, as did the Laura (French) versions; but it is of interest to note that the Macfarlane translation of 1850 said, "rescue education from the influence of a ruling class."

(4) INFLUENCE OF RULING CLASS. Since this paragraph does not make a specific proposal on education, it is not clear what exactly is supposed to °wrest [or rescue] education from the influence of a [or the] ruling class.° Perhaps the assumption, going back to Par.102, is that capitalism has disappeared as a precondition for society's assumption of responsibility for education.

Par. 105

(1) CLAPTRAP. This expression of the A.E.T.'s is much stronger and more emotive than the original's °phrases.°

(2) INTIMATE / HALLOWED. The original's adjective °intimate° was changed by the A.E.T. to the more contemptuous-ironic °hallowed°. As for the form °co-relation° in the A.E.T., there was no good reason for it as against the simple form, °relation(s)°.

(3) FAMILY. For the references to °family ties,° see the discussion in Par.101/3. For the next reference to abolition of the family, see Par.188.

Par. 106-111

(1) COMMUNITY OF WOMEN. Advocacy of some sort of 'community of wives,' or holding of wives in common (not polygamy), was associated not with any prominent nineteenth-century communist but with Plato (in the *Republic*, for the Guardian class) and with Campanella's utopia *The City of the Sun*; also with some views of primitive-communal tribal relations. In his *Economic and Philosophic Manuscripts of 1844* Marx had associated it with "crude communism," which he denounced as the "infinite degradation" in which woman is conceived simply as spoils, etc. (See MECW 3:294f, where however no target is named.) Engels' two drafts of the Manifesto likewise included repudiations of the notion that a "community of women" was associated with communism; see his first draft (Ques. 20, MECW 6:102) and his *Principles of Communism* (Ques. 21, MECW 6:354). In the Manifesto,

I suspect, the issue is introduced so prominently not because it was then a big issue among leftists but mainly to turn the tables on the bourgeois propagandists.

(2) WIFE AS INSTRUMENT OF PRODUCTION. Marx's 1844 manuscripts (see the preceding point) had already attacked "the *community of women*, in which a woman becomes a piece of *communal* and *common* property." This led to the dictum that the "relation of man to woman...reveals the extent to which man's *natural* behavior has become *human*."

(3) A.E.T. EDITING. There are several places in these paragraphs where the A.E.T. engaged in some rewriting for the sake of sharper or more emphatic language, but with little or no effect on the meaning. In Par.109, the change from °highly moral horror° to the A.E.T.'s °virtuous indignation° is only literary. In Par.111, °a community of wives° becomes °a system of wives in common° (which is certainly clearer); °official and frank° becomes °openly legalised°; °official and unofficial° becomes °public and private°; and so on.

(4) BOURGEOIS MARRIAGE. Although the family institution has by now been discussed more than once, the only direct reference to °marriage° as such occurs in Par.111. The point made has to do with its present-day hypocrisy and (in terms of *tu quoque*) its immorality, but there is no indication that an institutional change is proposed. Engels' *Principles of Communism* had raised two other aspects: (a) sexual morality in general, putting forth the "purely private relation" principle; and (b) the private-property foundation of bourgeois marriage (see MECW 6:354).

Par. 112

(1) FATHERLAND / COUNTRY. In Par.112 and Par.113, where the original spoke of the °Vaterland°, the A.E.T. said °country°, °countries°. This was an unfortunate choice, and has helped to muddy the waters ever since. °Fatherland° had, and has, political-emotive reverberations that go far beyond °country°. For one thing, °country° is a fact; °fatherland° is a state of mind. The Macfarlane translation caught this, with some exaggeration, rendering it 'patriotism' in Par.112, and 'Fatherland' in Par.113. French translations have no difficulty: they make it *patrie*. It is confusing to be told that you have °no country° (as in Par.113 in the A.E.T.) and then reminded that, well, yes, there are such things you have to take into account after all.

(2) ABOLISH NATIONALITY. The word °nationality° does suggest the juridical fact represented by °country°, and it will be noted, below, that workers are not told they have no nationality. On the contrary, the paragraphs below (which see) go about defining the workers' relationship to °nationality° somewhat more carefully than the swinging dismissal of °Fatherland°. Totally negative attitudes toward national differences were by no means new or unknown on the left; besides the long history of ideas about a world federation of states and international amalgamations, there was the famous example of Anacharsis Cloots, the Citizen of the World, in the French Revolution. In fact, it was the growth of modern nationalism that was enrooting *new* narrow ideas about Fatherland and nationality in a world that had long been under the impress of a medieval sort of cosmopolitan Catholicism; antinationalism was not a wild new idea. But in the Manifesto Marx would not have been interested in simply echoing the utopian visions of world comity that were already well

known, in line with his strong reaction in general against utopian dreaming. In Par.112-117, he was interested in counterposing class lines to national lines, class struggle to national struggle, not in visions of ecumenical reconciliation. For the state of mind of the socialist left in the forties, one should read Engels' 1845 article "The Festival of Nations in London," for its scorn of bourgeois ideologists' "fraternization of nations," their fanciful "abrogation of nationalities," their phrases about "perpetual peace" (through Free Trade, for example). Here he argued that the bourgeoisies of different countries "can never transcend nationality"—"Only the proletarians can destroy nationality" because they have common interests, enemies, struggles; hence "their whole disposition and movement is essentially humanitarian, antinationalist." (MECW 6:6.)

Par. 113

(1) NO FATHERLAND / COUNTRY. See Par.112/1. The target is patriotism, that is, nationalism in a pejorative context. The nation is taken primarily as the arena of struggle. The dictum °The workers have no Fatherland° had a limited meaning for Marx, as we see in these paragraphs' series of qualifications; but for a different sort of political animal the question existed on a more abstract plane. It had a special future in the anarchist movement (which refused to "recognize" the state anyway), and reached its apogee in the French "wild man," Gustave Hervé, who became notorious for his *antipatriotisme*—until his shrill rejection of national distinctions flipflopped onto its other side to become an equally wild-eyed social-patriotic chauvinism in World War I. Hervé liked to quote the Manifesto, of course, but only the words that said "Les ouvriers n'ont pas de patrie." In 1866 Marx himself encountered the ultimatistic "abolition" of nationality in fantasy when French Proudhonists (Lafargue then among them) told the International's General Council that (as Marx reported)

all nationalities and even nations were "antiquated prejudices."... [They expected that] the whole world waits until the French are ripe for a social revolution. Then they will demonstrate the experiment to us, and the rest of the world...will follow suit...

The English laughed very much when I began my speech by saying that our friend Lafargue and others, who had done away with nationalities, had spoken "*French*" to us, i.e., a language which nine-tenths of the audience did not understand. I also suggested that by the negation of nationalities he appeared, quite unconsciously, to understand their absorption by the model French nation. [Letter, June 20, 1866]

The last sentence explained part of the meaning of Hervéism.

(2) NATIONAL CLASS. The point that the nation is the political *arena* of struggle had already been made, perhaps better, in Par.57, which see. The concept of the °national class°—which the A.E.T. rendered °leading class of the nation°—was a Hegelian one, which Engels rightly assumed would not be accessible to the English audience. A °national class° was one which, in a given historical conjuncture, represented the historic tasks and interests of the whole nation. To Hegel, for example, the Prussian bureaucracy was the "universal

class" *par excellence* since it took care of the generalized communal interest of the entire polity. By 1843 Marx had revised Hegel by rejecting the bureaucracy for this position and nominating the proletariat (see KMTR 1, Chap. 3). The proletariat would °constitute itself as the nation° by coming to power. (The A.E.T., by the way, cleverly gave this an extra--Hegelian meaning by simply italicizing the word °the°.) For more on the content of this conception of the proletariat as the °national class,° see KMTR 2:70-72.

Par. 114

(1) NATIONAL DIVISIONS AND ANTAGONISMS. From our modern hindsight, this paragraph was onesided in speaking only of the cosmopolitanizing effects of the bourgeoisification of the world. The *German Ideology* had already said more: "while the bourgeoisie of each nation still retained separate national interests, large-scale industry created a class which in all nations has the same interest and for which nationality is already dead" (MECW 5:73). In Par.54, the Manifesto had claimed that modern bourgeois social conditions "have stripped him (the proletarian] of all national character," thereby (as in so many other Manifesto passages) stating tendencies as accomplished facts, without also investigating countervailing forces. But the important thing about this entire section, to the movement for which the Manifesto spoke, was not its apparent claims about the level reached by proletarian class-consciousness, but something else: the attitude toward °national divisions and antagonisms° which it preached, not what it predicted or portrayed.

Par. 115

(1) NATIONAL DIVISIONS UNDER PROLETARIAN RULE. See the last remarks, under Par.114/1. In the present paragraph the Manifesto speaks in terms of continuation of a trend. Engels' two Manifesto drafts had said nothing about nationality or national divisions in present society, but he had asked: "Will nationalities continue to exist under communism?" He answered that the nationalities won to communism would tend to "merge with one another" as the private-property foundation was superseded (MECW 6:103, 354). The second sentence of Par.115 recalls Engels' Question 19 in *Principles of Communism*: "Will it be possible for this revolution to take place in one country alone?" The answer was a flat "No," followed by a summary of the way in which world bourgeois development had made all countries interdependent; the communist revolution will "be no merely national one," but "a worldwide revolution...worldwide in scope," indeed "taking place simultaneously" in the major advanced countries though at different rates. (The 1848 revolution answered this description pretty closely.) In comparison, Marx's formulation in the Manifesto was quite cautious. In his *Critique of the Gotha Program* (1875) Marx referred back to the Manifesto's treatment of the national framework as "the immediate arena of its [the proletariat's] struggle" (referring especially to Par.57), but he found that the Gotha program was defective in internationalism because it had "not a word...*about the international functions* of the German working class." This attacks the Gotha program's failure to put forward the need for

international °united action at least of the civilized countries° (to use the Manifesto's words), such as a revolutionary International.

Par. 116

(1) EXPLOITATION OF NATIONS. Marx no doubt had traditional colonialism in mind here.

Par. 117

(1) PARAGRAPHING. The decision of the A.E.T. to merge this paragraph with Par.116 seems to be its own peculiarity, not a feature of any German edition. The merger may make it seem that Par.117 is a conclusion from Par.116; the separate paragraphing makes them independent points.

(2) WAR. Even if the Manifesto's date were not known, the fact that would place it in the early part of its century is this: this passage is the only reference to the problem of war, and a glancing one at that.

Par. 118

(1) DETAILED DISCUSSION. The A.E.T. turned this into °serious examination°: but isn't the Manifesto's examination 'serious'? It sounds like a case of apophasis. But the Manifesto *had* made some 'serious' remarks on "laws, morality, religion" as bourgeois ideas, in Par.54.

(2) RELIGION. Although Par.54 had called religion a "bourgeois prejudice," and in the present paragraph °religious...standpoints° are treated disrespectfully, the Manifesto stopped short of any formal rejection of religion as such or of any avowal of atheism, as was common in communist circles at the time. Engels' two Manifesto drafts had gone further, in answering the question, "Do Communists reject the existing religions?" He answered that they do, and that communism will make "all existing religions superfluous and abrogate [or supersede] them." (MECW 6:103) The repeated use of "*existing* religions" obviously left the door open for *new* religions, probably as a concession to some wing of the movement, such as the Weitlingites. Marx and Engels were, by this time, thorough atheists themselves, but they already seem to have adopted the practice which they stressed even more in later years: atheism was not to be made a party platform plank, a programmatic requirement of the movement.

Par. 119-121

(1) MATERIALIST CONCEPTION OF HISTORY. These paragraphs constitute Marx's third more or less formal statement of his new view of historical social change. There

had been a short explanation in his *Poverty of Philosophy* (1847), but it had first been set forth in the unpublished *German Ideology*. The Manifesto's paragraphs were no doubt based on this work, even using some of its language. In his Manifesto preface of 1883 Engels—after a concise statement of the theory—stressed that "this basic thought belongs solely and exclusively to Marx." This was an exaggeration, underplaying his own role; and in the preface to the A.E.T. he stated the case more accurately. Here he referred to his *Condition of the Working Class in England* (which would have been path-breaking by itself if Marx had never lived) but reported that in the spring of 1845, when he met Marx in Brussels, Marx had the conception completely worked out.

(2) MATERIAL. In Par.119, this word was explanatorily added by the A.E.T.: °conditions of life° (or conditions of existence) became °conditions of his material existence°. Here Marx used °life° to mean real, actual life as against ideas and intellectualizations about reality; hence, while the word °material° guides the reader to the meaning, it may somewhat circumscribe it if interpreted narrowly. However, the A.E.T.'s clarification was justified by other uses of °material° in the Manifesto. But in Par.121, where the same phrase °conditions of life° occurs again in the same way, the A.E.T. did not add anything.

(3) INTELLECTUAL PRODUCTION. In Par.120: for the meaning of °intellectual° in this connection, see Par.96/1.

(4) RULING IDEAS. This aphoristic statement in Par. 120 had previously been written, in very similar terms, in the *German Ideology* (MECW 5:59). But this work had not been published. The A.E.T. gave an extra notch of emphasis to the statement when it changed °an age° to °each age.° We may also note that the first sentence of Par.120, a rhetorical question, was left without a question mark in the original edition of 1848.

(5) INTENSIVE 'NUR.' See Par.10/1 for the problem. In the original (Par.120) the intensive use of °but° (translating °nur°) occurs in the aphoristic statement on °The ruling ideas...° Fortunately the A.E.T. dropped it. In 1848 Marx did not suspect he would be accused of believing that ideas had no autonomy whatever but were "merely reflections" of material factors. (For a convenient assemblage of Engels' later letters on the subject, see *MESW* 3:483-506.)

(6) EVEN PACE. As a translation of the phrase °gleichen Schritt°, the A.E.T.'s °even pace° was certainly justifiable, word for word. But the German form is a set phrase, not a scientific differentiation of 'even' (or 'equal') pace as against uneven or approximate pace. Unfortunately the literal meaning of even pace falls in with the claim that Marx held ideas to be "mere reflections" with no life of their own, attached to material factors like shadows. This is a convenience for critics who search Marx's every word for evidence of what they know in advance must be there, viz., evidence of a woodenheaded theory about the automatic-mechanical reflection of material by ideological factors.

Par. 122

(1) LAST THROES. The word °last° in this A.E.T. expression does not reflect anything in the original; the A.E.T. merely used a set phrase.

(2) ENLIGHTENMENT / RATIONALIST. In changing °the ideas of the

Enlightenment° to °rationalist ideas,° the A.E.T. used the English term then popular on the left for *antisupernaturalism*, modulating into atheism. The Laura (French) versions likewise appealed to 'national memory, rendering it *les idées philosophiques*, that is, the ideas of the *philosophes*.

(3) SPHERE OF CONSCIENCE. The last word °conscience° appears to be the result of a printer's error in the 1848 editions; the A.E.T.'s word °knowledge° (in °domain of knowledge°) should be accepted. The correction was made beginning with the 1866 German edition. The printer's error was probably caused by the use of °Gewissens° (°conscience°) at the beginning of this sentence; at the end of the sentence the word should have been °Wissens° (°knowledge°)—a bit of a play on words. But the 1848 printer made it °Gewissens° the second time too.

Par. 123-124

(1) QUOTE MARKS. The quote marks were added to the German editions beginning with 1872. The omission of such quote marks has always been commoner in German than in English, and so I have felt justified in adding them to the translation. Some reprints of the A.E.T. (for example, in *MESW* 1:125) place quote marks at the *end* of Par.123 also, but this violates the sense, since Par.123-124 form a continuous statement.

(2) A.E.T. OMISSION: POLITICAL. In Par.123: the list of °ideas° in the first sentence includes °political° and ends with °etc°. The A.E.T. omits °political° and drops the °etc°. But in the second sentence which gives a corresponding list, °politics° makes a reappearance in the A.E.T., only it becomes °political science° (by which the A.E.T. no doubt means political theory in general). Hence the omission of °political° in the first sentence must have been inadvertent.

(3) A.E.T. EDITING. In Par.123: (i) The A.E.T.'s °Undoubtedly° was moved to the fore; the German °allerdings° (which I rendered °to be sure°) was further down in the sentence. (ii) The broad-ranged German word °Recht° (°jurisprudence° or °law°) is explained in Par.98/4. In Par.124: (iii) The A.E.T. added °all°, twice, before °religion° and °morality°. This did not affect the meaning but it underlined the idea of atheism. (iv) The original's °historical development° was changed in the A.E.T. to °historical experience°.

Par. 126

(1) ALL PAST CENTURIES. Regarding this statement (in the A.E.T., about °all past ages°), take into consideration the qualification explained by Engels in his second footnote to the A.E.T.; see Par.7/1.

(2) FORMS OF CONSCIOUSNESS / GENERAL IDEAS. The A.E.T. replaced °forms of consciousness° with °general ideas°, no doubt to lighten the burden on unphilosophical Anglo-Saxon brainpans. The original German itself badly needed amendment, because of its awkward threefold repetition of the word °forms°. The 1890 German edition simplified the reading, cutting out one of the °Formen°, so that the reading was as follows: "...moves in

certain common forms, in forms of consciousness which pass away..."

Par. 127

(1) RELATIONS. I have remarked more than once on the A.E.T.'s apparent reluctance to use the term 'property *relations*,' 'production *relations*,' etc. where the German for 'relations' is *Verhältnisse*; see Par.33/6b, Par.43/2. All the more reason to note that here °Eigenthums--Verhältnisse° does become °property relations°.

Par. 129

(1) SEEN ABOVE. Seen where? where did the Manifesto refer previously to the idea of this paragraph: Marx was perhaps referring to Par.58 (see Par.58/1) and to Par.67 ("conquest of political power by the proletariat").

(2) THE TERM 'DEMOCRACY.' In 1848 this term had a specific political meaning which not only became obsolete by the end of the century but was completely forgotten, so that later discussions and disputes over this paragraph of the Manifesto became increasingly irrelevant. These disputants thought that 'democracy' meant what we would today call a democratic regime with voting rights, with more or less free speech, etc.; for the history of the term, see KMTR 1:84-87 and 2:176n, 211f. Engels' two Manifesto drafts show the meaning of the term very clearly, and also throw light on the source of the Manifesto statement. Engels, by 1847, was writing repeatedly in favor of forming a class alliance under proletarian leadership comprising also the small peasantry and the petty-bourgeoisie (see Par.28/3, Par.52/3). This class alliance in movement was *the Democracy*, or the Democratic movement; its goal, called democracy or Democratic government, was the winning of governmental power *by the coalition*, which would establish a 'democratic constitution' (used in the same sense). Engels argued at this time (for example, in *Principles of Communism*) that the Democracy in power, inaugurating a 'democratic constitution,' would bring about *proletarian* rule "directly or indirectly"—outside of England, indirectly through a series of radical onslaughts against capital possibly leading to a "second fight." In other words, in this conception the victory of the Democracy would be a stage in a pattern of 'permanent revolution' *leading to* proletarian power at a rate depending on the level of social conditions and of the proletariat, *but not beginning with proletarian rule*. In Engels' draft, the transition at first is de-emphasized, as in the first sentence answering Question 18:

> In the first place it [the revolution] will inaugurate a *democratic constitution* and thereby, directly or indirectly, the political rule of the proletariat.

The stages appear as Engels explains the word "indirectly." This, then, is the background to the formulations in the Manifesto about 'democracy.' It is especially important for the next point.

(3) WINNING OF DEMOCRACY. In the original (leaving the A.E.T. aside for the

moment) the words °the winning of democracy° (°die Erkämpfung der Demokratie°) were set in apposition with the proletariat's winning of proletarian rule: what did this mean? The words are cryptic, even in 1848 terms. In my opinion, this cryptic expression of 1848 was Marx's way of *intentionally* avoiding a definite statement on a moot question. What these words would have meant if written by Engels is perfectly clear, as explained in the preceding point: °the winning of Democracy° would have meant the victory of the Democratic bloc of classes, but not (yet) proletarian rule except perhaps for England. *But Marx did not at this time accept this perspective of Engels'*. The fact that he wrote nothing accepting this idea might be indecisive, but besides, as we have seen, the Manifesto left no room for the class alliance with the petty-bourgeoisie etc. which Engels called the Democracy. To be sure, there is no record of his opposing Engels' view, either. In fact, as far as one can tell, Marx's position when he sat down to write the Manifesto was that he had not yet adopted a programmatic view on this question. In this sense, the enigmatic four words of the Manifesto were a way of hedging, not of making a statement.

In the Manifesto, the ensuing paragraph, Par.130, starts off immediately with an account of what would be done by the proletariat's °political rule°, including a ten-point program of demands. But in the *Principles of Communism*, on the contrary, Engels had stated clearly that the ensuing program of measures and demands were proposed for execution *by the Democracy*. There is nothing in the Manifesto that allows for a transitional period of Democratic power; the transitional period envisaged is simply the first steps of proletarian rule. As mentioned in Par.28/3, immediately upon the outbreak of the 1848 revolution, Marx fully adopted Engels' perspective and went through the revolutionary period with it; but this was not the end of the problem. For the epilogue, see KMTR 2, Chap. 10.

(4) BATTLE OF DEMOCRACY. In terms of the preceding explanation, the A.E.T.'s translation °to win the battle of democracy° has the sole merit of being virtually as cryptic as the original. No one knows, for example, what °the battle of democracy° meant, and so anyone could interpret it to suit. Does it mean 'battle for democracy'? This is how it has been read more often than not, especially with the latter-day meaning of 'democracy,' which could not have been intended in 1848.

Engels left one legacy that may help, *if* he had a hand in this part of the Laura (French) version No. 3, which was published as "revised by Frederick Engels." The first two Laura versions had rendered the passage as "la domination de la démocratie," which was as ambiguous as anything else. But Laura-3 was quite different: "la conquête du pouvoir public par la démocratie" (the conquest of state power by [the] democracy). Marked changes like this, I think, must have been due to Engels' suggestions. In this translation we have the *only* version that reflected the 1848 meaning of °winning of democracy°. But it cannot gainsay the fact that Marx put a veil of haze over the concept at a point in time when he was still uncertain or opposed.

(5) REVISED A.E.T. OF 1932. In this version (see Part I, chapter 28, section 3), the expression °to win the battle of democracy° was changed to the following: °to establish democracy°. (This rendering was taken from the Pauls' translation.)

Par. 130

(1) POLITICAL RULE. As mentioned (Par.129/3), this paragraph makes clear immediately that it is discussing the course to be followed *after* the proletarian conquest of power, executed by a workers' state.

(2) BIT BY BIT / BY DEGREES. One of the odd features of later Revisionist (Bernsteinian) argumentation was its persistent effort to justify reformist "gradualism" by this paragraph's reference to gradual measures (°nach und nach°), although the Bernsteinians were talking about transforming capitalism 'bit by bit' without any revolutionary conquest of power at all. See point 1 above.

(3) HANDS OF THE STATE. The Manifesto (see also Par. 133, Pt. 5-7) was one of the few writings in which Marx spoke in terms of *state* ownership of the means of production. He usually left open the question of the forms of social ownership, which might include workers' associations and cooperatives. The emphasis in the Manifesto reflected the emphasis in the movement for which it was written at the time. State ownership (by a workers' state) was, to be sure, one form of social ownership for Marx.

(4) THE 1872 CODICIL. In their preface to the 1872 German edition of the Manifesto, Marx and Engels listed a number of points in which "here and there some detail might be improved" in the original document. One of these points was the following:

> One thing especially was proved by the [Paris] Commune, viz., that "the working class cannot simply lay hold of the ready-made state machinery, and wield it for its own purposes."

The preface then referred the reader to the source of the quote, namely, the *Civil War in France*. This codicil was not attached directly to any particular paragraph of the Manifesto, but it probably belongs under Par.130. The general problem is that of revolutionary strategy immediately after a conquest of power; what Par.130-131 discuss is solely economic policy—the codicil added a basic political consideration.

Par. 131

(1) DESPOTIC. A common usage in political writings of the time, this adjective was a stronger form of 'coercive,' 'enforced by stern measures.' Cf. Par.38/2.

(2) CONDITIONS OF PRODUCTION. In spite of Par.127/1 (which see), the A.E.T. is now back again with its reluctance to use the term '*relations* of production,' etc.

(3) TRANSITIONAL MEASURES (PROGRAM). 'Transitional' is the term (already in use by 1848) for the type of measures described in this paragraph: that is, programmatic measures which point *ahead* of themselves; which, as they are put into operation, compel further steps, which °drive beyond their own limits° (A.E.T.: °outstrip themselves°). Now, as later, the movement usually spoke of either 'minimum' demands (immediate reforms) or 'maximum' demands (involving socialism), but 'transitional' demands or measures do not fit under either category—they are intended to begin with immediate measures that however

°necessitate further inroads upon the old social order°. This last clause was indeed inserted into the Manifesto itself by the A.E.T., which thereby inserted an explanatory note into the body of the text. Engels' *Principles of Communism* had already described this type of measures, but it was speaking of the program of a Democratic regime:

> Of course, all these measures cannot be carried out at once. But one will always lead on to the other. Once the first radical onslaught upon private ownership has been made, the proletariat will see itself compelled to go always further... [MECW 6:351]

Marx referred back to this program of measures, in a letter of 1881, with an interesting remark: "transition measures which, as likewise noted in the Manifesto, are and must be self-contradictory" (that is, beset by internal contradiction). This referred, with a Hegelian reminiscence, to the sort of "contradictions" that solve their °inadequate and untenable° character by the fact that they must °drive beyond° it in practice—like a mountain climber who takes an 'untenable' step that cannot be held, only 'outstripped.'

(4) TRANSFORMING THE WHOLE MODE OF PRODUCTION. Here, in the last phrase of this paragraph, is the *only* statement tying up the ten-point program (Par.133) with the goal of a socialist reorganization of the economic system and the abolition of capitalism. See below, Par.133 (General)/2 regarding the fact that none of the ten points themselves call for such basic anticapitalist measures.—For the word °Umwälzung°, which the N.E.V. renders °transforming° while the A.E.T. makes it °revolutionising°, see Par.17/1.

Par. 132

(1) QUALIFICATIONS. The following comments apply to the ten-point program as a whole, and also to the first sentence of Par.133. All together, then, the program is introduced by three qualifying statements: (i) the program will be °different° for °different countries°; (ii) it applies to the °most advanced countries° (only); and (iii) it applies °fairly generally° even in those countries.

(2) LATER QUALIFICATIONS. See Par.130/4 with reference to the 1872 preface. Here Marx and Engels pointed out some of the respects in which the text was now outdated, the first reference being to the ten-point program. The new statement started out with the original qualifications:

> The practical application of the principles will depend, as the Manifesto itself states, everywhere and at all times, on the historical conditions for the time being existing, and, for that reason, no special stress is laid on the revolutionary measures proposed at the end of Section II. That passage would, in many respects, be very differently worded today. In view of the gigantic strides of modern industry in the last twenty-five years, and of the accompanying improved and extended party organization of the working class, in view of the practical experience gained, first in the February Revolution [of 1848], and then, still more, in the Paris Commune, where the proletariat for the first time held political power for two whole months, this program

has in some details become antiquated. [MESW 1:98f]

(3) OFFICIAL PROGRAM? Many or most scholars who have studied the background of the Manifesto have expressed the opinion that the "items in the transitional program were not drafted exclusively by Marx and Engels. They were formulated by the communists [of the CL] at a congress and were arrived at by collaboration." (Ryazanov, *The Communist Manifesto of Marx and Engels,* 180; see also Struik, *Birth of the C.M.,* 209.) However, Ryazanov goes a little beyond the facts: there is no direct evidence that the June or November 1847 congress of the CL actually adopted these planks as such. Another possibility is that these points represented a less formal consensus of the CL membership or leadership, a consensus that Marx wrote into the Manifesto. However that may be, there is widespread confidence that here, more than in other passages of the Manifesto, Marx was setting down not simply ideas of his own that would also be satisfactory to the CL but a list of measures *already* agreed on by communist propagandists. I must add that I quite agree with this opinion, which arises from two sources: (i) As we will see, all these demands already had, in 1848, long careers as popular leftist proposals. We find them plentifully in the socialist-communist literature of the time, but not so much in Marx and Engels themselves. (ii) These are the demands, with variations, that figure in previous documents of the CL and its predecessor League of the Just, and also in Engels' draft *Principles of Communism* (which see in MECW 6:350). The language distinctive of the contemporaneous movement permeates these demands to a greater extent than the rest of the Manifesto: already mentioned have been the matter of state ownership (Par.130/3) and the very popular socialist talk about 'industrial armies' which is found here (see Par.133, Pt. 8). Some of this carried over to another set of demands that require mention. In March 1848, on behalf of the CL's Executive established in Paris, Marx and Engels drew up the "Demands of the Communist Party in Germany" as a *supplement* to the propaganda use of the Manifesto itself. As the title shows, this seventeen-point program was conceived in the same spirit as the Manifesto, under the same auspices ("Communist Party"), not put forward in the name of Marx and Engels personally. This program may have had to be adopted by the CL in Paris before being published; we do not know. Some comparisons with the March "Demands" are made below under the various points of the program.

Par. 133 (General)

(1) INTRODUCTION TO PROGRAM. For the introductory sentence, see Par.132/1. From here on, under each point of the program, I note the corresponding plank of Engels' draft *Principles of Communism,* where a similar (twelve-point) program was given under Question 18, as measures to be adopted to implement "Democracy" (see Par.129/2). Among the planks in Engels' program that were not carried over to the Manifesto were: (i) part of its plank 1 calling for "compulsory loans" as a means of limiting private property, and (ii) its plank 10, for "The demolition of all insanitary and badly built dwellings and town districts," i.e., what was later invented as slum clearance. Contrariwise, the Manifesto's ten points included some measures not contained in Engels' draft, such as the "single tax" idea in point

272

1, and in point 10 the partial elimination of child factory labor (unless this was implicit in Engels' plank 8).

(2) ABOLITION OF CAPITALISM? Although this ten-point program is presented as the program of a workers' state after a proletarian conquest of power (see Par.130/1), not a single point of the program calls for a direct attack on the central economic power of capital, its ownership of the means of production. There were planks that proposed social ownership of land (point 1), credit and banks (point 5), and transportation (point 6), but none that demanded encroachments on capitalist ownership of, say, factories. In contrast, the corresponding program in Engels' *Principles of Communism* had done so: its plank 2 called for "Gradual expropriation of landed proprietors, factory owners, railway and shipping magnates, partly through competition on the part of state industry and partly directly through compensation in assignats [paper money]." (See also his plank 4 cited below.) The problem is underlined when we recall (see Par.129/2) that Engels' program was designed for the "Democratic" transitional stage, not directly for a victorious proletarian state.

The explanation is Marx's "transitional program" approach, for which see Par.131/3 and 4. In his introduction to the ten-point program (Par.131) Marx had stated that this program was 'a means of transforming the whole mode of production, by instituting a series of measures which would "drive beyond their own limits" and necessitate further inroads upon the old social order. The measures themselves, he openly agreed, were "economically inadequate"—that is, did not attack the mode of production at its root, capitalist ownership; but they were "unavoidable" as a means of getting the workers' state to that stage. The statement of the socialist goal is not in the ten-point program but is presented in Par.131. After the experience of the 1848—1849 revolution, Marx was going to adapt this "transitional" pattern to the new perspective embodied in the "Address to the Communist League" of March 1850. Here he looks forward to a first stage of the coming revolution in which the social-democrats (the "petty-bourgeois Democracy") would be in power and propose "more or less socialist [reform] measures"; the Communists should propose measures asking not for communism but for encroachments on the social order, "direct attacks upon private property," etc. (See MECW 10:286.)

Par. 133, Point 1

(1) EXPROPRIATION / ABOLITION. The A.E.T. softened °expropriation° to °abolition,° no doubt because °expropriation° suggests outright confiscation without compensation or at any rate sounds harsher. Land socialization or nationalization was a common leftist demand; Marx had advanced it as early as the *Economic and Philosophic Manuscripts of 1844*. It was the first socialistic measure endorsed by the International (1868), against Proudhonist opposition. The Manifesto's general insensitivity to the peasant question (cf. Par. 28/3) was illustrated by the unqualified nature of this first point, which made no distinction between the largest landed proprietor and the smallest peasant. Engels' draft *Principles of Communism* was a little better: the beginning of its second plank demanded "gradual expropriation of landed proprietors..." (see also under point 7 below). A couple of months after the Manifesto, the March 1848 "Demands of the Communist Party" refrained

273

from making any proposals that threatened small peasant property: its seventh demand called only for the state ownership of "princely and other feudal estates." This marked the beginning of a thought-out peasant policy by Marx.

(2) 'SINGLE TAX.' The second part of this point (°use of ground rent to pay state expenses,° somewhat reworded by the A.E.T.) was later compared by Marx to Henry George's single-tax proposal. Marx wrote (letter of June 20, 1881):

> His basic dogma is that *everything would be all right* if ground rent were paid to the state—(you will find this sort of payment also among the transition measures included in the *Communist Manifesto*.)

After tracing the idea through the early political economists, Marx added: "We ourselves, as already mentioned, adopted this appropriation of ground rent by the state among numerous other *transition measures*" in the Manifesto, but (Marx points out) it was Colins who first turned it into a socialist panacea. In the *Poverty of Philosophy* (chap. II, Sec.4) Marx had pointed out that economists like "Mill, Cherbuliez, Hilditch and others" had demanded that all rents go to the state in place of taxes—"This is a frank expression of the hatred the industrial capitalist bears toward the landed proprietor..." This point is an example of a pattern we will meet again: two proposals, apparently similar, are really essentially different insofar as one is proposed as *the* solution to the Social Question by itself, and the other is proposed merely as an auxiliary measure in a program for a socialist workers' government. See other cases under points 3 and 5 below.

Par. 133, Point 2

(1) INCOME TAX? It was the A.E.T. that specified *income* tax, not the original. Was Marx thinking only or mainly of income tax in 1848, when he wrote °progressive tax°? Not likely; at that point a plank about income tax would have been relevant only to England. For a broader discussion of taxation by Marx only two years later, see the review of Girardin's book on the subject in 1850, covering taxes on land, capital, etc. but not income (MECW 10:326); see also the discussion on taxation in the March 1850 "Address to the CL" (MECW 10:286). Neither the Macfarlane (English) translation of 1850 nor the much later Laura (French) versions of the Manifesto mentioned the income tax. True, England had gotten to know the income tax by 1798, when it was introduced as a war emergency measure, and again in 1842, when it was revived without this qualification, and the Chartists had taken it up as an issue; but such a demand in 1848 would not have had actuality for the Continent.

(2) PROGRESSIVE TAX. What the Manifesto did call for was not only a °heavy° but a °progressive° system of taxation; the A.E.T. expanded the latter term to °progressive or graduated° (the two adjectives being equated, not set as alternatives). Engels' draft *Principles of Communism* had also called for "progressive taxation." The March 1848 "Demands" (No. 15) called for "The introduction of steeply graduated taxes" (that is, progressive taxation) plus "the abolition of taxes on articles of consumption." In the March 1850 "Address to the CL" a distinction was made between merely "proportional" taxation and "progressive" taxation,

274

the latter with steeply rising rates.

Par. 133, Point 3

(1) INHERITANCE. This was another popular pre-Marx demand of the socialist-communist movement. Opposition to inherited wealth had been the special plank of the Saint-Simonians; indeed it virtually represented the full extent of their socialism, such as it was. Engels' draft *Principles of Communism* discussed inheritance twice. In plank 1 it called for "high inheritance taxes, abolition of inheritance by collateral lines" (brothers, nephews, etc.); in plank 11, "Equal right of inheritance to be enjoyed by illegitimate and legitimate children." The March 1848 "Demands" (No. 14) stated: "The right of inheritance to be curtailed." As the last-named case shows, Marx did not repeat the demand for pure-and-simple abolition of inheritance subsequent to the Manifesto. Much later, like the Saint-Simonians and other primitive leftists, Bakunin made an attack on inheritance the central issue of his revolutionary policy instead of an attack on capital, especially during his incursion into the International; and in response Marx refused to raise the demand for the abolition of inheritance, explaining why in a resolution (see *GCFI* 3:322). He emphasized that the abolition of capitalist private property would eliminate the effects of inheritance, and favored only raising demands for its limitation.

(2) A.E.T. ADDITION: ALL. The A.E.T.'s insertion of the word °all° served to underline precisely the respect in which the Manifesto was *not* representative of Marx's later views.

Par. 133, Point 4

(1) TRADITION OF EMIGRE EXPROPRIATION. This demand goes farther back, perhaps, than any of the others, viz., to the period of the French Revolution and its tradition of confiscating the property of aristocrats who fought against the revolution. The demand had also been heavily emphasized by the followers of Babeuf, and no leftist doubted its necessity. The almost identical plank in Engels' *Principles of Communism* ended with "...rebels against the majority of the people."

Par. 133, Point 5

(1) CREDIT AND BANKS. Demands for providing easier credit and for reforming or controlling the banking system figure among the oldest proposals of social dissenters of all sorts, and were far from being distinctively socialistic. In earlier forms, such demands are even older than the émigré plank of point 4. For example, in practice Proudhonism was mainly a program for a "mutual" credit system and a "people's" bank; the Saint-Simonians had been largely concerned with recasting the banking system rather than the socioeconomic system. In the typical cases of what Marx called petty-bourgeois socialisms (Par.146/1), such demands were substitutes for social revolution, whereas revolutionaries raised demands about

banking and credit as auxiliary reforms and inroads on capital. Engels' *Principles of Communism* (plank 6) had raised the Manifesto's demand in almost the same words, ending with "the suppression of all private banks and bankers." The March 1848 "Demands" (No. 10) stated: "A state bank, whose paper issues are legal tender, shall replace all private banks"; it discussed this measure as a means of undermining finance capital.

Par. 133, Point 6

(1) DELETION: WHOLE. Beginning with the 1866 German edition, the word °alles° (°whole°) was taken out of the text. This was no doubt an editorial emendation; the °whole° transportation system, taken literally, included more than capitalist enterprises. The A.E.T. followed the revised text.

(2) A.E.T. MODERNIZATION. The A.E.T. expanded °transportation system° to °means of communication and transport.° The addition of °communication° reflected the fact that, between 1848 and 1888, the telegraph came into regular use and the telephone system was being born (the United Telephone Company was formed in England in 1880).

(3) COMPARATIVE PLANKS. Engels' *Principles of Communism* (plank 12) demanded "Concentration of all means of transport in the hands of the nation." The March 1848 "Demands" (No. 11) spelled out—railways, canals, steamships, roads, the mails, etc.—to be taken over by the state, with free use by the poor.

Par. 133, Point 7

(1) ABOLITION OF CAPITALISM? Note that this plank calls for socialistic encroachments on the capitalist monopoly of production, but—as explained in Par.133 (General)/2—it does not entail the abolition of capitalism as a mode of production.

(2) NATIONAL FACTORIES. As part of a certain amount of editing and rewording of this paragraph, the A.E.T. took care to eliminate the term national factories (turning it into °factories and instruments of production owned by the state°). For one thing, in 1888 this was an obsolete term, having gone under long ago with the debacle of Louis Blanc's *ateliers nationaux* (national workshops) in the 1848 revolution. Ryazanov, in his annotation to the Manifesto, insisted that Marx's °national factories° "must not be confused with" Blanc's conception of national workshops, but his argumentation was historically and politically weak. Blanc's essential conception was generally accepted on the left in the 1840s, and the question should not be confused by the fact that the "national workshops" established by the French government were a caricature of the proposal. Ryazanov thought that Marx reflected the idea of "co-operative production backed up with State aid," but this is simply not so. (Marx rejected *Lassalle's* version of this general idea.) In the March 1848 "Demands" No. 16 used Louis Blanc's own term °national workshops' (*Nationalwerkstätten*) in a demand for their establishment, adding (in another echo of the demand current in France): "The state guarantees a livelihood to all workers and provides for those who are incapacitated for work." Engels' *Principles of Communism* had referred to 'national factories' in two different

planks. His plank 7 was very similar to the Manifesto's point 7, beginning "Increase of national factories, workshops, railways, and ships," and continuing with the proposal for land improvement and cultivation. His plank 4 stated:

> Organization of the labor or employment of the proletarians on national estates, in national factories and workshops, thereby putting an end to competition among the workers themselves and compelling the factory owners, as long as they still exist, to pay the same increased wages as the state.

Par. 133, Point 8

(1) INDUSTRIAL ARMIES. This proposal was originated by Fourier, adopted by Weitling and Dézamy, and was very popular among all sorts of leftists, especially as a program of jobs for all. For Fourier, 'army' was a metaphor; he was not proposing to regiment labor under generals and colonels. (It is only ignoramuses like S. T. Possony who point with horror at this proposed introduction of slave labor,—unaware that probably the first real "socialistic" proposal for a militarily regimented army of workers came much later with Bellamy's *Looking Backward*.) Later the proposal was merged with another leftist idea, this for putting standing armies to productive use; compare the March 1848 "Demands," No. 4. In Engels' *Principles of Communism* plank 5 was almost the same as the Manifesto's point 8. While the socialist movement was quite willing to use the 'army' metaphor in these innocent times before the development of Prussian-style militarism, Marine boot camps, Rooseveltian CCCs, or prison chain gangs, Marx and Engels had already begun associating the regimentation of labor with the conditions of capitalist production. In fact, the Manifesto itself had previously referred to °industrial armies° in Par.15, to describe the organization of labor in the modern factory. In his *Condition of the Working Class in England* Engels had described the tyranny of factory owners' rules for the regimentation of their hands, and taken up the military analogy:

> ...it may be asserted that such a severe discipline is as necessary here in a great, complicated factory as in an army. This may be so, but what sort of a social order is it which cannot be maintained without such shameful tyranny? Either the end sanctifies the means, or the influence of the badness of the end from the badness of the means is justified. [MECW 4:468]

These factory workers, subjected to "military discipline," live "under the sword, physically and mentally." Marx's denunciation of labor regimentation in the capitalist factory reached a high point in *Capital* I, where indeed the 'industrial army' metaphor was revived: "An industrial army of workmen, under the command of a capitalist, requires, like a real army, officers (managers) and sergeants (foremen, overlookers) ..." (Chap. 13.) Cf. also Marx's use of the metaphor 'industrial reserve army' in *Capital*. By this time European militarism had reached a new level.

(2) REVISED A.E.T. OF 1932. This version (see Part I, chapter 28, section 3) changed

°liability° to °obligation.°

Par. 133, Point 9

(1) ANTITHESIS / DISTINCTION. Beginning with the 1866 German edition, the °antithesis° (°Gegensatz°) of town and country was changed to °distinction° (°Unterschied°) between town and country, thus eliminating some Hegelian overtones. The A.E.T. followed the revised text. However, when the term recurs in Par.188, the German editions do not make a corresponding change, retaining °Gegensatz° (°antithesis°); but the A.E.T. made the change to °distinction° there too.

(2) A.E.T. ADDITION. The A.E.T. inserted an explanation of the town/country disjunction in the form of an added clause: °by a more equable distribution of the population over the country.° (I take it that the last °country° used by the A.E.T. meant the national territory, not 'countryside'—an unfortunate confusion.) While this addition offered a partial interpretation, it was rather inadequate and might give the impression that the proposal involved only some population redistribution. The first part of the paragraph—the proposal for combined agriculture and industry—was presented in the Manifesto as an approach to the goal and therefore a partial explanation of it; but, for no good reason, the A.E.T. simply dropped the words that made the connection (°making for°).

(3) TOWN AND COUNTRY. The social goal put forward in this paragraph, to reverse the teratological urbanization of capitalist society, had been raised in Par.28. Though not the originator of the idea, Marx had taken up this aim in previous writings, such as his *Poverty of Philosophy* (Chap. II, Sec. 2). Engels' *Principles of Communism* plank 9 (cited below), did not address it directly, but under Question 20 Engels covered the issue with a paragraph. In later life Marx and Engels discussed this question frequently; see, for example, Engels' *Anti-Dühring* (Part III, Chap. 3).

(4) COMBINING AGRICULTURE AND INDUSTRY. There were many socialist proposals around in the 1840s for the erection of industrial-agricultural institutions in which workers would work in association for productive and recreational purposes. One of the best known was Flora Tristan's. Plank 9 in Engels' *Principles of Communism* was similar:

> The erection of large palaces on national estates as common dwellings for communities of citizens engaged in industry as well as agriculture, and combining the advantages of both urban and rural life without the onesidedness and disadvantages of either.

Of this, the Manifesto's point 9 retained only the idea of combined agricultural-industrial enterprises. In the March 1850 "Address to the CL," the proposal was made to use confiscated "feudal property" (land held by aristocratic proprietors) for "workers' colonies" in which "rural proletarians" would cultivate land on a large scale. There were other forms of this idea.

Par. 133, Point 10

(1) FREE EDUCATION FOR CHILDREN. For this question, see Par.103/3. Free education for children was one of the earliest and most popular of leftist demands from Babeuf on. In the March 1848 "Demands," No. 17 called for "Universal and free education of the people"—a formulation not limited to children.

(2) PUBLIC SCHOOLS. The Manifesto called for °public education.°—The A.E.T. preferred to change this to °education...in public schools°—even though in England the term 'public schools' had, already for decades, meant the great private schools of the ruling class.

(3) CHILD LABOR AND EDUCATION. The combination of instruction and experience in productive labor, within an educational framework and with strict limits, was the standard view of the socialist-communist movement in the nineteenth century. The aim of combining mental and material (manual) labor had been pioneered by Owen and Fourier, and was strongly maintained by the International later, as well. The conception entailed doing away with the horrendous child-labor exploitation of the capitalist system while giving children productive (including technological) experience as a part of their schooling. These views later merged into the modern progressive-school movement.

Par. 134

(1) TERM: ASSOCIATED. The first sentence has three terms that need attention, the first being °associated individuals.° The A.E.T. revised this to read: °a vast association of the whole nation.° In part this change was brought on by the fact that the Manifesto used °associated° with much of its 1840s meaning. 'Association' was one of the first terms for what later took 'socialism' for its common name. It was particularly the term of choice for the Fourierists, but it was freely used in the movement. The term °associated individuals,° then, meant more to a reader in 1848 than would be visible to an 1888 reader. The A.E.T. rewrote the phrase to give it a more modern-sounding context, gratuitously adding the word °vast°. What resulted was emphasis on °the whole nation,° but I doubt that this was the purpose of the change. Note the use of °association° also in Par.135, which see.

(2) TERM: PUBLIC POWER. This term was a synonym for *state power* or the *state*; it was the French term *Pouvoir Public*.

(3) TERM: POLITICAL CHARACTER. This term means *state character*. In this usage, the word 'political' means: pertaining to the state or state functions. Some of the colloquial connotations of 'political,' especially in America, must be ignored. In the next sentence, °political power° is an exact synonym for 'state power.'

(4) THEORY OF THE STATE. This paragraph marks a milestone in the development of Marx's theory. The *German Ideology* had definitely put forward a class view of the state and the necessity for a revolutionary class to take political (state) power (see KMTR 1, Chap. 8). But its statement was not as clear-cut and encompassing as this Manifesto passage, which inaugurates Marx's theory of the state in mature form.
This paragraph plays the same role for another aspect of Marx's theory: the eventual dying-

out of the state under communism. This was not simply the ancient idea of the out-of-hand "abolition" of the state by a decree, but rather a view of the gradual elimination of state functions after a period of societal transformation.

(5) ELIMINATION OF CLASSES. As with the theory of the state (see preceding point), this paragraph was a notable early statement of Marx's theory of class society. It had already been forcibly stated in the *Poverty of Philosophy* (last page):

> Does this mean that after the fall of the old society there will be a new class domination culminating in a new political power? No.
> The condition for the emancipation of the working class is the abolition of all classes...

But this statement was onesided in ignoring the transitional period of workers' rule, about which Marx had already written. The Manifesto passage put both phases in perspective. When in 1850 a socialistic editor criticized Marx's *Class Struggles in France* for putting emphasis on workers' rule rather than on the abolition of class distinctions, Marx sent in a reply which mainly simply quoted the aforementioned passages in the Manifesto and the *Poverty of Philosophy* plus the full passage that had been criticized. (MECW 10:387)

(6) 'WHEN' OR 'IF'? Note that in the third sentence the references to revolution, forcible change, etc. are introduced by °when° in the N.E.V. and by °if° in the A.E.T. This is a problem that affects other writings too, and deserves a word here. In English the difference between these two conjunctions is often quite significant: 'if' may imply that the statement is uncertain; 'when' may appear to take fulfillment for granted. "When you come" and "if you come" may have different meanings. The different translations stem from the German word *wenn*, which often means 'if' and often means 'when' in the sense of 'whenever.' Now as a matter of fact the English 'if' is also sometimes used in the sense of 'whenever'—as it is here in the A.E.T. In any case, the Manifesto sentence used the indicative mood, not the subjunctive, and this reinforces the translation °when° (i.e., whenever). It is not incorrect to render it 'if' but it may be misleading.

(7) SOME SLIGHT GERMAN REVISIONS. The following note, which has no substantive importance, will interest only those who notice that the first edition of the Manifesto had a typographical error in the next-to-last line of this paragraph.—The phrase

°of class antagonism and of classes in general° was represented in the first edition by °des Klassengegensatzes der Klassen,° which makes poor sense because there should have been a comma strategically inserted as follows:

> ...des Klassengegensatzes, der Klassen...

The N.E.V. (being a translation of the first edition) uses this reading, inserting the word °and° where the comma comes in. The 1866 German edition corrected the typographical error by making a change; it did not simply supply the missing comma but rewrote a little, as follows:

...des Klassengegensatzes, die Klassen...

The effect of this slight change from der to die was to change the reading to this:

...abolishes the preconditions of existence of class antagonism and [abolishes] classes in general...

To be sure, the difference in meaning is barely visible. Anyway, for some reason the A.E.T. ignored the change adopted by the German editions and went back to the same reading used by the N.E.V.

Par. 135

(1) ASSOCIATION. For this term, see Par.134/1. Compare the similar use on the last page of Marx's *Poverty of Philosophy*:

The working class, in the course of its development, will substitute for the old civil society an association which will exclude classes and their antagonism...

(2) FREE DEVELOPMENT. This paragraph sets the end-goal of socialism or communism as the °free,° unfettered °development° of the individual human being to the maximum possible, or at least as establishing the preconditions for this development. A similar statement had been included in Engels' first draft of the Manifesto: the Communist aim was

To organize society in such a way that every member of it can develop and use all his capabilities and powers in complete freedom and without thereby infringing the basic conditions of this society. [MECW 6:96]

The CL had been developing this viewpoint about the role of individual freedom in the period when it was merging forces with Marx and Engels. In September 1847 its one-issue organ, the *Kommunistische Zeitschrift* had carried a programmatic editorial (probably written by Karl Schapper, after a period of discussions with Marx and Engels on a new approach for the League) which stated the following inter alia:

We are not communists who want to destroy personal freedom and make the world over into a big barracks or a big workhouse. There certainly are communists who take the easy way out and want to deny and abolish personal freedom, which in their opinion stands in the way of harmony; but we have no desire to purchase equality at the price of freedom. We are convinced and will seek to show...that in no society can personal freedom be greater than in one based on communality [*Gemeinschaft*].

In 1894 Engels received a request from an Italian socialist: please supply a motto from Marx for a new socialist periodical—a motto that would concisely counterpose the spirit of the new socialist era against Dante's aphorism about the old world (some rule and others suffer). The motto that Engels suggested (letter of January 9) was this paragraph of the Manifesto.

III

SOCIALIST AND COMMUNIST LITERATURE

Par. 136: Title, Section III

(1) MARX'S OUTLINE. Outside of one manuscript page (see Par.98/1), the only Manifesto manuscript material extant is a list of topics to be covered, jotted into a notebook dated December 1847 (MECW 6:576). A first draft of this outline listed only a point 1, as follows:

1) [Critique] Critical utopian systems (communist).

Brackets indicate a stricken word. A second draft had six points:1) Reactionary socialism, feudal, religious petty-bourgeois.

2) Bourgeois socialism.
3) German philosophical socialism.
4) Critical utopian systems of literature. Owen, Cabet, Weitling, Fourier, Saint-Simon, Babeuf.

5) Direct party literature.
6) Communist literature.

The last two points were not written up for the Manifesto; neither were some of the names in point 4. The main change in organization was the incorporation of point 3 into point 1. "Religious" socialism was made a part of the subsection on "feudal" socialism.

(2) THE 1872 DEMURRER. In their 1872 preface to the Manifesto, the authors pointed to this section as one of the parts affected by the passage of time:

...it is self-evident that the criticism of socialist literature is deficient in relation to the present time, because it comes down only to 1847...

This is one of the reasons why it later became standard practice in the Marxist movement and outside of it to refer to Section III in particular as the "obsolete section." This was unfortunate, since this preconception made it difficult for new readers to understand the extent to which the underlying ideas of the "obsolete" tendencies criticized in the Manifesto still conditioned socialist thinking and practice, even if in new forms.

(3) SOCIALISTS. Engels explained the then difference between the labels 'socialist' and

'communist' in his 1888 preface to the A.E.T.; there was a similar passage in his preface to the 1890 German edition. In 1847, said Engels, 'socialist' referred to the utopian sects (Owenites, Fourierists, etc.) or to various sorts of "social quacks" who flogged panaceas to tinker society back to health without infringing on capital. 'Socialists' connoted non-working-class ideologists who looked to the "educated classes" for support. In contrast, workers who came out for revolutionary social change called themselves communists, with "a crude, rough-hewn, purely instinctive sort of communism." In 1847, then, socialism was a "respectable" bourgeois or petty-bourgeois movement, communism a working-class movement, not "respectable" at all. Engels added that he and Marx called themselves communists because they believed that "the emancipation of the working class must be the act of the working class itself." (See note 2 on Main Title.) To this account the following may be added. (a) Both terms were almost mint-new: they had appeared in German only five years before that. And neither term had yet ousted all other labels for the new ideas ('associationism,' 'communalism,' and a dozen others). (b) While the defining idea of 'communism' was some sort of communal ownership of productive property, the defining idea of 'socialism' is not given in Engels' discussion. The term did not necessarily imply *any* transformation of the private-property status quo. The central notion was concern with the Social Question, as distinct from concern merely with political democratic-liberal aspirations (like constitutions). The Social Question was the danger looming from masses of poor people in the new industrial society. Socialism meant literally *social*-ism, and embraced any and all ideas of social amelioration regardless of whether they had anything socialistic about them in the modern sense. It had another side: it was the alternative to *individual*-ism, the new bourgeois ethic of dog-eat-dog. (See KMTR 1:97—99; see also Par.85—86/1.) (c) Regarding the socialists' hostility to political concerns, see Par. 190/1.

1. Reactionary Socialism

Par. 136: Title, Subsection 1

(1) REACTIONARY SOCIALISM. Since the word 'reactionary' has tended in recent times to become a mere cuss-word, like 'fascist pig,' we should make clear the definite meaning it had for Marx—its literal meaning. This has already been illustrated in Par.52: "reactionary, for they seek to turn back the wheel of history." Specifically, this meant: turn society back to *prebourgeois* conditions. Hence, historically, 'reactionary' meant: looking back in the direction of feudalism or the semifeudal absolutism out of which bourgeois society arose. The opposite term, 'progressive,' was applied at least to that part of the bourgeoisie that strove to eliminate all feudalistic and semifeudal remnants and establish a modern democratic-constitutional state. Under the heading °Reactionary Socialism° the Manifesto takes up the socialisms emanating from two classes: the feudalists of all sorts, in Germany grouped (however sullenly) around the Crown and its bureaucracy; and the petty-bourgeoisie, which is viewed here as the chief social ally of the feudalists (see Par.52/3). The latter current is divided into two subsections, to be sure, but this was only a way of organizing the material.

(a) Feudal Socialism

Par. 136

(1) FEUDAL. All definitions of 'feudalism' are doubtless controversial, but for present purposes it is important to understand that Marx viewed the absolutist state and the society it dominated as the last stage of the feudal era, one in which an autonomized state power rested on the social support of the (broken and domesticated) aristocracy and on the state bureaucracy as its political arm. This absolutist state, it is true, became increasingly bourgeoisified; but it is not our present task to draw a line of demarcation. For a whole historical period it was, in Marx's view, the aim of absolutism to defend whatever was still retainable in feudal privileges, while trying to keep the bourgeoisie content to be its tool, its supplier, its milch cow, but not its master. Depending on context, then, the term 'feudal' may be used by Marx not only to refer back to medieval times but also to point to the ongoing social situation in Germany.

(2) FEUDAL SOCIALISM. Engels' draft *Principles of Communism* had a substantial passage on feudal socialism, the "adherents of feudal and patriarchal society which has been and is still being daily destroyed..." (Question 24). For more of this passage, see Par.140/1. Marx and Engels, being concerned with the 'feudal socialism' of their own day, did not mention the problem (often called the puzzle) of the late-medieval socialisms beginning with Thomas More's *Utopia*. I suggest that the Manifesto's discussion sheds light on this "puzzle." The most useful way of seeing the historical roots of More and Campanella is to view their utopias as essentially idealized versions of the Good Absolute State, which, having broken the power of decentralized feudal landed property, has not yet yielded to the economic domination of the bourgeoisie. (See point 1 above.) The °feudal socialists° discussed by Marx were, consciously or not, agents of the absolute state's effort to keep the bourgeoisie as its tool not its master. In this framework, the first socialists (the More-Campanella type) were feudal socialists. While °feudal socialism° as an active current died long ago, more modern analogues survived for some time: for example, see Par.48/1 and Par.139/1,2.

(3) FOOTNOTE ON RESTORATION. Engels' footnote in the A.E.T., explaining that the Manifesto referred to the French Restoration of 1814—1830, was not one of the footnotes added to the German edition of 1890.—About °the old phrases of the Restoration period°: Henry Jacoby has pointed out that the partisans of these cries against absolutist bureaucratism (who had raised them well before the Restoration) capitulated in practice to the new Leviathan state. All the more did their catchwords °become impossible.°

(4) PARAGRAPHING. The A.E.T. broke this paragraph up into two, unlike the German editions. In this respect it was followed by the Laura-3 (French) version.

(5) TEXTUAL PROBLEM. Regarding the last sentence, Andréas (page 7) gives detailed consideration to the problem of what he thinks represents an error, probably a typographical error, in the text of the first edition, followed by an attempt at emendation in the second edition. It mainly concerns the word °bereitete...vor°; Andréas argues persuasively that °vor° should have been deleted, and later was. What it amounts to, minus complications, is that one should change the N.E.V.'s rendering °prepared to get redress° to °managed to get redress.° Obviously the meaning is unaffected.

(6) A.E.T. REVISION. Rewriting the second half of the last sentence, the A.E.T. dropped °more or less° and added °of coming catastrophe.° The first change seems simply literary, and the second seems to be an attempt to explain °ill-boding° (or °sinister°).

Par. 137

(1) MENACE OF THE FUTURE. Why was °feudal socialism° any °menace of the future°—"half" menace or any at all? The remark is unexplained, and any interpretation can only be tentative. In accordance with my own predilections, I think this was an insight into a phenomenon later ignored: the ongoing influence of reactionary (*prebourgeois*) values as an ingredient in antibourgeois ideologies, including socialisms of various sorts. In the ensuing century, socialists rarely questioned the equation *anticapitalism = socialism*. Yet there were going to be a number of individual figures, if not a movement, exemplifying the continued existence of antibourgeois disaffection from a standpoint alien to the working class. This is the genus of °reactionary socialism° of which the °feudal socialism° of the 1840s was becoming an extinct species.

Par. 138

(1) DEBT TO HEINE. The governing image in this paragraph (coat of arms on backsides) was taken by Marx from the then recent (1844) poem of political satire, *Germany, a Winter's Tale* (Cap. 3, st. 12) by Heinrich Heine. Heine ridiculed the introduction of the spiked helmet for the Prussian cavalry, taking it as a symbol:

> It suggests medieval nobles and squires,
> Knights errant and lords superior,
> Who bore true faith upon their breast,
> Coats of arms upon their posterior.

Heine's poem immediately became immensely popular; Marx expected his readers to recognize the allusion without being told. This poem had a special relation to Marx: Heine, in Hamburg, had sent Marx (in Paris) the unpublished manuscript, asking him to get it into the Paris *Vorwärts!* (as was done) and also to write an introduction for it (not done).

Par. 139

(1) FRENCH LEGITIMISTS. Most commentators, like Ryazanov, think Marx was referring to the period of Louis Philippe's Orleanist monarchy of 1830—1848, when the Legitimists (royalists of the Bourbon faction) were in opposition on the right. Attacking the Citizen King, monarch by the grace of the bourgeoisie, some (a minor current) combined their antibourgeois animus with sympathy for the poor victims of the new bourgeoisified

society. Two figures of this tendency may be mentioned as championing some reforms of workers' conditions: (i) Count Charles Forbes de Montalembert (1810—1870), London-born publicist and politician. At first associated with Lamennais in the Catholic social-reform movement, he eventually capitulated to the church's pressure and became hostile to liberalism. (See an 1858 article by Engels, MECW 16:91.) (ii) Vicomte Alban de Villeneuve-Bargemont (1784—1850), economist and administrator under Napoleon and the restoration. His chief work, *Economie Politique Chrétienne* (1834), read by Marx in 1845, looked to curbing capitalist excesses, heralding social-Catholicism.

(2) YOUNG ENGLAND. A "party" (tendency) in Parliament of Tory figures who sought to counteract the political dominance of the bourgeoisie, in the name of an idealized aristocracy (fantasizing "Merrie England," seventeenth-century Cavaliers, etc.)—see Par.48/1. To this end they held out a hand to the "enemy of their enemies," the new industrial working class, and played an important part in exposing the new horrors of industrial conditions and in gaining some reforms (factory and mine reforms, public holidays, model tenements, and above all the Ten Hours Act of 1847, for which see Par.47/2). Their philanthropic souls failed to beat with equal sympathy for the rural toilers who provided their own class with their traditional revenue, and they opposed the Reform Bill of 1832. Active for about five years or so in the mid-1840s, this tendency had already petered out at the time the Manifesto was published. Disraeli was often regarded as its leading figure; but it was Lord Ashley (later called Lord Shaftesbury) who was most responsible for the Ten Hours victory. Another prominent member was Lord John Manners, who was one of the more overt admirers of the fantasized feudality; another, William E. Perrand. Outside of Parliament, taking the ideological tendency as such, the leading writer was Thomas Carlyle, especially in the pre-1848 period, when his antibourgeois animus and his glorification of the medieval past were strongest. On the pre-1848 Carlyle, see two writings by Engels (MECW 3:444 and 4:578, including also a footnote on young England); on the post-1848 Carlyle, see MECW 10:301.

(3) A.E.T. OMISSION: BEST. The A.E.T. dropped the statement that the two named tendencies were the °best° examples of feudal socialism. Perhaps Engels had a better candidate in mind; perhaps the omission was inadvertent.

Par. 140

(1) FEUDAL SOCIALISM VS. THE BOURGEOISIE. Engels' *Principles of Communism* (see Par.136/2) had a corresponding passage which said much the same thing as the Manifesto, including:

> From the ills of present-day society this group draws the conclusion that feudal and patriarchal society should be restored because it was free from these ills.

And Communists oppose this tendency because it strives after the impossible, and because it seeks to establish the rule of the aristocracy, the guild-masters and the manufacturers, with their retinue of absolute or feudal monarchs, officials, soldiers and priests, a society which was indeed free from the vices of present society, but brought at least as many other evils in its train and did not even hold out the prospect of the emancipation of the oppressed workers through a communist organization... [MECW 6:355]

(2) FEUDALISTS. This term (in German °Feudalen°) is an ideological term, not socioeconomic; that is, it refers to representatives or ideologists of the feudal or absolutist state and society. The point made in Par.136/1 has to be kept in mind here. In European terms, a °feudalist° meant a representative of *prebourgeois* ideas and values.

Par. 141

(1) A.E.T.: ITALICS. It is perhaps unnecessary to say that the A.E.T.'s italicization of °régime° means only that it is taken to be a foreign word; it is not emphasized.

(2) DESTINED. The A.E.T.'s use of this word merely translated the future tense in the Manifesto. Very sharp people should not argue from it that the Manifesto held a theory of predestination.

(3) BLOW UP / CUT UP. The A.E.T.'s version °cut up root and branch° is its translation of an expression (°in die Luft sprengen°) which is translated by the A.E.T. in Par.56 as °sprung into the air° (see Par.56/4).

(4) PARAGRAPHING: MARX'S 1850 REPRINT. When Marx reprinted Section III of the Manifesto in his 1850 magazine *NRZ-Revue* (see Part I, chapter 10), the most extensive editorial change he made was to the paragraphing. There were twelve cases of amalgamation of two or more paragraphs into one, and two cases of the reverse—division of a paragraph into two. Thus Par.141, 142 and 143 were merged into a single paragraph. The other cases will be noted under the first paragraph affected.

Par. 142

(1) A.E.T.: ITALICS. The A.E.T. italicized °revolutionary° for emphasis, but this emphasis is only implicit in the original.

Par. 143

(1) A.E.T. ADDITION: GOLDEN APPLES. The A.E.T. inserted °dropped from the tree of industry° to flesh out the metaphorical reference to the golden apples that tempted Atalanta. The Laura-3 (French) version, incidentally, followed suit. All the Laura versions, besides, interpolated another phrase, "all the chivalric virtues," to introduce the three virtues listed.

(2) FIDELITY. The German °Treue° means °fidelity°, and not °truth° as in the A.E.T. In this sense 'truth' is obsolete in English, though 'true (to)' can still work.

(3) ENGELS' FOOTNOTE. This needling reference to the Prussian Junkers' unsnobbish enthusiasm for bourgeois profits, with its sharp point ending with °Schnaps,° recalls that in 1876 Engels had published a long essay in the German Social-Democratic press titled "Preussischer Schnaps in deutschen Reichstag" (MEW 19:37). Republished as a pamphlet, it was banned by the German government, which had no sense of humor about such serious matters.

Par. 144

(1) PARSON / PRIEST. The A.E.T. used °parson° where a Continental version might say 'priest'; the German °Pfaffe° can mean either one. The Manifesto's term for °clerical socialism° echoes this word: °pfäffische Socialismus.° It might be rendered 'priestly socialism' or 'parsonical socialism,' sharing some of the scornful character of the second.

(2) FEUDALIST / LANDLORD. Instead of °feudalist° the A.E.T. used °landlord.° An editorial footnote in MECW 6:508 "corrects" this to "feudal lord," but this is not quite accurate; for the meaning of 'feudalist,' see Par.140/2.

(3) PARAGRAPHING. Marx's 1850 reprint of Section III (see Par.141/4) amalgamated Par.144 and Par.145.

Par. 145

(1) THE 'HEITIGE' MISPRINT. In the first edition of 1848, the last sentence of this paragraph carried a misprint that caused trouble until 1872. It should have begun: °Der heilige Socialismus°.—'holy socialism' or 'sacred socialism' (as the Macfarlane translation had it) or °religious socialism° (this last being the version used in the N.E.V.). Instead, the typographical gremlins made the word °heitige.° The second edition of 1848 "corrected" this mistake to °heutige° ('present-day' socialism) which made little sense in context. When Marx reprinted Section III in his 1850 magazine *NRZ-Revue* he brought in the correct reading °heilige.° But Sigfrid Meyer's edition of 1866 was essentially based on the second edition, and he evidently did not have the *NRZ-Revue* available, and so Meyer went back to the reading °heutige.° Marx and Engels caught up with the error in preparing the 1872 edition, but this time they threw out the original word and made it read °christliche°—and this stuck for the subsequent career of the Manifesto. Naturally the A.E.T. followed it. Two comments can be added. (i) The 1872 change to °Christian socialism° was an act of updating; it was not likely that Marx would have written this in 1848, when neither the term nor the idea were yet prominent. (ii) Note that Macfarlane had the correct reading in advance of any revision. This is strong evidence for the thesis that she received at least some direct help from Engels or Marx. (For more evidence see Par.164/2.)

Par. 146

(1) TITLE: PETTY-BOURGEOIS SOCIALISM. For the definition of the petty-bourgeoisie, see Par.44/3; for the Manifesto's attitude toward this class, see Par.52/3. The Manifesto's internal organization in this section does not well reflect Marx's views. °Petty-bourgeois Socialism° and (in the next subsection) °German or True Socialism° are treated coordinately, but in fact one finds out (Par.165) that the latter is a species of petty-bourgeois socialism too. And, as we will see, in Par.172 Proudhon, who was a prime exemplar of petty-bourgeois socialism, is treated as a representative of a different trend. In the present subsection *b*, the only example of petty-bourgeois socialist cited is Sismondi. If we look at the corresponding treatment in Engels' *Principles of Communism* we find a different way of organizing what is essentially the same analysis. Engels' "three groups" of socialists were mainly divided by political coloration, with their class roots mentioned as part of the analysis, rather than as the label. Thus, petty-bourgeois socialists, together with unclass-conscious proletarians, were grouped under the "Democratic socialists"—a term guaranteed to be misunderstood today. The label meant the left wing of the unrevolutionary Democracy, for which see Par.129/2 and Par. 193/3: in other words, Democrats concerned with social reform but not anticapitalist.

(2) A.E.T. EDITING. The A.E.T. made two slight alterations. (i) Instead of °in modern bourgeois society,° it expanded to °in the atmosphere of modern bourgeois society.° (ii) Instead of the °small peasantry,° it spoke of the °small peasant proprietors°—to explain, I suppose, how they became °forerunners of the modern bourgeoisie.°

(3) A.E.T. CORRECTION. In the original, °this class° refers back to °the medieval burgesses and the small peasantry,° not to °the modern bourgeoisie.° Obviously it should have been plural, and in fact the A.E.T. writes °these two classes.°

Par. 147

(1) "DISAPPEARANCE OF THE MIDDLE CLASSES." We now continue this subject (the "disappearance" theory allegedly held by Marx) from preliminary discussions in Par.16/3, Par. 41/1, and Par.51/2. The °new petty-bourgeoisie° of the first sentence denotes the petty-bourgeois elements that flourished in early capitalism, previously referred to under such labels as 'tradespeople,' 'small industrials,' etc., and no doubt including small bourgeois elements too. In the present paragraph we learn that even this petty-bourgeoisie is not "disappearing" (let alone "*the* middle classes" in some global sense): just the reverse, it °continually re-forms itself afresh.° True, individual members of this class are °constantly° being proletarianized, but the class itself limps on in a more or less ruined state. Secondly, when the word °disappear° does crop up, it is not as part of a prediction of the galloping elimination of the class. The Manifesto says that some day this class will disappear °as an independent part of modern society°—which is not identical with simply disappearing. In fact, *this* prediction (if one wishes to call it that) was an obvious one and has already been

unquestionably verified, though the term date implied by the Manifesto was suitably vague. Thirdly, and most important: even if this type of 'middle class' were to °disappear altogether,° instead of merely ceasing to be °an independent part of modern society,° it would still not mean the "disappearance of the middle classes" in some absolute fashion; for the Manifesto climaxes this paragraph with an altogether different sort of prediction. That is: this historical petty-bourgeoisie °will be replaced°... And here we come to a serious deficiency in the A.E.T., which however could have been seen only in hindsight *after* the "theory of the disappearing middle classes" had been invented and posthumously attached to Marx. (I do not think Engels can be fairly condemned for failing to see this development in his crystal ball.) For the Manifesto states that, at least in part, this petty-bourgeoisie will be °replaced in commerce, manufacturing, and agriculture by labor overseers and stewards—that is, by superintending or managerial employees of capital hired to oversee the labor process in the interests of the owners. Elements of this general sort (today we would also emphasize technological employees) are certainly new in the mass, and certainly somewhere in the middle of the social structure, and so they can be called "new middle-class" elements for whatever the label is worth. But the A.E.T. obscured this statement by the Manifesto through its translation of the key phrase °durch Arbeitsaufseher und Domestiken,° which it rendered: °by overlookers, bailiffs and shopmen.° In particular, the import of °Domestiken° (which cannot mean *household* servants in this context) was lost, and the terms 'bailiffs' and 'shopmen' have nothing to do with either the word or the context.

Finally, we must now emphasize that the alleged "disappearance" theory, though usually "proved" by quotes of a sort from the Manifesto, is most thoroughly quashed when one looks at Marx's mature economic writings—where, indeed, this theory has to be discovered if it really existed. For this investigation, see KMTR 2:619—624, which highlights Marx's anticipation of "new middle class" developments.

(2) PARAGRAPHING. Marx's 1850 reprint of Section III (see Par.141/4) amalgamated Par.147 and Par.148.

Par. 148

(1) PETTY-BOURGEOISIE / INTERMEDIATE CLASSES. Toward the end of the first sentence, the A.E.T. said °these intermediate classes° instead of the original's term °the petty-bourgeoisie,° because the reference had been to two class groups, viz., the petty-bourgeoisie and the small peasantry. (Incidentally, the A.E.T. dropped the qualifier °small,° for no good reason.) To be sure, the Manifesto's use of °petty-bourgeoisie° to cover both the urban and the rural intermediate stratum had justification, in the sense that the peasantry can rightly be regarded as the petty-bourgeoisie on the land (cf. Par.44/3). Indeed, this has to be borne in mind if representatives of the peasants as a class are to be labeled 'petty-bourgeois socialists.'

(2) SISMONDI. Léonard Simonde de Sismondi (1773—1842) was a Swiss economist and historian. As historian, he was notable for emphasis on social and economic influences. As economist, though originally a follower of Adam Smith, he turned against liberal economics with the publication of his *Nouveaux Principes d'Economie Politique* (1819) and his *Etudes sur*

l'Economie Politique.(1837); criticized capitalism; argued for the reality of economic crises (from an underconsumptionist standpoint); and heralded a mild sort of state-socialistic ideology. Marx had a great deal of admiration for Sismondi's main contribution to political economy, his analysis of economic crises and the essential capitalist contradiction which leads to them; in fact, called him "epoch-making in political economy" for this reason (see *Theories of Surplus Value*, III, Chap. 19, Sec. 12, and Chap. 21, Sec. 2). Alongside Ricardo as the greatest figure of bourgeois political economy, Marx twice ranged Sismondi as the first great critic of that ideology (*Grundrisse*, 843; Afterword to *Capital* 1873). At the same time Marx's economic writings are peppered with notes on Sismondi's mistakes and inadequacies. This two-sided view of Sismondi developed from Marx's economic studies, of course; in the Manifesto, the focus is more on the Swiss writer's relation to the socialist movement, as was true also in the 1847 book *The Poverty of Philosophy*, (See Par.150/2 below.) While even later Marx would not have changed his view about the petty-bourgeois roots of Sismondi's standpoint, I do not know any later passage in which he pointed to this man as *the* leading representative of 'petty-bourgeois socialism'—an honor which was more justifiably assigned to Proudhon, as we will see.

(3) A.E.T. EDITING. In the last sentence the change in tense (from °is° to °was°) merely reflected the date of publication. When Marx started work on the Manifesto, Sismondi was only five years dead.

Par. 149

(1) "SCHOOL OF SOCIALISM." In the first sentence of this paragraph, as in the last sentence of the preceding one, it is the A.E.T. that speaks of a °school of Socialism,° not the original. Sismondi founded no school of either socialism or political economy, in the sense of a more or less conscious tendency. Marx's language referred only to Sismondi's being °the chief figure in this literature°—that is, the literature of the type of socialistic ideology described. Who else might have been included in this tendency, as Marx saw it at the time? Ryazanov's commentary suggested two likely candidates, French writers of the period who answered part of the Manifesto's description and who reflected Sismondi's influence at least in part: (i) Eugène Buret (1811—1842), journalist and writer on economics, who in 1840 won a prize for his chief work, *De la Misère des Classes Laborieuses en Angleterre et en France* (published 1841). He then made a research trip to Algeria but died before working up his material. Buret favored government-sponsored prolabor reforms in the spirit of Sismondi. (ii) Jérôme Adolphe Blanqui (1798—1854), economist, liberal brother of the revolutionist L. A. Blanqui. An Orleanist, disciple of Adam Smith and J. E. Say, a free-trader, he made contributions to the study of workers' conditions and slums. His chief work was his *Histoire de l'Economie Politique en Europe* (1837).

(2) A.E.T. EDITING. (i) °Concentration...in a few hands°: the A.E.T. added the last four words. (ii) °Ruin of the petty bourgeois°: so in the A.E.T.; but the original spoke not of petty-bourgeois but of °small burghers° or bourgeois (°kleinen Bürger°). About this slight difference, see the comments in Par.44/3.

(3) PARAGRAPHING. Marx's 1850 reprint of Section III (see Par.141/4) amalgamated

Par.149 and Par.150, except for the last sentence of the latter. (On this, see Par.150/4.)

Par. 150

(1) FORCIBLY. The A.E.T. omitted this word (in the German °gewaltsam°)—no doubt in order to avoid a misunderstanding. The socialistic writers considered in this paragraph were not in favor of forcible measures; the Manifesto used the word simply for emphasis.

(2) REACTIONARY. As elsewhere—cf Par.136 (T1)/1—this word is used in its literal sociopolitical sense. Marx made a similar comment on Sismondi in his *Poverty of Philosophy*:

> Those who, like Sismondi, wish to return to the correct proportion of production [as they see it], while preserving the present basis of society, are reactionary, since, to be consistent, they must also wish to bring back all the other conditions of industry of former times. [MECW 6:137]

(3) UTOPIAN. The content of this term is discussed at large, below, under Par.178 (T3)/1. While the present use shares that content-meaning, it also reverberates with the more popular sense 'impossible' or 'impractical.' The extant manuscript page of the Manifesto (see Par.98/1) ends with a paragraph that struck the same note:

> The Communists do not put forward any new theory of property. They state a fact. You deny the most striking facts. You have to deny them. You are backward-looking utopians.

Backward-looking' (literally, backward-turned) is a good alternative to °reactionary.°

(4) PARAGRAPHING. Marx's 1850 reprint of Section III (see Par.141/4) amalgamated Par.149 and Par.150, but the last sentence of Par.150 (calling this tendency °reactionary and utopian°) became a separate paragraph. This gave the latter statement heavy emphasis.

Par. 151

(1) CORPORATE GUILDS. For the A.E.T.'s term, see Par. 14/6. In the present paragraph the original said the °guild system.°
(2) PATRIARCHAL. For the term, see Par.20/1.

Par. 152

(1) A.E.T. ADDITION. Along with some rewriting, the A.E.T. inserted a completely new clause: °when stubborn historical facts had dispersed all intoxicating effects of self-deception.° Although it is perhaps the most extensive addition made to the text in the guise

of translation, its aim was purely explanatory, since the brief sentence of the original is certainly cryptic. The word °intoxicating° also prepared for the 'hangover' metaphor to follow (for which see point 3 below).

(2) A.E.T. EDITING. The A.E.T. replaced °In its further development° with °Ultimately,° and replaced °this tendency° with °this form of Socialism.°

(3) THE 'KATZENJAMMER' METAPHOR. The phrase °feigen Katzenjammer° in the original is, to be sure, hard to represent in English. A °Katzenjammer° is a hangover, the morning-after feeling (admittedly °miserable°). The adjective, which means 'cowardly,' is not carried over to the A.E.T. version, which attempted an approximation. The Macfarlane translation of 1850 was even freer: "This kind of Socialism has run to seed, and exhausted itself in silly lamentations over the past." The Laura (French) versions caught the 'cowardly' note. The first two Laura versions said, "this socialism could only shed cowardly tears" (perhaps echoing Macfarlane's emphasis on lamentation). Laura-3 obviously resorted to translating the A.E.T. rather than going back to the original: it made an insertion similar to the English one, and said, "this form of socialism abandoned itself to a cowardly melancholy."

(c) *German or True Socialism*

Par. 153

(1) TITLE: 'TRUE SOCIALISM.' This was one of the labels attached to the type of socialistic ideology expressed by Moses Hess in the 1840s, but for a few years only. (During a long life Hess shifted ideologies every few years, ending up with Lassalleanism and Zionism.) Other representatives of this trend encountered in the writings of Marx and Engels were Karl Grün, Otto Lüning, Andréas Gottschalk of Cologne, Hermann Kriege in America. It was not a 'school' in any formal sense, not a group, not even a definite theory, but mainly a philosophical concept of the Social Question (hence called 'socialism') under the backward German conditions of the day, strongly influenced by Feuerbach. This 'philosophical socialism' (another label for it) looked to a nonclass "humanism," in fact a humanitarianism, to accomplish those social tasks in Germany which in France (they saw) had been carried through by the "proletariat"; the spirit of Love (which is not to be confused with mere love) was to mobilize the philosophical elite against bourgeois selfishness. The positive side of this tendency was due to its antibourgeois animus, which led to some trenchant criticisms of the status quo; the other side of this coin was these writers' tendency to scorn and denounce bourgeois-democratic political reforms (like gaining a constitution) as liberal traps, to be eschewed. It was this last aspect that awakened Marx's and Engels' fiercest opposition, for it meant that this standpoint could be used by the feudal-absolutist ruling class under Crown and bureaucracy to confuse the forces of political democratization leading to a bourgeois-democratic revolution; in this sense, 'True Socialism' was an ally, wittingly or not, of the reactionary status quo. Instead of fighting bourgeois liberalism because it did not go far enough, they lent themselves (and their radical reputations) to a reactionary alternative to liberalism. None of the foregoing is gainsaid by the fact that Hess, personally, was the best of the lot, much better in Marx's view than (say) Grün, and a man

who tossed off many other sparks besides this one.

(2) A.E.T. EDITING. The A.E.T. made two slight changes. (i) It deleted the adjective °literary° modifying °expression of the struggle.° Perhaps Engels felt, as we sometimes feel nowadays, that 'literary' had a bit of a derogatory tone to it, as if to say 'merely literary.' The word had no such flavor in the original; it simply referred to the °literature° mentioned at the beginning of the sentence. (ii) The A.E.T. inserted the words °in that country,° to make doubly clear that the °bourgeoisie° in question was the German class, that the point being made applied specifically to Germany.

(3) UNEVEN DEVELOPMENT OF NATIONS. In a line of thought that merges right into the next paragraph, Marx here makes an important point which was later called the "law" or pattern of "uneven and combined development," in particular the consequences of a lack of correspondence in the sequence of material and intellectual conditions. France's sociopolitical forward leap, the conquest of political power by a new class, could impact on Germany in thought, in ideological form, but the new and modern social conditions could not be as easily imported. In Germany, then, there was a disjunction, a dislocation of political theory and social practice, which is explained in Par.154.

Par. 154

(1) UNEVEN DEVELOPMENT OF NATIONS. See the preceding note, Par.153/3. All the paragraphs from Par.153 to Par.159 inclusive form the explanation, probably the first systematic exposition of this concept in socialist literature. For another use of this idea, see Par.162; see also Par.196 to 198/3.

(2) OMITTED SENTENCE; OMITTED PHRASE. The A.E.T. dropped an entire sentence in the middle of the paragraph: °It was bound to appear to be idle speculation about the True Society, about the realization of Human Nature.° There is no clue to a possible motivation—leaving aside sheer error, of course. Even the Laura-3 version, which copied the A.E.T. in many respects, did not follow suit. Perhaps this omission, or deletion, is related to another one, which concerns the same sentence. Beginning with the 1872 German edition, the phrase °about the True Society° was dropped from the text. Again, there seems to be no very obvious reason for making this change in a "historical document": did the editor (apparently Liebknecht in 1872) or the authors think that this expression derogated any and all speculation about a new society's forms? Perhaps, though the words were scornful only of °idle° speculation, and the context was a very specific one. Perhaps, by extension, the same consideration persuaded Engels to drop the whole sentence in 1888? It does not sound like a very good reason.—Incidentally, the N.E.V.'s capitalization of °True Society° and °Human Nature° seeks to reflect the ironic undertone, but of course this device is not used, and cannot be used, in the German original.

(3) "PRACTICAL REASON." The quote marks make this an overt allusion to Immanuel Kant's work *Critique of Practical Reason* (1788). As John Lewis has explained:

The philosophy of Kant is the ideology of the young [German] bourgeoisie which was in need of a critique of the philosophic and legal concepts of the feudal epoch, but

294

which at the same time was so weak that it was compelled to compromise with absolutism, and was unable to develop more than a timid liberalism. [Introduction to Philosophy: 122]

In the *Critique of Pure Reason* Kant showed that the three great problems of metaphysics, God, Freedom, and Immortality, are insoluble by speculative thought; and in the *Critique of Practical Reason* he argued that one has to believe in these three concepts anyway because no morality (that is, no morality satisfactory to his preconceptions) is possible without them. See also the next point.

(4) KANT AND WILL. The last part of this Manifesto paragraph is closely related to, indeed probably based on, a passage in the *German Ideology* which may be usefully presented here:

> The characteristic form which French liberalism, based on real class interests, assumed in Germany we find again in Kant. Neither he nor the German middle class, whose whitewashing spokesman he was, noticed that these theoretical ideas of the bourgeoisie had as their basis material interests and a *will* that was conditioned and determined by the material relations of production. Kant, therefore, separated this theoretical expression from the interests which it expressed; he made the materially motivated determinations of the will of the French bourgeois into *pure* self-determinations of *"free will*,*"* of the will in and for itself, of the human will, and so converted it into purely ideological conceptual determinations and moral postulates. Hence the German petty-bourgeois recoiled in horror from the practice of this energetic bourgeois liberalism as soon as this practice showed itself, both in the Reign of Terror and in shameless bourgeois profit-making. [MECW 5:195]

(5) EXPRESSION...SIGNIFIED. In the editions of 1848 there was a flagrant case of the nonagreement of subject and verb—singular subject, plural verb:

> ...die Willensäusserung der revolutionären französischen Bourgeoisie bedeuteten...
> ...the expression of the will of the revolutionary French bourgeoisie signified...

Of course, the trouble does not show up in English. When Marx reprinted Section III in 1850, he corrected the mistake by making the verb singular in form; an English translation of this version would be unaffected. But this reprint was not available when the German edition of 1866 was published, and in this edition Meyer's correction was to make the noun plural: "expressions of the will...." It was the 1866 change that "took," and became accepted as standard.

(6) A.E.T. EDITING. (i) In the first sentence, the original's °semiphilosophers° (°Halbphilosophen°) became °would-be philosophers° in the A.E.T. (ii) The original's °Schöngeister° was rendered °beaux esprits° in the A.E.T., and I have followed suit. This translation is both correct and philologically exact, yet one of the odd editorial footnotes in MECW (6:510) objects to it as an alteration of the original, which it insists on translating as "lovers of fine phrases." In the Revised A.E.T. of 1932 (see Part I, chapter 28, section 3), the

rendering is "men of letters," which is entirely erroneous. (iii) Still in the first sentence, the original's °conditions of existence° became °social conditions° in the A.E.T. The latter is a narrower concept.

Par. 155—156

(1) PHILOSOPHY AND SOCIAL CONTE#T. For the further elucidation of these two paragraphs, besides the passage in the *German Ideology* cited in Par.154/4, I would recommend the chapter by John Lewis cited in Par.154/3.

(2) PARAGRAPHING. Marx's 1850 reprint of Section III (see Par.141/4) amalgamated these two paragraphs.

Par. 157

(1) TALES OF...SAINTS. In Marx's 1850 reprint of Section III, this expression (°Heiligengeschichten°) was changed to "portrayals (or representations, pictures) of saints"(*Heiligenbildern*). Like other changes made in the 1850 reprint, it was ignored in subsequent editions, in this case just as well.

(2) MANUSCRIPTS. Old manuscripts that were erased and overwritten are called palimpsests.

(3) A.E.T. EDITING. In the fourth sentence: (i) Instead of the original's °money relations° (a vague phrase), the A.E.T. was more concrete with °economic functions of money.° (ii) The A.E.T. changed the last philosophical title from one with a Hegelian cast to one made of more general philosophic jargon.

Par. 158

(1) ANALYSES / HISTORICAL CRITICISMS. Instead of the original's reference to °French analyses° (°Entwicklungen,° lit., developments, the working out of a line of analysis), the A.E.T. said °French historical criticisms.° I doubt that there was good reason to insert °historical° since the French writings involved also dealt prominently with current societal problems.

(2) 'PHILOSOPHY OF ACTION.' The title of an essay by Moses Hess, "Philosophie der That," published in 1843. Another rendering might be "Philosophy of the Deed," with reminiscences of Goethe's Faust. For Hess see Par.153/1. Note that the label °true socialism° is given here as only one of several appellations; it has stuck, historically, mainly because of the emphasis it got from the title of this subsection.

(3) 'SCIENCE OF SOCIALISM.' Contrary to an often-repeated myth, Marx made no claim to have been the first to put forward a 'scientific' socialism; as this paragraph illustrates, the claim was already a cliché by the time the Manifesto was published. Since 'scientific socialism' means nothing but a socialism based on a scientific analysis of society (hopefully

or putatively so), it was a natural thing to claim almost from the beginning. That Marx and Engels argued that their theory was scientific in this sense was just as natural, but they did not claim a copyright on the label.

(4) PARAGRAPHING. Marx's 1850 reprint of Section III (see Par.141/4) amalgamated Par.158 and Par.159.

Par. 159

(1) SOCIALIST-COMMUNIST. The hyphenation in the opening phrase °French socialist-communist literature° follows a correction introduced in the German editions from the 1866 edition on. Previously, in the 1848 editions, the reading had been as follows: "The French-socialist communist literature..." as if the hyphen had been misplaced by error.

(2) IRONIZING QUOTES. The A.E.T. added quote marks around °French onesided-ness° to display the irony; the original got along without them in 1848, but from 1872 the German editions started using quote marks too. In the rest of the same sentence, capitalization of the Big Abstractions is used for the same purpose, both in the A.E.T. and in the N.E.V.

(3) PROLETARIAN / PROLETARIAT. The original wording °proletarian° was changed to °proletariat° in Marx's 1850 reprint of Section III, but this alteration was not followed by subsequent editions. When Engels used °proletariat° in the A.E.T., it was probably his own rediscovery of the thought that the latter was more appropriate in counter-position to °Humanity.°-

Par. 160

(1) A.E.T. EDITING. There are two slight changes in the A.E.T. version: (i) The adjective °clumsy° has been dropped before °school exercises° (which in the A.E.T. reads °schoolboy task°); and (ii) while the A.E.T. added °its poor stock-in-trade,° it changed the metaphor from a °market peddler° to a °mountebank.°

(2) LOST ITS...INNOCENCE. From here through Par.164, the Manifesto discusses the role played by True Socialist views in the contemporary political struggle, for which see Par.153/1.

Par. 161

(1) FEUDALISTS AND ABSOLUTE MONARCHS. For °feudalists° see Par.140/2. It is essential to keep in mind that, in Marx's view at this point, the ruling class in Germany and in particular Prussia was still the *pre*bourgeois coalition of Crown and feudal (or semifeudal) aristocracy, with the absolutist bureaucracy as its state arm. Arrayed against this ruling class of the old regime was the still revolutionary bourgeoisie, fast becoming dominant economically but timid about reaching out for political power in its own name. Waiting in

the wings was the proletariat, already engaged in its inevitable class struggle against capital, but still cheering the bourgeoisie on to the conquest of state power so as to clear the decks for its own ascent. In this context, note the use of °liberal movement° as a synonym for the bourgeois-democratic constitutionalist movement. It must not be supposed that °liberal° has the connotations commonly associated with the word in modern American politics. It is in this constellation of class forces that the Manifesto proceeds to denounce the role of True Socialism.

(2) PARAGRAPHING. Marx's 1850 reprint of Section III (see Par.141/4) amalgamated Par.161 and Par.162.

Par. 162

(1) QUOTE MARKS ON 'TRUE.' As it had done in the subsection title, the A.E.T. added disclaimer quote marks around °"True"° in the label "True Socialism." it will continue to do so in Par.165—166. The original editions used no quotation marks to express an opinion of the tendency; but the German editions of 1872 and 1883 began the practice of enclosing the entire name "True Socialism" in quote marks. Note that the MEW text follows the A.E.T.'s practice.

(2) COURSE OF POLITICS / MOVEMENT. When the A.E.T. wrote that True Socialism had the opportunity °of confronting the political movement with the Socialist demands,° the modern reader will get a false reading. It sounds as if this tendency was setting its demands before a "movement," a word which nowadays has organizational implications. But we have had occasion to remark more than once (see Par.50/2 and Par. 53/3) that the German word for °movement° (°Bewegung°) here means a course of historical development, the "movement" of history, politics, etc. itself. The True Socialists are criticized here not because they set demands before a "movement" but because they followed the practice °of counterposing the socialist demands to the actual course of politics.° (Admittedly, I have added the word °actually° in order to make the meaning a little clearer.) The actual course of political development was calling for °representative government° and the rest of the list of political reforms that follow in the paragraph, but the True Socialists set themselves in opposition to this paramount need of the time: this is what the Manifesto is saying. It cannot be overstressed that in the 1840s Marx and Engels were among the few socialists or communists who combined revolutionary programmatic views with *support* for bourgeois-democratic political reforms, who argued that °representative government ... bourgeois freedom of the press ... bourgeois liberty and equality,° etc. should be supported even though they were not enough. For the next hundred and fifty years the socialist movement will continue to be bedeviled by a self-sterilizing left wing which made allegedly revolutionary attacks on bourgeois democracy and parliamentarism, with many true statements and cogent arguments, only to substitute less democratic forms, not more democratic ones.

(3) MISPARAGRAPHING. The 1848 editions made the confusing error of beginning not only a new sentence but a new paragraph after the first clause of the first sentence, the clause ending °actual course of politics° (or, in the A.E.T., °with the Socialist demands°). Although my N.E.V. follows the first edition, I have not reproduced this error, since it does not make

298

sense. This paragraph break has also been ignored in the paragraph numbering.

(4) LAW / LEGISLATION. The A.E.T.'s formulation °bourgeois legislation° may be taken erroneously to mean bourgeois laws; but the reference here is not to particular laws—it is to °bourgeois law° in general (°Recht,° system of law or jurisprudence in this case). See Par.98/4.

(5) MATERIAL / ECONOMIC. Here, as before (see Par. 98/8), the A.E.T. replaced °material conditions° with °economic conditions.° The same comments apply.

(6) UNEVEN DEVELOPMENT. For this idea, which occurs in the present paragraph, see Par.153/3,

Par. 163

(1) A.E.T. DELETION. The A.E.T. dropped °German° before °absolute governments,° making the statement more general. The plural form °governments° refers to the thirty-odd states and principalities that then made up °Germany.°

(2) A.E.T. EDITING. The list of the absolute governments' followers has been somewhat edited in the A.E.T.'s formulations. For °priests/parsons,° see Par.144/1. The °schoolmasters° have been promoted to °professors°; the °cabbagejunkers° (°Krautjunkern°) have been Englished into °country squires,° which does not adequately reflect the derogatory force of the German term; the °bureaucrats° have become mere °officials° (which is a pity especially because the terms 'bureaucrat' and 'bureaucracy' were still brand-new when the Manifesto was written, in fact had not yet appeared in English). At the end of the sentence the A.E.T. dropped the adjective °rising° (or aspiring) for the bourgeoisie.

Par. 164

(1) A.E.T. MEDICAL METAPHOR. With °bitter pills° and °dosed,° the A.E.T. resorted to a medical metaphor which is not in the original but which works very nicely. Behind this formulation is the textual problem that is discussed in the next point.

(2) TEXTUAL PROBLEM. The 1848 editions spoke of the way the governments °handled° the workers' uprisings; the German word used here was °bearbeiteten° (treated or dealt with). When Marx reprinted this Section III of the Manifesto in the *NRZ-Revue* of 1850, he changed °bearbeiteten° to °beantworteten° ('replied to'). In this form the sentence would read:

...with which these same governments replied to the German working-class uprisings.

Now of course this may have been a revision rather than a correction; but in general Marx did no revision in this reprint, and this change does not look like an attempt to revise the formulation. It is more likely, as Andréas believes, that Marx was trying to re-establish what should have been the original reading. At about the same time that Marx made this correction in his magazine, Macfarlane made the identical change in her own translation.

(This likewise tends to support the thesis that it was a textual correction rather than a revision; and gives us another reason to argue—as in Par.145/1—that Macfarlane must have gotten some direct help from Marx or Engels.) The Hirschfeld edition of the early 1860s followed the correction made in the *NRZ-Revue*, but the 1866 edition published by Sigfrid Meyer (who did not have access to copies of that magazine) reverted to the 1848 reading; thus °bearbeiteten° hung on. As mentioned, the A.E.T. by-passed the problem by introducing a new metaphor of its own. Since Marx's 1850 correction should be accepted as authoritative, it is fortunate that no question of meaning depends on it.

(3) A.E.T. ADDITION. The A.E.T. inserted an additional phrase, °just at that time,° to locate the event in time, since its medical metaphor (see point 1 above) lacked the chronological implication of the original.

(4) PARAGRAPHING. Marx's 1850 reprint of Section III (see Par.141/4) amalgamated Par.164, 165 and 166 into a single paragraph, except for the last sentence, for which see Par.166/1.

Par. 165

(1) ROLE OF THE PETTY-BOURGEOISIE. For the Manifesto's previous denunciation of this class as °reactionary,° see Par.52/3. That paragraph discussed it under the label °Mittelstände° (°intermediate strata°); here it is more clearly called the °Kleinbürgert(h)um° (the usual word for the °petty-bourgeoisie°). In the present paragraph the indictment is if anything even harsher, for now the assertion is made that this class is °the actual social foundation° of the society of the status quo. All this meant was that the petty-bourgeoisie provided the mass popular base for the regime, not that it was the ruling class. Oddly enough, it was the preceding subsection whose title promised analysis of the petty-bourgeoisie, but which did *not* dispatch that class with the same severity. This oddity, indeed, betrays Marx's motivation: it was True Socialism in particular, not simply petty-bourgeois socialism in general, that excited his deepest antagonism, for the reason explained in Par.153/1, namely, the way in which True Socialism lent a radical cover to absolutism. (For more on this, see KMTR 2:197—99.) The Manifesto reiterated its standpoint in Par.196.

(2) GOVERNMENT (SINGULAR). In Marx's 1850 reprint of Section III, °government° became singular (°...a weapon in the hands of the government°) in spite of the fact that it had been used in the plural in the two preceding paragraphs. This was probably an error; cf. Par.163/1.

(3) PHILISTINEDOM. In this paragraph we meet °Pfahlbürgerschaft° in the second of its two meanings; see Par. 12/1. In Par.12, and again in Par.146, this term (or a cognate) deployed its historical meaning referring to early bourgeois elements, there translated °burgesses.° In the eighteenth century *Pfahlbürger* merged with *Spiessbürger* to acquire the meaning 'philistines,' which meaning it bears in the paragraph before us. But, as the context makes clear, it makes 'philistinedom' virtually synonymous with 'petty-bourgeoisie,' and so I have combined the two (°petty-bourgeois philistinedom°). As we will see below, the A.E.T. does essentially the same thing in Par.168, though in the present paragraph it uses only the translation °Philistines°—In English 'philistine' usually has a purely cultural or charac-

300

terological import, rather than the socioeconomic implication it often takes on in German. Note that the other term for 'philistine,' viz. *spiessbürgerlich*, appeared in Par.20, and a cognate will come along in Par.169. Cautionary mention must be made of a misguided editorial footnote in MEW 4:487, referring to the A.E.T.'s translation °German Philistines° as if it represented an *alteration* from the original.

Par. 166

(1) PARAGRAPHING. The close-knit sequence in thought between the last sentence of the previous paragraph and the first sentence of this one illustrates how artificial some of these paragraph breaks are in the Manifesto. Cf. comments, Par.42/1, Par.70/2. Marx's 1850 reprint of Section III (see Par.141/4) amalgamated Par.164—166 into one paragraph, but the last sentence (It spread like an epidemic.) was added to Par.167.

(2) TWO BIRDS, ONE STONE. The German idiom here is 'two flies with one swat'—a notably easier task than is demanded by the English language.

Par. 167

(1) A.E.T. EDITING. The A.E.T. made a few changes to prune the "flowers of rhetoric" adorning the Manifesto's own language. (i) It omitted the adjective which the N.E.V. renders °belletristic° (°schöngeistigen°—see Par.154/5 for *Schöngeister*). (ii) It left out the hard-to-explain reference implicit in °liebesschwülem,° which became merely °sickly,° in the phrase °steeped in the dew of sickly sentiment.° About a year and a half before writing the Manifesto, Marx and Engels had occasion to dissect the political-mystical treatment of a transcendental Love (the capitalization is needed to indicate that it had little to do with love) by a True Socialist journalist named Hermann Kriege; see KMTR 2:154 for the case. (iii) The adjective °knöchernen° (made of bone) is well served by the A.E.T.'s phrase °all skin and bone°; the N.E.V. makes it °fossilized.° (iv) The A.E.T. left out °a few of° and added the adjective °sorry,° to modify the reference to eternal truths. (v) In the original, °Eternal Truths° had neither capitalization nor quote marks to alert the reader to its ironic use; I have added capitalization for this purpose (see the comment in Par.123—124/1). Andréas does not record that any German edition added the quote marks in Marx's and Engels' lifetime, yet the MEW text of the Manifesto displays them; perhaps they were imported from the A.E.T. (vi) The A.E.T. inserted °wonderfully° to doubly underline the irony, and incidentally to skillfully split an infinitive.

Par. 168

(1) PARAGRAPHING. Marx's 1850 reprint of Section III (see Par.141/4) amalgamated Par.168 and Par.169.

(2) PHILISTINEDOM. See Par.165/3 for °Pfahlbürgerschaft° (°philistinedom,° or

°petty-bourgeois philistinedom°). In Par.168 the A.E.T. made it °the petty-bourgeois Philistine,° though in Par.165 it had used only °Philistine.°

Par. 169

(1) PHILISTINE (SPIESSBÜRGER). The °philistine° here is the °Spiessbürger,° a narrowminded babbitt; it is a more common term for the species than the one we have met so far (cf. Par.12/1 as well as the preceding point), also rather more contemptuous. The A.E.T. signalized the change by rendering it °petty Philistine.°

(2) A.E.T. EDITING. (i) Although the A.E.T. says °model nation ... typical man,° the adjective in the original is the same: the German word °normal° (°standard,° regular). (ii) The A.E.T.'s °villainous meanness° is rather stronger and more extreme than the original. (iii) In opposing communism the True Socialists drew the °final conclusion° of their views, but did not go to an °extreme length,° as the A.E.T. has it. (iv) As we have seen before, the original edition did not deem it necessary to use quote marks to disclaim remarks like the °crudely destructive tendency of communism°; nor were they used in Marx's 1850 reprint. These quote marks appear in the MEW text and other modern editions, but Andréas does not mention where they were first introduced. The A.E.T. used the quote marks here as elsewhere. (v) Instead of °elevation above all class struggles,° the A.E.T. used the stronger language, °impartial contempt of° etc. (vi) The insertion of °now (1847)° in the A.E.T. was, of course, an editorial explanation.

(3) ENGELS' FOOTNOTE. The footnote in the A.E.T. was virtually identical with the one in the 1890 German edition. The statement that the representatives of this tendency ceased after 1848 to °dabble° in socialism was not applicable to Moses Hess, its godfather, but then Hess's name was not mentioned in the Manifesto in connection with it. Engels' footnote takes as its target Karl Grün (1817—1887). During the 1840s Grün advocated socialistic views of the sort attacked in the Manifesto, and also popularized Proudhon's ideas. In 1842 he suffered the radicalizing experience of being expelled from Baden for editing the *Mannheimer Abendzeitung* from too leftist a standpoint; he emigrated to Paris in 1844 and, the following year, published one of the earliest accounts of the French movement, *Die sociale Bewegung in Frankreich und Belgien*. A deputy to the Prussian assembly during the 1848 revolution, he later taught in Frankfurt and Vienna, but never took part in the working-class or socialist movement.

2. Conservative or Bourgeois Socialism

Par. 170: Title, Subsection 2

(1) CONSERVATIVE. Just as, in the title of Subsection 1—see Par.136 (Tl)/1—the term 'reactionary' was used in its literal political meaning, so too °conservative°: i.e., supportive of the status quo; not looking backward to prebourgeois society or forward to a more progressive one. The trouble with this term, as used in the Manifesto, is that it applied to

France but not to Germany, where the supporters of the real political status quo had just been denounced in Subsection 1 as "reactionary socialists." In other words, the trouble was that the bourgeois revolution had not yet taken place in Germany, but Marx was already thinking in the framework of a terminology (derived from France and England) which assumed that the state power was bourgeois. The difficulty shows itself in another way: Marx argued, with more or less emphasis at various times, that the German bourgeoisie was still revolutionary (see Par.19 of the Manifesto and the comment in Par.51/1) if only in relation to the feudalists and their supporters. Then were not bourgeois social reformers also "revolutionary" in the same sense? Marx would have opined, with justice, that this was not an educationally useful way to explain their role; but with the same justice °conservative° was not a useful designation for the social tendency described. I do not think Marx used it again in this way.

(2) BOURGEOIS SOCIALISM. For the meaning of °socialism° in this combination, see Par.136 (TIII)/3, which makes clear that °socialism° then encompassed *social reform* that was directed to the "Social Question," even if entirely innocent of any anticapitalist idea. This is what the Manifesto means by °bourgeois socialism°. A good statement about the same tendency was contained in Engels' *Principles of Communism* (Ques. 24):

> The second group consists of adherents of present society in whom the evils inseparable from it have awakened fears for its survival. They therefore endeavor to preserve present society but to remove the evils bound up with it. With this end in view, some of them propose measures of mere charity, and others grandiose systems of reform which, under the pretext of reorganizing society, would retain the foundations of present society, and thus present society itself. These *bourgeois socialists* will also have to be continuously fought by the Communists, since they work for the enemies of the Communists and defend the society which it is the Communists' aim to destroy.

Par. 170

(1) A.E.T. DELETION OF EMPHASIS. The A.E.T. eliminated the emphasis on °social ills° (or °social grievances° in its own version). Incidentally, emphasis in the original editions of 1848 was, as usual, indicated not by italics but by l e t t e r s p a c i n g, which was not always used for the purposes we are accustomed to. As is explained in KMTR 1:26, it was often a device like a pointed arrow, to call attention to a topic (or a name, etc.). In the present paragraph, I would guess, it was used to highlight a key idea, the key to the meaning of the passage.

Par. 171

(1) ECONOMISTS. The Manifesto's reference to °economists,° without any qualification, as if they constituted a reform tendency, would be surprising if we did not know

that this is precisely how the term had been used for the century preceding— mainly in France. In the eighteenth century, *les économistes* meant the early Physiocrats, by and large. To be sure, by the time of the Manifesto this usage was out-of-date, particularly in England.

(2) CHARITY ORGANIZERS. In Marx's 1850 reprint of Section III, this was replaced with "charity organization." Besides being in the singular, which does not make sense, the term is out of place in what is a list of *people;* it was probably a misprint or a misreading of the manuscript.

(3) TEMPERANCE FANATICS. This was the A.E.T.'s version of °founders of temperance societies,° and no doubt reflected Engels' opinion of the anti-alcohol movement, as a lover of good wine and spirits. Incidentally, the German socialists had a long record of fighting against drunkenness and alcoholism in the working-class movement without however supporting attempts at prohibition.

(4) PARAGRAPHING. Marx's 1850 reprint of Section III (see Par.141/4) amalgamated

Par.171 and Par.172.

Par. 172

(1) PROUDHON. At the time of the Manifesto, Pierre Joseph Proudhon (1809—1865) was one of the best-known socialists in France, though he did not usually call himself a socialist. He had published his first work, a great success, *Qu'est-ce que la Propriété?* (1840). His answer, "Property is theft" an aphorism borrowed from Brissot, became famous. His chief work came in 1846: *Système des Contradictions Economiques ou Philosophie de la Misére.* Marx's reply of 1847, *Misére de la Philosophie (Poverty of Philosophy)* took off from the subtitle. In this book Proudhon had already come out for "an-archie" and inveighed against all authority, but it was not his early anarchism (still virtually unknown as an ideology) that drew attention; his main nostrum for society's ills was a mutual-credit bank. Marx's book dissected his economic analyses and his social views. In addition, Marx's opinion of Proudhon was set forth in two long letters, one to Annenkov, December 28, 1846, and another (printed as an article) to Schweitzer, January 24, 1865. In all of these writings, Marx explained Proudhon as a representative of petty-bourgeois ideology—an interpretation well founded not only on Proudhon's ideas but also on his personal development. The fact that the Manifesto presents him not in the sections on petty-bourgeois socialism but as a representative of °bourgeois socialism° is not only surprising but impossible to justify in terms of Marx's own analyses before and after the Manifesto. What justification is possible I presented in KMTR 2:295 fn; but it would be simpler to say that there was a wide area common both to bourgeois social reform and various sorts of petty-bourgeois socialism; and Proudhon, who was diffuse and amorphous in his positive ideas, certainly straddled this area. This provides some reason for the choice, but not much justification. Perhaps Marx felt this later: while in the original edition this statement about Proudhon was set off in a paragraph by itself, in Marx's 1850 reprint of Section III the sentence was merged into Par.171.

Par. 173

(1) A.E.T. EDITING. The A.E.T. rewrote some of the language without making any significant change. To begin with, it replaced °the conditions of existence of modern society° with °all the advantages of modern social conditions.° Further along, where the original had bourgeois socialism developing °a partial or complete system° (in the singular—meaning, in German, that each bourgeois socialist developed a system of his own), the A.E.T. made the construction plural as is proper in English: °various more or less complete systems.° The difference is in grammar, not in content.

(2) NEW JERUSALEM. The heaven on earth promised in Revelation 21—22: "And I saw a new heaven and a new earth... the holy city, new Jerusalem, coming down from God out of heaven..." It represents the tendency in religious sect life to await the social utopia from a dispensation from above. Also implied may be a reference to the Church of the New Jerusalem, founded on the doctrines of the Swedish mystic Emanuel Swedenborg (1688—1772), to whom "the heavens were opened" in 1745. It spread to a considerable following in England (as well as America and some parts of the Continent); the first General Conference took place in England in 1817, and it was strongest in Lancashire. In 1848 a Swedenborgian "Union of the New Church" was founded in Germany. But the term °New Jerusalem° had no necessary connection with the Swedenborgians.

From 1866 on, the German editions of the Manifesto changed the text slightly, replacing °in order to enter the New Jerusalem° with °and enter...° The A.E.T. did not follow this, but rather expanded the whole reference with several added words: °and thereby to march straightway into the social New Jerusalem.°

(3) PARAGRAPHING. Marx's 1850 reprint of Section III (see Par.141/4) divided this paragraph into two. The first paragraph comprised the first three sentences; the second began with °The bourgeoisie conceives the world...°

Par. 174

(1) PRACTICAL FORM. From 1866 on, the German editions made a slight change in the text: instead of °more practical° form, it said °only more practical form.° The A.E.T. did not follow this change, but made another, giving a different order to the three adjectives before °form of socialism.°

(2) FORM OF SOCIALISM. In the same clause as the preceding point, this phrase has been given some editorial attention. Although the text has not been changed, modern reprints like MEW give an emendation in editorial brackets to make it read °form of this socialism° in German. This happens to be the A.E.T.'s formulation. To be sure, it implements the sense of the passage. Marx's 1850 reprint of Section III made an emendation here too, so that the phrase became: °form of conservative socialism.° The intent was obviously the same as that of the editorial brackets.

(3) TRIED. Andréas is concerned about the fact that this verb (°suchte°) is in the past tense, and thinks that it must have been a mistake in 1848; that neither the authors nor

translators later noticed the mistake (as in the A.E.T.) because by that time 'bourgeois socialism' had in fact become a theory of the past. Perhaps it *was* a mistake, but the argument is faulty, for 'bourgeois socialism' in the Manifesto's sense (social reform) certainly did not die out. Andréas does not take account of the fact that this paragraph is not about 'bourgeois socialism' in general (as in the preceding paragraph) but about a specific form of this tendency—which however has no representative named for it. By using the past tense Marx certainly pushed this type of bourgeois socialism into the past, but we really cannot be sure whom he was talking about.

(4) CHANGE / REFORM. Where the original referred to °political change,° the A.E.T. made it °political reform.° This is not using °reform° pejoratively, for the Manifesto's viewpoint is clearly opposed to those who counterpose economic change to political reforms. Indeed, here the Manifesto anticipates a dispute in the socialist movement which was only barely visible in 1848: it condemns the standpoint that later came to be known as 'economism'—the depreciation of political issues in favor of exclusive concentration on economic demands.

(5) MATERIAL / ECONOMIC. We have noted previous cases where the A.E.T. replaced °material° with °economic° to modify °conditions of existence°; see Par.98/8. In the present paragraph, the original itself uses the two interchangeably, in apposition. The term °material conditions° is given first, as the more accurate one; but in case it is not understood, the text adds °economic° to indicate the idea.

(6) RELATIONS OF PRODUCTION. We have seen that in some cases (see Par.33/6b, Par.43/2, Par.131/2) the A.E.T. displayed reluctance to use this term, preferring 'conditions of...' But, as once before (Par.127/1), it does use °relations of...° in the present paragraph.

(7) REVOLUTIONARY WAYS. Instead of the original's expression °in revolutionary ways,° the A.E.T. said °by a revolution.° Perhaps Engels thought this was more explicit.

(8) COST OF STATE ADMINISTRATION. In the last sentence the Manifesto makes a point which is very important but which has not been emphasized by the socialist movement: one of the consequences of, and by the same token one of the motivations for, bourgeois-democratic political reform is the question of lower administrative cost explained in this paragraph; among other things, dictatorship is a very expensive enterprise, in several ways. Socialists should argue that a democratic workers' state means *cheap government* in the long run; but this gets us onto a different subject.

Par. 175

(1) FIGURE OF SPEECH. This sentence makes an effective aphoristic put-down, but frankly, I'm not sure what it means. Webster's gives the nontechnical definition of °figure of speech° as "an extravagant statement; an untruth"; but is Marx saying here that bourgeois social reform is merely a deception or a flourish? The last sentence of the next paragraph gives some color to this interpretation. The modern reader may be tempted to think that Marx was questioning the *socialistic* bona fides of this tendency, in line with modern notions that draw a hard line between socialism and mere social reform; but there is no reason to

believe so, since 'socialism' is used loosely throughout the Manifesto.

Par. 176

(1) PRISON REFORM: THE CELL S#STEM. When the Manifesto was written, the cellular prison was still quite new. In the late eighteenth century John Howard and others had exposed the unspeakable horrors of the typical English prison, not only for convicted felons but for innocent detainees; there was a wave of penal reform; the idea of the separate cell for individual prisoners gained support. In the 1830s select committees of Parliament came out for the cell system; in 1840 Pentonville prison was started; and when the Manifesto appeared Pentonville was the model for new prison construction. Similar developments took place in America and on the Continent. The A.E.T. refused to translate °Zellen-gefängnisse° (cellular prisons) but generalized the idea to °Prison Reform.° MECW 6:514 has a misleading editorial footnote translating this term as "solitary confinement."

Par. 177

(1) TEXTUAL REVISION. Apparently the first two words, °Its socialism,° were felt to be ambiguous (what was the antecedent of °Its°?) and so, from 1872 on, the German editions were changed to read: °The socialism of the bourgeoisie consists...° This was not a happy change, since the original was talking about the socialism *of the bourgeois socialists* not the "socialism of the bourgeoisie," whatever that might be thought to be. The A.E.T. avoided this problem by rewriting the whole line, leaving out the word °socialism° altogether; its first word °It° presumably referred to the °bourgeois socialism° under discussion.

3. Critical-Utopian Socialism and Communism

Par. 178: Title, Subsection 3

(1) UTOPIAN. This term, derived from the title of Thomas More's famous work of 1516, was in use long before the Manifesto and had been attached to a variety of nouns. But the combination 'utopian socialism' may have been used for the first time in the Manifesto; at any rate no one has cited a prior appearance. The same goes for the term 'utopian socialist.' (Cole's *History of Socialist Thought* indicates that it was first published in J. A. Blanqui's *History of Political Economy*, but this is erroneous.) Yet the idea was around; for example, Karl Grün's *Die sociale Bewegung in Frankreich und Belgien* counterposed "utopianism" to "scientific socialism" in 1845. To be sure, the Manifesto uses a hyphenated form only, °critical-utopian socialism and communism,° for reasons we see below. The Manifesto's section on utopian socialism offers no definition of the term, the nearest thing to it being Par.183. Unfortunately, during three centuries of use, 'utopian' picked up a variety of connotations: it could imply that something was (a) impossible or impractical, (b) ideal or ideally perfect, (c) imaginary or

fanciful, or (d) futuristic; or any combinations of these together with pejorative adjectives like 'visionary,' 'perfectionist,' 'chimerical.' With this arsenal of meanings, anyone can prove that anyone else is 'utopian' in some sense, and this game has been played out in countless books. Some of these are colloquial usages; here we are concerned only with the term's scientific meaning for Marx. The defining characteristic of the utopian approach was its method, the leap into speculative abstraction, instead of deriving proposals for social change from the actual forces at work in society. While this criticism overlaps some of the pejorative adjectives listed above, it is not congruent with any of them. As time went on, Marx and Engels grew more appreciative, not less, of the contributions made by the utopian innovators, particularly Fourier and Owen; witness Engels' encomiums in *Socialism: Utopian and Scientific*. (One of the infallible indicia of marxological ignorance is the oft-repeated assertion that Marx or Engels used 'utopian' as simply a "term of opprobrium," or that they merely "cavalierly dismissed" the utopians. These claims—I have quoted actual statements—were apparently based on an exhaustive study of Engels' title.) See also Par.189/4. The Manifesto's discussion largely focuses on the utopians' weaknesses, which it explains historically, but their positive contributions are set forth in Par.188.

(2) CRITICAL. By inventing the hyphenated description °critical-utopian,° Marx made the positive side of this tendency coordinate with its weak aspect, and thereby emphasized the former, to be further developed in Par.188. This appreciation had already been embodied in the (then still unpublished) manuscript of the *German Ideology* which had opined that "the Saint-Simonian criticism of existing conditions" was "the most important aspect of Saint-Simonism," and "the critical side of Fourier" was "his most important contribution" (MECW 5:505, 510). This concerned their critical analysis of bourgeois society, as distinct from their speculative leap to what should replace it.

(3) UTOPIAN COMMUNISM. This term is less often heard than 'utopian socialism'; there were fewer utopian communists, for one thing. It applies to utopians who, for one reason or another, called themselves 'communists.' The chief figure of this sort was Cabet; for his use of the appellation see note 2 on the Main Title. Another was Wilhelm Weitling, whose name is not mentioned in the Manifesto. In fact, although the Manifesto says °socialism and communism° more than once, it does not mention the name of a single utopian communist; in Par.180 the communists referred to are apparently included in the °etc.° To be sure, the designation 'communist' was sometimes used in the Owenite movement, for all terminology was still in a state of flux; in the *Holy Family* Owen was called the founder of English communism (MECW 4:131), and in an 1845 article by Engels written for the Owenite organ, "Rapid Progress of Communism in Germany," virtually everyone became a "communist." The communists who do figure in this subsection, the communists of the Babouvist tradition and of the French secret societies of workers, are those who in Par.178—179 are put aside from the 'utopian' designation.

Par. 178

(1) NOT SPEAKING HERE. Of course, the Manifesto does go on to speak of the tendency represented by °Babeuf, etc.°: the next paragraph, Par.179, is devoted to a general statement about it; another case of apophasis or paraleipsis (preterition). But this statement

has the character of a parenthetical insertion; the implication is that a discussion of this tendency does not belong in the Manifesto. Why? The present paragraph seems to say that it is not discussed *because* it °expressed the demands of the proletariat.° That is, the implication is the following: *Babeuf represented a form (if only a primitive one) of proletarian communism, i.e., of our own tendency, and here we are discussing only alternative tendencies...* In his original outline for Section III—see Par. 136 (TIII)/1—Marx had included Babeuf under the heading "Critical utopian systems of literature," a designation that would be hard to justify under his own strict definition; perhaps he decided, rightly, that Babeuf did not properly come under this heading. The situation is clearer in Engels' *Principles of Communism*, which in Question 24 undertakes to describe three socialist currents but never discusses different kinds of communists; for "the Communists" are taken to be those in whose name the program is being written; Babeuf is never mentioned at all. True, the Manifesto entitled its Section III "Socialist *and Communist* Literature" but the second appellation actually applied only to those self-styled communists for whom the Manifesto was *not* speaking. The *German Ideology* had shown awareness of two kinds of self-styled communists:

> The few nonrevolutionary communist bourgeois who made their appearance since the time of Babeuf were a rare occurrence; the vast majority of the communists in all countries are revolutionary. All communists in France reproach the followers of Saint-Simon and Fourier with their peaceableness ... [MECW 5:226]

The Manifesto's refusal to discuss the communist tendencies as if they were alternative tendencies, as if they were "out-siders" from the standpoint of the Manifesto's writers, must be understood in connection with another fact: the fact that the name of the Communist League nowhere appears in the document (see note 3 under Main Title). The "Communist party" included communists who were outside the CL—such at least was the Manifesto's perspective—and current differences inside this "party" were not directly taken up by the Manifesto.

(2) BABEUF. François Noël Babeuf, called Gracchus Babeuf (1760—1797), was the founder of the first socialist or communist *movement* organized to achieve a new anticapitalist social order. His views came largely from Morelly and his interpretation of Rousseau. From 1793 on, he was active in Paris as a revolutionary journalist, lastly editor of *Le Tribun du Peuple* (under the name Gracchus B.) with a platform calling or sans-culotte power, pointed against the Directory, rallying many former followers of Robespierre and Hébert. In 1796, convinced that the revolution had been betrayed, he established an insurrectional committee with links to the army, Paris artisans, leftists in the provinces, etc. Sylvain Maréchal drafted the "Manifesto of the Equals" as platform of the movement (which was called the Conspiracy of the Equals). Denounced by an informer, the insurrectional committee was arrested in May, and tried from October to next May. Babeuf was one of two sentenced to death; they committed suicide with a dagger, but were guillotined anyway. Babouvism gained European currency in the 1830s through the publication of a book by Babeuf's lieutenant Buonarroti, *La Conspiration pour l'Egalité dite de Babeuf* (1828); translated into English by Bronterre O'Brien (1836). In the *Holy Family* Marx traced the roots of socialism in the French Revolution not to the Jacobins or even their Hébertist left wing but to (a) the social left wing of the

Girondists, organized in the Cercle Social of Claude Fauchet; (b) the radical-plebeian representatives of social democracy whom their enemies sneered at as the "Enragés," naming Théophile Leclerc and Jacques Roux specifically; and (c)--

> The revolutionary movement...which finally with *Babeuf's* conspiracy was temporarily defeated, gave rise to the *communist* idea which...Buonarroti reintroduced in France after the Revolution of 1830. [MECW 4:119]

True, "the *Babouvists* were crude, uncivilized [i.e., not modern] materialists, but developed communism too derives *directly* from *French materialism*." (MECW 4:131) No one should regard Babeuf "as the theoretical representative of communism" (as the *German Ideology* said); his contribution was different. The left-wing drive in the French Revolution "derived its support from the insurgent proletariat," wrote Engels in 1845, and "Babeuf's conspiracy for equality revealed the final consequences of the democracy of [17]93—insofar as these were at all possible at that time." (MECW 6:5) Shortly before working on the Manifesto, Marx wrote on how the communist movement arose out of the bourgeois revolution:

> The first manifestation of a truly active communist party is contained within the bourgeois revolution, at the moment when the constitutional monarchy is eliminated. The most consistent *republicans*, in England the *Levelers* in France *Babeuf, Buonarroti* etc., were the first to proclaim these "social questions." The *Babeuf Conspiracy*, by Babeuf's friend and party comrade Buonarroti, shows how these republicans derived from the "movement" of history the realization that the disposal of the social question of *rule by princes* and *republic* did not mean that even a single "social question" has been solved in the interests of the proletariat. [MECW 6:321f]

In the °etc.° after Babeuf's name we have the only reference to the other communists whom the Manifesto refuses to discuss by name. Among these Marx would have included Théodore Dézamy and Jules Gay, whose writings influenced him at the time he was first reading about socialism; Auguste Blanqui and Armand Barbès were well-known leaders of the French communist secret societies of the day; Wilhelm Weitling emulated them among German worker émigrés. For Cabet's self-styled communism, see note 2 on the Main Title. Is it true that their movements °expressed the demands of the proletariat°? Not if the modern proletariat is meant, that is, the class of wage-workers, for industry based on wage-labor was only weakly developed; yes, if we consider what they themselves would have called the proletariat, that is, people dependent on their own labor, mainly artisans. There is a terminological confusion here that is historically conditioned.

(3) A.E.T. ADDITION. The word °always° was added: °always given voice...° It seems to be superfluous since the same idea is expressed five words back.

Par. 179

(1) A.E.T. EDITING. The wording was a bit changed in several places. (i) Near the beginning, the A.E.T. left out °class° in the expression °class interests° (or in its own version °its own ends°). (ii) As in other cases already noted, °material conditions° was changed to °economic conditions.° (iii) The ending of this sentence was substantially expanded in the A.E.T., beginning °conditions that had yet to be produced,° to the conclusion of the sentence. To be sure, no new thought was introduced, only much increased emphasis on the idea already there. (iv) At the end of the paragraph, °leveling° was spelled out to mean °social leveling,° and the statement about it was made more pejorative: instead of °a crude leveling,° it said °social leveling in its crudest form.° (v) The A.E.T.'s insertion of °these attempts° in the middle of the first sentence was unnecessary, and may be more confusing than helpful.

(2) REACTIONARY. Once again, the literal meaning; see note 1 on Par.136 (TI)/1.

(3) ASCETICISM. For a good explanation of the role played by asceticism in the early communist movement, see Engels *Peasant War in Germany* (beginning of Chap. 3), where of course it is discussed in terms of the medieval situation. In the modern movement it tended to die out (or, as Engels says in the work cited, lose its revolutionary meaning) "when the development of modern productive forces infinitely multiplies the luxuries, thus rendering Spartan equality superfluous." The degree to which it hung on in the communist sects was a barometer of primitiveness.

(4) LEVELING. This is the pejorative term describing demands for social or economic equality. Marx's term in German is °Gleichmacherei° (lit., equal-making), hence it does not necessarily contain a reference to the Levelers of the English (Cromwellian) revolution, whose collective name was applied to them in derision. A Puritan grouping on the left wing of the revolution, led by John Lilburne, the English Levelers fought for a constitutional democratic republic, political and religious liberty, and social reforms. Its mass support was especially in the lower ranks of the army; Cromwell crushed it among the soldiers in 1649. On its own left were the True Levelers or "Diggers," led by Gerrard Winstanley, with socialist-communistic views. By °a crude leveling° Marx meant demands for equality unleavened by any social program or ideas that would make greater equality possible in the course of a social transformation; equality-mongering as an end in itself.

(5) PARAGRAPHING. In Marx's 1850 reprint of Section III (see Par.141/4) this paragraph was divided in two. The first paragraph comprised the present first sentence; the second began with °The revolutionary literature...°.

Par. 180

(1) PROPERLY SO CALLED). Which °socialist and communist systems° would be so called improperly? I think the one-word insertion (°eigentlich°) reflected an unvoiced feeling about the then amorphousness of the term 'socialist'—explained in Par.136 (TIII)/3. The socialists °properly so° called were those whom we would today call socialists, because in some way or to some extent they expressed anticapitalist views, not merely proposals for social reform or answers to the Social Question.

(2) AND COMMUNIST. On the absence of °communist° names from this paragraph, see Par.178 (T3)/3 and Par.178/1.

(3) SAINT-SIMON. Count Claude Henri (de Rouvroy) de Saint-Simon (1760—1825) was one of the three great socialist innovators (the other two being named with him in this paragraph). He stands on a borderline: although he was a seminal source of socialistic ideas at the start of the movement, his own writings did not propose social solutions that are socialist in a modern sense (anticapitalist). His main contribution to the mix of ideas was stress on scientific social planning (from above, hierarchically, by a power elite). Nor did he really offer a utopia of his own, despite his common classification as a utopian socialist. It was only in his last work, *Le Nouveau Christianisme* (1825), that he did stress the working class—as a source of recruitment. This orientation was followed by the Saint-Simonian "school" or "religion" (sect) organized by Bazard and Enfantin after the master's death. It was this movement that had the greatest impact on the early formation of European socialism; it was much more than simply a reflection of Saint-Simon's ideas, and historically much more important. The best work on the man himself is F. E. Manuel, *The New World of Saint-Simon* (1956); but there is no good treatment in English of the movement. The unsuperseded study of the latter is S. Charléty, *Histoire de Saint-Simonisme* (1896).

(4) CHARLES FOURIER. The family name of François Charles Marie Fourier (1772—1837) was originally spelled Fourrier, as we find it in the first edition of the Manifesto. The writings of Fourier and Saint-Simon constituted the fountain from which French socialism flowed for about its first quarter century. Son of a well-to-do Besançon shopkeeper, he conceived an early hatred of the chicanery and inefficiency of business and the bourgeoisie. He settled in Lyons (1800); published his first writings there; moved to Paris (1828), and worked as a traveling salesman and bookkeeper. His first disciples came around 1816; in 1834 Jules Lechevalier opened the *Revue du Progrès Social* to Fourier's ideas. The first organ of the *école sociétaire* (the Fourierist tendency) appeared in 1836 as *La Phalange*. His new social order, which he called the "phalanx," was based on a model community, the *phalanstère* (phalanstery), which he described in detail. The movement generally used the term *association(ism)* rather than socialism. His leading disciple and the organizer of the Fourierist movement was Victor Considérant, under whom Fourierism became a respectable social-reform group, publishing the influential organ *Démocratie Pacifique*. The leading American Fourierist was Albert Brisbane; the best-known Fourierist community, Brook Farm. Aside from his proposed social order (which was not actually fully socialist in the modern sense), Fourier was noteworthy for his advanced views on women's rights and sexual liberation, views that were played down by his own disciples but were especially admired by Marx and Engels. Engels' *Socialism, Utopian and Scientific* offers a veritable panegyric on Fourier. In 1845, when Marx and Engels were planning to issue a "Library of the Best Foreign Socialist Writers," Engels translated and published a work of Fourier's on trade (see MECW 4:613).

(5) OWEN. Robert Owen (1771—1858) was the great British (Welsh-born) pioneer of socialism and cooperativism. He began as a self-made, successful cotton manufacturer in Manchester. Moving to New Lanark, Scotland (1800), he reconstructed the mills and the town into a model industrial community. Since profits increased despite great benefits to the workers, the New Lanark experiment became world-famous. But his attempts to establish model (utopian) communities elsewhere, as in New Harmony, Indiana, were failures. Besides,

312

he developed nonconformist views on religion, marriage, and other sensitive subjects, and was unable to convince the British government and the capitalist class to jettison their social system. For a while he turned to an alliance with the young trade-union movement, but he was basically hostile to working-class organization and looked to his own benevolent dictatorship as the mainspring of change. His chief contribution was made through the activity and influence of the Owenite movement he inaugurated. There are a number of biographies of the man, but it would be more important still to have an adequate study of the movement; a contribution is made by J. F. C. Harrison' *Quest for the New Moral World* (1969). Soon after his arrival in England, Engels began writing (autumn 1843) for the Owenite organ *The New Moral World*, as well as for the Chartist press, and continued until 1845.

(6) DESCRIBED ABOVE. The A.E.T. moved this expression to the middle of the sentence in order to show that it modifies the word °period°; the German original makes this clear by means of grammatical agreement, unavailable in English.

(7) THE PARENTHETICAL REFERENCE. The parenthesis at the end of the paragraph was left out in Marx's 1850 reprint of Section III. Perhaps he felt that the °period of the struggle between proletariat and bourgeoisie° was described also in Section II or III; or perhaps he dropped it only because the reprint did not include Section I. On the other hand, the A.E.T. added °Section I° to the title reference.

(8) QUOTE IN 'HERR VOGT.' Chapter 4 of this 1860 polemic (MECW 17:88f) gave a long citation from the Manifesto, all in a single continuous paragraph, which however was actually made up of several paragraphs. It comprised: all of Par.180 except the parenthetical reference at the end, all of Par.181—183, and parts of Par.189; but there are some changes noted under the respective paragraphs, below. Besides (not noted below) there are revisions of spelling and language forms, and the addition of emphasis (letter spacing in the original, italics in reprints like MEW)—the emphasis being relevant to the line of thought in *Herr Vogt* not the Manifesto.

Par. 181

(1) A.E.T. ADDITION. The words °as yet in its infancy° were inserted in the second sentence, to explain why the utopians saw the proletariat as lacking class °initiative° or °independence.° This change was perhaps related to the revision discussed in the next point.

(2) A.E.T. REVISION. The second sentence was recast by the A.E.T. in a way which, I think, was illegitimate as translation and unwise in content. What in the original was charged against the utopians as a *failure in perception* on their part was, in the A.E.T., explained as simply due to the immaturity of the proletariat itself; to carry this revision out, the A.E.T. even wrote in a few additional words (see preceding point). The revised version could even be interpreted to mean that there *was* no class °self-activity° (or °initiative°), etc. to be perceived; but this was both historically inaccurate (at least in Marx's view) and unfaithful to the words of the Manifesto. The change made by Engels (for it must have been made by him, not Sam Moore) goes well beyond simply adducing the immaturity of the proletariat

313

as a factor. All this may remind us of a previous occasion when Engels defended one of the great utopians against a criticism by Marx: see Engels' footnote on Saint-Simon in Volume 3 of *Capital* (Chap. 36). And Engels was wrong there too, in my opinion; but this is not the place to argue the question.

(3) A.E.T. EDITING. In the same sentence, there are two cases where the A.E.T. version involves a slight nuance: instead of °historical self-activity,° it says °historical initiative°; and instead of °political movement characteristic° of the proletariat, it speaks of °independent political movement.°

(4) QUOTE IN 'HERR VOGT.' See Par.180/8. In this work, citing the present paragraph only twelve years after first publication of the Manifesto, the two main verbs are put into the past tense: the utopian currents had become historical references.

Par. 182

(1) EVEN PACE. On this expression, see Par.119—21/6.

(2) A.E.T. RECASTING. Instead of °they...do not find,° the A.E.T. turned the sentence around to say: °the economic situation...does not as yet offer to them...° The effect is essentially the same as that explained in Par.181/2, above, though here the change is less objectionable because the difference is slighter. In fact, it would be hard to see why the change was made at all if we did not have the model of the previous alteration.

(3) A.E.T. EDITING. In the last sentence, the A.E.T. added °therefore° and the word °new° twice, in each case making the thought explicit.

(4) PARAGRAPHING. Marx's 1850 reprint of Section III (see Par.141/4) amalgamated Par.182 and Par.183.

(5) QUOTE IN 'HERR VOGT.' See Par.180/8 on the citation of the present paragraph in the 1860 work by Marx.

Par. 183

(1) SOCIAL / HISTORICAL. The original's reference to °social° activity (or action) was changed by the A.E.T. to °historical° action. It is hard to see why the change was made, or how it can be justified, since here the counterposition is with °personal° inventive activity (or action), and the °historical° aspect is part of the immediately following clause.

(2) FANCIFUL / FANTASTIC. The tendency to translate °phantastisch° as °fantastic° is understandable, but it is overdone, and here it is misleading. The usual connotation of °fantastic° in English is irrational, wild, bizarre, chimerical, grotesque, freakish; but (apart from some aspects of Fourier) the utopians' approach emphasized *fancy* rather than fantasy or extravagant freaks of thought. In any case, the counterposition in the present paragraph is °historical° versus °fanciful° (or, in the A.E.T., °historically created° versus personally °contrived°), not phantasmagoric versus sobersided.

(3) A.E.T. ADDITION: SPONTANEOUS. Instead of °the gradually advancing° (or ongoing) °organization of the proletariat into a class,° the A.E.T. spoke of °the gradual,

spontaneous° class organization. The insertion of °spontaneous°, I presume, was intended to heighten the contrast with the °fanciful ... concoction° of a °specially contrived° social order. It should not be regarded as a contribution to a later debate about 'spontaneity' versus party organization, a debate that was of course still unknown.

(4) QUOTE IN 'HERR VOGT.' See Par.180/8. The quotation in this work included all of the present paragraph. The text was slightly altered to omit two definite articles, which however do not figure in the English translation anyway.

Par. 184

(1) SUFFERING CLASS. The view of the working class °as the most suffering class° was the viewpoint especially of the Saint-Simonians; at least they laid the greatest emphasis on it. But it was the initial approach to a working-class orientation on the part of the early socialists in general, *including Marx himself*. He began writing (autumn 1842) of human suffering as the "popular language of distress," and focused the Social Question on "the existence of a suffering humanity that thinks and of a thinking humanity that is oppressed." His first economic studies transformed the Economic Question from one of suffering to one of social struggle. In his *Economic and Philosophic Manuscripts* of 1844 the prime emphasis for the first time was laid on the struggle rather than the suffering; and while he still mentioned that man is a "*suffering being*," this is done to explain why he is also a "*passionate being*." (For the references, see Suffering in the index to KMTR 1.)

(2) PARAGRAPHING. Marx's 1850 reprint of Section III (see Par.141/4) amalgamated Par.184 and Par.185.

Par. 185

(1) POSITION IN LIFE / SURROUNDINGS. In the first sentence, the original said °position in life° (or life situation, or social status, °Lebenslage°); and besides this is adduced as part of the utopians' motivation for depreciating °class antagonism.° To render this simply °surroundings° is a surprising abandonment of the Manifesto's line of thought. This is the third time now that we find the A.E.T. softening the Manifesto's criticism of the utopians, at the expense of the translation's accuracy in letter and spirit. (Cf. Par. 181/2, Par.182/2.) Moreover, the same word °Lebenslage° is used in the very next sentence, obviously to make a counterposition; but the relationship of the two sentences has been destroyed by the A.E.T.'s rendering. (In the second sentence, the A.E.T. turns °Lebenslage° into °condition.°)

(2) A.E.T. EDITING. Other changes made in this paragraph by the A.E.T. are of the language-editing sort. In the first sentence, °all° was added to the expression °all class antagonisms,° and the noun itself was made plural, but the difference in meaning is of no consequence. In this sentence the main verb in the German text was plural, but it is English grammar that required the change to singular, not a change in meaning. In the third sentence, °without distinction° was expanded to °without distinction of class,° but the meaning was already implicit.

Par. 186

(1) PEACEFUL MEANS OR REVOLUTIONARY ACTION. The counterposition of these two perspectives on political methods makes clear the viewpoint of the Manifesto. For a positive statement, see Par.202 below.

(2) NECESSARILY DOOMED. The original's description of the °experiments° as those °that naturally fail° is here intensified and made more portentous with: °necessarily doomed to failure.° This formulation was, no doubt, necessarily doomed to be used to "prove" a theory of predestination; see Par.141—142/2.

Par. 187

(1) FANCIFUL / FANTASTIC. For this paragraph's use of °fantastic° (twice), see the comment in Par.183/2.

(2) CORRESPONDS TO / ARISES FROM. The utopians' °depiction of the future society° (says this paragraph) °corresponds to° the immaturity of the proletariat. In the editions of 1848, the German word for °corresponds to° was °entspricht°; the same word was used in Marx's own 1850 reprint of Section III. But in the German edition of 1872, and remaining so in subsequent German editions, this word became °entspringt° (arises from). There was no evident reason for this change, and .entspringt. does not sit comfortably in the sentence; Andréas thinks that it was a question of a printer's error that somehow stuck. Yet the A.E.T. ignored the change and apparently went back to the original formulation.

(3) INSTINCTIVE YEARNINGS. This phrase was put into the A.E.T. without a presageful (let alone instinctive) foreknowledge of later theories about yearnings. The original simply spoke of a 'drive' (or an urging) in the proletariat that pointed ahead to (or presaged) a °general reconstruction of society°: hence my rendering °presageful thrust.°

Par. 188

(1) THE / THESE WRITINGS. As in Par.148 (which see), the A.E.T. made the meaning of the original explicit by saying °these° instead of the definite article.

(2) CRITICAL ELEMENTS. See Par.178 (T3)/2; see also Introductory Note, page 68.

(3) FOUNDATIONS / PRINCIPLE. Instead of °all the foundations° of existing society—or the N.E.V. might have said °all the fundamentals°—the A.E.T. referred to °every principle° of existing society. The latter rendering will do if we view the 'principle' of a society as its objective component, not simply a subjectively held concept.

(4) POSITIVE PROPOSITIONS / PRACTICAL MEASURES. The former corresponds to the original, the latter to the A.E.T. To be sure, these terms do not mean the same thing, but the difference in context is slight. More interesting is the fact that the reference to °the future society° which followed immediately was dropped from the A.E.T.—perhaps to de-emphasize the well-known fact that the utopians fantasized about the future, or perhaps to avoid seeming to praise them for this preoccupation.

316

(5) TOWN-AND-COUNTRY ANTITHESIS / DISTINCTION. See Par.133, Point 9/1, for its account of what happened to the present paragraph, Par.188, with respect to the town-and-country question.

(6) ABOLITION OF THE FAMILY. Since the utopians are praised for proposing the abolition of the family (Fourier is meant in the first place), this passage must be considered with the others in assessing the Manifesto's position on this question. See Par.100/2, Par.101/1—3, Par.102/1, Par.105/3.

(7) PRIVATE GAIN. The original text spoke of the abolition of °private gain° (°des Privaterwerbs°), a term which the A.E.T. took eleven words to render: °the carrying on of industries for the account of private individuals.° MECW's editorially footnoted translation of the original term, "private profit," is erroneous. (For the use of the term *Erwerb* in German, see KMTR 1:160—62.) The A.E.T., that is, Engels, was unwilling to say simply °private gain° because this was historically inaccurate: the utopians did not propose the abolition of all °private gain°; this would credit them with advocating far too broad and sweeping a social transformation. It was, then, a difficult thing to handle in translation, hence the eleven words for one. My own version could stick with °private gain° the only accurate rendering, because my task is not that of Engels in 1888. But incidentally, all three of the Laura (French) versions likewise stayed with "gain privé."

(8) WAGE-LABOR / WAGE SYSTEM. Instead of the abolition °of wage-labor,° the A.E.T. made it abolition °of the wage system°—an improvement from the standpoint of scientific terminology.

(9) PROCLAMATION OF SOCIAL HARMONY. This points in the first place to Fourier and the Fourierist movement, which laid special stress on 'harmony' inside its utopian society; but other socialistic sects glorified harmony too. For example, New Harmony, Indiana, was not a Fourierist colony.

(10) CONVERSION OF THE STATE INTO ADMINISTRATION... The A.E.T. changed the °state° into °functions of the State°. The implication of this change is that the state survived, with modified functions; and this was certainly true of Saint-Simon's ideas, which are pointed to by the un-quotemarked allusion to substituting the administration of "things" for the administration of "men." This statement of Saint-Simon's is sometimes called anarchistic—a misunderstanding of Saint-Simon's views, which were closer to envisioning the administration of men *as if* they were things. The A.E.T. muffed the implicit reference to Saint-Simon by using the word °superintendence° instead of °administration.°

(11) PURELY UTOPIAN SENSE. For this, see Par.178 (T3)/1.

Par. 189

(1) CRITICAL UTOPIAN. The absence of a hyphen between these two words is not a misprint; in the German it is not a hyphenated description as it is in the title of Subsection 3.

(2) A.E.T. ADDITION: MODERN. In the second sentence, the A.E.T. added °modern° to °class struggle.° The change seems unnecessary.

(3) FANCIFUL / FANTASTIC. In the same sentence: for the difference between these

two words, see Par.183/2.

(4) FOUNDERS AND DISCIPLES. The third sentence is a key to Marx's and Engels' attitude toward the utopian socialists, often misunderstood. Toward Saint-Simon, Fourier and Owen themselves, their attitude was one of very great admiration; the sects formed by the disciples played a different role, however, from that of the seminal innovators. In the 1840s, it was the °reactionary sects° that represented the tendency. Few who write about Marx and the utopians grasp the fact that he made a sharp differentiation.

(5) REACTIONARY SECTS. For °reactionary,° which is used with its literal meaning, see Par.136 (Tl)/1. For °sects° and Marx's attitude toward them, see Par.61/1.

(6) A.E.T. EDITING. The fifth sentence was edited by the A.E.T. in two respects. (i) Where the original merely said °consistently,° the A.E.T. gave this heavy emphasis by making it a whole phrase set off by commas: °and that consistently.° (ii) The A.E.T. added °class° to °antagonisms,° spelling out the meaning.

(7) SOCIAL UTOPIAS. These words in the sixth sentence are followed by references to three of the best-known utopians, not identified by name since the reader was expected to know them: Fourier (phalansteries), Owen (home colonies), Cabet (Icaria). In a footnote to the A.E.T. appended after °Icaria,° Engels explained Fourier's and Cabet's term, but not Owen's (presumably English readers would know it). In a similar footnote to the 1890 German edition, Engels said a word about all three. More on these references below.

(8) INDIVIDUAL / ISOLATED. In the sixth sentence: the utopians, said the original, founded °individual phalansteries°; the A.E.T. called these °isolated° ones, thereby intensifying the characterization well beyond the original. The change was inadvisable, not only because it is inaccurate as translation, but also because not all phalansteries can be said to have been 'isolated.' But each one was an °individual° attempt to solve the Social Question, rather than a society-wide effort.

(9) PHALANSTERIES. The model community imagined by Fourier was called a *phalanx*; its great central building was a *phalanstère* (in English, phalanstery); the A.E.T. used the French form. The latter term was and is sometimes used erroneously or loosely for the whole community. In his footnote to the A.E.T., Engels explained *phalanstères* as "Socialist colonies on the plan of Charles Fourier" but in his 1890 note he stated more accurately that it "was the name of the societal palaces planned by Fourier." Judging by the context, the Manifesto itself used °phalanstery° to mean the whole community or colony.

(10) HOME COLONIES. This was Owen's term for his proposed model communities (utopian colonies) to be set up in the home country rather than the wilds of America. The German text, incidentally, used the English word °home° in the term °home-Colonien.° Engels' 1890 footnote (see point 7 above) said: "Home colonies (colonies in the home country) was Owen's name for his communistic model societies." Marx could have found the term in Engels' *Condition of the Working Class in England*.

(11) ICARIA; CABET. Etienne Cabet (1788—1856) was, in point of time, the third and last of the great triumvirate of French utopians. His central contribution was his book *Voyage en Icarie* (1840), which blueprinted the details of a utopia In the form of a novel. Around it he organized a sect whose followers were called Icarians—Icarian communists, communists, or of course Cabetists. For a while in the 1840s Cabet had influence in the London group, the League of the Just, which was to become the Communist League. The Cabetist-Icarian

group was active in France up to early 1848, but it stood aside from the revolution, and decided to flee the turmoil. Cabet sailed for America in December, burying his movement in France; in the next years he tried to found an "Icaria" in the United States. Cabet himself became a U.S. citizen (1854); but the colony collapsed after much dissension. Engels' footnote to the A.E.T. explained that "*Icaria* was the name given by Cabet to his Utopia and, later on, to his American Communist colony." His 1890 footnote said that it "was the name of the utopian land of fancy, whose communist institutions Cabet described." The A.E.T. was misguided in quote-marking the name °"Little Icaria"° and capitalizing the word °little°; this was inaccurate both as translation and as history.

(12) DUODECIMO...NEW JERUSALEM. °Duodecimo° (or 12mo) described a book page size made by folding a printer's sheet into twelve leaves, five by eight inches or a fraction more. Used figuratively as here, it meant 'small' or 'miniature.' The Revised A.E.T. of 1932 (see Part I, chapter 28, section 3) replaced °duodecimo editions° with "pocket editions" (following the Pauls' translation). For °New Jerusalem,° see its previous use in the Manifesto, Par.173/2. In connection with these words, see point 17 below.

(13) CASTLES IN SPAIN. While the source of this expression is French (*châteaux en Espagne* or *d'Espagne*), the Manifesto uses it (°spanischen Schlössern° without marking it as foreign. On the other hand, some British authorities view °castles in Spain° as a Gallicism (still, after some centuries of use in English); and the A.E.T. followed the best British punditry in preferring °castles in the air.°

(14) PHILANTHROPY. Where the original referred to °the philanthropy of bourgeois hearts and moneybags,° the A.E.T. dropped the word °philanthropy° altogether, and in rewriting this clause offered no substitute for it. I can see no reason for this, except inadvertence.

(15) REACTIONARY OR CONSERVATIVE. The A.E.T. inadvertently left out the word °or,° offering the nonsense term °reactionary conservative socialists°; but in the teeth of common sense this reading has been piously reproduced in all A.E.T. reprints that I have seen except MECW.

(16) ONE 'MORE' TOO MANY. This point is solely for people who read the original German of 1848 very, very closely. In the original edition, and in German editions up to 1872, there was an otiose °mehr° in the words translated as °differentiated from them only by more systematic pedantry.° For the record, this passage went as follows:

...unterscheiden sich nur mehr von ihnen durch mehr systematische Pedanterie...

The 1872 German edition eliminated this first °mehr° and replaced it with °noch°. Now the good news: neither German reading affects the English translation; at any rate the original reading cannot be brought over into English without confusion, and so the N.E.V. has ignored it (as did Macfarlane's translation in 1850).

(17) QUOTE IN 'HERR VOGT.' For this long citation from the Manifesto, see Par.180/8. Only parts of the present paragraph are included: the first sentence (with a slight change in language), the third sentence, and part of the sixth. The passage ends with °duodecimo edition of the New Jerusalem,° and Marx adds:

In the last words *Cabet's* Icaria, or, as Techow calls it, his "bower-of-bliss-cowshed," is expressly referred to as a "duodecimo edition of the New Jerusalem."

Par. 190

(1) AGAINST...POLITICAL MOVEMENT. Here Marx notes one of the outstanding characteristics of the utopian socialist sects, namely, their hostility to political issues, which they associated with bourgeois-democratic demands like a constitution, free press, etc. In fact, to them the very name *social*-ism implied *antipoliticalism*; concern for the Social Question *rather than* concern about such things as political freedom. This is one reason why Marx considered them "reactionary sects" (see Par.189).

(2) A.E.T. EDITING. In the second part of this sentence, the A.E.T. inserted the parenthetical °according to them,° to avoid possible misunderstanding.

Par. 191

(1) OWENITES. Besides the activities of Owen himself (see Par.180/5), the movement shaded out in other directions. Owenism was influential in shaping the cooperative movement; and at one point touched the young trade-union movement when the Grand National Consolidated Trades Union flourished. Organizations and cooperative societies were established with more or less connection with Owen himself, beginning in 1821 with the Co-operative and Economical Society formed mainly by London printers. Owen's own moral writings were needfully supplemented by the acute economic analyses of the so-called Ricardian socialists, like the active Owenite William Thompson, also Thomas Hodgskin, John Francis Bray, John Gray, and others. Owen published a series of organs to expound his views; Engels himself began his English journalism in the columns of his *New Moral World*. By the 1830s the center of gravity of the movement had shifted from London to the industrial north.

(2) FOURIERISTS. Following Fourier's death in 1837, the Fourierist tendency was organized under the leadership of Victor Considérant (1808—1893), who founded and edited the daily *Démocratie Pacifique* (1843—1851). Breaking with those Fourierists who were interested only in utopian colonies, he pointed toward the broader goal of establishing a popular movement with a liberal appeal—a reformist, social-democratic type of sect rather than one oriented toward founding colonies, a sect that did not appeal primarily to workers. Important in the 1840s, this movement came to an end following the 1848 revolution. Considérant's writings have a historical importance quite apart from those of Fourier; they belong to the origins of social-democratic reformism.

(3) CHARTISTS. Chartism was the British working-class movement for democratic political reform organized around the 1838 drafting of the "People's Charter," the centerpiece of which was universal suffrage. The movement was active during the 1840s and petered out in the early 1850s. Engels first made contact with the Chartists in Manchester (1843) and soon started writing for the *Northern Star*, the leading Chartist organ. His book

Condition of the Working Class in England included a valuable report on the Chartist movement as of the mid-1840s. Marx and Engels maintained relations mainly with the left wing of the Chartist movement—this was also the socialist wing—first with George Julian Harney, then Ernest Jones. Many of their references to Chartism really applied mainly to this left wing. In their view, the Chartists were "the first working men's party of modern times," as Engels wrote in *Socialism, Utopian and Scientific*. Cf. Par.62/1, Par.67/2.

(4) RÉFORME TENDENCY. The A.E.T.'s version °Réformistes° (which follows the German term °Reformisten°) is obviously open to misunderstanding. It meant the political tendency around the influential Paris daily *La Réforme* (1843—1850), founded by Ledru-Rollin, edited by Ferdinand Flocon et al. In the period leading to the 1848 revolution, it was the organ of the left wing of the liberal-radical opposition in France, a coalition of liberal democrats (headed by Ledru-Rollin) with a socialistic wing looking to Louis Blanc. (For the right wing, see Par.1/7.) Engels contributed articles to its columns in 1847 and early 1848. This group had the misfortune of coming into power on the wave of revolution and doing nothing but discrediting itself. For more on this tendency, see Par.193/3.

(5) COME OUT AGAINST. A moment's thought is necessary to see what point this paragraph is making. It is the last indictment in a series of charges against the utopian socialist sects. In the case of both England and France, these socialists are censured for opposing a nonsocialist tendency that was definitely to their right in terms of socialist theory. The Chartist movement as a whole was far from being socialist, and the dominant leaders of the *Réforme* group were its liberals. The big difference, to Marx and Engels, was that the movements which the socialists scorned were not sects but real popular movements. Within these movements, Marx and Engels thought, was the starting point for the future proletarian movement of the country. Behind this antisectist approach were the views explained in the notes on Par.61—65; and see Par.193/3 below.

IV
POSITION OF THE COMMUNISTS ON THE VARIOUS OPPOSITION PARTIES

Par. 192: Title, Section IV

(1) COMMENTS IN LATER PREFACES. Marx and Engels made general comments on this section in two prefaces. In their preface to the German edition of 1872, the first preface they wrote to the Manifesto, they listed the respects in which "Here and there some detail might be improved"—see Par. 130/4, Par.132/2, Par.136 (TIII)/2. The last item said it is self-evident

that the remarks about the position of the Communists on the various opposition parties (Section IV), although in fundamental lines still correct today, yet in practice are antiquated today, because the political situation has been entirely transformed and the course of history has removed from the world most of the parties there enumerated.

In their preface to the Russian edition of 1882, they commented on what was missing in the Manifesto:

> What a limited field the proletarian movement still occupied at that time (December 1847) is most clearly shown by the last section of the Manifesto: the position of the Communists in relation to the various opposition parties in the various countries. Precisely Russia and the United States are missing here.

The preface went on to discuss the role of these two countries then and now: "How very different today!" (However, the Manifesto did not completely ignore the United States: see Par.192/2 below.)

Par. 192

(1) SELF-EVIDENT / MADE CLEAR. The A.E.T. version of this paragraph may be understood, or misunderstood, to say that Section II already explained (°made clear°) the question heading this section; but in fact this paragraph says only that from Section II this question °is self-evident,° i.e., may be easily deduced. In point of fact, the 1848 revolution showed how far from self-evident this very difficult question was; and by 1850 Marx and Engels came out with a considerably altered view of many aspects of the issue, embodied in their "Address to the Communist League" of March (MECW 10:277). At the same time Marx's and Engels' assertion of 1872 that they still maintained the fundamental lines of the Manifesto's approach was quite true; what changed was largely the very important matter of the application of these "fundamental lines" to the reform-socialistic groups who were taking on the name social-democrats (see Par.193/3). In any case, the revolution did not essentially affect their attitude toward the two groups named in this paragraph, the British Chartists and the American "agrarian reformers."

(2) AGRARIAN REFORMERS IN AMERICA. Marx means the so-called National Reformers. The name of the organization was actually the National Reform Association, founded in 1845 as a political-action movement by George Henry Evans, who published the *Working Man's Advocate*, later *Young America*. Its basic concern was land reform: every worker to get 160 acres (which was to be the limit on all farms)—with the slogan "Vote yourself a farm!" It was for land nationalization; against land profiteering. It also came out for a ten-hour day, the abolition of slavery and the standing army, etc. Its ranks included many German émigré workers. After a few small reforms, it petered out during the latter 1840s, having mainly operated to involve a few workers in a back-to-the-land movement. Marx first had to adopt a position on this movement in 1846, when a German Weitlingite named Hermann Kriege, editing the *New York Volks-Tribun* as an allegedly Communist organ, had adopted its Free Soil program as his substitute for communism, along with a number of other eccentricities. In a "Circular Against Kriege," Marx and Engels condemned his political course while explicitly leaving room for communist support to the National Reform movement as one that would (or could) develop into a proletarian and communist movement. (See KMTR 2:420f.) But the communists had to point out that the Free Soil program

being advocated was an illusion. In an article on Heinzen in 1847, Marx referred to the American group in very complimentary terms:

> Just as in *England* the workers form a political party under the name of the *Chartists*, so do the workers in *North America* under the name of the *National Reformers* and their battle-cry is not at all *rule of the princes* or the *republic*, but *rule of the working class* or the *rule of the bourgeois class*. [MECW 6:324]

Indeed, this gave them too much credit, but one sees how their name is in Marx's mind just before he sat down to write the Manifesto. In Engels' draft *Principles of Communism*, in a passage similar to the Manifesto's Section IV, the Americans were mentioned in the same way:

> In *America*, where a democratic constitution has been introduced, the Communists must make common cause with the party that will turn this constitution against the bourgeoisie and use it in the interest of the proletariat, that is, with the national agrarian reformers. [MECW 6:356]

The interest of all these mentions of the National Reformers does not lie in the fact that the American movement was much overvalued, but in the fact that Marx and Engels were obviously looking about, in America as elsewhere, for a class-based movement that was not simply a socialistic sect, and were ready to hail it even though it was still far from socialist ideas, provided that it represented a working class in self-motion.

Par. 193

(1) REPRESENT THE FUTURE OF THE MOVEMENT. We have already noted (see Par.65/3) that this statement is closely related to the antisectist views expressed so strongly in Par.61—65. In particular, it enlarges on the statement that makes up the second part of Par.65. In the present paragraph the nonsectist viewpoint is put forward in terms of what alliances to make in the coming revolutionary period, how to link up today and tomorrow. This sentence is the general introduction to Section IV, and really should have been a separate paragraph by itself.

(2) A.E.T. ALTERATIONS. (i) Instead of °interests of the working class,° the A.E.T. made it °the enforcement of the momentary interests of the working class.° I do not see why Engels felt it necessary to expand the language in this way. His insertion of °momentary° is particularly dubious. (ii) In the second part of the same sentence, the A.E.T. reinforced °represent° with °and take care of°; I suppose the idea was to get away from the passive feeling of °represent.°

(3) FRANCE: THE SOCIALIST-DEMOCRATS. By the °socialist-democratic party° Marx means the movement discussed above in Par.191/4, the tendency around the organ *La Réforme*. In the period before the 1848 revolution, Marx and Engels (particularly Engels in Paris) did make considerable efforts to establish an alliance with these socialistic elements;

Engels talked with both Ferdinand Flocon and Louis Blanc to this end. Although they preserved a critical attitude toward the *Réforme* people, as the Manifesto shows, they were disappointed and disillusioned by their thoroughgoing retreat to the right following the 1848 revolution. The term °socialist-democratic° meant the socialistic wing of the Democratic camp; for the meaning of the Democracy, see Par.129/2. In the very next paragraph, Par.194, the same tendency is called °democratic socialists°; this meant the socialists who supported the Democracy, unlike the utopian socialist sects who eschewed politics—see Par.136 (TIII)/3, Par.190/1; hence the terms were interchangeable. The A.E.T. used the label °Social-Democrats,° and this was in use too, especially after 1848; but this designation obviously invited misunderstanding by 1888, when it sounded like the German Social-Democratic Party. Therefore the A.E.T. carried a footnote, as you see, to explain things. The footnote was notably accurate in making clear that the name indicated "a section of the Democratic or Republican party"—though it should have explained that there was no such organized 'party' (cf. note 3 on the Main Title)—a section "more or less tinged with Socialism." The corresponding footnote in the 1890 German edition was hung, of course, on the appellation °social*ist*-democratic party,° and it went as follows:

> The party in France then calling itself socialist-democratic was the one represented politically by Ledru-Rollin and literarily [i.e., in socialist literature] by Louis Blanc; hence it was poles apart from the present-day German Social-Democracy.

Engels' draft *Principles of Communism* had a passage offering the same standpoint on the tendency which it called "democratic socialists" (but without special reference to France). It may help to clarify the references in the Manifesto; here it is. It is treated as the third of three kinds of "socialists" discussed; they "in the same way as the Communists desire part of the measures listed" in the draft's program of transitional measures, but

> not, however, as a means of transition to communism but as measures sufficient to abolish the misery of present society and to cause its evils to disappear. These *democratic socialists* are either proletarians who are not yet sufficiently enlightened regarding the conditions of the emancipation of their class, or they are members of the petty-bourgeoisie, a class which, until the winning of democracy and the realization of the socialist measures following upon it, has in many respects the same interest as the proletariat.

It then proceeded to take up the question of policy handled in the Manifesto's Section IV:

> At moments of action the Communists will, therefore, have to reach an understanding with these democratic socialists, and in general for the time being pursue as much as possible a common policy with them, insofar as these democratic socialists do not enter the service of the ruling bourgeoisie and attack the Communists. It is obvious that this common action does not exclude the discussion of differences with them. [MECW 6:355f]

324

While in 1888 the A.E.T. was concerned about misunderstanding the term to refer to the contemporary Social-Democracy, nowadays we must be equally sure to understand that 'democratic socialists' did *not* mean socialists who held (in the modern sense) democratic views on what in 1848 would be called freedoms and popular rights.—The two notes following are on the two men mentioned in Engels' footnote.

(4) LEDRU-ROLLIN. Alexandre (Auguste) Ledru-Rollin (1807—1874) was a lawyer by profession; his family name was Ledru, to which he appended Rollin himself. Elected a deputy in 1841, he became the leading parliamentary figure in the left wing of republican liberalism, allied with Louis Blanc's socialist circle in *La Réforme*. In the 1848 revolution, he became interior minister in the Provisional Government and a member of its Executive Commission. As a moderate, he supported Lamartine in the May 1848 crisis, thus losing mass support without becoming palatable to the Right. After the bungled semiputsch of June 1849 he fled to England, where for two decades he played the role of impotent Democratic leader in exile. Returning to France (1869), he stood aside from the Paris Commune and other events, and faded out of history as a ghost of yesterday's radicalism. Together with Ferdinand Flocon, he was one of history's lessons in the futility of riding two horses in different directions especially in time of revolution.

(5) LOUIS BLANC. Jean Joseph Charles Louis Blanc (1811—1882) was born in Madrid, son of a functionary in Joseph Bonaparte's Spanish government. He first became prominent as a historian with his *Histoire de Dix Ans*, dealing with 1830—1840 (published 1841 1844). He was an editor of *Revue Indépendante* (1841—1848) with Pierre Leroux and George Sand, and the editor of *Revue du Progrès* (1839—1842), in which he published his first important socialist work, *Organisation du Travail* (1839), proposing workers' cooperative production financed by the state as the final solution. A prominent member of the *Réforme* tendency and active in the "banquet" campaign leading up to the 1848 revolution, Blanc entered the Provisional Government, and, as its socialistic wing, was put in charge of the "national workshops" under the Luxembourg Commission, which were set up to fail and thus discredit socialistic solutions. Although he was a mild pink who disapproved of revolutionary militancy, he was used as a scapegoat; he made a speech and then fled to London. In emigration (till 1870) he finished his Robespierrist history of the French Revolution, and published pamphlets. Back in France, he was elected to the Assembly, where he condemned the Paris Commune, but supported some radical-democratic measures. Historically, Louis Blanc represented an early version of reformist socialism with a strong state-socialistic cast.

(6) REVOLUTIONARY TRADITION. The original formulation in the Manifesto—°phrases and illusions deriving from the revolutionary tradition°—is likely to be misunderstood today. It appeared in a passage about France, and it meant specifically the kind of 'revolutionary' phrasemongering that hung on from reminiscences of the French Revolution of 1789—1794. It was not, then, about °the revolutionary tradition° in general. This meaning was exactly conveyed by the A.E.T. in its good reformulation: °traditionally handed down from the great Revolution°. (The three Laura-versions, incidentally, allowed the original words to stand, since the French would understand.)

Par. 194

(1) SWITZERLAND: THE RADICALS. This 'party' (that is, political tendency) was a small current on the left wing of Swiss politics, active mainly in the French-speaking cantons of Geneva and Vaud. (For the use of the appellation °democratic socialists° in this paragraph, see Par.193/3 above.) In Geneva the radical journalist James Fazy (1796—1878) had led a democratic revolt in October 1846, from which the Radicals gained strength. The year before, at Lausanne (capital of Vaud), the conservative cantonal administration had to yield before a popular rising; the radical Henri Druey (1799—1855), whom Engels later equated with Louis Blanc, became head of the cantonal government. In 1847 these radicals took a prominent part in beating back the Sonderbund (the seven conservative-clerical cantons which sought to split away from the more progressive federal government). On this occasion the Brussels Democratic Association, of which Marx was vice-president, sent an "Address to the Swiss People" praising Swiss democracy (see its catalog of progressive gains in MECW 6:625). Engels' draft *Principles of Communism* had a similar appreciation:

> In *Switzerland* the radicals, although still a very mixed party, are yet the only people with whom the Communists can have anything to do, and, further, among these radicals those in the cantons of Vaud and Geneva are the most advanced. [MECW 6:356]

But in face of the 1848 revolution, these Swiss radicals showed what their radicalism was worth. As Ryazanov wrote, "When the German socialists and even the democrats were obliged, after the unsuccessful rising in May 1849, to seek hospitality in Switzerland, both Fazy and Druey proved faithful henchmen of the European reaction." Marx's post-revolutionary opinion of Fazy can be found in several passages of his *Herr Vogt*, where he is often called the Bonapartist "dictator of Geneva."

Par. 195

(1) POLAND: NATIONAL REVOLUTION. The national-democratic struggle of the Poles against the three powers that had partitioned their land, Russia, Austria, and Prussia, was the international issue that had the widest and most enthusiastic support from all leftists, and all kinds of leftists, all over Europe, throughout the nineteenth century. Marx's and Engels' writings on this question alone would fill more than one volume. Marx probably first encountered Polish revolutionists in emigration in Paris (1843—1844) and certainly in his Brussels days (early 1845 to 1848); there he met the Polish revolutionary historian Joachim Lelewel, and they became fast friends. In Marx's mind, the question of revolution in Poland was inextricably bound up with the question of destroying the reactionary power of Russia, but this connection was not yet reflected by the Manifesto. As usual, the word °party° in this paragraph does not mean a political (electoral) party in the current sense, but rather a tendency or movement; the chief organization of the Polish national emigration, from 1832 on, was the Polish Democratic Association. It should be noted that neither in the Manifesto

nor in subsequent writings did Marx or Engels insist that the Polish national movement had to be socialist; this question is continued in point 3 below.

(2) CRACOW INSURRECTION OF 1846. The Polish revolt of 1831—1832 had taken place under aristocratic leadership and without a social program; its defeat fostered the rise of a new leadership which proposed to link the national aspirations of the people to a democratic social program, which meant in the first place to a program of radical agrarian reform in the interests of the peasantry. In February 1846, after a year's preparation, an insurrectionary movement led by Ludwik Mieroslawski and Henryk Dembinski proclaimed a national government in Cracow (then, with its environs, a republic that had been set up in 1815 by the Congress of Vienna, under the sway of the partitioning powers). The movement was crushed by Austrian and Russian forces in March, and in November Cracow was incorporated into Austria. Because of its democratic social character, the Cracow insurrection brought about a great burgeoning of mass support to the Polish national movement by all left-of-center elements in European politics, most particularly by all working-class movements. This is what the Manifesto is pointing to in its reference to °the party that insists on an agrarian revolution° etc.; see the next point.

(3) POLAND: AGRARIAN REVOLUTION. About the same time that the Manifesto was coming off the press and the February Revolution was breaking out in Paris, a London meeting was held commemorating the Cracow insurrection's second anniversary; and at this meeting both Marx and Engels enlarged on the Manifesto's remark about the nature of the Polish revolution. What they emphasized was that "only a democratic Poland" (that is, a Poland with a social program in the interests of the Democracy)" could be independent, and a Polish democracy was impossible without the abolition of feudal rights..." The overthrow of the controlling despotism had to be linked with a revolutionary agrarian program (land to the peasants). The national cause had to be united with the cause of social liberty "by emancipating the Jews and peasants, by having the peasants participate in the ownership of the soil, by reconstructing Poland on the basis of democracy and equality." (For these references, see KMTR 2:429f.) This remained their general view on the fusion of a national with a social program in a country like Poland.

(4) FIRST EDITION ERROR. The first editions of the Manifesto made a sentence break before the final clause of the sentence, that is, after the words °national emancipation,° leaving a grammatical rump. This was corrected beginning with the 1866 edition. The N.E.V. ignores this peccadillo.

(5) A.E.T. EDITING. (i) Instead of °Among the Poles,° which includes the very important Polish emigration, the A.E.T. made it °In Poland,° which does not and is therefore inaccurate both as translation and as fact. (ii) The word °insists° does not reflect the original. (iii) The word °prime° has been added to °condition° (or °precondition°) to emphasize its importance. (iv) The word °fomented° is a mistake because of its pejorative connotation; as the Oxford English Dictionary notes, this word is used °especially in a bad sense.°

Par. 196—198

(1) GERMANY: REVOLUTIONARY POLICY. These three paragraphs taken together

(and they should be so taken) set down in advance the line which Marx and Engels were going to follow in Cologne on the outbreak of the revolution, through the *Neue Rheinische Zeitung* and their own activity in the local and regional Democratic Association and Workers Association. To be sure, by the time the revolution was winding down in 1849, they had substantially modified their approach. The revolution, they expected, would be—or at least begin as—a bourgeois-democratic revolution, that is, one that would oust the monarchic-absolutist-feudal-bureaucratic regime from power and install the bourgeoisie as the ruling class in the state, hopefully through a democratic republic. The proletarian, or communist, left wing of this revolution should therefore support a takeover by the revolutionary bourgeoisie, politically and militarily: firstly, to make sure that the bourgeoisie really carried through this historical task, pressing it from the left flank, and secondly, in order to create the best possible ground for continuing the proletariat's own class struggle

against the new bourgeois state power. But (as Par.197 emphasizes) at no time would this entail a class truce. An escape clause is inserted into Par. 196: °as soon as the bourgeoisie acts in a revolutionary way°; and it does not predict whether the bourgeoisie *will* so act; but in fact Marx expected the bourgeoisie's political forces to act with a degree of revolutionary militancy that far exceeded what actually happened. In retrospect Engels' formulation, °whenever it [the bourgeoisie] acts in a revolutionary way,° seems to take account of the fact that in 1888 that he knew the Manifesto's expectations had been disappointed. The main body of the German bourgeoisie capitulated before the absolutist regime, and quailed in terror before the task of imposing the sovereignty of parliament upon the Crown, which came out of it reinforced. Marx had to draw the conclusion that this German bourgeoisie could not be relied on to make its own revolution, the bourgeois-democratic revolution; that the bourgeois-democratic revolution and the proletarian revolution, which they had originally seen as two stages, would have to be telescoped into one revolutionary process, under the hegemony not of the revolutionary bourgeoisie but of the proletariat. This was the essence of the perspective of Permanent Revolution. However, Par.197 already contains the basic formulation of the Permanent Revolution pattern: after the overthrow of the old regime, the proletarian struggle against the new bourgeois power will °immediately begin.° And Par.198 adds that the German bourgeois revolution would °be only the immediate prelude to a proletarian revolution.° But events pushed Marx to a still more radical formulation of Permanent Revolution, which was set forth in detail in the "Address to the Communist League" of March 1850: the tasks of the bourgeois revolution would have to be carried out by the proletarian revolution. The foregoing is a highly condensed summary of four chapters of KMTR 2, Chap. 7—10, which trace Marx's and Engels' policy during the revolution step by step. This is a very complicated story, and cannot be done justice here. Certainly Marx did not expect all the complications when he drafted the Manifesto; fifteen years later (Feb. 13, 1863) he would remark in a letter to Engels: "the easygoing delusions and the almost childish enthusiasm with which, before February 1848, we greeted the era of revolution have gone to the devil." But the experience of the revolution opened a new era also in Marx's political thought; the Manifesto was a summary of the prelude to the maturing of his political views.

(2) ENGELS' DRAFT. On this important question, Engels' formulation of the position in his *Principles of Communism* should be studied along with the Manifesto. It forms the final

paragraph of his draft:

Finally, in *Germany* the decisive struggle between the bourgeoisie and the absolute monarchy is still to come. Since, however, the Communists cannot count on the decisive struggle between themselves and the bourgeoisie until the bourgeoisie rules, it is in the interests of the Communists to help bring the bourgeoisie to power as soon as possible in order as soon as possible to overthrow them again. The Communists must therefore always take the side of the liberal bourgeois against the governments but they must ever be on their guard against sharing the self-deceptions of the bourgeois or believing their false assurances about the benefits which the victory of the bourgeoisie will bring to the proletariat. The only advantages which the victory of the bourgeoisie will provide for the Communists will be (1) various concessions which make easier for the Communists the defence, discussion, and spreading of their principles and thus the unification of the proletariat into a closely knit, militant and organized class, and (2) the certainty that from the day when the absolute governments fall, comes the turn for the fight between bourgeois and proletarians. From that day onwards the party policy of the Communists will be the same as in the countries where the bourgeoisie already rules.

(3) UNEVEN DEVELOPMENT OF NATIONS. In Par. 198 Marx clearly presents a conception about German development which expresses the pattern later dubbed "uneven and combined development." For previous expressions of this idea, see Par. 153/3, Par. 162/6. Germany, he writes, is carrying out the bourgeois revolution "under more advanced conditions" of development ("civilization") and with a more advanced proletariat than was true in the case of the bourgeois revolutions in France and England, and this explains why in Germany the bourgeois revolution will be°the immediate prelude to a proletarian revolution°.

(4) QUOTE IN 'HERR VOGT.' In Chapter 4 of this work, Marx quotes Par. 196 plus the first clause of Par. 197 (up to °bourgeoisie and proletariat°), ending with an °etc.°—all in one continuous paragraph, as in other citations from the Manifesto in this chapter. He says of this that one "could have found my view of the attitude to the bourgeois movement adopted by the German in particular expressed very clearly in the Manifesto." This was written a dozen years after the revolution, with no indication that Marx felt that any qualification was needed.

(5) AGAINST THE PETTY-BOURGEOISIE. We have already more than once noted (Par. 52/3, Par. 165/1) that the Manifesto not only condemns the petty-bourgeoisie as reactionary but sees it as arrayed in a class front of reaction along with the absolutist state and the semifeudal ruling class. The present paragraph does this for the third time, and this time it is clearest of all in its portrayal of the petty-bourgeoisie as lined up with °the absolute monarchy° and °feudal landed property° in one reactionary front facing the revolutionary (or potentially revolutionary) alliance of the Communists and the bourgeoisie. In a curious editorial footnote to its reprint of the A.E.T., at this point MECW tells the reader that instead of°the petty-bourgeoisie° the original German text said "philistinism," though it adds

the actual German word, °Kleinbürgerei,° in brackets. Now it is true that "philistinism" is a possible dictionary definition of *Kleinbürgerei* (which is a somewhat more contemptuous form of *Kleinbürgertum* or *-schaft*), but surely not in the context of the Manifesto! And part of that context are the two other passages to the same effect. Even more curious is the fact that, in its translation of *Herr Vogt* (MECW 17:91), the same passage from the Manifesto is not given in the A.E.T. version (as all citations from the Manifesto are in the MECW) but in the new translation put forward in the aforementioned editorial footnote, namely, substituting "philistinism" for °petty-bourgeoisie°. The effect is to suppress the actual viewpoint about the petty-bourgeoisie which Marx wrote into the Manifesto—and which he shortly afterwards dropped for good.

(6) A.E.T. EDITING. In Par. 196: we have already seen the significant difference between °as soon as° in the original and °whenever° in the A.E.T. (see point 1 above); and in the same sentence, the °feudal landed property° (meaning the landowners, by metonymy) is Englished, or Britishized, into °feudal squirearchy°. In Par. 198, the A.E.T. has done some recasting of the 'because' clauses, but the meaning is unaffected.

Par. 199

(1) SUPPORT EVERY REVOLUTIONARY MOVEMENT. At the risk of repetition, we note that this statement does *not* say that the Communists support every socialist or communist movement, and in fact the latter position was not Marx's by a long shot. In paragraph after paragraph, the Manifesto has now emphasized that its criterion for support of a movement is not in the first place political-ideological but primarily this question: what class forces, what real and progressive social strata or tendencies, are represented by this movement? what masses has it set into self-motion, for what ends? In 1875 Marx was going to formulate this antisect approach aphoristically: "Every step of real movement is more important than a dozen programs." (MESW 3:11) This principle is further rounded out by the next paragraph, under which see Par. 200/2.

Par. 200

(1) PROPERTY QUESTION. This term was current at the time, meaning the form of property ownership one advocated: private property (in production) or communal property? Or, of course, various socialistic attempts to straddle the issue, or combine forms, as in the case of the Saint-Simonians and Fourierists. It must be remembered that those who advocated any form of communally owned property in the means of production were called communists—see note 2 on the Main Title, and Par. 136 (TIII)/3.

(2) BASIC QUESTION OF THE MOVEMENT. Far from contradicting the principle enunciated in Par. 199, this statement complements it. The state of a movement's position on the property question does not determine whether the Communists will *support* that movement, but where the Communists support a movement they will °emphasize the property question° as the basic one; that is, they will function as the revolutionary left wing

of that movement. For example, the position of the Chartist movement on the °property question° was far from socialistic or communistic, but English communists (so Marx and Engels would argue) should enthusiastically support the movement as a whole while acting as a loyal left wing that advocated a socialist/communist position on the °property question°. (The Chartist left wing around Harney or Ernest Jones exemplified this approach, in Marx's eyes.) It was, then, not a question of dissolving one's revolutionary opinions in a mass movement but, rather, of bringing those opinions to the fore within that movement. Two bisymmetrically opposite approaches were thus rejected: (i) the line of those who put radical views on the shelf, or in their back pockets, in order to get along in a popular movement, and (ii) the line of those who refused to support and build a progressive class movement on the ground that it had an inadequate program on the °property question.° Historically speaking, the archetypal case was going to be those very r-r-revolutionary people who refused to support reformist trade unions on the grounds of revolutionary impurity; that is, who put ideology above the class role of a movement, and yet somehow considered themselves Marxists.

(3) BASIC / LEADING QUESTION. The A.E.T.'s replacement of °basic question° (°Grundfrage°) with °leading question° raises only a slight nuance, but insofar as it is raised, the A.E.T. rendering must be considered unwise.

Par. 201

(1) ALLIANCE AND ACCORD. The A.E.T.'s rendering of °Verbindung und Verständigung° as °union and agreement° introduces an ambiguity, which to be sure exists to some extent also in the German. The question is whether the Manifesto is saying that the Communists work for the unification (merger, fusion) of the democratic parties or only for their alliance in the sense of collaboration and working together—in later terms, organic unity or united front? Given Marx's view of the contemporaneous movements, there can hardly be any doubt that he meant the second of these two choices; and in any case 'organic unity' would have meaning only as applied to firm organizations, and most of these movements were not embodied in such structural forms. The A.E.T. would have done better to have avoided a word like °union,° under the circumstances.

(2) DEMOCRATIC PARTIES. Again risking repetitiveness, we point out that Marx does not even raise the question of °alliance and accord° of the *socialist or communist* groups; cf. Par.200/2 above on Marx's antisect views.

Par. 202

(1) OPENLY DECLARE. While here, for rhetorical effect, the Communists °disdain° to continue to be a secret society, there was really an important question of political perspective involved. See Par.5/1 near the other end of the Manifesto.

(2) FORCIBLE OVERTHROW. See Par.58/2 for the Manifesto's first enunciation of this idea.

(3) SOCIAL ORDER / CONDITIONS. It is surprising that the A.E.T. avoids rendering °Gesellschaftsordnung° by the obvious (and correct) expression °social order,° and instead has the Communists seeking the overthrow of °all existing social conditions°—which is too tall an order by half. Taken literally, this is virtually a definition of nihilism; but in fact it is simply an ill-considered rendering.

(4) LET THE RULING CLASSES TREMBLE. They did. Though the statement sounds very elocutionary, it is best taken as a sober fact of history. True, our 20-20 hindsight tells us that a communist revolution was not on the order of the day in 1848, but the German bourgeoisie had not yet become convinced of that; it sweated with fear of violent subversion from below. The mass uprising in Berlin on March 18, 1848, which launched the revolution in Germany, did make the bourgeois statesmen and leaders (in addition to those of the absolutist regime) tremble for Law and Order and the fate of Civilization. Then in June the workers' uprising in Paris was a second gigantic shock that pushed the bourgeoisie in the same direction. Marx and Engels believed that the main reason the German bourgeoisie showed itself to be so craven, as compared with the French of 1789, was its fear of revolution from below on its left flank. The bourgeois paladins ran to shelter themselves and their blossoming system under the troops and truncheons of the Crown; they preferred to let time bourgeoisify the old regime over decades rather than overthrow it and have done. (See KMTR 2:219—28.)

(5) COMMUNISTIC. Nowadays the form °communistic° instead of °communist° sounds either old-fashioned or approximate; that is, it tends to connote 'vaguely or amorphously communist' rather than fully communist. But this form was far more common in English, in and out of the movement, in the 19th century. Although this is its only occurrence in the A.E.T., it marks no difference.

(6) NOTHING TO LOSE. Whole forests have been cut down to supply the paper on which perspicacious thinkers have pointed out that workers *do* have something to lose besides their chains, at least in some fortunate countries, and it has never proved difficult to make a property inventory. Few have noticed, however, that the A.E.T. (with which alone they are mostly acquainted) has left out a couple of small words. What the Manifesto says is that °IN IT°—that is, in the course of the communist revolution—°the proletarians have nothing to lose but their chains.° In short, the Manifesto is not concerned with estimating whether workers have so much to lose that they should refrain from plaguing the bourgeoisie with a communist revolution; it assumes (as stated in Par.198) that the revolution is around the corner and unstoppable. Even without the two little words, the import of the famous aphorism is such that they might be taken for granted; instead the passage has been treated as an assessor's appraisal, in the true commercial spirit. For a remark bearing on an analogous claim by the True Socialists, see Par.162.

Par. 203

(1) HORTATORY WATCHWORD. As the typography shows (the line is centered and in spaced text in the original edition), this concluding slogan was not printed as a paragraph of text, but for convenience we consider it as the last paragraph. It appeared for the first time

in the masthead of the single published number of the Communist League's projected organ, *Kommunistische Zeitschrift* in September 1847, replacing the old nonclass motto of the League of the Just, "Alle Menschen sind Brüder!"—(All people are brothers!)—which ignored the fact that some people are sisters. Andréas notes the fact that a very similar slogan made its appearance, about the same time, in a toast given at a meeting of German, English and French Democrats on September 20: "May the proletarians of all countries unite communally for the defence of their rights!" ("Mögen die Proletarier aller Länder sich gemeinschaftlich vereinigen zur Vertheidigung ihrer Rechte!") He opines that "the paternity of the new slogan can be ascribed to Engels" (page 4), but on singularly flimsy grounds; the question remains wide open.

INDEX

WHAT IS INDEXED? This index covers the Annotations section only. The preceding matter (Preface, etc.) is not indexed. But a desired passage of the Manifesto can usually be located from indications given in this index.

In general, this index includes all proper names—persons, periodicals, organizations, etc.—except a few that occur so frequently it would be more productive to look up a narrower subject. Not indexed are the geographical names America, Britain, England, Europe, France, Germany, London, Paris, Prussia, United States; plus the cognates of these names. Not indexed also are the names of Marx and Engels; the Communist Manifesto; book titles in general, except anonyma (look up the author's name instead). References to MEW and MECW are not indexed, except for the entries "MECW errors" and "MEW errors."

Subject headings are indexed quite thoroughly. They are in boldface type, lest they get lost amidst other matter.

A large part of the index has been devoted to listing the numerous locutions—phrases, terms, words—that are discussed as such in the notes. These have to be distinguished from subject headings: they do not indicate subject areas; it is the locution itself that is indexed. These locutions therefore are entered (in lightface) preceded by the degree-mark symbol (°).

The German-language locutions that are discussed in the notes are also indexed, also preceded by the degree mark. To distinguish the German forms immediately, they are followed by an asterisk (*). For example: °also*—it is the German *also* that is meant.

Finally, as mentioned in the introduction, this index includes abbreviations used in this work. There is no other list of abbreviations.

FORM OF INDEXING. Index references are given in the following form: paragraph number, slash mark, note number. The slash mark (/) always introduces the number of the note(s) under the given paragraph. For example: 72/3 refers to note 3 under Par.72. There may be more than one note number after the slash mark; for example, 131/1,4 refers to notes 1 and 4 under Par. 131. As you have seen, some paragraph numbers are complex; for example, Par.119-121 treats three paragraphs together. Note 1 under this head would be indexed like this. 119-121/1.

Annotations dealing with section titles like "Par.70: Title, Subsection 2"—are indexed with a "T" after a colon. For example, 170:T/1 refers to note 1 on the title over Par. 170. On the other hand, note on Par.170 itself would be indexed so: 170/ (as usual).

But in one case a paragraph number has more than one title dependent on it. This is Par.136: first comes the title of Section III, then the title of Subsection under that section. Using as example note in each case, the index references would look as follows:

136:T(III)/1 [Note on title of Sec.III]
136:T(ss.)/1 [Note on title of Subsec.]
136/1   [Note on Par.136 itself].

The Main Title, at the beginning of the Annotations, is not tied to a paragraph number. The four notes on the Main Title are indexed as follows: MT/1, MT/2, etc.

Par.133 has ten subsections, dealing with the points of the Ten-Point Program. The point number is included in the index reference. For example: 133:8/ refers to note following the heading "Par.133, Point 8."

The instruction "See" is used for "See also" as well.

INDEX TO MENTIONS OF AND QUOTATIONS FROM
THE WRITINGS OF MARX AND ENGELS

Wage-Labor and Capital. 37/4; 82/1.
Wages [1847]. 82/1.
Wages, Price and Profit. 82/1.

By Engels

Anti-Dühring. 8/3; 133:9/3.
The Communist Confession of Faith [or The Communist Credo]. 106-11/1; 115/1;
    118/2; 129/2; 135/2.
The Condition of the Working Class in England. 20/2; 28/1; 33/3; 4s/1; 100/2; 101/3;
    103/3; 119-21/1; 133:8/1; 189/10; 191/3; 192/2.
The Festival of Nations in London. 112/2.
A Fragment of Fourier's on Trade. 180/4.
The Housing Question. 28/1; 67/2.
Introduction to Marx's Wage-Labor and Capital. 37/4.
Letters by Engels. MT/l; 135/2.
Marx and the NRZ. 81/1.
The Origin of the Family [etc.]. 7/1,4; 101/2; 100/2.
Outline of a Critique of Political Economy. 32/1; 33/3.
The Peasant War in Germany. 56/3; 179/3.
Preface to Capital, I, English ed. 14/3; 58/2; 138:T(III)/3.
Preface to the Communist Manifesto, 1883. 119-21/1.
Preface to the Communist Manifesto, 1890. 138:T(III)/3.
Prussian Schnaps in the German Reichstag. 143/3.
Principles of Communism. 5/1; 8/1; 11/1; 18/11; 27/2; 28/3; 33/3; 41/1c; 58/2; 103/3;
    108-11/1,4; 115/1; 118/2; 129/2,3; 131/3; 132/3; 133:Gen/1,2; 133:1/1; 133:2/2;
133:3/1;
    133:4/1; 133:5/1; 133:6/3; 133:7/2; 133:8/1; 133:9/3,4; 138/2; 140/1; 148/1; 170:T/2;
    178/1; 193/3; 194/1; 196-98/2.
Rapid Progress of Communism in Germany. 178:T/3.
Socialism, Utopian and Scientific. 178:T/1; 180/4; 191/3.
Trades Unions. 48/1.

340

°estates (social). See: social estates.
estates assembly. 9/1; 18/9.
estates-based monarchy. 18/9.
°Eternal Truths. 167/1.
ethnology. See: anthropology.
Evans, George Henry. 192/2.
°even pace. 119-21/6; 182/1.
°every foreign country. 48/2.
exaggeration as method. 8/11; 54/6; 56/3.
°exchange, means (or mode) of. 17/2; 31/2; 33/2.
°exclusive political rule (by bourgeoisie). 18/11.
°executive of the modern state. 18/12.
°existence for the few. 89/3.
°existence of the laborer. 84/1.
°existence of the worker. 83/3.
°existing up to now. 41/1a.
°exists at all. 89/3.
°exploitation of the world market. 26/2.
°exploitation of nations. 116/1.
°expression...signified. 154/5.
°expropriation / abolition. 133:1/1.
expropriation of émigrés. 133:4/1.
°extinction. 52/2.
°extreme length. 169/2.
°factories and instruments of production owned
    by the state. 133:7/2.
factory labor, effect on worker. 37/2.
factory legislation. 47/2.
family. 22/1; 54/3; 100/2; 101/1,2,3; 102/1;
105/3;
    188/6.
familylessness. 101/3; 102/1.
°fanciful / fantastic. 183/2; 187/1; 189/3.
°far surpassing. 23/2.
°fatherland / country. 112l/; 113/1.
Fauchet, Claude. 178/2.
Fazy, James. 194/1.
February Revolution. See: Revolution of 1848-49.
°feigen Katzenjammer* 152/3.
Ferrand, William B. 139/2.
°feudal lord. 144/2.
feudal socialism. 44/2; 48/1; 136/2; 137/1;
    140/1.
°feudal squirearchy. 196-98/6.
°Feudalen* 140/2.
feudalism. 14/1,2; 20/1; 136/1.
°feudalist(s). 140/2; 144/2; 161/1.
Feuerbach, Ludwig. 100/2; 153/1.
°few hands, in a. 149/2.
°a few of. 167/1.
°fidelity. 143/2.
°figure of speech. 175/1.
°final aim. 38/5.
°final conclusion. 169/2.
°finally disappear. 51/2.

financial measures / demands. 133:5/1.
First International.
    See: International Working Men's
    Association.
Flemish. 6/3.
Flocon, Ferdinand. 191/4; 193/3,4.
°fomented. 195/5.
°forbidden [added]. 99/6.
force, use of. 43/4; 58/2; 202/2.
°forcibly [omitted]. 150/1.
°Formen* 126/2.
°forms [repeated]. 126/2.
°forms of consciousness. 126/2.
°fossilized. 167/1.
Fourier, Charles. 50/1; 100/2; 133:8/1; 133:10/3;
    136:T(III)/; 178:T/1,2; 178/1; 180/4; 183/2;
    188/6,9; 189/4,7,9; 191/2.
Fourierism, Fourierists. MT/1,2; 134/1;
    180/4; 188/9; 191/2; 200/1.
°foundation / principle. 188/3.
°founders of temperance societies. 171/3.
founders and disciples. 189/4.
°form of [this] socialism. 174/2.
Frankfurt (Ger.). 169/3.
Fraternal Democrats. 62/1.
°free competition. 32/1.
°free development (of the individual). 135/2.
°free education. 133:10/1.
free labor. 27/1; 87/1.
Free Soil movement (U.S.). 192/2.
free trade. 87/1; 112/2.
°freedom. 87/1; 88/2.
freedom of the press. 62/2.
French Revolution of 1789+. 18/4; 29/1; 30/1;
    50/1; 58/2; 112/2; 133:4/1; 178/2; 193/5,6;
202/4.
°functions of the state. 188/10.
°future society [omitted]. 188/4.
Garnier-Pagès, Louis Antoine. 1/7.
Gay, Jules. 178/2.
GCFI = *The General Council of the
    First International* [five unnumbered
    volumes]. Moscow: n.d. [1963-68?].
°Gegensatz* 133:9/1.
°gegenüber* 62/2.
°geistig* 96/1.
°geknechtet* 38/3.
°gemeinschaftliches* 79/2.
°general results. 66/4.
general strike. 45/1.
Geneva (Switz.). 194/1.
George, Henry. 133:1/2.
°German or True Socialism.
    See: True Socialism.
°gesprengt* 31/5; 56/4. Cf. 141/3.

343

°getrennten* 62/2.
°gewaltsam* 150/1.
°Gewissens* 122/3.
Girardin, Emile de. 133:2/1.
Girondists. 178/2.
°Glaubensbekenntnis* MT/1.
°gleichen Schnitt* 119-21/6.
Goethe, Johann Wolfgang von. 158/2.
Götrek, Per. 6/3.
°golden apples [etc.]. 143/1.
Gotha Congress. 51/1; 115/1. See: Marx's
"Critique of the Gotha Program."
Gottschalk, Andreas. 153/1.
°government(s). 165/2.
gradualism. 130/2.
°gradually. 41/2.
Grand National Consolidated Trades Union.
191/1.
°gravediggers (metaphor). 35/1; 60/3.
Gray, John. 191/1.
Greece (classical). 28/1,2; 99/5.
Gregory XVI. 1/3.
Greville, C.C.F. 47/2.
°grosse Industrie* 15/2.
Grün, Karl. 153/1; 169/3; 178:T/1.
guild system, guilds. 14/1,2; 14/6; 20/1; 151/1.
°guildsman, °guild-master. 8/1,2; 14/4; 38/1;
Guizot, François. 1/6.
°Halbphilosophen* 154/6.
°hallowed. 105/2.
Hammen, Oscar J. 1/1.
°handled. 164/2.
Hapsburgs. See: Austria.
°harmony. 188/9.
Harney, George Julian. 62/1; 67/2; 191/3; 200/2.
Harrison, J.F.C. 180/5.
Haxthausen, Baron August von. 7/2.
Hébert, Jacques Roux, and Hébertists. 178/2.
Hegel, G.W.F. 20/1; 113/2.
Hegelianism and Hegelian elements.
46/1; 47/1; 54/2; 67/3; 113/2; 131/3; 133:9/1;
157/3.
°heilige Socialismus* 145/1.
°Heiligenbildern, °Heiligengeschichten* 157/1.
Heine, Heinrich. 138/1.
Heinzen, Karl. 192/2.
°heitige* [misprint] 145/1.
°Heranbildung* 97/1.
°Herrschaft* 58/1.
Hervé, Gustave. 113/1.
Hess, Moses. MT/1; 153/1; 158/2; 169/3.
°Hetzjagd* 1/2.
°heutige Socialismus* 145/1.
°highly moral horror. 106-11/3.
Hilditch, Richard. 133:1/2.

Hirschfeld, Rudolph. 164/2.
°historical action. 183/1.
°historical change. 70/1.
°historical criticisms. 158/1.
°historical development/experience. 123-4/3.
°historical initiative. 181/3.
historical materialism.
See: materialst conception of history.
°historical movement. See: °movement.
°historical self-activity. 181/3.
history.
See: ancient history; materialist conception of
history.
°hitherto existing. 14/1; 41/1a.
Hodgskin, Thomas. 191/1.
Holy Alliance. 1/2,4,5.
°holy socialism. 145/1.
home colonies. 189/7,10.
hortatory watchword. 203/1.
House of Burgesses. 12/1.
Howard, John. 176/1.
°huckstering. 88/1.
Hugenots. 1/6.
°hundred years (of bourgeois rule). 30/1.
Hungary and Hungarians. 6/3.
Icaria; Icarians. MT/2; 189/7,11,17.
See: Cabet; Cabetism.
ideological superstructure. 26/4; 54/5; 96/3.
°idiocy of rural life. 28/1.
°Idiotismus* 28/1.
°if / when. 134/6.
illegitimate children (inheritance by).
133:3/1.
Immaculate Conception. 1/3.
°immediate aim. 67/1.
°impact. 104/1,2.
°impartial contempt. 169/2.
imperialism. 27/2; 48/2.
°imported wares. 43/3.
°in any case. 31/1.
°in die Luft sprengen* 141/3.
°in Poland. 195/5.
°incoherent mass. 44/1.
income tax. 133:2/1.
°indefeasible. 20/4.
°indem* (construction). 98/2.
India. 27/2.
Indians (American). 7/4.
individual, individuality,
individualism.
85-86/1,2;   88/2;   91/2;   92/1;   135/2;
136:T(III)/3.
°individual phalansteries. 189/8.
°individual property. 55/2; 91/1,2.
°industrial. 14/5; 15/3; 41/1c; 52/1.

paragraphing. 42/1; 70/2; 72-74/2; 77/1; 78/1;
79/1; 103/2; 117/1; 136/4; 141/4; 144/3;
147/2;
149/3; 150/4; 155-56/2; 158/4; 161/2; 162/3;
164/4;
166/1; 168/1; 171/4; 172/1; 173/3; 179/5;
182/4;
184/2.
parenthetical reference. 180/7.
parents. 103/1,3.
Paris Commune (1871). 18/4; 130/4; 132/2;
193/4,5.
°parson. 144/1; 163/2.
°parsonical socialism. 144/1.
°partial or complete system. 173/1.
°party. MT/3,4; 47/1; 62/1,2; 195/1.
party organization.
See: organization questions.
°past, in the. 70/1.
past tense, change to. 181/4.
°patriarchal relations, °patriarchalism. 20/1; 38/1;
136/2; 140/1; 151/2.
°patrie (Fr.). 112/1.
patriotism. 113/1.
Paul, Eden and Cedar. 129/5; 189/12.
Der Pauperismus und die Volksschule. 1/1.
pauperization* 59/2.
°pawnbroker. 40/1.
peace. See: war question.
peaceful means. 186/1.
peasantry and peasant questions.
28/1,2,3; 44/3; 52/3; 56/3; 133:1/1; 148/1.
See: The Democracy.
penal reform. 176/1.
Pentonville Prison. 176/1.
People's Charter. 191/3. See: Chartism.
permanent revolution. 129/2; 196-98/1.
°persönliche Eigenthum* 91/2.
°Persönlichkeit* 85-86/1.
°person, °personalism. 85-86/1.
°die Person* 91/2; 92/1.
°petit-bourgeoisie (Fr.). 44/3.
°petty-bourgeois, °petty-bourgeoisie. 14/5; 40/1;
44/3; 59/1; 149/2.
petty-bourgeois socialism. 146/1; 148/2;
165/1; 172/1.
petty-bourgeoisie and the Democracy.
See: The Democracy.
petty-bourgeoisie, role of. 16/3; 41/3; 44/3;
52/3; 56/3; 136:T/1; 147/1; 148/1; 165/1,3;
168/2; 193/3; 196-98/5.
°pfäffische Socialismus* 144/1.
°Pfaffe* 144/1.
°Pfahlbürger(schaft)* 12/1; 46/2; 165/3; 168/2.
La Phalange (Paris). MT/1; 180/4.

phalanstére, phalamstery; phalanx.
180/4;
189/7,8,9.
°philanthropy [omitted]. 189/14.
°philistine(dom), °philistinism. 12/1; 165/3; 168/2;
169/1; 196-98/5.
°philosophical socialism. 153/1.
°Philosophie der That* 158/2.
philosophy and social context. 155-56/1.
°philosophy of action, °philosophy of the deed.
158/2.
°phrases / claptrap. 105/1.
Physiocrats. 171/1.
Pius IX. 1/3.
Plato. 100/2; 106-11/1.
Poland and the Polish. 6/3; 195/1,2,3,5.
polar classes. 8/1; 11/1,2.
°police-spies, °policemen. 1/8.
Polish Democratic Association. 195/1.
°political. 46/1b.
°political [omitted]. 123-24/2.
°political change. 174/4.
°political character. 134/3.
political economy (Marx's). 15/3; 30/2; 36/1;
37/4,5; 45/2; 82/1,2; 91/1; 94-95/1; 96/1;
148/2.
°political movement. See: °movement.
°political party. 47/1.
political power (state power). 18/12; 58/1;
67/2; 129/1; 130/1,2; 134/2,3.
°political reform. 174/4.
°political rule. See: political power.
°political science. 123-24/2.
°political struggle. 46/1.
°poor stock-in-trade. 160/1.
Pope. 1/3.
Populists (Russian). See: Narodniks.
°position / status. 78/3.
°position in life. 185/1.
°positive propositions. 188/4.
Possony, S. T. 133:8/1.
°pouvoir politique (Fr.). 134/2.
°power to subjugate...labor. 93/1.
°practical form. 174/1.
°practical measures. 188/4.
°practical reason. 154/3.
predestination. 186/2. See: inevitability.
Preamble (of CM). 6/4.
prebourgeois society. 9/2; 18/2; 28/2; 54/1;
161/1.
See: feudalism; Middle Ages, classical history,
etc.
°presageful thrust. 187/3.
°priest. 144/1; 163/2.
°prime (condition). 195/5.

348

primitive society. 7/1,3.
°principle / foundation. 188/3.
prison reform. 176/1.
°private gain. 188/7.
private property (as programmatic point).
MT/2; 72-74/1. See: property.
°Privaterwerb* 188/7.
°professors. 163/2.
profit-seeking. 94-95/1.
program of demands. 129/3.
See: Ten Point Program.
progressive. 136:T(ss.1)/1.
progressive tax. 133:2/1,2.
°proletarian, °proletariat. 7:T/1,3; 9/5; 35/1;
159/3.
proletarian ascendancy. 67/2.
°proletarian familylessness. 101/3; 102/1.
°proletarian rule. See: political power.
proletariat. 11/2; 41/1; 53/1; 56/3; 113/2;
178/2.
°prolong and reproduce. 83/4.
°proper, °properly so called. 180/1.
°property and hard work. 75/1.
property, individual (personal) or
private. 55/2; 72-74/1; 75/1; 80/1; 89/2; 91/1;
93/1;
94-95/1; 100/2; 106-11/4.
property, petty-bourgeois. 76/1.
°property question. 200/1,2.
°property relations. 127/1. But see: °conditions
(for Verhältnisse).
°proposal. 100/2.
protective legislation for women. 47/2.
Proudhon, Pierre Joseph. 45/1; 146/1; 148/2;
169/3;
172/1.
Proudhonism, Proudhonists. 113/1;
133:1/1; 133:5/1.
°public power. 134/2.
°public schools. 133:10/2.
Puritans. 179/4.
°pushed into the background. 16/3.
quotation marks, use of. 123-24/1; 159/2;
162/1; 167/1; 169/2; 189/11.
°race / kind. 37/3.
Radicals (English). 47/2.
Radicals (French). 1/7; 191/4.
Radicals (Swiss). 194/1.
°rate of wages. 45/2.
°rationalist ideas. 122/2.
°reactionary [term]. 52/3; 136:T(ss.1)/1; 150/2,3;
170:T/1; 179/2.
°reactionary conservative. 189/15.
°reactionary sects. 189/5; 190/1.
°reactionary socialism. 136:T(III)/1; 136:T(ss.1)/1.

°reactionists. 23/1.
°Recht* 98/4; 123-24/3; 162/4.
recruits from bourgeoisie. 49/2; 50/1.
°reform. 174/4.
Reform Bill of 1832. 139/2.
La Réforme (Paris). 1/7; 191/4,5; 193/3,4,5.
Réformistes. 191/4.
°régime [italicized]. 141/1.
°relations (of production, etc.).
See: °conditions (used for Verhältnisse).
religion. 54/5; 118/1,2; 173/2; 180/5.
°religious socialism. 136:T(III)/1; 145/1. See:
Christian socialism.
°rentier. 41/1e.
°represent the future of the movement. 193/1.
representative government. 162/2.
°re-produce. 83/4.
The Restoration (French). 136/3; 139/1.
°restore by force. 43/4.
restrictive clause. 64/1.
°retired tradesmen. 41/1e.
Revelation (in Bible). 173/2.
Revised A.E.T. of 1932 (see p.). 40/2; 54/7;
129/5; 133:8/2; 154/6; 189/12.
Revisionism. 51/2; 130/2.
°revolution. 17/1; 174/7.
See: permanent revolution.
Revolution, French.
See: French Revolution.
revolution in one country. 16/2.
Revolution of 1830. 1/6.
Revolution of 1848-49. MT/3; 1/4,6; 11/2;
115/1; 129/3; 133:Gen/2; 133:7/2; 169/3;
189/11;
191/4; 192/1; 193/3,4,5; 196-98/1,2; 202/4.
°revolutionary [italicized]. 142/1.
revolutionary action. 186/1.
revolutionary policy in Germany.
196-98/1,2.
°revolutionary tradition. 193/6.
°revolutionary ways. 174/7.
Revue du Progrés (Paris). 193/5.
Revue du Progrés Social (Paris). 180/4.
Revue Indépendante (Paris). 193/5.
Rheinische Zeitung (Cologne). MT/1; 2/1.
Ricardian socialists. 191/1.
Ricardo, David. 82/1; 83/2; 148/2.
°rising bourgeoisie. 163/2.
Robespierre, Maximilien. 178/2.
Robespierrism. 193/5.
Rome (ancient). 8/3; 99/5.
Rome (city). 1/3.
Rotteck (K.W. von) and Welcker (K.T.) lexicon.
1/1.
Rousseau, Jean Jacques. 178/2.

CPSIA information can be obtained
at www.ICGtesting.com
Printed in the USA
LVHW052222131119
637300LV00001B/1/P

9 781642 590388